CHARLES A. BEARD was one of America's most distinguished historians. Born in Knightstown, Indiana, he studied at DePauw, Oxford, Cornell, and Columbia universities. He later taught at Columbia and served as president of both the American Historical Association and the American Political Science Association. His books include *An Economic Interpretation of the Constitution of the United States*; *The Economic Origins of Jeffersonian Democracy*; *The Economic Basis of Politics*; *The Rise of American Civilization* and *The American Spirit* (with Mary Beard); *American Foreign Policy in the Making, 1932-41*; and *President Roosevelt and the Coming of the War, 1941*. He died in 1948.

THE IDEA OF NATIONAL INTEREST

THE IDEA OF NATIONAL INTEREST

AN ANALYTICAL STUDY IN AMERICAN FOREIGN POLICY

BY

CHARLES A. BEARD

WITH THE COLLABORATION OF
G. H. E. SMITH

EDITED WITH NEW MATERIAL BY
ALFRED VAGTS AND WILLIAM BEARD

Q

QUADRANGLE PAPERBACKS
Quadrangle Books/Chicago

First QUADRANGLE PAPERBACK edition published 1966 by Quadrangle Books, Inc., 180 North Wacker Drive, Chicago 60606. Manufactured in the United States of America.

25/05

PREFACE

SEVERAL years ago, a student in Columbia College, Leo Perla, sought an answer to the question: What is "National Honor"?[1] The formula was constantly used in diplomacy to explain and justify policy and was widely employed by statesmen and publicists in efforts to prevent the adoption of, or to qualify, treaties and other international agreements which might tie the hands of the Government of the United States— "impair its sovereignty." In his volume, Mr. Perla catalogued and analyzed numerous and often conflicting views expressed under the head of "national honor," clarified the issues, and made a valuable contribution to thought about diplomacy and policy. Perhaps he compelled some statesmen who had been using the term freely and loosely to examine their fundamentals.

As a student of history having occasion to pore over thousands of pages of diplomatic documents, congressional debates, and state papers, I noticed what appeared to be a decline in reliance upon the term "national honor" and the growing use of the formula "national interest" to explain and justify policy. In the summer of 1931, it occurred to me that an inquiry should be made into the meaning of this expression as employed by statesmen and publicists. Remembering that Mr. Perla's study had been made with the advice and counsel of Frederick P. Keppel, then Dean of Columbia College, later President of the Carnegie Corporation, I wrote to Mr. Keppel suggesting that someone be engaged to conduct such an inquiry into "national interest." The expression is in constant use. What does it mean?

Acting on this suggestion, Mr. Keppel took up the matter with the Social Science Research Council, and the Council agreed that such a topic would be an appropriate subject for investigation. Then to my surprise, Robert T. Crane, Secre-

[1] Leo Perla, *What Is "National Honor"?* (Macmillan, 1918).

vii

tary of the Council, informed me that, since I had proposed the theme, I should undertake to carry out the project. Though busy with other studies I consented and the Carnegie Corporation made a generous appropriation to the Council to cover the expenses of the inquiry.

Work was begun on April 1, 1932. The story of the inquiry is a long one and must be shortened here. Many minds have been engaged in the exploration. John D. Lewis, formerly a graduate student at the University of Wisconsin, went through thousands of pages of American history in a search for the content of the term "national interest" as employed by statesmen. Louis B. Domeratzky, of the Department of Commerce, rendered invaluable aid in the field of foreign commerce, furnishing voluminous statistical and documentary information and giving priceless counsel. Paul D. Dickens, specialist in foreign loans and investments for the Department of Commerce, made a study of the purposes to which foreign loans floated in the United States had been applied by borrowers. And many other officers of the Government of the United States and students of diplomacy served as guides through the wilderness of diplomatic formulas.

From beginning to end, G. H. E. Smith, formerly a student at the University of Michigan, has been connected with the inquiry. Chapters VII and VIII are largely his work. His services have been so valuable and indefatigable that his name has been properly associated with mine on the title page, although ultimate responsibility for planning and carrying out the work rests on my shoulders. I am also indebted for assistance to Dr. Alfred Vagts, who has devoted years to the study of American-German relations at the Foreign Office in Berlin and the State Department in Washington. Although not engaged on this project, Dr. Vagts has freely given me the benefit of his intimate acquaintance with the unprinted archives of Germany and the United States.

For purposes of publication, the results of the inquiry have been divided into two parts. The first, the present volume, is analytical and descriptive—a matter-of-fact inquiry into the meaning and use of the formula. It is concerned with what the lawyers call "relevant facts in the case." In the second volume, an effort will be made to construct a consistent and tenable philosophy of national interest. Thus an attempt has been made to distinguish as far as possible, for the benefit of the reader, between things that have been said and have happened and things that may be said and made to happen under the head of national interest.

For all shortcomings of this work and for all opinions expressed the responsibility is mine.

Some passages from this volume were given as lectures at the University of North Carolina on the Weill Foundation in the winter of 1933.

CHARLES A. BEARD.

CONTENTS

INTRODUCTION

IN THE contemplation and writing of *The Idea of National Interest*, Charles A. Beard had in part an immediately political aim: to renew consideration of the idea amid the great changes in policy occurring under the New Deal. But his other, overriding purpose was historiographic: to trace the European origins and American development of a great and abiding concept not limited to an era—indeed, in many ways more relevant today than when he wrote.

In 1934 Beard published two books. The work on national interest was accompanied by a sequel, *The Open Door at Home: A Trial Philosophy of National Interest*, setting forth more specific proposals to promote the best interests of this country in its dealings with foreign nations. In both works the collaborator was an able researcher, the late George H. E. Smith, whose tireless industry matched that of Beard himself.

Of the two works, the first has outlived the era with a remarkable freshness. The phrase "national interest" is more frequently invoked today, and in more diverse quarters, than when the book first appeared. Whether Beard's book helped to stimulate the regrowth of the idea, as well as providing its genealogy, would be hard to say—beginnings are always a dark area in historiography. But certainly the book remains unique in its field; historians and political scientists have not attempted since to develop the theme at length, or to answer the challenge issued thirty years ago by a man who himself spanned both disciplines: to define and investigate a formula by which governments supposedly live and for which men are still asked to die.

At the time Beard wrote, what he called "the high noon of 'normalcy'" was past; the glow of hope and national awareness that had been mirrored, seven years before, in

Charles and Mary Beard's *Rise of American Civilization,* had given way to sober reappraisal of national goals. With the deepening economic depression, spreading over the world after the crisis of 1929, came a questioning of old formulas, in particular those of the Adam Smith laissez-faire school. Adam Smith had maintained that the individual "neither intends to promote the public interest, nor knows how much he is promoting it" but is "led by an invisible hand to promote an end which was no part of his intention." According to the laissez-faire school, it was unnecessary to think about the national or public interest; nature, unseen, would provide for a mysterious "harmony" of all interests and, whatever men did, would assure a happy and prosperous world. This easy faith was shaken as European nations turned to autarchy and the hand of government in the New Deal era was laid heavily on private industry.

The setting, then, for Beard's study of the idea was provided by these events—the deep crisis of belief in a natural harmony of interests accompanying the world-wide economic upset. Men asked whether this laissez-faire theory could still be supported, whether this natural harmony would ever be restored, or whether a new gradation of interests within the nation, and among nations, must take its place. In a chapter on the "Harmony of Interests," an English contemporary of Beard, Edward Hallett Carr, whose *The Twenty Years' Crisis, 1919-1939* appeared in London in 1939, pictured the demoralization of that period.

A stimulus to Beard's thinking was undoubtedly the appearance in Germany, just ten years before, of Friedrich Meinecke's *Idee der Staatsraison,* a work on state reason which was not translated into English until 1957 and then under the somewhat oblique title of *Machiavellism.* Meineke devoted several chapters of his work to discussing the origins and early transformation of the notion of interests of princes and estates into "state interest" after the rise of modern national states. His study of the path-breaking book by the Duke of Rohan (1635) and Courtilz de Sandras' *The New Interests of the Princes of Europe* (1685) encouraged Beard to carry the investigation much further.

Going beyond Meinecke, who, very much the "continental," had not pursued the idea into the Anglo-Saxon world, Beard sought to trace the evolution of "state interest" into true "national interest." State interest in the period covered by Meinecke might mean subjugation of a people to the will of bureaucracies; the national interest which concerned Beard involved a determination of the true needs and will of the peoples.

To understand the background and significance of Beard's original and seminal work, we must see it as the first American contribution to *Interessenlehre,* a great body of lore and doctrine dealing with political interests, which developed over several centuries in Europe. This thread of *Ideengeschichte,* this unfolding, ever-changing, yet always connected history of ideas stretches over almost exactly three hundred years from the early work of Rohan, to Meinecke and Beard, and includes the many separate studies of national interests such as *The Interest of Holland* by Pierre de la Court (1662) and *The Present Interests and Pretensions of the Powers of Europe* by Jean Rousset (1735), as well as the work of Abbé Dubos on *The Interests of England Misunderstood* (1703), which included an early prophecy of the revolt of the American colonies because of England's misconception of her best interests.

Many diverse personalities have contributed to the great stream of *Interessenlehre,* from Richelieu and Cromwell, Frederick the Great, Montesquieu, Adam Smith, and Jeremy Bentham, to Thomas Paine, Gladstone, and Lenin. Many of these have had, like Beard himself, immediate political purposes beyond a purely theoretical exercise. This was especially true of those critics of the *ancien régime* before the French Revolution, who believed that the governors of the autocratic states were damaging the interests of the nations in the pursuit of narrow self-interest. Thus the philanthropist Abbé de Saint Pierre, who must be counted as one of the fathers of the idea, denounced the War Minister of Louis XIV as a man who put his private pocket above the needs of the people: he "has loved money. That is one reason the more for prolonging the war; for the particular interests

in person near to kings often decide the public interest"
(*Annales politiques,* London 1758, published posthumously).

Beard knew that the national interest had also been
appealed to in the United States, almost from the beginning
of the republic. But the phrase had appeared only spo-
radically. Often tacitly understood, it had never been made
the center point of argumentation, the theme of history or
of political science, until Beard—who had already been
president both of the American Historical Association and
the American Political Science Association—produced this
history of the venerable *verbum magistralis* and, in effect,
transplanted and tried to acclimatize in the New World a
European strain of thought.

Though the author supposed the moment ideal for the
purpose, the book was in fact coolly received by an American public not prepared to understand this new genealogy
of an idea, this novelty in political literature. The lack of
critical appreciation disappointed Beard; the sales of the
book were a mere 5,000 until it went out of print a decade
later (as compared with 15,000 of the *Open Door* or the
tens of thousands sold by some of his other works). Still,
like Beard's earlier *An Economic Interpretation of the Constitution of the United States,* the book was destined to
have a life much longer than its slender sales indicated.

Probably the concept was out of tune with the still largely
idealistic atmosphere and phraseology of the New Deal era.
Although a copy of the book was sent to Hyde Park, where
the author had on occasion been a guest, it cannot be said
to have influenced the thinking of Franklin D. Roosevelt
on foreign affairs. Willing as he was to admit the place of
interests in politics, FDR saw his own role as that of arbitrator, telling an academic audience in 1936 that it was
"the problem of government to harmonize the interests" of
all groups in the nation; and he went on to say that "The
science of politics, indeed, may properly be said to be in
large part the science of adjustment of conflicting group interest" (March 23, 1936). Abroad, he sought also to be
an arbitrator among nations, rather than the definer and
promulgator of a definite national interest. In his message

to Congress of January 11, 1944, he declared that the countries of the world had an international, a supranational interest which demanded that "all freedom-loving nations shall join together" in creating a single "just and durable system of peace." This idea materialized as the United Nations, the charter of which proclaimed that its "armed force shall not be used, save in the common interest."

To many Liberals of the era, as to Roosevelt, there was something repellent about pure national interest, a concept that proceeded from a cold and rationally weighed advantage that would, if necessary, override such sacred principles as Christian charity or ancient friendship—"friendship, however strong it might be, cannot prevail against interest," in the chill words of a Venetian ambassador of the eighteenth century. Some trace of its Machiavellian origin clung to the phrase, making it the very antithesis of generous idealism; it seemed as shameful to the New Deal thinkers as to a French Liberal in 1826, that "the Statue of Liberty should be put on a base of material interest."

Nor were Marxists drawn to the study. Their thinkers, from Babeuf and Proudhon to Lenin, had indeed produced fragmentary and at times ambiguous and contradictory statements on the subject; class war they saw as essentially a conflict of interests, but they thought rather of the interests determining the policy of the nation than of the nation deliberately defining and promulgating its interest. Proudhon would see that "the class war, the antagonism of interests, the manner in which the interests enter upon their coalitions, determine the political regime, consequently the choice of government," but Marxists were not concerned with exploring the "true interests" of nations. Rather, they assumed that national interest would soon, like other manifestations of property and group interest, vanish when the state itself "withered away."

Before many years had passed, however, a certain alteration in the American mood was noticeable. Beard himself, in the evening of his life, could note a gradual resurgence of the phrase "national interest," a definite shift of emphasis in political discussion; the successors of Roosevelt were to confront the ruthlessly pursued, hostile interests of other nations, especially those represented by Stalin, interests with a strong nationalistic tinge even when communist, as Russian quarrels with Red China amply demonstrate. But it was after Beard's death in 1948 that the real spate of nationalist claims appeared; then the ideal of cooperation among democratic nations was challenged by Charles de Gaulle, a declarant of the narrowest national aims (see his *Mémoires de Guerre*, Paris, 1959, III, 40, 98, 179, 679), and in his way a figure as harsh as Richelieu, the old embodiment of the French tradition of national interest, to whom the Duke of Rohan had once dedicated his writings. It was the intransigence of de Gaulle which, by 1964, made Under Secretary of State George Ball admit that the North Atlantic Treaty Organization's real problem had become the members' "limited sense of world responsibility—as distinct from national interest."

In the same postwar period, many of the exotic "new nations" spoke out in what they called their national interest, showing that this lesson in political science at least had been well learned from imperialist tutors. Korean professors opposing a treaty with Japan assailed it as "bringing immense damages to our national interest," while farther to the south, a premier of Cambodia condemned student demonstrations against negotiations with France, the country's former overlord, as "contrary to national interests" (*New York Times*, July 13, 1965 and May 23, 1952).

While the concept of national interest was thus gaining strength abroad, it was receiving a greater attention in the United States. Presidential statements reflect this steady increase: Truman and Eisenhower rarely employed the phrase, but John F. Kennedy stressed it on more than one occasion. In his State of the Union message on January 29, 1961, he deplored the fact that "The unity of NATO has been weakened by economic rivalry and partially eroded by national interest," and on August 30, 1961, he went further: "The termination of the moratorium on nuclear testing by the Soviet unilateral decision leaves the United States under the necessity of deciding what its own national interests require." But it was with Lyndon B. Johnson that the words and idea were firmly lodged in the White House.

"This nation is prepared and will always be prepared to protect its national interests," declared Johnson on July 27, 1965, explaining further that the decision to send larger American armed forces into Viet Nam was made because "we felt our national interest required it." Quite clearly Johnson felt that the argument, if unspecific, was as strong and overriding as the claim made at nearly the same time that American "honor" was engaged in that unfortunate country.

The very next month Johnson applied pressure to labor and management in the steel industry to settle their differences without a strike, by insisting on the same formula: "We're going to do everything we can to ask both parties to be responsible and to act in the national interest" (August 30, 1965). The foreign policy of this country was linked with the solution of the domestic problem, and with "American boys still fighting in South Viet Nam," the negotiators must take into account "the overall greater national interest" (August 25, 1965). When agreement was won, Johnson praised both sides but proffered a special bouquet to the labor leaders: "They represented their interests with skill and conviction, but they always put the interests of their nation first" (September 3, 1965).

Below the presidential level, numerous federal executive agencies have had occasion to refer to the national interest, especially in those areas where domestic and international concerns most obviously overlap. Beard himself pointed out that "few important aspects of domestic development fail to have some bearing upon foreign relations." This seems true where customs tariffs, protective of certain groups, have been called in question. The Eisenhower administration set up a "Public Advisory Board for Mutual Security" composed of business, farm, and labor leaders as well as academicians, which published a *Trade and Tariff Policy in the National Interest* (Washington, 1953). The board urged that to achieve "U.S. national and international objectives," decisions on trade policy be based on national interest, that in cases where "choice must be made between injury to the national interest and hardship to an industry, the industry be helped to make adjustments" at state expense.

The same formula has played a part in the efforts of the Department of Labor to cope with strikes that seem capable of affecting defense efforts or foreign trade. Secretary of Labor Arthur Goldberg, faced with nation-wide strikes during the Kennedy administration, announced that henceforth when the government moved into collective bargaining, it would define and assert the national interest and not simply mediate the particular issues. The current regime, he said, "had the courage to draw economic guidelines" to protect the national interest in a world in which "domestic inflation, wages, profits, and price levels can create international crises."

International travel is a third area where national interest has become an important consideration for federal executive activity. Indeed, perhaps of all offices of the executive branch, none has invoked the phrase more readily than the Immigration and Naturalization Service, as when justifying the arrest and deportation of undesirable aliens (*New York Times,* January 3, 1953). The Departments of State and Justice have denied visas to foreigners seeking to visit the United States, after failing "to find anything in the national interest" to justify their admission. Passports have been denied to certain native communists who wanted to go abroad, notably to Red China and Cuba, and on occasion the validity of a passport has been restricted to ensure the holder's return to the United States "on the grounds that his further travel in Europe was not in the national interest" (*New York Times,* September 19, 1950, and January 21, 1954).

In not a few instances, national interest has been invoked to defend the secrecy in governmental processes, to preserve the inviolability of personnel files, military information, secret police reports, and details of diplomatic negotiations. Often, too, federal executive officers argue, sometimes with a hint of the imperiousness of the Absolutist age, that the size of their budgets should not be questioned lest the national interest suffer. Thus a director of the United States Information Agency, defending items of his proposed budget before a congressional committee, has declared that deeper cuts "would not be in the national interest" (June 15, 1965).

Many conflicts have been provoked by the insistence on secrecy, the withholding of material from members of Congress and advocates of "open diplomacy." The executive holds that its branch is best equipped to decide when revelation is in the public interest: "Our Presidents have established, by precedent, that the members of their Cabinets and other heads of Executive Departments have an undoubted privilege and discretion to keep confidential, in the public interest, papers and information which require secrecy," a privacy essential in negotiations with foreign governments (*New York Times,* May 7, 1954). The legislative branch, in opposition, maintains that Congress has a paramount right to information enabling it to perform its work, a right overruling decisions made in the executive departments. A memorable test case on this point, in which the national interest was invoked and the problem brought home vividly to the American public, was the demand of the late Senator Joseph McCarthy for such information. The Senator declared in less than suave language that he wanted once and for all a decision on "this question of whether or not we—the Senate—are the lackeys to obey and afraid to overrule a decision made by some in the Executive Department" (*New York Times,* April 16, 1953).

In other ways, too, the legislative branch has alluded to the national interest when dealing with controversial matters. Thus Senator J. W. Fulbright (*New York Times,* July 16, 1965), in discussing negotiations conducted by the Firestone Tire and Rubber Co. with the communist government of Rumania for the building of a synthetic rubber plant, emphasized the national interest at stake, which, to him, seemed to favor such a plan. Likewise, Republican Senator William F. Knowland drew attention to the issue when, speaking of Viet Nam, he asked his colleague Mike Mansfield: "Do you believe it is in our national interest to have all of Asia pass into Communist hands?" (May 15, 1954).

While the clarification of the national interest has been customarily left to the executive branch, with relatively little assistance from Congress, the judiciary has at times participated in the process, when appealed to by public or private parties. Thus the Supreme Court has sided with the executive rather than Congress when the latter demanded information withheld by one of the administrative agencies, said to be acting as "the President's alter ego" and sharing his immunity against such demands (May 8, 1945). On the other hand, in cases of appeals against federal regulations in passport cases, based on claims pertaining to the national interest, the government has fared less well.

Occasionally, too, the courts have been called upon to uphold the power of the national government to determine through treaties what is in the national interest, overriding local authorities. A case in point is one in which the State of Missouri (*Missouri v. Holland,* 252 U.S. 416) raised the issue whether a 1916 treaty with Great Britain, referring to the protection of migratory birds, and a 1918 act of Congress giving effect to the treaty did not exceed federal powers, thus invading the rights of the states. The Supreme Court, speaking through Justice Holmes, asserted that "Here a national interest of very nearly the first magnitude is involved. . . . It can be protected only by national action in concert with another Power. . . . It is not sufficient to rely on the states."

From even such a cursory review, one point is clear: there is in the American system of government and politics no fixed or final arbiter on the question of what constitutes national interest. The phrase has been employed by all three branches of government, though used most extensively by the executive. Political ideas have ever, like the planets, had their special "houses," that is to say, certain ideas have been preferred by some political entities, groups, and interests, to the rejection of others. The "house" par excellence of the idea of national interest has been the executive.

Some pundits have held, like Walter Lippmann, that this

is as it should be. Congress, which has made relatively little use of the idea, habitually, according to Lippmann, "does not succeed in representing the national interest," whereas the executive is "defining and promoting the public interest" as against the ever-changing opinions and interests of the voters, whose "opportunities of judging great issues are in the very nature of things limited" (*The Public Philosophy*, Boston, 1955, Chap. IV).

Charles Beard sent a copy of his *Idea of National Interest* to President Roosevelt, and in the last pages he expressed the hope that "a new conception, with a positive core and nebulous implications" of that idea, already rising out of the past in the New Deal era, would find its "formulation at the hands of a statesman as competent and powerful as Hamilton or Jefferson." But there is no doubt that the book was addressed not to the leaders of the nation alone but to that nation itself, and in particular, to that group of political scientists, the teachers and students of political ideas, to which Beard himself belonged. Here, he supposed, among those outside government circles and more or less apart from strong specific interests, political or commercial, ethnic or regional, it should be possible to "detect and discount the self-interest group," as Lippmann phrased it, and to discuss, clarify, and proclaim the national interest.

"No one has explored the nature and implications of the formula," he said (p. 26). Yet if citizens are to support the government which proclaims it, "soldiers are to die for it, and foreign policies are to conform to it, what could be more appropriate than to ask: what is national interest? An inquiry into the substance of the formula becomes a pressing task of political science."

So far, a meager harvest has been the response. Some recent articles might be cited, such as those of Grayson Kirk ("In Search of the National Interest," *World Politics*, V, 1952) or Kenneth W. Thompson ("Beyond National Interest: A Critical Evaluation of Reinhold Niebuhr's Theory of International Politics," *Review of Politics*, XVIII, 1955). The phrase has raised its head in legal writings (Miller, "The

Public Interest Undefined," 10 *Journal of Pub. Law* 184, 1961). There have been some historical analyses, such as *In Defense of the National Interest* by Hans J. Morgenthau (New York, 1951), as well as articles on the question of whether various past administrations have preserved or injured the national interest, among them Daniel M. Smith's study of Woodrow Wilson ("National Interest and American Intervention, 1917," *Journal of American History*, 1964-65).

Here and there, pungent and appropriate remarks on the subject will be found, such as the observation on the American scene by Harold D. Lasswell that "often the phrase 'national interest' is used when what is meant is that a certain bank wants the State Department to do something" (*World Politics and Personal Insecurity*). George F. Kennan, among others, has pointed out the gross neglect of the national interest by various administrations which failed to cope with the serious problem of America's unfavorable balance of payments (*Realities of American Foreign Policy*, Princeton, 1954, p. 12); Kennan observed that our government "has not, as a rule, attempted to examine each specific thing Americans are doing abroad, with a view of judging whether it was desirable from the standpoint of national interest."

On the whole, surprisingly little has been added to the basic work published by Beard and Smith in 1934. There seems, under the circumstances, ample justification for reprinting the present volume. With the mounting American involvement in world affairs and the increasing calls upon the formula at all levels, from the lofty to the trivial, in the private and domestic as in the public and international realms, there appears a new need for a background work to assist modern scholars in filling what James M. Prothro (*Journal of Politics*, XV, 1953, pp. 67ff.) has called "the most pressing need of American politics," namely, "an effective and responsible theory of interests, concerned with protecting the rights of individuality in the humane as well as in the economic sense."

Such a task would not be light. It might well call for "civil courage" like that of the Abbé de Saint Pierre, an early formulator of the concept of national interest, when he was ejected from the Academy of France for refusing to grant the byname of "The Great" to Louis XIV—the Sun King, he averred, might be "The Powerful," but one who prosecuted warfare without regard to the interests of the nation could never be called great.

And there will remain the problem of translating theory into action. The great philosopher Leibniz, looking back in 1707 on the disappointments of his career as diplomatic negotiator for more than one court, consoled himself: "My principle is to work for the public good, regardless of whether I please anyone or not. I believe this is to imitate the Divinity which takes care of the universe, whether or no men are grateful."

Until it was selected by Quadrangle Books, *The Idea of National Interest* was long out of print. As here offered to a wider public, it contains the original text of the 1934 edition, with slight modification. Heeding the advice given by Smith himself, who was largely responsible for their preparation, Chapters VII and VIII (giving statistics on "The American Stake Abroad") have been removed because they were seriously out of date. Likewise deleted has been the Appendix to the original edition, dealing with foreign loans floated during 1920-29. Lastly, the material covered by the old Chapters VII and VIII and the old Appendix has been supplanted by a fresh Appendix prepared by Charles A. Beard's son, William, who had worked in the past with his father on various books dealing with American government.

ALFRED VAGTS

Sherman, Connecticut

THE IDEA OF NATIONAL INTEREST

CHAPTER I

THE PIVOTS OF DIPLOMACY

"FOREIGN policies are not built upon abstractions. They are the result of practical conceptions of national interest arising from some immediate exigency or standing out vividly in historical perspective." [1] In this brief sentence, Charles E. Hughes, speaking as Secretary of State, presented the central conception of modern diplomacy, and it may be added that in practice he applied it with striking precision.

Although especially pointed in statement, the formula of Secretary Hughes was not new to American thought. It reaffirmed an old doctrine accepted, as we shall see, by leaders among the founders of the American Republic, and it gave conservative and official sanction to a creed which had been refurbished during the closing years of the nineteenth century by Alfred T. Mahan, the philosopher of the sea power in history. Indeed, if there is any system at all beneath the voluminous writings of Mahan, it is that national interest is the prime consideration in foreign policy. In one place, he flatly declared: "Self-interest is not only a legitimate, but a fundamental cause for national policy; one which needs no cloak of hypocrisy. As a principle it does not require justification in general statement, although the propriety of its application to a particular instance may call for demonstrations. . . . Not every saying of Washington is as true now as it was when uttered, and some have been misapplied; but it is just as true now as ever that it is vain to expect governments to act continuously *on any other ground than national interest.* They have no right to do so, being agents and not principals." [2]

[1] *Annals of the American Academy of Political and Social Science*, Vol. CXI, Supplement, p. 7.

[2] *The Problem of Asia*, pp, 97, 187 (italics mine). See also Mahan, *The Interest of America in Sea Power—Present and Future* (1898).

I

On another occasion, Mahan confirmed this doctrine of national interest in a manner somewhat more sweeping, though similar: "It is as true now as when Washington penned the words, and always will be true, that it is vain to expect nations to act consistently from any other motive than that of interest. That, under the name of Realism, is the frankly avowed policy of German statecraft. It follows from this directly that the study of interests—international interests—is the one basis of sound, provident policy for statesmen. . . . Governments are corporations, and corporations have no souls . . . must put first the interests of their own wards . . . their own people." [3]

As Mahan implies, the conception of national interest as the principal rule of diplomacy is not confined to the United States. It is to be found in the *Realpolitik* elaborated by German writers on international relations, in the documents that pour from the chancelleries of other European countries, and in the ceremonial usages of the Orient. From the Italian dispatches of the sixteenth century to the state papers of the latest crisis it appears with striking insistence. On July 31, 1914, when with a grim foreboding of future events the German ambassador in Paris asked the French minister for foreign affairs, "What the attitude of France would be in case of war between Germany and Russia," the minister prepared in reply the laconic formula: "France will have regard to her interests." [4] The following day, when the neutrality of Luxemburg was threatened by Germany, the French minister informed his representative in the duchy that such an act "would compel France from that time to be guided in this matter by care for her defense and her interests." [5]

Even Soviet Russia, though committed broadly to the principle of communist internationalism, does not contemplate, in any case at present, the loss of her identity in a world society composed of individuals ruled from one center of power, but operates on considerations arising from state, if not national, interest. Her position is thus officially declared by Karl Radek,

[3] Admiral Mahan, *The Interest of America in International Conditions*, quoted in Perla, *What is "National Honor"?*, p. xii.
[4] *The French Yellow Book*, No. 117.
[5] *Ibid.*, No. 129.

editor of *Isvestia*, the organ of the Communist party in Soviet Russia: "The Soviet Union is strong enough to defend her territorial integrity and her interests. Concentrating her efforts on building up peaceful industries for meeting the needs of her own population, keeping aloof from armed interference with the affairs of foreign nations, the Soviet Union will seek a peaceful settlement of all conflicts which may arise between her and her neighbors. She will base her policy exclusively on her own interests, which correspond with the interests of peace both in the East and in Europe. But she will know how to defend her vital rights. Those who think that she will sacrifice them because she is afraid of a conflict are just as wrong as those who believe that she will become a tool of foreign interests." [6]

Although none of the thinkers and statesmen who thus present the doctrine of national interest speak in the language of exact science, they apparently conceive interest as a reality open to human understanding and as a kind of iron necessity which binds governments and governed alike. It binds them so closely that there is no escape, except possibly for an insignificant minority; it cuts across the social divisions reflected in political parties and compels "a united front"—an integrated, totalitarian State. Such, at least, was the contention of President Taft and President Coolidge (below, pp. 119, 132), and it was positively formulated in the address by Secretary Hughes from which the opening lines of this chapter are taken.

After saying that foreign policies are the result of practical conceptions of national interest, Mr. Hughes continued: "When long maintained, they express the hopes and fears, the aims of security or aggrandizement, which have become dominant in the national consciousness, and thus transcend party divisions and make negligible such opposition as may come from particular groups. They inevitably control the machinery of international accord which works only within the narrow field not closed by divergent ambitions or as interest yields to apprehension or obtains compensation through give and take. Statesmen who carry the burdens of empire do not for a moment lose sight of imperial purposes and requirements." While this

[6] *Foreign Affairs*, July, 1932, p. 557.

is not a deterministic sequence, in the scientific sense of the terms, it has some characteristics of the inexorable: the reality, national interest, is posited; policy is the result of practical conceptions of it; when long-maintained, policy becomes an inescapable rule for the nation—a rule written in the nature of things, partaking, it would seem, of the stern mandate imposed by the law of gravitation.[7]

NATIONAL INTEREST A MODERN CONCEPTION

Although employed as if it were a fixed principle, somewhat like the law of gravitation, the idea of national interest is, relatively speaking, a newcomer among the formulas of diplomacy and international morality. In the nature of things it could not have served the statesmen of antiquity. In that long period of history the relations of states and peoples were not conducted according to any system of international law and diplomacy. Egyptians, Persians, Jews, Greeks, and Romans did not freely grant to other peoples that equality which, though crude and imperfect in practice, is accepted in theory among the great states of modern times, nor did they conceive of their world as a family of nations or balance of power. Substantial interests were pursued, no doubt, by one powerful state or empire after another. Both negotiation and arms were employed to realize these interests. The argument of gain was abundantly used to induce soldiers and the populace to make war on neighboring societies. But, since there were no systematic relations, there was no common formula, accepted by all, on which relations were expected to turn. So far as the Romans needed verbal justification for the deed, they found it in *utilitas rei publicæ* or in *reipublicæ ratio et utilitas*.[8]

Nor in the early middle ages were circumstances favorable to the development of the conception of national interest. The teachings of Christianity, from which policies of state, so far

---

[7] *"Interessen* (materialle und ideelle), nicht Ideen, beherrschen unmittelbar das Handeln der Menschen. Aber die 'Weltbilder,' welche durch Ideen geschaffen wurden, haben sehr oft als Weichensteller die Bahnen bestimmt, in denen die Dynamik der Interessen das Handeln fortbewegte." Max Weber, quoted in Marianne Weber, *Max Weber* (1926), pp. 347f.

[8] Meinecke, *Die Idee der Staatsräson*, p. 32.

as they were articulate, and rules for private conduct were frequently drawn, lent no countenance to the idea. Christians did, to be sure, render unto Cæsar the things that were Cæsar's; they admitted that there was no power save from God; and they sanctioned prayers for the magistrates and for the good of the Roman state. "But," as Westermarck truly says, "the emperor should be obeyed only as long as his commands do not conflict with the law of God—a Christian ought rather to suffer like Daniel in the lion's den than sin against his religion; and nothing is more foreign to him than affairs of state. Indeed in the whole Roman Empire there were no men who so entirely lacked in patriotism as the early Christians. They had no affection for Judea, they soon forgot Gallilee, they cared nothing for the glory of Greece and Rome. When a judge asked them which was their country, they said in answer, 'I am a Christian.' And long after Christianity had become the religion of the Empire, St. Augustine declared that it matters not, in respect of this short and transitory life, under whose dominion a mortal man lives, if only he be not compelled to acts of impiety or injustice. Later on, when the Church grew into a political power independent of the State, she became a positive enemy of national interests. In the seventeenth century a Jesuit general called patriotism 'a plague and the most certain death of Christian love!' " [9]

For centuries after the Roman Empire was shattered, there were no national states. Wandering tribes led by war lords conquered, divided, and fought over fragments of the former Roman dominion. The milling around of nomadic peoples and tribes gradually slowed down and small states soon arose, but they were not national states. They were feudal principalities ruled over by war lords supported by their military retainers. These fragments were divided, combined, and handed about with little or no respect for race, language, geography, or trade. Slowly the feudal holdings coalesced into larger duchies, principalities, and kingdoms; the war lords became dukes, princes, and kings; their power and right to rule gradually came to rest upon a broad acceptance of the perpetuation of noble blood and lineage.

[9] Westermarck, *Origin and Development of the Moral Ideas*, Vol. II, p. 179.

The tie which bound the active part of the population, namely, the various grades of feudal lords, was a personal tie of allegiance, not a bond with the earth or people. "To a man of the middle ages 'his country' meant little more than the neighborhood in which he lived. The first duty of a vassal was to be loyal to his lord; but no national spirit bound together the various barons of one country. A man might be the vassal of the King of France and of the King of England at the same time; and often, from caprice, passion, or sordid interest, the barons sold their services to the enemies of the kingdom. . . . Far from being, as M. Gautier asserts, the object of an express command in the code of chivalry, true patriotism had no place there at all. It was not known as an ideal, still less did it exist as a reality, among either knights or commoners. As a duke of Orleans could bind himself by a fraternity of arms and alliance to a duke of Lancaster, so English merchants were in the habit of supplying nations at war with England with provisions bought at English fairs, and weapons wrought by English hands." [10]

Strictly speaking neither secular *Politik* nor reason of state is to be found in the philosophy of the early middle ages.[11] The barbarian invaders brought with them the tribal gods of war, but no large conceptions of government. They were led by commanders whose motive was plain conquest and booty, with no ethical trimmings or fine-spun notions of policy. *Am Anfang war die Tat;* in the beginning was the deed. And the deed alone was sufficient, because in the raw struggle for life, the war lords did provide for their followers an acceptable measure of subsistence and protection by their own skill in achieving a crude social organization and in manipulating it through the incessant conflicts of the middle ages. Not until after some assurance of bare survival was attained did it become necessary to go beyond the deed and establish some reason for it. The dominant interest of the lords who conquered and built extensive states, as of the vassals who followed them, was the seizure of new lands, the collection of booty, and the levying of taxes.

---

[10] Westermarck, *Origin and Development of the Moral Ideas,* Vol. II, p. 180; the sale of munitions to enemy countries is, of course, not unknown in recent times.

[11] F. Meinecke, *Die Idee der Staatsräson,* p. 33.

Not until war lords were converted to Christianity and sur-
rounded themselves with clerics who could read and write were
they bothered about explanations or justifications of their own
actions, or of the system in which they found themselves.

The purpose was unvarnished and was not challenged until
the ethics of Christianity came into vogue, and later the revived ethics of the pagan writers of Greece and Rome. Christianity itself was often employed in the early middle ages as a
covering justification for wars against infidels and heretics,
although such wars almost invariably promised and yielded
rich earthly returns. After Clovis, convinced that the God
of the Christians had aided him in winning the battle of Strass-
burg against the Alemanni, was baptized with his whole army,
he served the "true faith" by conquering the King of the Bur-
gundians who clung to "the Arian heresy." Then, finding that
the "fair lands of Aquitaine" were also in the hands of "unbe-
lieving Arians," Clovis combined religious motives with conquest
and exploitation. The subjugation of England by William of
Normandy had papal approval; from time to time the pope lent
aid to one Christian king against another for reasons of ec-
clesiastical politics; and after the pope and high dignitaries of
the Church acquired large domains themselves they frequently
sanctioned wars among Christians for practical reasons.

But neither the Church nor Christian writers, as such, could
consistently lend any support to one Christian king against
another or furnish any philosophy of politics to sustain the
pretensions of particular monarchs or the secular claims which,
in time, came to be covered by the phrase dynastic interests.
The pope might give aid and comfort to one king against another less loyal or compliant, but not on any theory of royal or
national advantage. He might, on a rare occasion, prefer the
growth of the Holy Roman Empire to the development of independent and recalcitrant kingdoms, but in his eyes one faithful monarch stood on the same footing as all others.

Indeed the weight of the Church was, on the whole, against
the spread of centrifugal influences under the cover of dynastic
and national enterprise. Of necessity this was true. In organization, faith, and conception, the Church was universal, at
least for Europeans. Its clergy formed one intellectual and

religious brotherhood, spoke and wrote in one tongue—Latin, and thought in terms of an all-embracing union of the faithful. Though clerks often served kings, sometimes too well for the good of the Church, they could not throw off their greater loyalty to the papacy and write a philosophy of nationalism in any form. "To place worldly interests above the claims of the Church was impious. When Machiavelli declared that he preferred his country to the safety of his soul, people considered him guilty of blasphemy; and when the Venetians defied the papal thunders by averring that they were Venetians in the first place and only Christians in the second, the world heard them with amazement." [12]

THE CONCEPTION OF DYNASTIC INTEREST

Evidently, then, the Christian faith, if open to various interpretations, could furnish no formula adequate to the requirements of any particular political interests under the hegemony of the Church during the middle ages. In the circumstances, individual overlords and monarchs found in secular life other sanctions to serve them in their struggle for power, riches, and domain. At length, "the will of the prince" and later "dynastic interest" appeared as convenient formulas for secular rulers, as feudal principalities were merged into rising states. Thus the idea of fealty to the overlord expanded into loyalty to the king or reigning house; and the support thus established was further strengthened by the employment of mercenaries to be sustained by growing tax levies.

At first, these sanctions were assumed and frankly employed as such, without a covering of popular ideology. Under the law of God and nature, the will of the prince was supreme— in the legal theory of the middle ages. If the prince waged war, made alliances, annexed territories, and adopted diplomatic policies, that was sufficient for his subjects, at least, as long as it was sufficient. For centuries, accordingly, the relations of European countries turned wholly or chiefly on princely or dynastic considerations and such interests meant in substance increases in territory, vast accumulations of personal

[12] Westermarck, *op. cit.*, Vol. II, p. 181.

property, fortunate family alliances, and bitter personal and family rivalries; and, in the later period, the enlargement of royal revenues through the enrichment of merchants and agriculturists. Ambassadors appeared as royal agents, and royal agents they remained as long as kings retained absolute dominion.

It would be a mistake, accordingly, to follow the theorists and treat the formula, "dynastic interest," as if it were an ideal and logical system of thought, consistent in all its parts and regularly employed by statesmen as a controlling principle to the exclusion of practical considerations. In fact, it covered substantial realities and was seldom, if ever, invoked in the collective actions of monarchs before the appearance of the republican specter. At bottom and stripped of all trappings, dynastic interest originally meant the interest of each monarch in holding fast to the territories and privileges which he already possessed, in keeping a firm grip upon the activities of his subjects, in extending his domains at the expense of his neighbors, and in the aggrandizement and perpetuation of his house. All this brought riches in lands, palaces, chattels, and money, quite as material as those collected by, let us say, modern merchants engaged in a foreign trade, for the protection of which national interest is invoked. Dynastic interest as a general principle came to the front only when revolutionary republics and restless populations drove frightened monarchs to make common cause to stave off impending eclipse.

All formulas associated with dynastic diplomacy thus had their basis in the realities of dynastic interest. The elaborate language of royal and imperial intercourse deceived no one within the circle; the ambassador in glittering court costume could work as hard at gaining a crumb of territory for his avaricious lord as a black-coated minister of modern times does in winning an oil concession abroad for those whom his government serves at home. The transition from the diplomacy of dynastic interest to that of national interest did not mark, therefore, as great a break as the change in pomp and circumstance would seem to indicate.

To trace the rise and decline of "dynastic interest" as a diplomatic formula would require a re-writing of European history for centuries and obviously lies outside the scope of this inquiry. Yet it is relevant to speak of the doom of that conception and to give a practical illustration of the manner in which it was finally blotted out, for practical purposes, by the triumph of cold, impersonal, national interest.

That the diplomacy of dynastic interest was sinking into oblivion near the close of the nineteenth century was made clear, even to its defenders, by the secret negotiations which went on in Europe over the coming war between the United States and Spain. When in the autumn of 1897, General Woodford, the American Minister at Madrid, presented to the Spanish government a protest against its conduct in Cuba and demanded a cessation of hostilities, the German Emperor, William II, was moved by a surge (*Aufwallung*) of feeling for monarchical solidarity to raise with the German Foreign Office the issue of intervention in behalf of Spain by the European states, possibly by the Continental states only, whose monarchical form of government, he thought, would be threatened by the independence of Cuba. There were even rumors in the press that the Kaiser might address a note to the Government of the United States in the same tone as his famous dispatch during the Transvaal affair a short time before. At all events he was profoundly stirred by the peril to the dynastic interest inherent in the Spanish-American controversy.[13]

But as soon as the Kaiser took up the question with his foreign office, his ardor for action in support of dynastic interest was immediately chilled by the cold waters of commercial interest. Although there was no lack of sympathy for the dynastic principle in Berlin, the futility of acting upon it directly was speedily demonstrated. With due display of tact, Herr von Bülow telegraphed, for the Kaiser's information, that he hoped, in seeking to meet the intentions of the All Highest, to prevent England and France—in case of common action in favor of Spain—from holding off themselves and gaining economic advantages at Germany's expense. If Eng-

---

[13] Owing to the revolution in Germany which tore open the secret archives, it is possible to trace an outline of the affair in German diplomatic documents: *Die Grosse Politik der Europäischen Kabinette, 1871–1914*, Vol. XV, pp. 3–30, upon which the above record is based. What French, English, and Spanish papers may sometime show is a matter for interesting speculation.

land and France stood aside, he said, the result of common action would not only be doubtful but could bring positive harm to Germany in the form of adverse political and economic consequences.

Then Herr von Bülow came down to the nub of the matter. He recalled for the Kaiser's benefit that the English exports to America amounted to $170,000,000, German to $94,000,000, and French to $66,000,000; while American exports to England totalled $406,000,000, to Germany $97,000,000, and to France $47,000,000. He also directed the attention of His Majesty to the fact that the new American tariff law authorized the President of the United States to grant special favors to foreign countries through reciprocal agreements. Such was Germany's economic position considered in dollars and marks equivalents. On the other hand, Russian, Austro-Hungarian, and Italian trade and shipping interests were far below those of England, Germany, and France. Five words of sympathy for the Kaiser's dynastic interest; a whole note on the politics and economics of commercial interest. Perhaps the proportion of words represented the weight of dynastic interest in the scales of diplomacy in the new capitalistic age. Herr von Bülow was adroit in dealing with William II, but clear and firm.

In transmitting this paper to His Imperial Majesty, Prince zu Eulenburg, of the Kaiser's retinue, agreed sympathetically with the monarchical principle, expressed doubts about the coöperation of England and France, and hinted that a secret suggestion from Germany to Austria would perhaps be the right way to proceed. He added that Austria was the state from which a proposal in favor of Spain should naturally come. The Austrian Minister, Count Goluchowski, had continually made efforts to interest Germany in the matter; and it would be well if he, reasonably sure of Germany's approval, would take over the business of initiation in favor of the Queen-Regent at Madrid. For this plan Prince zu Eulenburg had the endorsement of William II. It depended, he said, upon the realities of the situation. One must choose the most effective method for reaching the goal. Should there be difficulty in enlisting the support of the French Republic for the dynastic principle, it might be possible to unite the powers on another platform, namely, that their colonial possessions ought to be protected against over-seas covetousness *(Begehrlichkeiten)*. Evidently dynasties were not strong enough to assert themselves openly in their own defense; commercial interests were more powerful; yet by indirection the latter might be used for dynastic ends. Things had changed fundamentally since the allied monarchs moved upon the French Republic after the outbreak of the first Revolution.

In response to Prince zu Eulenburg's expression of views, Herr von Bülow etched the realities of the situation in sharper lines. In order to help the Spanish monarchy without bringing economic and political injuries to Germany, it was desirable, on the one hand, to act if possible with England and France; in any case, with France, against America; and, on the other hand, to avoid the assumption of leadership themselves. How was France to be enlisted? The French were financially and economically more deeply involved in Spain than were the Germans, while an injury to American relations would affect Germany more seriously than it would France. Russia and Austria-Hungary had only slight economic interests in the United States, as compared with Germany, France, and England, and would risk next to nothing in seeking to block American action in Cuba. Given this situation, von Bülow thought that it would be most satisfactory to Germany if France and Russia, or France alone, or England alone, would take the initiative. Perhaps the goal would be reached quickest if Germany, with complete secrecy, should approach the Vienna cabinet—the natural attorney for the Spanish Queen-Regent— with the proposal that Austria make sure of French, Russian, and English support for common procedure in favor of Spain against the United States—"in accordance with the measure of the All Highest's command." To this solution of the problem, the Kaiser gave his approval in a marginal note on the document. Thus it was generally agreed in German governing circles that independent action by Germany in behalf of the dynastic principle would arouse jealousy in England and France and run against German interests. The dynastic principle was precious, of course, but economic considerations were regarded as "decisive in controversies between Europe and

America," and all diplomatic shuffling had to be done within the frame set by economic interests.

It would be irrelevant to trace the tortuous windings of European diplomats in their efforts to protect dynastic interest while safeguarding economic interest. Sufficient for the purposes of this study is the summary: None of the governments or monarchs who spent days and weeks in fruitless negotiations behind the scenes could or at least dared to risk practical interests in an effort to uphold the dynastic principle or the fortunes of any dynasty. The diplomacy of dynastic interest revealed its futility. The dusk of dynastic interest had come; and darkness fell upon it at the end of the World War.

Incidentally, during the negotiations, the principle of universality, represented by the Church, was likewise defied, for all efforts of the pope to save the Spanish house from war were equally futile. On the one side, he entered into the secret negotiations of royal governments and, on the other, he sought to bring direct pressure upon President McKinley through Archbishop Ireland. This, too, came to nothing. The Church Universal was as powerless as William II or Queen Victoria to prevent the war or save the Spanish dynasty from the humiliation of defeat. Like its ancient associate and frequent foe, monarchy, the Church had become impotent in the presence of conflicting national interests.

The abandonment of the dynastic conception was not due, therefore, to a sudden substitution of ideas. In the long process leading up to its eclipse there had been a decided shift in substantial interests. As we have seen, dynastic interest originally meant the interest of the particular monarch in holding fast to the territories he already possessed, in extending his domains, and in the aggrandizement of his house. Dynastic interest was not an abstraction springing from the realm of pure reason and employed as such to move governments, armies, and navies. It embraced, in fact, lands, palaces, goods, chattels, and revenues differing in degree rather than in kind from those enjoyed by the subjects of monarchs, though clothed in the majesty of public law. And long before the age of the dynasts had drawn to a close, they were subjected to the restrictions and pressure of other interests which were growing up among their peoples—interests quite apart from, if not in conflict with, the mere maintenance of ruling families and their personal advantages. Hence the transition from dynastic to national interest was not as sharp as the outward history of monarchies would seem to imply to superficial observers. Although the change had far-reaching repercussions in externalities, it was primarily an internal transformation, involving principally the question: For whose benefit is diplomacy carried on and whose will is to determine the policy and exercise the greatest control.

REASON OF STATE AS THE PIVOT OF DIPLOMACY

Closely associated, though by no means identical, with the formula of dynastic interest is that of *ragione di stato, raison d'état, Staatsräson,* reason of state. In searching for the origin of this concept we are carried back to Machiavelli. While it is true that he did not compress his system of politics into this or any other slogan, he undoubtedly laid the foundation upon which all later systems of state-reason were built. Although the term was widely used in many senses, good and bad, justifying both low intrigue and high measures of public welfare, the system of politics to which the name of Machiavellianism was popularly given carried definite connotations in the minds of realistic statesmen. It meant maintaining in power the practising government, whether republican or royal, crushing dangerous opposition at home, extending dominion and influence abroad, and enriching the ruling class of the state. In the attainment of these great ends all means were justified—intrigue, bribery, secret alliances, wars, annexations, and indemnities. Obviously such a system of politics can work effectively only under a régime of secrecy—*arcana imperii;* it is incompatible with parliamentary institutions, published treaties, and a free press. Moreover, however cynically pursued by many modern statesmen, it runs counter to many sentiments which interfere with, if they do not block, its effective functioning.

In its diluted forms, reason of state provided no practical guide to statesmen, no fulcrum for diplomacy, no working basis for international relations. It was largely an opportune device, a defense mechanism, too uncertain in its application to give continuity or unity to diplomatic practice. In the hands of Giovanni Botero, *ragione di stato* is a combination of Machiavellian shrewdness and respect for religious institutions. Ammirato was equally, or even more, vague, for he defined reason of state as nothing more than the *contravenzione di ragione ordinaria per rispetto di publico benefitio o vero per rispetto di maggiore e piu universal ragione.*[14] Obviously such abstractions furnish no guide for statesmen in dealing with concrete situations.

Nor have any of the efforts in modern Europe to give working substance to state-reason been more successful. When Meinecke says that state-reason consists of the maxims of state affairs, the law of state motion, telling statesmen what they must do to maintain the state in health and strength, he does not illuminate the path of diplomats confronted by imperial and trade rivalries, foreign investments, inter-governmental debts, defaulted bonds, or disorders in backward countries. Hence the use of reason of state, either in the Machiavellian sense or as modified by later interpretations, has slowly dropped out of the documents of practical politics. It now abides mainly with closet philosophers. When foreign offices, confronted by inconvenient questions from parliamentary bodies, decline to give out information, they do not appeal to any reason of state, but to the new slogan, "public interest." [15]

Naturally, the decline in the use of such *termini technici* came first in countries like England and Holland where monarchies were early challenged by popular bodies. In absolute monarchies, possessing supreme and exclusive governing power, the term, "state reason," could be easily used to fortify the position of rulers and their bureaucracies. There the idea, equivalent to *suprema lex*, order, royal command, was unanswerable and final. But in England the case was different. Attempts of the Stuarts to fasten authoritarian concepts upon

[14] Meinecke, *op. cit.*, p. 151.

[15] Joint resolutions of the American Congress, calling upon the executive for information and reports upon foreign policies, invariably include the phrase "if compatible with the public interest," indicating the modern form into which "state-reason" has passed.

the estates of the realm failed utterly. The English Parliament, accustomed to argumentation and to answering royal ministers and even kings in sharp language, would have none of the absolute irresponsibility that hid itself behind *raison d'état*. For, at bottom, state reason meant that the monarch and a small group of persons around him claimed omniscience with respect to the state's true interest. With the establishment of parliamentary supremacy, the idea of state reason and state interest became largely obsolete in England, surviving longest in the language of the courts of law in dealing with high treason and other state cases. As use of the term declined, such notions as the interest of England, the public interest, and national interest took its place (below, p. 24).

THE FORMULA OF NATIONAL HONOR

Among the reasons of state, peculiarly appropriate to feudal orders and monarchies, there early appeared a formula known as the "honor of the prince," which was easily transformed, with the growth of democracy, into the idea of "national honor." As its Latin origin implies, the term "honor" was associated with the requirements of rank; an *honestus vir* was a man of high status, possessing property in keeping with his condition; and certain signs and ceremonies of respect, such as salutations and genuflections, were associated with his position in society. In feudal times the characteristics of honor were found in the *code duello*. Ordinarily they did not pertain to pecuniary matters but to insults, aspersions of character, defamation, signs of contempt, and the virtue of women. To give a king's ambassador a lower place at a public spectacle or at a conference table than His Majesty felt proper in view of his conceptions of grandeur and position was an affront to his honor, to his dignity and his status.[16] From feudal and monarchical orders the formula passed over to republics and

[16] The troublesome question of rank and position in diplomatic practice, especially at congresses and conferences, has become less pressing only in recent years as the nations consent to alphabetical arrangements and other abstract standards. The whole code of precedence based upon honor and degrees of eminence has not, of course, been completely obliterated; it has merely become less important.

democracies and was widely employed in political and diplomatic usage and literature.

Like other slogans of politics, the term was never minutely analyzed or defined, but it was treated as covering something transcending in nature all material and economic interests. Indeed from the standpoint of national honor, the latter were deemed ignoble, and appeals to them unworthy of patriotism. This did not mean that statesmen who employed the term, national honor, were more opposed than princes to wars for material interests; on the contrary, in their opinion, national honor often coincided with winning substantial advantages by arms; yet, as a rule, exponents of the code were inclined to regard with contempt arguments against war based on the pecuniary consideration that war does not "pay."

In many instances, however, "honor" provided a convenient manœuvring ground for the attainment of economic or political advantage. A cause in which economic matters were involved was not to be rejected, if questions of national honor could also be drawn into the scene, but honor was the supreme concern. The case was clearly put in an address before the Naval War College in 1897 by Theodore Roosevelt, whose public papers and private writings are strewn with the terms "righteousness" and "national honor." In calling for battleships as against arbitration treaties, he said: "A really great people, proud and high spirited, would face all the disasters of war rather than purchase that base prosperity which is bought at the price of national honor. . . . We ask for a great navy partly because we think that the possession of such a navy is the surest guaranty of peace, and partly because we feel that no national life is worth having if the nation is not willing, when the need shall arise, to stake everything on the supreme arbitrament of war and to pour out its blood, its treasure, and tears like water rather than submit to the loss of honor or renown." [17]

So widely spread was the conception of national honor as the supreme consideration of diplomacy and international relations, in republican America no less than in imperial Germany, that the Hague Conference of 1899 placed it first on the

[17] Bishop, *Theodore Roosevelt and His Time,* Vol. 1, p. 77.

reservations of states. In recommending that parties unable to settle controversies by negotiation should submit them to inquiry by an impartial commission, the Conference included only matters "involving neither honor nor vital interest." For many years thereafter it was customary for governments in drawing arbitration treaties to make similar reservations. That signed by Great Britain and the United States, in 1908, for example, in stipulating that certain differences should be referred to the Hague Tribunal, contained the significant addendum: "Provided, nevertheless, that they do not affect the vital interests, the independence, or the honor of the two contracting states." As the follower of the *code duello* could not submit a matter touching his pride to a court of law in an action for pecuniary damages, so no nation could suffer the arbitration of any point involving honor. As Lord John Russell said, in speaking of the Alabama claims: "That is a question of honor which we will never arbitrate, for England's honor can never be made the subject for arbitration." [18]

Yet on close scrutiny the meaning of national honor in concrete terms proved to be exceedingly elusive. Mr. Perla's symposium of opinions on the subject, published in 1918, revealed an array of diverse and conflicting ideas respecting the content of the phrase, the association of pecuniary interests with it, the occasions on which it should be invoked, and the means of satisfaction. In his careful analysis the irrationality and emotional perils of the concept stood clearly revealed.

As trade, commerce, and other economic relations became increasingly the major subject matters with which international questions were associated, and as the exercise of national sovereignty changed from the personal control of a monarch to that of a popular representative body, the formula of national honor became more and more inadequate. So long as pride, dignity, position, and the aggrandizement of royal families and their retinues, and similar matters of personal and emotional content constituted significant subjects of international discourse, the mere assertion of national honor was sufficient. By their very nature such matters were not debatable. Each personal sovereign and later each sovereign nation was

[18] Perla, *What is "National Honor"?*, p. 36.

the sole judge of its own conduct. There was no basis, no objective standard, for calling these matters into question and settling them.

When, however, economic issues gained a preponderance in international relations, much of the ground upon which the original conception of national honor rested was destroyed. Economic questions, treating of material things, of industry, trade, tariffs, exchange, and the like, are open to statistical enumeration, to reason and logic, to debate and persuasion. Acceptable standards can be applied, and differences of opinion do not involve any indictment of opponents on principles of honor. The very nature of such questions usually precludes their absolute determination at the will of, or by the action of, a single person or a small group. At all events, the use of reason is not excluded.

As soon as the prime subject matters of international intercourse took economic forms, the views and standards of many different peoples and groups became applicable, without insult to any; and "honor" in this connection became debatable, was stripped of absolutism. Moreover, since it was generally impossible to raise an issue of honor that did not also involve pecuniary risks, losses, or gains, it was increasingly difficult to keep pecuniary calculations from entering into the weighing of honor, openly or secretly. It was almost impossible to isolate pure "honor" and avoid imputations of interest. Thus honor as a single, insulated pivot of diplomacy was deprived of its finality.

As time passed, statesmen were led to lay diminishing emphasis on a formula that defied rational analysis, that had its sanction mainly in emotion and ceremony.[19] Perhaps they discerned a certain inconsistency, if not irony, in treaties by which "honorable" governments, which *ipso facto* could not insult one another, reserved from pacific settlement questions of insult against one another. At all events, the phrase, "national honor," already declining in efficacy prior to the World War, was abandoned in some respects and materially altered

---

[19] The assertion that a particular question is a matter "solely of domestic concern" illustrates one of the modern forms into which the original conception of honor is passing.

in others in the post-war years. The emotional and sentimental complex of national honor has not wholly disappeared; nor are appeals to it wanting in lighter political literature; [20] but as a working formula for international action it has become of distinctly secondary importance.[21]

The later arbitration treaties omit it. The climax is reached in the Kellogg Pact which condemns recourse to war for the solution of international difficulties, binds the signatories to renounce it as an instrument of national policy in their relations with one another, and obligates them to seek the pacific settlement of "all disputes or conflicts of whatever nature or of whatsoever origin they may be." The *code duello* is renounced and even matters of national honor are to be adjusted by peaceful processes, without recourse to arms. The transition from the sentiments of feudalism to the philosophy of calculation has been completed—in the pretensions of contemporary diplomacy.

[20] Thus, Senator McCumber, when questioning Secretary of State Robert Lansing concerning the power given to a "commission of inquiry" by certain labor provisions of the Treaty of Peace with Germany, signed June 28, 1919, asked: "But do you think it an appropriate thing for a great government to put itself in a position in which it should submit itself in honor or in any other way to be hauled up before a commission of this kind to answer as to what it should do with reference to its own labor?" Clearly indicating the insignificance of this aspect of the "honor" formula, Mr. Lansing replied: "I do not think there is anything out of the way about that at all." *Senate Doc.* 106, 66th Congress, Vol. 10, p. 178.

[21] Modern diplomatic negotiation frequently appeals to national honor, as for example in connection with the "sanctity" of treaties; but it does so only in support of a position taken rather than as a position per se—"honor" as an independent pivot of diplomacy. The most frequent modern use of the national honor formula is that by which internal, national action is influenced vis-à-vis international relationships. It was so used to bring about the repeal of the clause in the Panama Canal Act of August 24, 1912, which exempted American vessels engaged in the coastwise trade from the payment of tolls. Similarly, the "national honor" concept was employed in the debate concerning the devaluation of the gold dollar (Senator R. C. Patterson, *Cong. Record,* 73d Cong. 1st Sess., April 25, 1933, p. 2339); and again, in connection with the debate on the "joint resolution (H. J. Res. 192) to assure uniform value to the coins and currencies of the United States" (bearing upon the "gold clause" in financial obligations). (See Senator David A. Reed, *Cong. Record,* 73d Cong. 1st Sess., June 3, 1933, p. 4996). The number of instances of this kind is almost unlimited, especially when legislation on domestic affairs is likely to have repercussions outside American borders. This is one of the new ways of applying the old "national honor" formula.

THE RISE OF THE IDEA OF NATIONAL INTEREST

Responsive to the ever-changing physical conditions of the world, the character and occupations of its people, and the political and economic structure of society, the old formulas of international relations—will of the prince, dynastic interests, reason of state, and national honor—came into being, served their respective purposes in a rough way, and passed into history. Most of these formulas are today either entirely abandoned as pivots or fulcra of diplomacy, or their form is so radically altered as to render their operation and influence indirect and of minor importance. No diplomat is any longer seriously disturbed by the will of the prince.[22] Dynastic interests have long since passed into the discard with the eclipse of monarchical rule. State-reason and the feudalistic conceptions of national honor have broken down completely under the impact of economic relations and popular control of government. All these formulas now appear too abstract, too unreal, and too remote from modern conditions to be effective. In the light of modern demands for a foreign policy truly expressive of realities, stable, consistent, and capable of being handled by logical and analytical methods, these old formulas, with their personal associations, their emotional content, their uncertainties and needless hazards, are recognized as deficient.

With the emergence of the national state system, the increase in influence of popular political control, and the great expansion of economic relations, the lines of a new formula—"national interest"—were being laid down. The process by which the new formula came into general use was largely evolutionary, many of the elements of the old formulas, after much re-interpretation and adaptation, being incorporated in it. National interest, as a pivot of diplomacy, is now almost universally employed in international relations. Indeed, it may be said that national interest—its maintenance, advancement, and defense by the various means and instrumentalities of political power—is the prime consideraton of diplomacy. The term

---

[22] Although the power of dictatorships is often strong and absolute, the will of the dictator does not have the same moral sanction as the will of the prince once had.

evidently appeals to men of affairs as susceptible of rational comprehension, concrete definition, and specific usage. Unlike the abstractions and vagaries of the old formulas, national interest seems to bear a clear and positive relation to the tangibles which are the major concern of the modern world, especially to economic operations that can be cast or reflected in particular and general balance sheets.

Although no microscopic history of the idea of national interest has yet been written, some tentative conclusions respecting its origin and development are permissible. The term "interest" is old, being a derivation from the Latin. The word means: it concerns; it makes a difference to, or is important with reference to, some person or thing: *interest omnium recte facere*. In the middle ages, when religious affairs were the chief preoccupation of the intellectual class, it was often employed in spiritual relations—"the heavenly interests of mankind"— and did not necessarily carry material implications. With the spread of secularism and commerce it took on tangible substance—"worldly interests," as contrasted with things of the spirit. With the rise of political economy the term assumed material connotations, thrusting other usages into the background. In some circles it was employed in an invidious sense, in attacks on "vested interests," but the word of aspersion was often accepted by the aspersed; and statesmen were not ashamed to speak of "dollar" diplomacy. While the word retains, and may rightly retain, much of its ancient flavor, whenever it appears in diplomatic and political negotiations it can generally be broken down into substantial elements.

At all events, the use of national interest in diplomacy is particularly associated in time with the rise and growth of the national commercial state, and with the evolution of republican control over national affairs. The nations of Western Europe had scarcely emerged from the chaos of feudalism under the leadership of strong monarchs, when the era of discovery and world commerce opened. If nations were built up by dynastic interests, they soon broke the mold and outran the purposes of their makers. "Princes rule peoples," said the Duke de Rohan in 1638, "and interests dominate the princes." In the beginning the "interests" that ruled princes were interests as conceived by the princes and agreeable to them. As long as the prince merely commanded small groups of fighting men, he could freely consult his own pleasure and will; but as commerce increased, towns flourished, and society became compactly knit in an economic mesh, the prince himself became a victim of interests. National interest was largely developed through the compromise between interests dynastically conceived and interests as interpreted and enforced by the rising class power, and later by popular power.

This change in affairs was apparently observed first, and not strangely, in the commercial cities of Italy, and the philosophy of it was outlined in the documents known as the "Italian Relations"—reports of Italian ambassadors from the other countries of Europe. Commercial in interest and compelled to employ every possible stratagem to preserve themselves against destruction by powerful foes, the Italian cities sent out diplomatic agents who were, of necessity, realistic in their approach. These ministers reported not only on the intrigues of courts, but also on industry, commerce, legislation, and the customs and prejudices of peoples. By the middle of the sixteenth century they reached the conclusion that the great movements of politics sprang from deeply rooted forces of life, that the impersonal *interessi di stato* controlled the relations of states with one another, that each state was driven by the egoism of its own needs and interests, and that all other motives of policy were secondary.[23]

From Italy, it seems, the doctrine of interest spread to France where it was re-formulated for French usage by powerful writers during the first half of the seventeenth century. While direct connections are not yet established, it is not without significance that one of the thinkers of the new direction, Duke de Rohan, spent some time in Italy before he wrote his treatise, "De l'Interest des Princes et Estats de la Chrestienté" (1638). In due course the idea of national interest became associated with the concept of dynastic interest in various parts of Europe, giving wider content to that ancient historic formula.

Across the Channel in England, where dynastic interest was

[23] Meinecke, *op. cit.*, p. 188.

early subdued to parliamentary control and reason of state was early recognized as a mere covering formula for monarchical and bureaucratic pretensions (above, p. 15), the idea of "England's interest," "public interest," and "national interest" found a hospitable home by the end of the seventeenth century. Parliamentarians, publicists, and representatives of ruling classes used the new concept freely as equivalent to the sum of particular interests or a balance of interests in society. In this way they justified policies of government, on the comfortable assumption that a harmony of interests existed, that interest, though often mistaken, could "never lie"—to use the phrase of an old writer, and that national interest could be disclosed by adding together the dominant interests. As the circle of governing classes widened, the circle of interested parties widened, and the interest of society, meaning the vocal and efficient sections of it, supplanted the interest of the dynasty.

In the English colonies beyond the Atlantic, where feudal and monarchical sentiments became attenuated as the population grew, state reason was early regarded with suspicion, and popular interests bulked large in the thought of public men.[24] In their resistance to the British government, Americans acquired a habit of using terms like "the people," the "nation," or the "commonwealth" when speaking of *res publicæ* in a laudatory sense and of referring to government or state when employing derogatory language.[25] To Americans the state appeared as "a cold monster." As the British official class in the colonies and the British Admiralty increased their pressures on American economic life, under pretense of a general British interest,[26] the provincials developed a sense of community, local,

---

[24] When William Penn was threatened with the loss of his proprietary rights, he wrote to Robert Harley: "It is pretended the King's service, but I hope reason of state shall never be one to violate property." August 27, 1701. *Portland Mss.*, Vol. IV, pp. 19ff.

[25] Schmoller, *Jahrbuch*, 1894, p. 1241; citation of W. J. Ashley's writings.

[26] With a view to overcoming the resistance of local interests—"the interests of private landowners being often opposed to that of the public"—certain cases were transferred from local courts to the Admiralty courts. *Acts of the Privy Council of England; Colonial Series;* Vol. I, p. 194. A British admiral, stationed in the waters of the West Indies, complained of difficulties placed in his way by the authorities of Jamaica in 1702: "Private

or collective interest as against the weight above. Dynastic interest and state reason had no roots in the American heritage, and British usage had prepared the way for a transition to commonwealth or national interest.

Even from this cursory survey it seems evident that the transition from feudal formulas to the conception of national interest was not marked by a sharp break in ideas, akin to the opposition between the Ptolemaic and Copernican systems. It was a gradual transition from formula to formula. The conception of *unity* associated with dynastic interest remained. An element of compelling *absolutism* was retained: national interest was no less sovereign and inexorable than the will of the prince. Although national interest was opposed to dynastic interest, its official interpreters might exclude the nation from knowledge of specific operations in foreign affairs on grounds of "the public interest." The main citadel of the *arcana imperii* stood unscathed.

If the transition marked no sharp break, however, it was swift. As European commerce expanded to all parts of the world, wars between reigning families over territories in Europe became entangled with wars over colonies, backward places, and trade, thus spreading to the ends of the earth. Meanwhile commerce flourished, capital accumulated, and the trading classes rose in numbers and wealth until they overshadowed the aristocracies of the soil. Monarchs were gradually subdued by parliaments in which the middle class gained ascendancy. Monarchies became republican nations in fact, if not also in name. Science undermined the intellectual authority of the clergy who were concerned, theoretically at least, with other-worldly interests. Competition between capitalist countries for raw materials and markets became sharper and sharper. Political economy was transformed into economics, the science of private gain. Darwinism introduced a principle which was interpreted as implying an eternal struggle for existence on a material plane, as lending biological sanction to the primary significance of material interests. The church was

interest is what they aim at without regard to the King's order or security of this island, whose interest here will be either lost or ruined if left in their hands." *State Papers: Domestic. Anne,* Vol. I, p. 147.

divorced from the state and the desiderata of politics became fundamentally secular. At last the way was prepared for the unquestioned supremacy of national interest in international relations and of the idea as the guide to national action.

Yet no one has explored the nature and implications of the new formula. If citizens are to support the government which prosecutes it, soldiers are to die for it, and foreign policies are to conform to it, what could be more appropriate than to ask: What is national interest? An inquiry into the substance of the formula becomes a pressing task of political science. A beginning may be made with a study of the idea in the United States.

THE PROBLEM

The problem presented by the proposed inquiry is not one in exact science—an examination of a deterministic sequence, a physical process under law which can be expressed by a differential equation. Nor is it a problem of philology to be solved by an excursion in etymology, resulting in a dictionary definition. The question—what is national interest?—can be answered, if at all, only by exploring the use of the formula by responsible statesmen and publicists and by discovering the things and patterns of conduct—public and private—embraced within the scope of the formula. The problem, then, can be expressed in terms of formula, things, and patterns of conduct. Where the formula appears in the usages of statecraft it is appropriate to explore the substance covered by it. Where the things and patterns of conduct covered by it appear, with or without the formula, it is appropriate to relate them to the conception of national interest; for obviously statesmen do not always pronounce the formula every time they operate under the conception. Only in this way can unity of theme, continuity of practice, diversity of interpretation, and possible upshot be kept steadily in view until general conclusions are reached.

Of necessity the initial procedure must be historical, for the term, national interest, has been extensively employed by American statesmen since the establishment of the Constitution. The formula is an idea which has been developed in a long course of years. Conceivably, to be sure, a shallow time-depth could be taken—the use of the term during the past six months, the past ten years, or the past fifty years; but any such segmentation of history would be arbitrary. It would leave out of account relevant practices, usages, thought, and traditions which cannot be excluded if the fullness of the theme is to be covered. Yet there must be a beginning; and the break made in American institutional history by the establishment of the Constitution affords a starting point which is more than merely convenient. The adoption of the Constitution marked a new concentration of efficient forces in American politics, the creation of new machinery for giving expression to those forces in foreign affairs, and the coöperation of leading statesmen in laying down fundamental lines of foreign policy for the future. Moreover, it is within the framework of the Constitution that foreign policies coming under the head of national interest are still formulated and carried into execution.

Other considerations call for historical procedure. The formula, national interest, embraces two terms—national and interest. Now, it is a matter of common knowledge that the American nation was not created at one stroke in 1776 or in 1787. It is the product of a long historical development. Although the term, nation, was freely used by the Fathers, by Jefferson as well as Hamilton, it later came under a cloud, as the existence of the nation was challenged by those advocates of states' rights who placed loyalty to their respective commonwealths above loyalty to "the general government," as it was often called. Not until the great decision of 1865 was the issue settled and the existence and supremacy of the nation assured against all doubts and opposition, political or military. Thus, although the nation of the Fathers perdured and survived the trial by battle, the use of the term "national" in connection with "interest" rose and fell with the fortunes of the domestic conflict that divided the country. The substance of nationality continued in development, but the phraseology of politics varied. Since we are concerned with substance as well as formula, consistency of treatment requires respect for historical continuity.

Historical treatment is also required by the very nature of the diplomacy which turns upon national interest. Despite all calls for "a united front" and for the stoppage of politics "at the water's edge," American diplomacy, within certain broad limits, reflects party divisions at home, and is party diplomacy. Owing to the inherent characteristics of the American system, government is party government. And it is in historical time that parties succeed one another in control over the machinery and engines of foreign policy. Although some continuity is assured by general considerations, by the bureaucracy of the State Department, and by the permanent technicians of the Navy Department, fluctuations more or less violent have occurred and do occur in the interpretation of national interest. Since this is true, it follows that a wide historical span must be brought under review in a quest for the meaning of national interest.

The first step, therefore, is historical—an inquiry into the things and patterns of conduct covered by the formula, "national interest"—in their development from 1787 to the present moment. Such an inquiry can be objective, factual, and realistic, within the range of empirical scholarship. The things and patterns can be described with fair accuracy, in a manner approaching that of exact science; and typical applications of the formula can be disclosed by historical investigation. Such is the rule of reference controlling the exploration and arrangement of materials in this volume. When this task has been completed, the way is open for an evaluation of the doctrine, as well as the things and patterns of conduct covered by it, and for an attempt to construct out of the materials a philosophy of national interest, consistent in its several parts, to serve as a guide to policy and an interpretation of history in the process of unfolding. Inasmuch as the second step involves the necessity of choosing and asserting values, it is reserved for a separate volume to follow—to avoid confusing facts with assumptions and predilections.

Although the first step is historical, it does not call for a rewriting of American history. It implies at the outset an exploration of the original conception of national interest under the Constitution, with respect to things and patterns of conduct covered by it. That exploration yields two fundamental relevancies in the field of national interest—territory and commerce, including their connections with domestic affairs. By this disclosure attention is narrowed essentially to nationality, territory, and commerce, in their relation to the conception of interest, as the years of American history unrolled. Since in the study of all human affairs, limitations must be set, these limitations—territory and commerce in relation to national interest—seem to be justified by the nature of the problem before us and by the preliminary findings.

CHAPTER II

THE CONSTITUTION AS A CONCEPTION OF
NATIONAL INTEREST

WHEN the American Republic entered the family of nations
western civilization had already moved far away from the
conceptions of religious unity and simple dynastic interest
which had long prevailed in Europe. The solidarity of Chris-
tendom had been shattered by the Protestant revolt, the multiplication of sects, and the growth of scientific rationalism.
Whatever may have been the intrinsic merits of Catholic internationalism, its formulas possessed no binding authority
upon statesmen in Northern Europe and the United States;
and their efficacy was destined to be diminished in other
quarters by the overthrow of religious establishments and the
development of levelling democracies.

At the same time, absolute monarchies were in process of
dissolution. Everywhere the masses as well as the bourgeois
were restless. By two revolutions and the development of parliamentary practices kingship by divine right had been repudiated in England, the monarch reduced to a precarious position
in the state, and the ultimate supremacy of the middle classes
definitely assured. George III, it is true, often used the
language of old days in speaking of his prerogatives but no
member of Parliament was deceived by it; the will of the prince
was not the law, if sometimes the policy, of the land.

Exploration had paved the way for the spread of commerce
to the four corners of the world. Scientific inquiry into the
constitution of the universe and the history of mankind had
begun to shake tradition and dogma to the foundations.
Through improvement of steam power, a mobile prime mover
revolutionized industry. Associated with these material, secular, and practical concerns a rising class—shopkeepers, traders,

merchants, factors, entrepreneurs, and those engaged in auxiliary pursuits—had already challenged the supremacy of landed aristocracies, lay and clerical. This class, based upon the production and distribution of wealth through industrial activity, had begun to expand and occupy ever-larger areas of the intellectual and political life formerly closed to it.

Keenly cognizant of the great changes that were taking place throughout the world and fortunately endowed with a great heritage of resources, rich in the art of government, experienced in new forms of economic enterprise, and grounded in the traditions of an ever-expanding commercial life, the American Republic prepared to set the course of its national development.

THE CONSTITUTION: SECULAR, REPUBLICAN, AND PRACTICAL

Owing to the movement of world history and the circumstances of its own origin, the Government of the United States was both republican and secular. With the rejection of a monarchical form of government, dynastic interest as a formula for the conduct of foreign relations was irrevocably discarded. No fixed point of reference for guidance in affairs of state could be grounded in theological infallibility. That possibility was as remote as the creation of a new dynasty. The very idea was foreign to the spirit of the Fathers of the Republic. Catholics were few in number and Protestants were divided among themselves. Moreover, many leaders among the founders of the Republic were Deists, opposed to carrying religious controversies into the domain of statecraft. Accordingly God is not mentioned in the Constitution, and the only reference to religion consists of a prohibition forbidding Congress to make any laws respecting religious establishments or interfering with freedom of worship. In rejecting dynastic claims and theological dogma, the Fathers became realists in politics. They built the Government of the United States upon a collaboration of powerful economic groups and they chose national interest as the principal formula for guidance in international intercourse, basing it upon a foundation of substantial and

earthly considerations.[1] Unhampered by a traditional bureaucracy enamored of state reason, they started with a clean slate.

Yet nowhere in the Constitution of the United States is the
word "national" to be found. This is no accident. When that
document was framed in 1787 the American nation was a
dream of seers rather than an actuality; the bond of perpetual
union was to be sealed long afterward on the field of battle.
Leaders among the men who drafted our fundamental law, it
is true, ardently desired to diminish the strength of state or
local attachments and to fuse fundamental political loyalties
under one government, but they had to speak and act with caution. They could not command the allegiance of the masses.
Behind the closed doors of the convention they occasionally
used the term "national government," particularly during the
early stages of the proceedings. Indeed, on May 30, the convention resolved, by a narrow margin of states, "that a national
government ought to be established consisting of a supreme
legislative, executive, and judiciary." [2] But the debate which
ensued showed that the members in using the phrase "national
government" were thinking primarily of a government strong
enough to bring coercive powers to bear on individual citizens,
not of consolidating powers and forging racial unity. Fearing
that the expression would confuse the issue and produce fruitless debate, the convention struck it out on June 20 and
resolved that "the government of the United States ought to
consist of a Supreme Legislative, Judiciary, and Executive."
Thus the troublesome word "national" was definitely eliminated.

Nor are the words "We the people of the United States,"
which appear in the opening of the preamble, to be taken in a
national sense. When the draft of the Constitution was reported by the committee of detail on August 6, the text
opened "We, the people of New Hampshire, Massachusetts,
Rhode Island," and so forth. In other words the people of the
respective states were to form a more perfect union. But on
second thought it was evident that the formula was inappropri-

---

[1] For the conception of interests in domestic affairs, see Beard, *An Economic
Interpretation of the Constitution*. Macmillan, New York.

[2] Farrand, *Records of the Convention*, Vol. I, p. 20.

ate. One or more of the states might refuse to ratify the new instrument of government and it would be awkward and untrue to include recalcitrant states among the makers of the more perfect union. Accordingly, in the final draft, there appeared, instead of an enumeration of the states, the simple, but equally disintegrated, conception, "We, the people of the United States." Thus it happened that the great document which formed the legal basis on which a nation was finally erected went forth without any hint that a nation was to be substituted for a federation of "sovereign" states and that a loyalty to a distant center was to take the place of state loyalties.[3] There was strategy in the performance—a brilliant illustration of the truth that it is not expedient to force the hand of destiny.

NATIONAL INTEREST IN THE "FEDERALIST"

This did not mean, however, that the framers of the Constitution sought to conceal or could conceal the fact that there were, in the social composition of the thirteen states, realities, forces, and processes—material and moral—which were making for a growth of nationality. These were obvious: a common language, literature, an intellectual heritage, a similarity of laws, and a certain community of economic relations. Even superficial observers were well aware of all these things.

So general was the thought, that John Jay in the second number of the *Federalist* deemed it useful to his argument to refer to the nation and the forces making for national unity. He rejoiced that "independent America was not composed of detached and distant territories, but that one connected, fertile, wide-spreading country was the portion of our Western sons of liberty." He referred to the succession of navigable waters

---

[3] That some of the states looked upon others as separate and distinct entities, and that this attitude persisted even after the Constitution was fully accepted, may be seen from the following extract from an item in the United States *Gazette*, April 15, 1818: " . . . The shoemakers of Philadelphia had become so impressed with protectionist reasoning that they petitioned the Governor and State Assembly for legislation prohibiting the sale of New England shoes in Pennsylvania, on the ground that the New Englanders were a 'species of foreigners.' " Cited in Malcolm R. Eiselen, *The Rise of Pennsylvania Protectionism,* University of Pennsylvania, Philadelphia, 1932.

which formed a kind of chain around its borders and to the noble rivers which provided channels of easy communication for the mutual exchange of commodities. Then he laid emphasis on the common ancestry of the people, their common language, the similarity of their manners and customs, their attachment to uniform principles of government, their religious affiliation. "This country and this people," he exclaimed, "seem to have been made for each other."

Having called attention to these realities, Jay was bold enough to say that "To all general purposes we have uniformly been one people: each individual citizen everywhere enjoying the same national rights and protection. As a nation we have made peace and war; as a nation we have vanquished our common enemies; as a nation we have formed alliances and made treaties, and entered into various compacts and conventions with foreign States." Nothing was more natural, therefore, than the proposition that this people, this nation, should improve upon the plan of government made hastily in time of stress and should form a more perfect Union.

Although the framers of the Constitution refrained from incorporating the alarming word "national" in the document which they drafted, they made it perfectly clear to the country that the new instrument of government was designed to protect, realize, and promote certain great common interests which had been neglected under the Articles of Confederation. Some of these interests pertained to domestic affairs: the maintenance of order, the regulation of interstate commerce, the discharge of the public debt, and the protection of private rights. Others were involved in foreign relations: defense, the regulation of foreign commerce, the negotiation of treaties, and advancement of American enterprise on the high seas and in the markets of the world—European and Oriental. Many numbers of the *Federalist* are devoted to the exposition of these interests in realistic terms, and the authors of that remarkable series of state papers do not shrink from calling them "national" interests or from summing up their philosophy of foreign relations under the head of "national interest."

Deeply versed in the practices of diplomacy, the authors of the *Federalist* took a cold and secular view of the motives that actuate governments in their international relations. In Number IV, John Jay declared: "It is too true, however disgraceful it may be to human nature, that nations will make war whenever they have a prospect of getting anything by it; nay, that absolute monarchs will often make war when their nations are to get nothing by it, but for purposes and objects merely personal, such as a thirst for military glory, revenge for personal affronts, ambition, or private compacts to aggrandize or support their particular families, or partisans." For these and other reasons, Jay continued, a sovereign will often be led to engage in wars "not sanctified by justice, or the voice and interests of his people." But he was careful to point out that there are motives which effect nations, as well as kings, and lead them to engage in armed conflicts.

A fundamental source of war is commercial rivalry. This point Hamilton drove home with sledge-hammer blows. Opponents of a strong national government for the United States had said that "the genius of republics is pacific: the spirit of commerce has a tendency to soften the manners of men and to extinguish those inflammable humors which have so often kindled into wars. Commercial republics, like ours, will never be disposed to waste themselves in ruinous contentions with each other. They will be governed by mutual interest, and will cultivate a spirit of mutual amity and concord." Having stated the case for economic benevolence, Hamilton proceeded to demolish it. "Has commerce hitherto done anything more than change the objects of war? Is not the love of wealth as domineering and enterprising a passion as that of power or glory? Have there not been as many wars founded upon commercial motives . . . as were before occasioned by the cupidity of territory or dominion? Has not the spirit of commerce, in many instances, administered new incentives to the appetite, both for the one and for the other? Let experience, the least fallible guide of human opinion, be appealed to for an answer to these inquiries." (Number VI)

To clinch the argument Hamilton reviewed history from antiquity to his own day. "Sparta, Athens, Rome, and Carthage, were all republics; two of them, Athens and Carthage, of the commercial kind. Yet were they as often engaged in wars, offensive and defensive, as the neighboring monarchies of the same times. Sparta was little better than a well-regulated camp; and Rome was never sated of carnage and conquest. Carthage, though a commercial republic, was the aggressor in the very war that ended in her destruction. . . . Venice, in latter times, figured more than once in wars of ambition. . . . The provinces of Holland, till they were overwhelmed in debts and taxes, took a leading and conspicuous part in the wars of Europe. They had furious contests with England for the dominion of the sea. . . . In the government of Britain the representatives of the people compose one branch of the National legislature. Commerce has been for ages the predominant pursuit of that country. Yet few nations have been more frequently engaged in war. . . . The wars of these two last-mentioned nations [England and France] have in a great measure grown out of commercial considerations—the desire of supplanting, and the fear of being supplanted, either in particular branches of traffic, or in the general advantages of trade and navigation. . . ." (Number VI)

Bringing generalities down to concrete cases Jay gave a number of illustrations growing "out of our relative situation and circumstances" to indicate the grounds of possible international conflicts in the future. He showed that Americans were rivals of France and Britain in fisheries and could supply them with fish cheaper than they could supply themselves. Americans were also rivals of these two countries and "most other European nations" in navigation and transport. "As our carrying trade cannot increase, without in some degree diminishing theirs, it is more their interest, and will be more their policy, to restrain, than to promote it." American trade with China and India threatened the European monopoly. The extension of American commerce by American vessels in the waters of Asia could not fail to disturb the European nations which possessed territories in the neighborhood. Spain might close the Mississippi, and Britain the St. Lawrence, to American navigation in an effort to protect their natural advantages. For these and other reasons Jay argued that "a good national government" was necessary to safeguard American operations and protect the country against acts and policies of other governments conceived in the pursuit of their respective interests. In other words, Jay saw in the conflicts of economics the roots of international rivalries and in strong government a possibility of repressing the propensities of other countries to resort to war whenever they saw a chance to gain anything by it. On this theme he laid great emphasis.

That the authors of the *Federalist* desired to lay stress upon the protection and defense of national interests in appealing to the voters to support the new Constitution is also disclosed in the numbers dealing with the powers to be vested in the Union. These powers are classified under six heads and the first two are: "1. Security against foreign danger; 2. Regulation of intercourse with foreign nations." At the top of the list stands defense. "Security against foreign danger is one of the primitive objects of civil society. It is an avowed and essential object of the American Union. The powers requisite for attaining it must be effectually confided to the federal councils." (Number XL) The regulation of intercourse with foreign nations also "forms an obvious and essential branch of the federal administration. If we are to be one nation in any respect, it clearly ought to be in respect to other nations." (Number XLI) In discussing the provision which vests the treaty-making power in the President and Senate, Hamilton argued that the President and Senators "will always be of the number of those who best understand our national interests, whether considered in relation to the several states or to foreign nations, who are best able to promote those interests, and whose reputation for integrity inspires and merits confidence." (Number LXIII)

The nation whose interests are thus to be defended is not static; nor are its interests confined to its territorial boundaries and waters. "The commercial character of America" is marked by "the adventurous spirit." The country is endowed with enormous natural resources and inhabited by an enterprising people. The nation is dynamic. Its energies are to spread to the seven seas. And this will excite the jealousy and opposition of other countries. Only a powerful Union can make the latter conform to American requirements. "Under a vigorous national government, the natural strength and resources of the country, directed to a common interest, would baffle all the combinations of European jealousy to restrain our growth. This situation would even take away the motive to such combinations, by inducing an impracticability of success. An active commerce and a flourishing marine would then be the inevitable offspring of moral and physical necessity. We might defy the little arts of little politicians to control, or vary, the irresistible and unchangeable course of nature." (Number XI)

But the mere existence of a strong government would not be enough to secure a free way for American enterprise. The devices of diplomacy and the machinery of negotiation must be vested in its hands. More than this; it must have engines of coercion—the power of making commercial regulations and building and maintaining a navy. "By prohibitory regulations, extending at the same time throughout the states, we may oblige foreign countries to bid against each other for the privilege of our markets." By similar methods markets could be opened to American enterprise. "Suppose, for instance, we had a government in America capable of excluding Great Britain (with whom we have at present no treaty of commerce) from all our ports; what would be the probable operation of this step upon her politics? Would it not enable us to negotiate, with the fairest prospects of success, for commercial privileges of the most valuable and extensive kind, in the dominions of that kingdom?" (Number XL) A strong government could exert powerful economic pressure in all directions in the extension and realization of national interests.

If the methods of peaceful coercion fail, the sword is at hand. "A further resource for influencing the conduct of European nations toward us, in this respect, would arise from the establishment of a federal navy. There can be no doubt that the continuance of the Union, under an efficient government, would put it in our power, at a period not very distant, to create a navy, which, if it could not vie with those of the great maritime powers, would at least be of respectable weight, if thrown into the scale of either of two contending parties. This would be more peculiarly the case in relation to operations in the East Indies. A few ships of line, sent opportunely to the re-inforcement of either side, would often be sufficient

to decide the fate of a campaign, on the event of which interests of the greatest magnitude were suspended. . . . A
price would be set, not only upon our friendship, but upon
our neutrality. By a steady adherence to the Union, we may
hope, erelong, to become the arbiter of Europe in America;
and to be able to incline the balance of European competi-
tions in this part of the world, as our interests may dictate."
(Number XI)

Under such a system of policy the United States could become supreme in the Western Hemisphere. Such, at least, was
the view put forth by Hamilton in the eleventh number of the
Federalist: "Our situation invites and our interests prompt us
to aim at an ascendant in the system of American affairs."
Europe dominated Africa and Asia; the United States had
its own sphere of power. "Let Americans disdain to be the
instrument of Europe's greatness! Let the Thirteen States,
bound together in a strict and indissoluble Union, concur in
erecting one great American system, superior to the control
of all trans-Atlantic force or influence, and able to dictate the
terms of connection between the Old and the New World."
In short, national interest is supreme and it is interpreted to
imply the supremacy of the United States as against Europe
in the American Hemisphere.[4]

Besides believing that nations in general will make war when
there is a prospect of getting anything by it and that tap roots
of international conflicts, apart from dynastic considerations,
lie in commercial rivalries, Jay held that in the long run nations
can know what their interests really are. "It is not a new observation," he said, "that the people of any country (if, like
the Americans, intelligent and well-informed) seldom adopt,
and steadily persevere for many years in, an erroneous opinion respecting their interests." Although this flattering reference to American intelligence was connected with an appeal for
popular support for the Constitution, it may be taken as representing Jay's deliberate opinion that there are reliable processes by which national interests are disclosed and formulated
as a guide to governments. (Number III)

[4] An interpretation singularly prophetic, and fully realized, subsequently,
through the Monroe Doctrine and associated policies.

THE USE OF INTEREST: WASHINGTON, HAMILTON, AND MADISON

That the authors of the *Federalist,* in placing interest at the center of policy, correctly divined the course of action to be followed under the Constitution is demonstrated by the declarations of President Washington. In general and in detail he referred his decisions and measures to the bench mark of interest. "In every act of my administration," he wrote in 1795, "I have sought the happiness of my fellow citizens. My system for the attainment of this object has uniformly been to overlook all personal, local, and partial considerations; to contemplate the United States as one great whole; . . . and to consult only the substantial and permanent interest of our country." [5]   In making this statement near the close of his second term Washington did but repeat views advanced at the opening of his presidency, for in a public address on April 20, 1789, he had said: "Whatever may be the issue of our public measures, or however I may err in opinion, I trust it will be believed that I could not have been actuated by any interests separate from those of my country." [6]

When President Washington came to the question of national defense he expressed the belief that a free people should be armed and disciplined and "that their safety and interest require that they should promote such manufactories as tend to render them independent of others for essential, particularly for military, supplies." [7]   Turning to foreign affairs he called upon Congress for provisions which would enable him to discharge his duties in that sphere and for "a competent fund" for defraying expenses. These things, he insisted, are required by "the interest of the United States." [8]   In refraining from the broils of Europe, encouraging commerce with all countries, and maintaining friendly relations generally, Washington defended his course on the ground "that it is our policy and interest to do so." [9]   Confronted by the "conscientious scruples"

[5] *Works* (Sparks ed.), Vol. XI, p. 42.
[6] *Ibid.,* Vol. XII, p. 144.
[7] *Ibid.,* Vol. XII, p. 8.
[8] *Ibid.,* Vol. XII, p. 9.
[9] *Ibid.,* Vol. XI, p. 102.

of the Quakers he insisted that, while they should be treated with "great delicacy and tenderness," they should receive such accommodation "as a due regard to the protection and essential interests of the nation may justify and permit." [10]

In matters of concrete application Washington made reference to national interest. Was it a question of ratifying a treaty with the Creek Indians? Then it was to be recommended by the possibility of attaching them "to the interests of the United States." [11] The court of Lisbon made amicable advances for cultivating friendship and intercourse with the United States. "It was to our interest to meet this nation in its friendly dispositions and to concur in the exchange proposed." [12] The French have played havoc with American commerce. Washington inquires: "Could it be expected by France that this country would neglect its own interests . . . ?" [13] War breaks out in Europe and sympathies with France are expressed in many quarters. But Washington is "fully persuaded that the happiness and best interests of the people of the United States will be promoted by preserving a strict neutrality." [14] Relations with France are strained. "The interests of this country" make it necessary to send a special representative to fill the place of the present minister at Paris. [15] Whether it is a matter of large generality or specific detail, Washington is ever mindful of the national interest.

Near the close of his second administration Washington summed up the philosophy of national interest in his "Farewell Address" to his countrymen. He told them that it was of "infinite moment you should properly estimate the immense value of your national union to your collective and individual happiness." He dwelt upon the common ties of "religion, manners, habits, and political principles" which bound them together. "But," he continued, "these considerations, however powerfully they address themselves to your sensibility, are greatly outweighed by those which apply more immediately to your

---

[10] *Ibid.*, Vol. XII, p. 169.
[11] *Ibid.*, Vol. XII, p. 86.
[12] *Ibid.*, Vol. XII, pp. 92–93.
[13] *Ibid.*, Vol. XI, p. 523.
[14] *Ibid.*, Vol. XII, p. 202.
[15] *Ibid.*, Vol. XI, p. 144.

interest. Here every portion of our country finds the most commanding motives for carefully guarding and preserving the union of the whole." Then he proceeded to show that the several sections of the country, with their specialized economic activities, benefited from the unrestricted intercourse which was provided under the Constitution. Maritime, commercial, and manufacturing enterprise provided outlets for agricultural produce and in turn the agricultural sections furnished materials for industry and commodities for transport and exchange. Such were the considerations which outweighed the bonds of religion, manners, habits, and political principles and applied more immediately to the "interest" of the people of the United States. Such was the solid substance of national interest in the preservation of the Union.

From interest as the cement of national union Washington turned to national interest in international relations. "While, then," he explained, "every part of our country thus feels an immediate interest in union, all the parts combined cannot fail to find in the united mass of means and effort greater strength, greater resource, proportionately greater security from external danger"—from the interruption of peace by foreign broils, from domestic difficulties, from foreign attachments and intrigues. "Europe has a set of primary interests which to us have none or a very remote relation." Hence the United States will wisely refrain from becoming implicated in the European quarrels which touch American interests remotely, if at all. "Harmony, liberal intercourse with all nations are recommended by policy, humanity, and interest. But even our commercial policy should hold an equal and impartial hand, neither seeking nor granting exclusive favors or preferences; consulting the natural course of things; diffusing and diversifying by gentle means the streams of commerce, but forcing nothing; establishing with powers so disposed, in order to give trade a stable course, to define the rights of our merchants, and to enable the Government to support them, conventional rules of intercourse, the best that present circumstances and mutual opinion will permit, but temporary and liable to be from time to time abandoned or varied as experience and circumstances shall dictate."

Having charted the course of commercial policy to be pursued in international relations, Washington then warned his countrymen against forming attachments of sympathy with any foreign power, against expecting any bounties in any quarter. He urged them constantly to keep in view "that it is folly in one nation to look for disinterested favors from another; that it must pay with one portion of its independence for whatever it may accept under that character; that by such acceptance it may place itself in the condition of having given equivalents for nominal favors, and yet of being reproached for not giving more. There can be no greater error than to expect or calculate upon real favors from nation to nation. It is an illusion which experience must cure, which a just pride ought to discard."

To summarize, Washington believed that practical interest furnished the chief cement of national union, that nations in their intercourse with one another were governed by their interests, and that the young republic should profit from a knowledge of these stubborn truths. He did not flatter himself that his counsels would "control the usual current of the passions or prevent our nation from running the course which has hitherto marked the destiny of nations," but he did hope that they might produce some partial benefit, moderate the fury of the party spirit, and serve as a warning against the mischiefs of foreign intrigue.[16]

Washington's Secretary of the Treasury, Alexander Hamilton, expressed identical views of national interest as a substratum of the union and a guide for the conduct of foreign affairs; indeed, reasoning from his intimate relation with the first President and observing the frequency with which he prepared memoranda and suggestions for his chief, on invitation or his own motion, it might be truly said that Hamilton supplied a large part of the political philosophy which Washington expounded. While the Constitution was being framed Hamilton argued for the establishment of a president and a

---

[16] In a letter written in 1778 Washington laid down the maxim, "founded on the universal experience of mankind, that no nation is to be trusted farther than it is bound by its interests; and no prudent statesman or politician will venture to depart from it." New York *Times*, February 18, 1933.

senate enjoying life tenure with a view to creating a firm center of national interest. This principle he illustrated by reference to the British upper chamber. "The House of Lords," he declared, "is a noble institution. Having nothing to hope for by a change and a sufficient interest, by means of their property, in being faithful to the national interest, they form a barrier against every pernicious innovation whether attempted on the part of the Crown or of the Commons." [17] Since it was impossible to create an aristocratic body in the United States, Hamilton proposed, therefore, to give to "the rich and well born" a special position in the state—"a distinct and permanent share in the government." [18] Owing to the endless conflicts of society, he believed that the most powerful economic interest should be placed firmly at the very center of government.

Besides formulating, in defense of the Constitution, the theory of national interest presented in the *Federalist* (above, p. 35), Hamilton made use of the conception of "interest" in supporting ratification of the document before the state convention of New York. The financial difficulties of the old government, he argued, had been largely due to the fact that the states had been "incapable of embracing the general interests of the Union," had "almost uniformly weighed the requisitions by their own local interests," and had "only executed them so far as answered their particular convenience or advantage." [19] The proposed Constitution was an embodiment of national interest. "The powers of the new government," Hamilton explained, "are general, and calculated to embrace the aggregate interests of the Union, and the general interest of each state, so far as it stands in relation to the whole. . . . The local interests of each state ought in every case to give way to the interests of the Union. For when a sacrifice of one or the other is necessary, the former becomes only an apparent, partial interest and should yield, on the principle that the smaller good ought never to oppose the greater one." [20]

[17] Farrand, *Records of the Federal Convention*, Vol. I, p. 288.
[18] *Ibid.*, pp. 299ff.
[19] *Works* (Lodge ed.), Vol. I, p. 415.
[20] *Ibid.*, Vol. I, pp. 443, 452.

When called upon as Secretary of the Treasury to formulate economic policies for the new government, Hamilton operated on the conviction that its strength and permanence depended very largely upon attracting to it the support of the most powerful interests in society—financial, commercial, and industrial. The funding of the continental debt and the assumption of the state debts forced all public creditors to look to the Federal Government for regularity of interest payments and security of the principal. A similar function was performed by the first United States Bank. Discriminating customs and tonnage duties served to rally manufacturers and shippers around the new establishment. But, while making use of particular groups, Hamilton constantly referred to something transcendent—the national interest. Speaking on behalf of his Report on Manufactures, he said: "It is the interest of nations to diversify the industrial pursuits of the individuals who compose them. . . . It is the interest of a community, with a view to eventual and permanent economy, to encourage the growth of manufactures. . . . The encouragement of manufactures is the interest of all parts of the Union." [21]

Although Hamilton was not Secretary of State, he actively assisted President Washington in formulating and defending foreign as well as domestic policies—much to the chagrin of his bitter enemy in that Department, Thomas Jefferson. And whenever he operated in the field of foreign affairs Hamilton proceeded on the assumptions of national interest which he had expounded in the *Federalist*. One example taken from numerous cases will illustrate his method and reasoning. When war broke out between France and Great Britain in 1793 the question arose whether the Government of France had the right to demand American coöperation or the United States was bound to come to its aid under the obligations imposed by the treaties of alliance and commerce made in 1778 when France threw her lot in with the American revolutionists.

With great bitterness the issue was debated, the antifederalists insisting upon supporting the former ally in time of need against the old foe. In the midst of the turbulence Washington invited his "cabinet ministers" to give him their

[21] *Ibid.*, Vol. III, pp. 321, 352, 361.

opinions. Hamilton replied flatly "that there is a right either to refuse or consent, as shall be judged for the interests of the United States. . . . If there be such an option, there are strong reasons to show that the character and interests of the United States require that they should pursue the course of holding the operation of the [French] treaties suspended. . . . It would be to our interest, in the abstract, to be disengaged from them, and take the chance of future negotiation, for a better treaty of commerce." [22] On such principles Washington decided in favor of neutrality, making "the duty and interest of the United States" paramount.[23]

After the proclamation of neutrality was issued Hamilton came to the support of the administration with a powerful pamphlet in which he set forth the supremacy of national interest, coldly calculated and resolutely applied. "An individual may, on numerous occasions," he said, "meritoriously indulge the emotions of generosity and benevolence . . . even at the expense of his own interests. But a government can rarely, if at all, be justifiable in pursuing a similar course; and, if it does so, ought to confine itself within much stricter bounds. Good offices, which are indifferent to the interest of a nation performing them, or which are compensated by the existence or expectation of some reasonable equivalent, or which produce an essential good to the nation to which they are rendered, without real detriment to the affairs of the benefactor, prescribe perhaps the limits of national generosity or benevolence. It is not here meant to recommend a policy absolutely selfish or interested in nations; but to show that a policy regulated by their own interests, as far as justice and good faith permit, is, and ought to be, their prevailing one; and that either to ascribe to them a different principle of action, or to deduce, from the supposition of it, arguments for a self-denying and self-sacrificing gratitude on the part of a nation which may have received from another good offices, is to misrepresent or misconceive what usually are, and ought to be, the springs of national conduct. . . . It was not difficult to pronounce beforehand that we have a greater interest in the preservation

[22] *Works* (Lodge ed.), Vol. IV, pp. 33, 90, 95.
[23] Richardson, *Messages and Papers of the Presidents,* Vol. I, p. 156.

of peace than in any advantages with which France might tempt our participation in the war." [24]

The distinguished associate of Washington and Hamilton, one of the authors of the *Federalist,* James Madison, who has been called "the father" of the Constitution, also founded his system of politics on the realities of economic interest. Men have different and unequal faculties of acquiring property, he said; where these faculties are protected, the possession of different degrees and kinds of property results; "and from the influence of these on the sentiments and views of the respective proprietors ensues a division of society into different interests and parties." These interests he enumerates. "Those who hold and those who are without property have ever formed distinct interests in society. Those who are creditors and those who are debtors fall under a like discrimination. A landed interest, a manufacturing interest, a mercantile interest, a moneyed interest, with many lesser interests, grow up of necessity in civilized nations, and divide them into different classes actuated by different sentiments and views." And the principal task of modern legislation is the "regulation of these various and interfering interests." They give rise to factions and parties and there is no help for it. "The causes of factions cannot be removed, and we well know that neither moral nor religious motives can be relied upon as an adequate control." His solution of the problem was to enlarge the size of the state to include more interests and to prevent dominance by a majority of them through a system of checks, balances, and electoral refinements. In Madison's view, as expressed in Number X of the *Federalist,* there was no higher interest by which particular interests could be controlled.

Yet on other occasions he spoke of a "common interest." In the Virginia ratifying convention he declared his opinion that the deliberations of the House of Representatives would be directed "to the interest of the people of America." [25] A few days later in the same assembly he repeated the idea, saying

---

[24] *Works* (Lodge ed.), Vol. IV, pp. 166, 167, 186, 187. Thus Hamilton avoided the opposition of interest and morals by relegating generosity to the rear and so escaped the tragic antithesis of Western thought and experience.

[25] *Works* (Hunt ed.), Vol. V, p. 137.

that in the general council of the country "the sense of all America will be drawn to a single point. The collective interest of the union at large will be known and pursued. No local views will be permitted to operate against the general welfare." [26] On another occasion he set "general and national interests" over against "local considerations." [27] Addressing himself to international affairs, Madison remarked: "It is to be presumed that in transactions with foreign countries, those [federal authorities] who regulate them will feel the whole force of national attachment to their country. The contrast being between their own nation and a foreign nation, is it not presumable that they will, as far as possible, advance the interests of their own country?" [28] And long afterward, in the midst of the second war with Great Britain, he again referred to a common interest, transcending the special interests. "In addition to the thousand affinities belonging to every part of the Nation," he wrote to David Humphreys in 1813, "every part has an interest, as deep as it is obvious, in maintaining the bond which keeps the whole together." [29]

Such were the views of leading statesmen in the contest which resulted in the establishment of the Constitution and the inauguration of the new Federal Government; they are fairly typical of the opinions entertained by the chief actors in that historic drama.[30] Society is composed of special interests; governments reflect and are concerned with the regulation of conflicting interests; nations in their intercourse with one another are controlled primarily by their interests. There are other forces at work in politics—religious, moral, and irrational; but interest is the fundamental consideration, especially national interest in foreign affairs. And national interest, as formulated by Hamilton, the principal author of measures and policy in Washington's administration, had a positive and definite content: it meant a consolidation of commercial, manufacturing, financial, and agricultural interests at home, the promotion of trade in all parts of the world by the engines of diplomacy,

[26] *Ibid.*, p. 152.
[27] *Ibid.*, p. 187.
[28] *Ibid.*, p. 214.
[29] *Ibid.*, Vol. VIII, p. 241.
[30] Beard, *An Economic Interpretation of the Constitution*, Chap. VII.

the defense of that trade by a powerful navy, the supremacy of the United States in the Western Hemisphere, and the use of military and naval strength in the rivalry of nations to secure economic advantages for citizens of the United States. If, as Talleyrand said, Hamilton divined Europe, it may be properly added that he also divined the system of *Machtpolitik* under which European nations operated.

CHAPTER III

NATIONAL INTEREST IN TERRITORIAL EXPANSION

FOR the sake of convenience in tracing the application of the national-interest conception in the external relations of the United States, those relations may be divided into territorial and commercial, although in practice the two are seldom, if ever, divorced. There is also a certain historical warrant for this division of considerations. The political party or group which had been largely instrumental in bringing about the adoption of the Constitution and the economic measures that accompanied its going into force and was concerned primarily with financial and commercial affairs was soon ousted from power by Jefferson's agrarian party which laid particular emphasis on land and agricultural interests. It so happened, then, that from the inauguration of Jefferson in 1801 to the retirement of Buchanan, all the elected presidents except two were affiliated with the agrarian party, and that in this early period of American history all the acquisitions of vacant land for American farmers and planters were made. If the authors of the *Federalist* did not anticipate swift and wide territorial expansion as a phase of national interest, the party of Jefferson was not long in discovering in what direction the expansive forces of the nation were running, and at various intervals made significant additions of land to the original domain.

The broad division into land and commerce, which is historically convenient, has the sanction of political science. By common consent, the great commentators on statecraft have given attention to land, as well as to trade. Land forms the material basis of every nation. The location, configuration, and resources of its land are vitally connected with the course of its civilization and the strategy of that supreme national interest, defense. Therefore, the addition or loss of territory always has been and must ever be a matter of prime concern to statecraft in promoting national interest.

In this respect the United States does not differ fundamentally from the other countries of the world. The affirmation of history is clear. For more than one hundred years the foreign policy of America was periodically concerned with territorial expansion, and a conception of national interest underlay each step and all phases of the operation. Whether the covering formula was "manifest destiny" or "moral obligation to benighted peoples," every aspect of this development carried with it connotations of practical aims. If much was said meanwhile about the accidents of history, the lap of the gods, and unsolicited opportunities, there were in each case acts of will committed by directors of public policy who at least thought they were well aware of the practical upshot and immediate consequences of their decisions and movements.

When the course of American territorial expansion is examined in detail, it appears that there have been two distinct types of acquisition, each under different leadership motivated by distinct and different conceptions of national interest. The first is continental expansion—the struggle for land to round out the national domain, land to be tilled by free farmers or exploited by planters employing slave labor. It was a type of expansion which blended reasonably well with the background of the then existing world economy; and it was responsive to the political forces of a world engaged in establishing a system of national states. It was introduced into the life of the young nation under the auspices of the Jeffersonian party.

The second is over-seas expansion. It was associated in time and philosophy with the growing recognition of increasing national prestige and power. In turning toward this type of expansion, the nation was following the new economic course of Western civilization. Along with other nations, the United States was well on the way to a form of industrial maturity which had positive implications in domestic affairs and momentous repercussions in the world at large. It was a type of expansion not at all concerned with the acquisition of land to be tilled by American citizens or developed by their labors in other domestic pursuits. It was essentially extensive and ex-

ternal in its associations, seeking island trade centers, naval
bases, and spheres of control, in the attempt to enlarge upon
the opportunities for trade and investment. It saw nothing
out of the way in sweeping into the American orbit distant
lands with subject populations made up of aliens who, for the
most part, did not yield readily to assimilation to American
racial stock and nationality. It took place under the second
Republican party.

Both types of expansion were clearly discernible despite the
conflicting interests within each party and despite the shifts
between parties in response to the course of events and the
changing conditions of national and international life. Each
had its own peculiar center of economic gravity, political
philosophy, and financial support. There was little that was
fortuitous about these aspects of expansion even if, on occasion,
the current of events, the drama of their appearance, the
verbiage of their ideology, and the nature of their consequences
made it appear so.[1]

THE ACQUISITION OF LAND FOR THE EXPANSION OF AMERICAN CIVILIZATION

America's first great expansionist, Thomas Jefferson, founder
of the Democratic party, under whose auspices the first step
in expansion—the Louisiana purchase—took place, had a broad
and, on the whole, consistent conception of American civilization, its potentialities, and its interests. He believed that a
democratic republic could be securely founded only upon agriculture, accompanied by a wide distribution of land among the
cultivators in contrast to the concentration of estates which
formed the basis of aristocracies in Europe. With him this
was a reasoned conviction derived from experience and the
study of history. "Cultivators of the earth," he said, "are the
most valuable citizens. They are the most vigorous, the most
independent, the most virtuous, and are tied to their country,

---

[1] Writing of the American acquisition of the Philippines James Bryce believed
that "It was the Unforeseen that happened . . . the Americans drifted into
dominion. . . ." *The American Commonwealth*, New Revised Edition, Vol.
II, p. 584. The belief held by Bryce has been widely entertained by others,
in this country as well as abroad.

and wedded to its liberty and interests, by the most lasting bonds." [2] He also believed that the democratic principle of mild government dependent upon the intelligence of the masses would be secure "as long as we remain virtuous; and I think we shall be so, as long as agriculture is our principal object, which will be the case while there remain vacant lands in any part of America. When we get piled up upon one another in large cities, as in Europe, we shall become corrupt as in Europe, and go to eating one another as they do there." [3] The implications of this are clear.

Jefferson founded his party, and through the years built it up, on the assumption that there was a fundamental relation between agriculture and national stability and progress. According to its requirements he shaped his policy. In his political campaigning he bid, as he said, for the support of "farmers whose interests are entirely agricultural," and declared his opposition to government by commercial and financial affiliations. Farmers, he insisted "are the true representatives of the great American interest, and are alone to be relied on for expressing the proper American sentiments." [4] Traders, investors, and manufacturers, he thought, were not attached to the soil by bonds of interest and affection but were mobile and connected with similar groups in foreign countries; for this reason they were often prepared to sacrifice the country to their particular advantage—momentary gain. On such grounds he bitterly attacked his opponents, the Federalists, whose seats of power were in the cities, for their "British sympathies," their willingness to truck and huckster with Great Britain in the hope of enlarging their commercial opportunities. Agriculture, ran his formula, is the fundamental American interest, a guarantee of the perpetuity of American institutions, the source of patriotic devotion to the land and its government.

Agriculture, moreover, gave the nation a high degree of self-sufficiency and independence and made it possible for its government to avoid the intrigues, entanglements, and col-

[2] *Works* (Washington ed.), Vol. I, p. 403.

[3] *Ibid.*, Vol. II, p. 332. C. A. Beard, *Economic Origins of Jeffersonian Democracy*, pp. 415ff.

[4] *Works* (Washington ed.), Vol. VI, p. 197.

lisions common to European powers.[5] Jefferson did not want the American people to depend on "the casualties and caprice of customers" for their security and chief sources of livelihood. Trade, he was convinced, was accompanied by chicanery ruinous to morals; while agriculture was the nursery of independence in spirit and virtue in life. He thought, as we have seen, that the country would remain virtuous as long as agriculture predominated, "while there remain vacant lands in any part of America." This philosophy of politics is, of course, as old as Aristotle, but it is also as new as Spengler who finds in capitalism the cancer of internationalism and in agriculture the source of patriotism and the heroic virtues of the warrior.

With agriculture as the economic sheet anchor, Jefferson naturally advocated territorial expansion to provide new lands for farmers. As early as 1801 he wrote to Monroe: "However our present interests may restrain us within our own limits, it is impossible not to look forward to distant time, when our rapid multiplication will expand itself beyond those limits, and cover the whole northern if not the southern continent."[6] Later he endorsed the idea of annexing Florida, without a war if possible, by means of colonization and absorption. Still later, with some inconsistency, he approved a project for taking Cuba, on the ground that it would give us control over the Gulf of Mexico, the Isthmus, and neighboring countries. But here he stopped in his over-seas expansion. "Cuba," he said, "can be defended by us without a navy, and this develops the principle which ought to limit our views. Nothing should ever be accepted which would require a navy to defend it."[7] A navy, he held, divorced men from the soil, developed a bureaucracy which interfered with politics, incurred unprofitable expenditures, and was affiliated with the commercial interest and its party representation. Expansion to obtain land for farmers, —continental expansion which could be defended by a militia-army—such was the Jeffersonian conception of national interest

[5] It should be noted that later, after the European war had worked havoc with the export of American produce, Jefferson came to the conclusion, with Calhoun, that it would be well to balance agriculture with industries, dangerous as the latter were to morals and republican spirit.

[6] W. E. Curtis, *The True Thomas Jefferson*, p. 184.

[7] *Ibid.*, p. 185.

in territorial extension. The Louisiana purchase was his first great demonstration of this policy.

Although many Federalists were willing to approve the Louisiana cession on the ground that it opened the Mississippi River to commerce, the weight of opinion in Federalist circles was against the form in which annexation was authorized. Their spokesman in Congress, Griswold, insisted that the treaty was unconstitutional and impolitic. It was unconstitutional because it provided for the incorporation of foreign soil and people with the United States and for the admission of new states into the Union by act of Congress. It was impolitic "because we could not govern so vast a wilderness and a people so unlike our own in language, manners, and religion." [8]

Later this contention was even more strongly emphasized. When the proposal to admit Louisiana as a state came up in Congress, opposition from the commercial sections of the seaboard was placed frankly on the ground that by such action the political power of the commercial regions in the Federal Government would be diminished, that they would be overborne by a majority from the agrarian states, and that the balance of the original partnership of states would be destroyed. "Do you suppose," asked Josiah Quincy in the House of Representatives, "the people of the Northern and Atlantic states will or ought to look with patience and see Representatives and Senators from the Red River and Missouri pouring themselves upon this and the other floor, managing the concerns of a sea-board fifteen hundred miles at least from their residence, and having a preponderancy in councils into which constitutionally they never could have been admitted?" [9] Quincy's

---

[8] McMaster, *History of the American People,* Vol. III, p. 4.

[9] E. Quincy, *Life of Josiah Quincy,* p. 210. This attitude has appeared again and again through American history (see p. 58), and it has remained persistent even to our own times. At a recent Senate hearing, Joseph R. Grundy of Pennsylvania, when appraising the weight which should be accorded to the several states in the national councils, took a similar view and illustrated it by a number of interesting comparisons. He showed that Pennsylvania, with only two United States Senators, turned out an amount of manufactured products equal in value to twenty-five other states with fifty Senators. In another comparison he matched Pennsylvania against seven "farm" states as to farm acreage, number of farms and value of all property. In a third comparison he ranged seven "industrial" states against seven "agricultural" states,

answer was that it would be better to dissolve the Union than to have the commercial states submerged in an agrarian flood. Thus the agrarian interest became associated with the national outlook, and the commercial interest became particularistic in policy.

A similar cleavage between the commercial and agrarian interests occurred in connection with the annexation of Florida. The project had long been on the carpet. Jefferson approved it as early as 1791. The fulfillment of the scheme was a part of the Republican program for the war of 1812. The South, as J. W. Pratt shows, "was almost unanimous in its demand for Florida, for agrarian, commercial, and strategic reasons." [10] Support from Northern Republicans for the undertaking was won, it seems, by a promise that the rich lands of Canada were also to be acquired in the war on Great Britain.[11] The failure of the two factions to win their combined objective in the conflict which ensued was due largely to disaffection in their own ranks, to the lukewarmness of the Madison administration toward the Canadian expedition, and to the united opposition of Federalists and certain Northern Republicans to the Florida enterprise; but this failure did not destroy Monroe's determination to carry out the Southern part of the compact at the first opportunity. And the opportunity came. With the growing weakness of Spanish authority, Florida was beset by disorders and, as President Monroe said in his message of December 7, 1819, "was made the means of unceasing annoy-

apparently illustrating the relative insignificance of the latter. Upon the basis of these comparisons he made the following observations in his testimony: "These States that are enumerated here have been the most vocal on the floor of the Senate. . . . Frankly, when you come to analyze what they mean in the national life of the country, they haven't got any chips in the game at all." For these men that represent so little in the national economy to find fault and to obstruct and try to destroy a policy which has been responsible for building up these great reservoirs of taxation that have been for the great benefit and advancement of the country, . . . is a tragedy to mankind. . . . These Senators [from the smaller—materially—states] should talk darn small." Paraphrased and quoted from the *Hearings of the Sub-Committee of the Senate Committee on the Judiciary*, 71st Congress, 1st Session. Investigation pursuant to Sen. Res. 20 relating to Lobbying, pp. 500, 501. For the statistical comparisons, see pp. 466–474.

[10] J. W. Pratt, *The Expansionists of 1812*, p. 12.
[11] *Ibid.*, p. 13.

ance and injury to our Union in many of its most essential interests." At length, after tedious negotiations, Florida was duly incorporated in the United States by the final exchange of ratifications in 1821.

Between the acquisition of Florida and the next expansion of American territory the division of opinion respecting national policies which marked the conflict over Louisiana had not disappeared. On the contrary it had widened and sharpened. The industrial and commercial interests of the Northeast had multiplied, reviving in the form of the Whig Party the opposition which Federalism had once supplied. In the meantime, with the growth of cotton planting, slavery had been transformed from a somewhat lethargic domestic institution into a highly dynamic system of economy, pushing endlessly westward in search of virgin soil to exploit as the fertility of the old lands on the seaboard declined. In Jefferson's and Jackson's agrarian party, dominance passed almost entirely to the planters, particularly the cotton planters. To the Northwest, where the free labor system prevailed, the rapid opening of farming regions increased the numerical strength of the non-slaveholding wing of the Democratic party and contributed to the preponderance of free states.

Thus a triple motive was provided for the annexation of Texas and Mexican territory to the Pacific: the quest of additional cotton land, the lure of new homesteads for free farmers, and the determination of planting leaders to maintain their balance of power in the Union of States. On the other side, attacks on the acquisition of Texas and on the war with Mexico came mainly from the old centers of opposition to agrarian extension, namely, the commercial states of the seaboard, which still looked out upon the seas rather than westward across the continent; but their antipathy was softened somewhat by the belief that the addition of California would be favorable to the swiftly growing commerce on the Pacific and by the opportunity to speculate in Texas securities.

By this time the country was rent with the political dispute which culminated in the Civil War. In the circumstances, the discussion of the Mexican War and the acquisition of territory which followed it turned, not so much upon some grand conception of national interest, as upon interests frankly sectional in character. The leaders of the dominant party in Congress, the Democrats, made no concealment of their purposes. It was to add land for exploitation and to preserve the balance of the slave power in the Union. This was manifest in the resolutions for the annexation of Texas which provided that Congress might thereafter make four new states out of the territory thus added to the country. It was revealed in triumphant hostility to the Wilmot proviso which expressly provided for the exclusion of slavery from any territory acquired from Mexico, and in the fixed resolve of Southern leaders to hold all gains during the hardfought battle that ended in the Compromise of 1850—a compromise which left the question of slavery open in all the new regions except California where the rule of freedom had already been established by independent local action.

On the other hand, Whig leaders who opposed further territorial expansion at the expense of Mexico were equally clear in expounding the source of their objection—the enlargement of the agrarian representation in Congress which would endanger their economic position in the Government. More votes from agrarian states meant the undoing of protection for American industries. Webster illustrated the Whig case against annexation when he declared: "Texas was finally admitted, in December, 1845. . . . In July, 1846, those two Texan votes turned the balance in the Senate, and overthrew the tariff of 1842 [the Whig law abrogating the Compromise of 1833], in my judgment the best system of revenue ever established in this country. . . . In two years' time we shall probably be engaged in a revision of our system: in the work of establishing, if we can, a tariff of specific duties; of protecting, if we can, our domestic industry and the manufactures of the country; in the work of preventing, if we can, the overwhelming flood of foreign importations. Suppose that to be part of the future: that would be exactly the 'suitable time,' if necessary, for two Senators from New Mexico to make their appearance here!" [12] The implication was clear: keep new agrarian states out of the Union, refrain from additional annexations which

<hr/>

[12] *Works* (Ed. 1869), Vol. V, p. 292.

will make impossible the supremacy of the commercial and industrial interests in national politics.

With the acquisitions that marked the triumph over Mexico, and except for a minor acquisition primarily concerned with rounding out the national boundaries, the long epoch of national expansion under the auspices of the agrarian party came to a close. The Pacific Ocean had been reached at last. No more rich land for farmers and planters awaited easy conquest. The areas already added to the American heritage were wide enough to engross the labors of pioneers for many decades; the nineteenth century had almost drawn to a close before the Federal Land Office could announce the disappearance of free land and the frontier.

By that time many changes had been wrought in the party of territorial expansion. Its planting leadership in the South had been destroyed by arms. The intense pressure for more virgin cotton lands had been definitely relaxed. While American farmers were conquering the plains and fertile valleys of the West, the vacant areas of Canada were being occupied rapidly, so rapidly indeed that the pressure of Canadian competition in American and foreign produce markets dampened the old ardor for annexation in that direction. To the southward, the semi-arid lands of Mexico offered little temptation to a people engaged in breaking the prairies of the Northwest; while the adjacent islands of the Caribbean, already occupied by Spanish, mixed, Indian, and negroid peoples, extended no beckoning palms to free farmers. The curtain was lowered upon the drama of four acts—Louisiana, Florida, Texas, and California, and the play was never to be repeated. The pioneering flame died down, and, by the millions, the sons and daughters of Jefferson's stalwart and upstanding farmers became dwellers in cities.

Yet Jefferson's party continued to echo the original doctrines of its founder. While it supported the war on Spain in 1898, it looked with suspicion, if not complete disfavor, on the territorial expansion which followed that conflict. True to tradition, the Democrats declared in their platform of 1900: "We are not opposed to territorial expansion, when it takes in desirable territory which can be erected into states in the

Union, and whose people are willing and fit to become American citizens. We favor trade expansion by every peaceful and legitimate means. But we are unalterably opposed to the seizing or purchasing of distant islands to be governed outside the Constitution and whose people can never become citizens." If the purchase of the Virgin Islands and the operations of President Wilson's administration in the Caribbean did not square exactly with the perfect letter of the Jeffersonian law, it was perhaps because an inexorable drift of economic forces had torn the party of Jefferson away from its old moorings.

TERRITORIAL EXPANSION CONNECTED
WITH COMMERCE

While the Government of the United States under agricultural leadership, with planters in the foreground, was marching in seven league boots across the American continent adding new areas for farmers and slave owners, commerce and manufacturing were not idle, either in matters economic or in matters political. It is true that from the triumph of Jefferson in 1800 to the victory of Lincoln in 1860, the agrarian party carried every presidential election except two; but in the meantime, despite reverses and defeats in tariff battles, trade and industry steadily widened their domain, increasing the proportion of the national capital and of the population enlisted under their banners.

In the course of this industrial and commercial expansion, special attention was given to the Pacific area and the Far East generally—attention which was reflected in Congress, particularly by members of the Whig party and also in policies and acts of the Government during the tenure of Whig presidents (below, pp. 95ff.). With their usual vigilance and true to the traditions of empire, naval officers of the United States, freely afloat at sea in distant places, on their own motion cast about for stations and naval bases to serve as points of support for trade. If all the good agricultural land open for seizure had not already been preëmpted by the imperial powers of the Old World, they might have sought such additions as well, but in the circumstances they confined their operations to the acquisition of holdings principally useful for commercial and naval advancement.

Thus it came about that, after the continent had been rounded out by the conquest of California, the next territorial extension was made by Commodore Perry, in command of the naval expedition to Japan, as a part of his policy of providing adequate naval protection to American commerce in the East. On the way to the Orient, Perry stopped at the Bonin Islands, claimed by Japan for centuries. As they lay on the route from Honolulu to Shanghai, he became convinced of their strategic importance, and accordingly he bought a plot of ground for the erection of "offices, wharves, coal-shed, etc." Under instructions from Perry, Commander Kelly, in charge of the *Plymouth,* occupied the southern group of the islands in the name of the United States, raised the American flag, and renamed them "Coffin Islands," in honor of an American naval officer who had visited the place about thirty years previously. This occupation, however, proved to be temporary for the islands were abandoned after the negotiations with Japan proved successful.[13] Commodore Perry also got a foothold in the Lew Chew Islands by recognizing their independence from Japan and negotiating a treaty with the ruler granting certain rights to American ships visiting the ports.[14] Although the treaty was ratified by the Senate of the United States, the privileges granted did not develop into occupation.

The second territorial gesture in the Pacific, less official and even more evanescent, occurred at Formosa. The chief actors in this enterprise were Dr. Peter Parker, commissioner of the United States to China, and Commodore Armstrong, of the American naval force at Hongkong. The former, a medical missionary who owed his political preferment, in part at least, to the fact that his wife was a distant relative of Daniel Webster, discovered that two American citizens, engaged in exploiting the camphor industry in Formosa, had fallen into difficulties with the natives, had raised the American flag in the harbor of Takow, and were prepared to set up an independent state in

[13] Dennett, *Americans in Eastern Asia,* pp. 274ff.
[14] Hawks, *Narrative of the Expedition of the American Squadron to the China Seas and Japan,* p. 570.

Formosa, if the approval of the American Government could be secured. Parker forwarded this proposition to the State Department with the all-embracing suggestion that it should not "shrink from the action which the interests of humanity, civilization, navigation, and commerce impose upon it." Commodore Armstrong supported the scheme, but held that his present naval force was not strong enough to make occupation immediately practicable. Unfortunately for Commissioner Parker and Commodore Armstrong, Daniel Webster was now dead, the Whig party which he had led was dying, and the Democratic administration in power at Washington denied all "aggressive" aims, declaring that "the extension of our commercial intercourse must be the work of individual enterprise," and refused to do more than extend protection to life and property, thereby declining emphatically to approve annexation.[15]

After the collapse of the Formosa undertaking, the American nation was deeply engrossed in the great sectional conflict of which the Civil War was one phase; but as soon as the struggle was over territorial expansion was renewed—under different leadership and other conceptions of national interest. William H. Seward, then Secretary of State, had been a Whig of the Federalist school and long before 1861 had declared his belief in the desirability of adding new territory to the old heritage—Canada, Latin American countries, the Arctic regions of the Northwest; and he had proclaimed his conviction that the next great theater of American political and commercial action was to be the Pacific Ocean. In the wide reach of his imagination he saw Russia and the United States coming to grips on the plains of Manchuria in a contest over the partition of China. All these things Seward conceived in the name of manifest destiny and high national interest.

The first step in the realization of his dream was the acquisition of Alaska in 1867 which received the approval of the Senate, although the new possession brought little or no land for American farmers. Turning then to the Caribbean, Seward, through the good offices of the Navy Department, sponsored a treaty for a naval base in Santo Domingo, then another for

[15] Dennett, *op. cit.*, pp. 279ff.

the purchase of the Virgin Islands from Denmark, and a third assuring American control over the Isthmus; but the Senate, not yet prepared for such adventures, withheld approval, and Seward passed out of the State Department in 1869 saddened by this affront to his aspirations.

Notwithstanding the coolness of the Senate, expansive impulses were not checked. Three years later, an American naval officer, Admiral Meade, in command of the *Narragansett,* while cruising in the distant Pacific visited the Samoan Islands. These Islands, though small, inhabited by primitive peoples, and of slight economic value, had long been the scene of disputes among the German, British, and American commercial interests operating there. Considerable attention seemed to attach to the position of the Islands, for they lay in the line of trade routes from the Isthmus of Panama and Honolulu in the east to Australia in the southwest. While, as J. B. Henderson says, "they were of neither political nor commercial importance," [16] the Islands appeared to offer to Admiral Meade a strategic center for a naval base. Accordingly, without any authorization from his Government, entirely on his own motion, the Admiral negotiated an agreement with a chief at Tutuila, granting the United States a naval and coaling station in the harbor of Pago Pago and extending the "friendship and protection" of the United States to the grantor.

Disturbed by the commitments involved in the treaty, the Senate of the United States withheld its sanction. But as the result of persistent action on the part of President Grant, the threads thus spun were kept intact. The acquisition of the naval base was finally consummated in 1878 and a promise of friendly assistance was given to the Samoan chieftain, much to the alarm of old-fashioned politicians who saw in the arrangements an entangling alliance likely to prove troublesome in the future. Their prophecies, in fact, proved more than true; and yet after a collision with Germany, which brought the two countries to the verge of war, the United States emerged triumphantly in firm possession of the distant naval base and some surrounding bits of land.

Meanwhile territorial operations in the Caribbean were re-

[16] *American Diplomatic Questions,* p. 213.

vived. In connection with new attempts to secure possession of Santo Domingo, the theory of national interest was cogently expounded. After a treaty of annexation negotiated by President Grant's private secretary in 1869 was rejected by the Senate, the President, referring to the incident in his message of December 5, 1870, explained in detail the grounds of his advocacy. "I was thoroughly convinced then," he said, "that the best interests of the country, commercially and materially, demanded its ratification. Time has only confirmed me in this view. . . . The acquisition of San Domingo is desirable because of its geographical position. It commands the entrance to the Caribbean Sea and the Isthmus transit of commerce. It possesses the richest soil, best and most capacious harbors, most salubrious climate, and the most valuable products of the forests, mines, and soil of any of the West Indian Islands. Its possession by us will in a few years build up a coastwise commerce of immense magnitude, which will go far toward restoring to us our lost merchant marine. It will give us those articles which we consume so largely, thus equalizing our exports and imports. In case of foreign war it will give us command of all the islands referred to, and thus prevent an enemy from ever again possessing himself of a rendezvous upon our very coast. . . . San Domingo will become a large consumer of the products of Northern farms and manufactories." To these practical considerations others were added by the President. The people of the Island "yearn for the protection of our free institutions and laws, our progress and civilization." Prosperity there would tend to make slavery unsupportable in Cuba, Porto Rico, and ultimately in Brazil, and the Monroe Doctrine would be vindicated.

To the end of his administration President Grant insisted that such impressive arguments based on substantial interests warranted this territorial extension. In his last regular message he reviewed the economic advantages to be derived from the operation, dwelling particularly upon the advantages that would have been gained if annexation had been consummated when he first proposed it. In that case, he said, "the soil would have soon fallen into the hands of United States capitalists," and the emigration of American negroes to the Island would have been encouraged. "The emancipated race of the South would have found there a congenial home, where their civil rights would not be disputed." These views President Grant did not present to Congress for the purpose of renewing the issue of annexation, but merely "to vindicate my previous action in regard to it." [17]

Within a few years the movement for territorial expansion, conforming to the commercial type, was renewed in the Caribbean direction, with the Cuban revolution of 1895 as the occasion for action. Great and genuine as was the indignation throughout the United States at the horrors in Cuba which marked the contest between Spain and the revolutionists, it was accompanied by other considerations belonging under the head of national interest. There were many practical reasons for American intervention. The passion for annexation that sprang from the desire to extend the slave power to Cuba had, of course, disappeared with the abolition of slavery; [18] but other grounds for anxiety over the fate of the Island remained. Fundamental among them were incentives connected with

[17] Richardson, *Messages and Papers of the Presidents,* Vol. VII, p. 412.

[18] For efforts to extend the slave power to Cuba, see J. W. Foster, *A Century of American Diplomacy,* pp. 327, 345. The relation of Cuba to the United States had been a constant source of anxiety to American administrators. In his message to the House of Representatives in 1854, President Pierce declared: "In view of the position of the island of Cuba, its proximity to our coast, the relations which it must ever bear to our commercial and other interests, it is vain to expect that a series of unfriendly acts infringing our commercial rights and the adoption of a policy of threatening the honor and security of these States can long consist with peaceful relations." *Executive Doc.,* 33rd Cong., 2nd Sess., Vol. 10, p. 34. After consulting together, at the suggestion of Secretary of State William Marcy, with a view toward concerted action, James Buchanan, J. Y. Mason, and Pierre Soulé (American Ministers at London, Paris, and Madrid) in a letter under date of October 18, 1854, took the position: "Self preservation is the first law of nature, with States as well as with individuals. . . ."

"After we shall have offered Spain a price for Cuba far beyond its present value, and this shall have been refused, it will then be time to consider the question, does Cuba, in the possession of Spain, seriously endanger our internal peace and the existence of our cherished Union?"

"Should this question be answered in the affirmative, then, by every law, human and divine, we shall be justified in wresting it from Spain if we possess the power; and this upon the very same principle that would justify an individual in tearing down the burning house of his neighbor if there were no other means of preventing the flames from destroying his own home." *Executive Doc.,* 33rd Cong., 2nd Sess., Vol. 10, p. 131.

national defense, formulated under the ægis of the Monroe Doctrine. Entirely apart from the antagonism between the monarchical institutions of the Old World and the republican institutions of the New, which figured so conspicuously in the original Doctrine, the United States could not fail to regard the establishment of a first-rate military or naval power in Cuba as a menace to its security, involving huge outlays for defensive purpose and the constant peril of a serious war. Nor did the Government of the United States look upon the permanent possession of the Island by Spain as conducive to the most efficient development of insular economy and trade.[19]

Supplementary interests were plainly economic. The cane sugar growers of Louisiana could supply only a small part of the domestic requirement and the beet-sugar industry was in its infancy. Under reciprocity arrangements with Spain sugar had been allowed to come freely into the United States from Cuba for many years; in 1898 ninety-five per cent of Cuba's export to the United States was sugar and that amounted to a significant proportion of Cuba's foreign trade. During the rapid development of the Cuban sugar industry, which responded to the enormous demand of the American market, American capital and enterprise poured into Cuban plantations and mills. Then came the tariff of 1894 which put a duty on raw and refined sugars. This was followed by a heavy drop in the export of sugar from Cuba to the United States, widespread unemployment and distress in Cuba, revolutionary outbreaks, and the destruction of American property as well as American business with the Island.

In his message of December 7, 1896, President Cleveland explained how the Cuban revolution spread economic ruin throughout Cuba. After describing the methods pursued by bands of marauders which now in the name of one party and then of another, plundered the people and harried the country, the President said: "Such a condition of things would inevitably entail immense destruction of property, even if it

---

[19] In President Fillmore's administration, the United States rejected a proposal from England and France for a tripartite guarantee of Spanish possession of Cuba and a disavowal of any intention to acquire the Island. Foster, *op. cit.*, p. 327.

were the policy of both parties to prevent it as far as practicable; but while such seemed to be the original policy of the Spanish government, it has now apparently abandoned it and is acting upon the same theory as the insurgents, namely, that the exigencies of the contest require the wholesale annihilation of property that it may not be of use and advantage to the enemy. It is to the same end that, in pursuance of general orders, Spanish garrisons are now being withdrawn from plantations and the rural population required to concentrate itself in the towns. The sure result would seem to be that the industrial value of the Island is fast diminishing and that unless there is a speedy and radical change in existing conditions it will soon disappear altogether." [20]

While making due allowance for the sympathy of the American people for the suffering Cubans and for the efforts of the revolutionists to establish "better and freer government," President Cleveland pointed out that the United States had a concern with the situation "which is by no means of a wholly sentimental or philanthropic character. It lies so near to us as to be hardly separated from our territory. Our actual pecuniary interest in it is second only to that of the people and government of Spain. It is reasonably estimated that at least from $30,000,000 to $50,000,000 of American capital are invested in the plantations and in railroad, mining, and other business enterprises on the island. The volume of trade between the United States and Cuba, which in 1889 amounted to about $64,000,000, rose in 1893 to about $103,000,000 and in 1894, the year before the present insurrection broke out, amounted to nearly $96,000,000." [21]

Although it was the custom of the Spanish government to represent the revolution as the work of "the scum" of the island, that view was one-sided, to say the least. Secretary

[20] "The insurgents were attempting to paralyze the economic life of the island and so harass and cripple the Peninsular party, and incidentally they were working on the theory that until their belligerency should be recognized it was to their interest to destroy plantations and other property belonging to foreigners, and let the foreigners hold Spain responsible under international law." Henry James, *Richard Olney and His Public Services*, p. 157.

[21] *Messages and Papers of the Presidents*, New York publication, Vol. XIII, p. 6150.

Olney insisted that "the Cuban insurgents are not to be regarded as the scum of the earth. . . . In sympathy and feeling nine-tenths of the Cuban population are with them. . . . The property class to a man is disgusted with Spanish misrule, with a system which has burdened the Island with $300,000,000 of debt, whose impositions in the way of annual taxes just stop short of prohibiting all industrial enterprise, and which yet does not fulfil the primary functions of government by insuring safety to life and security to property." [22] In other words, substantial native interests in Cuba were on the side of American economic interests in the Island during the movement to throw off Spanish rule and stabilize the social order.

Yet President Cleveland, as leader of Jefferson's old agrarian party, then harassed by extreme agrarians known as Populists, was not prepared to wage war on Spain or forcibly intervene in behalf of Cuban independence. The initiative was left to the Republicans who, as heirs of the Whig and Federalist tradition, could interpret national interest in terms of commercial expansion and the enlargement of naval power. In their platform of 1896 the Republicans stated their case succinctly without any embroidery of political theory: "The government of Spain, having lost control of Cuba, and being unable to protect the property or lives of resident American citizens, or to comply with its treaty obligations, we believe that the Government of the United States should actively use its influence and good offices to restore peace and give independence to the Island." This declaration, with its inevitable implications, was accompanied by an appropriate navy plank: "The peace and security of the republic and the maintenance of its rightful influence among the nations of the earth demand a naval power commensurate with its position and responsibility. We therefore favor the continued enlargement of the navy and a complete system of harbor and coast defenses."

If, as seems highly probable in view of the documents now available, the independence of Cuba could have been obtained by diplomatic pressure on Spain, the administration of President McKinley did not choose that course. The mere emancipation of Cuba from Spanish dominion would not have given

[22] McElroy, *Grover Cleveland*, Vol. II, p. 247.

the United States a naval base at Guantanamo, commanding the Windward passage; nor would it have furnished the occasion for annexing Porto Rico, commanding the Mona passage, or for acquiring the Philippines which supplied a naval base for commercial expansion in the Orient, so long and so ardently demanded by American naval officers.

To be sure, no such comprehensive policy of expansion, if deliberately formulated by the American Government, was proclaimed officially to the country as a motive for war.[23] In the face of the Teller amendment to the resolution declaring war on Spain, which disowned motives of annexation and renounced any intention to impose restraints on the independence of Cuba, it would have been inexpedient to publish any such program, had it been privately entertained. Indeed the war sentiment stirred up in the United States scarcely ran beyond assistance to "the heroic Cubans" struggling for independence, as the American colonists had done more than a hundred years before, and the letters and papers of the time now open to students reveal no little confusion in official minds.

Yet the conformity of the outcome to the pattern of com-

[23] In his message of April 11, 1898 to Congress, President McKinley drew together all of the grounds for intervention—the cause of humanity, protection of the lives and property of American citizens, injuries to American commerce with the island, national defense—as follows:

"First. In the cause of humanity. . . . It is no answer to say this is all in another country, belonging to another nation, and is therefore none of our business. It is specially our duty, for it is right at our door."

"Second. We owe it to our citizens in Cuba to afford them that protection and indemnity for life and property which no government there can or will afford. . . ."

"Third. The right to intervene may be justified by the very serious injury to the commerce, trade and business of our people, and by the wanton destruction of property and devastation of the island."

"Fourth, and which is of the utmost importance. The present condition of affairs in Cuba is a constant menace to our peace, and entails upon this Government an enormous expense. With such a conflict waged for years in an island so near us and with which our people have such trade and business relations; when the lives and liberty of our citizens are in constant danger and their property destroyed and themselves ruined; when our trading vessels are liable to seizure and are seized at our very door by war ships of a foreign nation, the expeditions of filibustering that we are powerless to prevent altogether, and the irritating questions and entanglements thus arising—all these and others that I need not mention, with the resulting strained relations, are a constant menace to our peace, and compel us to keep on a semiwar footing with a nation with which we are at peace." *U. S. For. Rels.*, 1898, pp. 757–758.

mercial and naval expansion could not have been neater, had it been deliberately planned. Nor could it be accurately described as a historic accident, as was once the fashion; for it was the perfect upshot of a long chain of actions and leadership extending back over more than half a century. Daniel Webster, Commodore Perry, William H. Seward, and Admiral Meade had not wrought in vain. While many congressmen who voted for war did not look far ahead, Theodore Roosevelt, Henry Cabot Lodge, and Alfred Thayer Mahan saw beyond the smoke of battle—how far and with what vision the verdict of history remains unspoken.

Without in the slightest minimizing the lofty sentiments which accompanied the war of the United States on Spain, it remains a fact that the American interests associated with Cuban industry and trade derived practical benefits from forcible intervention and expanded under the rule of law later established in virtue of the Platt Amendment. After the war was over American claims for damages done during the revolution were adjusted on an equitable basis [24] and industry and commerce flourished as never under the Spanish régime. The American capital invested in Cuba, estimated by President Cleveland at a figure ranging between $30,000,000 and $50,-000,000 in 1896, rose to $141,000,000 within ten years after the conclusion of peace. At the beginning of 1931 the total investment of American capital was placed at $1,066,551,000, consisting of $935,706,000 in "direct" investments, such as sugar properties and enterprises, electric utilities, transportation and communication systems, and other tangible properties; and of $130,845,000 in "portfolio" investments comprising a broad range of securities. The volume of trade, which President Cleveland put at $96,000,000 in 1895, increased rapidly as soon as stability was assured in the Island, and within less than thirty years stood at $561,499,000—$199,-778,000 in exports from the United States to Cuba and $361,-721,000 in imports from Cuba into the United States. [25]

[24] Scott Nearing, *Dollar Diplomacy*, p. 173.

[25] For the year 1924. Figures for previous years, notably 1920, are much higher due to inflated price levels and currency disturbances. Total trade with the United States, exports plus imports, averaged $38,411,000 for the period 1896–1900; $185,124,000 for 1910–1914; and $480,899,000 for 1921–1925.

The reasons for the annexation of Hawaii ranged the whole scale from national defense to the white man's burden, but only two of them—the strategic value of the Islands and the close relation of their economic structure to American interests —emerged predominant. These two remained the substantial realities back of all the thinly-veiled motives which were advanced from time to time either to hasten or justify annexation. Thus, if "the attitude of the United States toward Hawaii was in moral effect that of a friendly protectorate," it was because "observing the spirit of the Monroe Doctrine, the United States . . . made a firm . . . declaration of the purpose to prevent the absorption of Hawaii or the political control of that country by any foreign power . . . [upon] . . . very important commercial and military considerations." [26] Also, while it "would be to the advantage of the commerce of the world that any stable and great power [like the United States] should have the occupation of those islands, rather than a weak and uncertain power . . . such as would be furnished by the native population of Hawaii," [27] nevertheless, with the possession of Hawaii and other naval bases, "a properly organized fleet of sufficient size . . . will hold the Pacific as an American ocean, dominated by American commercial enterprise for all time." [28] Similarly, back of all the broad abstractions of service to humanity, aid to world commerce, and the protection afforded by a "big brother" to a weak and indefensible Hawaii, lay the substantial naval and commercial interests of the United States. Among the many reasons for annexation it was even suggested that "we might look to the native islanders as a large source of supply for seamen." [29]

There was nothing unexpected in such an attitude. It was a natural consequence of the course of events. American

Since 1926 there has been a steady decrease, intensified by the fall in price levels since 1929, in values of total trade, from $411,088,000 for 1926 to $87,112,553 for 1932 (official, but unrevised). Source, *United States Commerce Yearbook*. Various, since 1922, and Monthly Summaries of Foreign Commerce of the United States.

[26] *Sen. Rep.* 227, 53d Cong., 2d Sess., p. 20.
[27] *Ibid.*, Appendices, pp. 431–433.
[28] *Ibid.*, Appendices, p. 133.
[29] *Ibid.*, Appendices, p. 281.

relations with the Islands were at first commercial. In the early part of the nineteenth century the Islands served as a port of call for Pacific shipping and as a base for the whaling industry. Later a number of Americans acquired plantations and soon had established a thriving trade in sugar. Pressed by the persistent efforts of the planters and commercial interests, and fearful lest some political control of the Islands should follow the threatened diversion of the sugar crop to the free port of Sydney, Australia,[30] the State Department, in 1875, concluded a commercial treaty admitting Hawaiian sugar to the United States without a duty.

American economic interests and control of the Islands expanded with great rapidity under the benefits derived from this treaty. The sugar output increased seven or eight times over that of the year preceding its conclusion. American exports to the Islands increased almost in the same ratio. A new merchant marine, with more than 90 per cent of the total tonnage American built, was created expressly for the service, with the mercantile houses profiting on the entire commerce both ways through high rates of freight, insurance, commissions, and exchange.[31] The trade in merchandise from 1870 to 1892, inclusive, according to estimates based upon reports of the collector-general of the customs of the Hawaiian Islands and from the United States Treasury Department, totalled $193,854,348 of which $55,183,611 was exported to the Hawaiian Islands and $138,670,737 was imported from there into the United States.[32] An apparently conservative estimate of American property holdings in 1893 sets the figure at $22,000,000, or nearly two-thirds of the total assessed valua-

[30] *Sen. Rep.* 227, 53d Cong., 2d Sess., Appendices, p. 103.

[31] *Ibid.*, Appendices, p. 104. For a calculation of $36,150,230 in gross profits and its distribution among the various commercial interests, see pp. 105 and 106 of the *Report*. For a "balance of payments" sheet showing benefits accruing to the United States under the reciprocity treaty, see p. 104 of the *Report*. A similar calculation showed a profit of more than seventy-three millions of dollars under the operation of the treaty. *Ibid.*, Appendices, pp. 776–777.

[32] *Ibid.*, Appendices, 776, 777. In 1929 the value of merchandise sent from the United States to Hawaii amounted to $82,951,000, and the amount sent by Hawaii to the United States totalled $106,313,000. Hawaiian trade with countries other than the United States is practically insignificant. Despite the sharp drop in commodity prices since 1929, Hawaiian-American trade has been affected only to a slight degree.

tion of $36,000,000 for all taxable property in the Island Kingdom.[33] A few years later, at the Senate hearings on annexation, Z. S. Spalding, who described himself as the largest personal producer of sugar on the Islands, estimated American investments to be between thirty and fifty millions of dollars depending upon the state of economic conditions. He further stated that nine-tenths of all the property was owned by whites, and that of this three-fourths was owned by Americans, the native Hawaiians having only "a very small proportion." [34]

Near the close of the century American control of the economic and political life of the Islands was practically complete. The Royal Government under Queen Liliuokalani was by that time a threadbare cloak tolerated only so long as it could be tossed about to serve one group or another in the local conflicts centering around economic interests.[35] The native population had steadily declined, while immigrant laborers from China and Japan, "who were excluded from participation in the government as voters, or as office-holders," [36] flooded in to work the broad acres of cane. The economic drift was clearly in the direction of the United States, despite the efforts of other nationalities to obtain a more secure foothold. Two economic developments intensified the drift toward American hegemony. The one had to do with United States trade with the Far East. It raised the question of the strategic value of American annexation of the Hawaiian Islands. The other was a matter of internal trade—the conflict over the sugar business on the American continent—a conflict which also forced the question of annexation.

At first Hawaiian sugars refined in San Francisco served only to supply the Pacific coast markets. With the rapid increase of production under the reciprocity treaty, supplemented by increasing supplies from Manila and Central America, sales of these sugars spread eastward into the Mississippi Valley, coming into direct competition wth the sugars of eastern refiners and Louisiana planters. The growers and processors

[33] *Ibid.*, Appendices, p. 771.
[34] *Ibid.*, Appendices, p. 249–250.
[35] *Ibid.*, p. 38.
[36] *Ibid.*, p. 21.

of these eastern sugars, believing that this competition was the direct result of the reciprocity treaty which discriminated against them, began an attack to terminate the treaty.[37] The conflict was intensified by another clash which took place within the field of Hawaiian sugar production itself. The monopolistic position of Claus Spreckels helped to bring about the competition of independent planters and the formation of an opposition refinery, C. Adolf Low & Company.[38]

At length, the conflict of Hawaiian sugar with Louisiana sugar and the output of the eastern refineries led to the passage of the McKinley bill which placed the Hawaiian product upon an equal basis with that of all other countries and gave a bounty of two cents per pound for home-grown sugar. Resentful now at what they believed was discrimination against them, and doubtful respecting the course to pursue, the Americans in control of the affairs of the Hawaiian Islands began to agitate for annexation.[39] Undoubtedly, they reasoned that, with Hawaii an integral part of the United States, they could enjoy, without further fear of interruption, the free market constitutionally guaranteed to American citizens and territories. The internal conflict between Spreckels and the independent planters also led to the same goal—annexation—since it split Hawaiian local politicians into two camps, with those hoping to advance their own interests through annexation arrayed against others seeking their interests through the power and control of the Royal House.

Meanwhile with the expansion of American trade in the Far East, the question of the strategic value of Hawaii came into prominence. As early as 1851, Admiral DuPont, well acquainted with Pacific affairs, declared that "the Hawaiian Islands would prove the most important acquisition we could make in the whole Pacific Ocean—an acquisition intimately connected with our commercial and naval supremacy in those seas." On kindred assumptions, the Department of State long resisted all operations and suggestions of European powers likely to interfere with the independence of the Hawaiian

[37] *Ibid.*, Appendices, p. 108–109.
[38] *Ibid.*, Appendices, p. 111–113.
[39] *Ibid.*, Appendices, p. 771.

Islands. In a message to Congress on December 31, 1842, written by Daniel Webster, President Tyler referred to the Islands as a center for whale-fishery, as a port of call for Pacific ships, and as a scene of American economic activities; and he declared that it was "in conformity with the interest and the wishes of the Government and people of the United States" to maintain the integrity and security of the Islands against outside intervention.[40] Nine years later, after France had made a naval demonstration against the authorities of Hawaii, Webster, as Secretary of State again, warned the French government that it should desist from measures directed against the sovereignty and independence of Hawaii and that the United States would not consent to see those Islands seized by any of the great commercial powers of the Old World.[41] By a treaty with the United States, made in 1878, the Hawaiian monarch agreed not to alienate any of his territory except to the United States; and in 1890 a supplementary treaty gave Americans exclusive use of Pearl Harbor.[42]

With the discussion of strategy, the question of the possession of the Hawaiian Islands was swept into the larger movement accompanying the growth of American economic and political power in the Pacific and, later through an Isthmian canal, in all other waters of the world.[43] The question broadened to include commercial expansion, national defense, and the whole philosophy of national interest in sea power. A strange interdependence emerged: the Hawaiian Islands became absolutely essential to an Isthmian canal and the latter equally essential to possession of the Hawaiian Islands, although at the time of the discussion the United States did not have possession of either one. The interdependence of Hawaii and the Nicaraguan canal was compared with Gibraltar and the Suez Canal.[44] Moreover, in the theory of naval policy, possession of the

---

[40] *Works of Daniel Webster,* Vol. I, p. 463 (Boston, 1869, 15th ed.)

[41] *Ibid.,* Vol. I, p. 477.

[42] American interest in the exclusive control of the Hawaiian Islands is cited as part of the historical background leading up to annexation. See *Sen. Rep., op. cit.,* p. 21.

[43] *Ibid.,* Appendices, p. 133.

[44] *Ibid.,* Appendices, pp. 431–433.

Hawaiian Islands was essential to the protection of the Pacific coast, and an augmented navy essential to the defense of the Hawaiian Islands.[45]

Such discussions brought the questions within the broad domain of sea power where Captain Alfred T. Mahan was thoroughly at home. After pointing out the parallels between the expansion of England through sea power and the inevitability of America's pursuing the same course, to the consequent benefit of the whole world, Captain Mahan, with his characteristic frankness and boldness of expression, observed: "If a plea of the world's welfare seems suspiciously like a cloak for national self-interest, let the latter be frankly accepted as the adequate motive which it assuredly is. Let us start from the fundamental truth, warranted by history, that the control of the seas, and especially along the great lines drawn by national interest or national commerce, is the chief among the merely material elements in the power and prosperity of nations. . . . From this necessarily follows the principle that, as subsidiary to such control, it is imperative to take possession, when it can righteously be done, of such maritime positions as contribute to secure command. If this principle be adopted there will be no hesitation about taking the positions—and they are many—upon the approaches to the Isthmus, whose interests incline them to seek us. It has its application also to the present case of Hawaii." [46]

All these motives of national concern—the economic exploitation of the Islands, the accompanying domestic struggles both in Hawaii and in the United States, the strategic position of the Island group both in relation to America's national defense and her inexorable march along the path of her destiny—matured rapidly in the closing decade of the nineteenth century. In the circumstances, the policy of the United States Government, as outlined by Secretary Bayard, during Cleveland's first administration, was "to wait quietly and patiently and let the islands fill up with American planters and American industries until they should be wholly identi-

[45] *Ibid.*, p. 23 of the *Report*.
[46] From an article in the March, 1893, number of *The Forum* magazine incorporated in *Sen. Report, op. cit.*, pp. 119–120.

fied with the United States. It was simply a matter of waiting until the apple should fall."

But events operated to hasten the ripening process; and in the eagerness to dispose of the matter the apple was shaken down by a revolution in which American citizens took a leading part. It was said that "The banks of Bishop and Spreckels are ready to help the Government with money. . . . [and that] Certain merchants are also ready to support the Government . . . ;"[47] while "Among the privates who went on guard duty [on behalf of the Provisional Government against the Queen] there was represented several million dollars."[48] Whether deliberately or not, the American minister John L. Stevens, acting under the all-embracing principle of "the protection of American life and property" authorized in the dispatches of Secretary Bayard,[49] supported the revolutionary movement. The major part of the whole affair took place in the presence of troops landed from the *Boston,* an American war vessel conveniently near in the harbor of the capital. The commander of the *Boston* acted under the regulations of the Navy Department for 1893, which elaborated the "protection of American life and property" principle.[50] That the support of the American minister and troops and the presence of the *Boston* contributed to the successful overthrow of the Royal Government, which was accomplished wholly without violence, there was little doubt. Nicoll Ludlow, Commander of the *Mohican,* an American naval vessel at Hawaii from February 10 to May 1, 1893, testified: ". . . the revolution would not have occurred in the way it did, and at the time it did, if the people who were the revolutionary party had not been assured of the protection and assistance of the United States forces there."[51]

---

[47] *Ibid.,* p. 38 of the *Report.*

[48] From the sworn statement of Dr. Nicholas B. Delamarter, a physician who testified on Hawaiian conditions, read into the *Sen. Rep.,* Appendices, p. 730.

[49] *Ibid.,* Appendices, p. 532.

[50] *Ibid.,* Appendices, p. 436, where the naval regulations are incorporated in the *Report.*

[51] *Ibid.,* Appendices, pp. 796ff. Elsewhere it was brought out in the Senate *Report* that the American Minister, the commanding officer of the *Boston,* and the Provisional Government officials (Sanford B. Dole—president) held

The apple-shaking operation was so obviously an American maneuver and was done with such apparent gusto, that President Cleveland refused to support the project for an immediate annexation of the Islands by the United States. There were, of course, political and moral grounds for the revolution made under American direction; it was said that the old monarchy was primitive, unenlightened, and reactionary in economic affairs; but the fundamental reasons for the acquisition of the Hawaiian Islands were doubtless stated correctly by the chairman of the committee on foreign affairs in the House of Representatives when the resolution of annexation was under consideration: "The importance of the question lies first of all in the necessity of possessing these islands for the defense of our western shore, the protection and promotion of our commercial interests, and the welfare and security of our country generally."

The annexation of Hawaii, early in July, 1898, was, therefore, not a sudden accident of history. It was the outcome of a long chain of measures, policies, and actions justified in "the national interest." Since the fourth decade of the nineteenth century American naval authorities and Secretaries of State had regarded annexation as a step indispensable to the expansion of American commercial interests in the Pacific theater, and the Spanish war offered the opportunity to break the resistance of Democratic opposition at home. Moreover, the date of final consummation is significant. It was July 8, after Dewey's victory at Manila, while the annexation of the Philippines was not yet officially determined. If there was any logic in the direction of affairs at Washington, then it foreshadowed the final determination to establish near the continent of Asia a base for the advancement of American commercial enterprise in the Far East.

Although great emphasis was laid by the Government of the United States on the weight of "moral obligation" in shaping its decision to acquire the Philippine Islands at the close of the Spanish war, this obligation was not the sole consideration.

innumerable conferences and coöperated in complete harmony before, during, and after the overthrow of the Royal Government and the establishment of the Provisional Government.

Practical interests also entered into the calculations, more or less, from the beginning of the conflict. American trade in the Orient had been an object of solicitude on the part of the Government from the foundation of the Republic. It was included by the authors of the *Federalist* in the list of commercial interests abroad deserving support by the political agencies to be established under the Constitution (above, p. 36). And during the long period that intervened between the inauguration of Washington and the inauguration of McKinley, Presidents, Secretaries of State, Secretaries of the Navy, and innumerable naval officers gave serious attention to the promotion of American commercial interest in the Far East. The promotion of commerce involved the securing of territorial footholds to serve as bases for the navy and as points of support for demonstrations of naval power against rivals and disturbers of the order necessary for regular traffic in goods.[52] The logic, once the premises were accepted, appeared irresistible. As expounded by Mahan (above, p. 76) the fundamental truth was that the control of the seas, especially along the great lines drawn by national interest, is the chief among the material elements in the power and prosperity of nations; and "From this necessarily follows the principle that, as subsidiary to such control, it is imperative to take possession, when it can righteously be done, of such maritime positions as contribute to secure command."[53] A review of these commercial activities, extensions of naval power, efforts to get naval stations, and declarations of policy on the part of the American Government and American naval officers shows that there was nothing new in the motives which actuated the McKinley administration in the conquest and acquisition of the Philippines.[54]

Whatever may have been the divided state of President McKinley's mind during and immediately after the Spanish war, it is certain that ardent members of his party, particularly

[52] For a practical expression of this view, see extracts from remarks of William F. Draper (*Cong. Record*, Feb. 4, 1894) incorporated into *Sen. Report* 227, *op. cit.*, Appendices, p. 133.

[53] From an article by Capt. A. T. Mahan in the March, 1893, number of *The Forum* magazine, incorporated into *Sen. Rep.* 227, *op. cit.*, p. 120.

[54] For an authentic and carefully documented summary, see Tyler Dennett, *Americans in Eastern Asia*, in 725 pages.

Senator Henry Cabot Lodge and Theodore Roosevelt, Assistant Secretary of the Navy at the outbreak of the war, had clearly in view the possibility of securing a permanent base in the Philippines for the extension of American power in the Orient. In a letter written to Mr. Lodge on September 21, 1897, six months before the declaration of war, Mr. Roosevelt stated that he had recently dined with President McKinley and had expounded his opinions to the President on action to be taken in case a war broke out with Spain. "I gave him a paper showing exactly where all our ships are, and I also sketched in outline what I thought ought to be done if things looked menacing about Spain, urging the necessity of taking an immediate and prompt initiative if we wished to avoid the chance of some serious trouble, and of the Japs chipping in." After sketching the lines of action along the Cuban coast, Mr. Roosevelt added, "Meanwhile, our Asiatic squadron should blockade, and if possible, take Manila." [55]

Resolved to have a man in charge of the Asiatic squadron, "who would act without referring things back to home authorities," Mr. Roosevelt, as Assistant Secretary of the Navy, selected Commodore Dewey. He advised Dewey to ask Senator Procter for support, and the Senator acted promptly by calling on President McKinley and getting a promise of the appointment before he left the White House. After receiving his commission, Dewey sailed for his post on December 7, 1898, and set to work to assemble the fleet at Hong Kong, as he said himself, "entirely on my own initiative, without any hint whatever from the department that hostilities might be expected. It was evident that in case of emergency Hong Kong was the most advantageous position from which to move to the attack." A little more than two months later, Assistant Secretary Roosevelt sent Dewey an order to gather the squadron, except the *Monocacy,* at Hong Kong, to "keep full of coal, and in event of war to see that the Spanish squadron does not leave the Asiatic coast, and then resort to offensive operations in the Philippine Islands." After the declaration of war, Secretary Long instructed Dewey to proceed at once to the Philippine Islands

[55] *Selections from the Correspondence of Theodore Roosevelt and Henry Cabot Lodge,* Vol. I, p. 278.

and use utmost endeavor. "Thus," claims Mr. Roosevelt's biographer, "was the famous battle of Manila fought and won by a commander whose appointment had been secured by Roosevelt against the wishes of Secretary Long and whose fleet had been thoroughly equipped for the conflict by an order that Roosevelt had sent on his own responsibility in the absence of his chief." [56]

On May 24, 1898, about a month after the opening of the war, Mr. Lodge wrote to Colonel Roosevelt, then with his regiment: "The one point where haste is needed is the Philippines, and I think I can say to you, in confidence but in absolute certainty, that the Administration is grasping the whole policy at last. . . . Porto Rico is not forgotten and we mean to have it. Unless I am utterly and profoundly mistaken the Administration is now fully committed to the large policy we both desire." The next day Colonel Roosevelt wrote to Mr. Lodge: "I earnestly hope that no truce will be granted and that peace will only be made on consideration of Cuba being independent, Porto Rico ours, and the Philippines taken away from Spain." A month later Mr. Lodge was able to write Colonel Roosevelt, forecasting precisely the ultimate action taken by President McKinley. He stated that he had recently dined with Mr. Day, Secretary of State, and Captain Mahan, the distinguished American formulator of *Machtpolitik,* and that he had "talked the Philippines" with Mr. Day for two hours. "He said at the end," continued Mr. Lodge, "that he thought we could not escape our destiny there. The feeling of the country is overwhelming against giving the Philippines back to Spain. That is clear to the most casual observer. Bryan has announced that he is against colonization, and Cleveland, in a ponderous speech, has come out against war as much as he dares and utterly against annexation. We shall sweep the country on that issue in my judgment." [57]

Thus, in spite of numerous references to fate, the accidents of history, the current of events, destiny, and gifts of the gods, it is clear that there was a positive connection between the

---

[56] J. B. Bishop, *Theodore Roosevelt and His Time,* Vol. I, pp. 92ff.

[57] *Correspondence of Theodore Roosevelt and Henry Cabot Lodge,* Vol. I, pp. 299ff.

decision to annex the Philippine Islands and the official activities of the Government of the United States in the Far East,
extending over a century of commercial development, accompanied by avowed resolutions of naval officers with respect to
naval bases and points of naval support for trade. Other evidence confirms this view. President McKinley, as Senator
Hoar said, "had to get his facts" about the Philippines, "almost wholly" from military and naval officers during the summer of 1898; [58] and numerous military and naval officers were
dispatched to Paris for the purpose of giving the American
Peace Commission their views on the policy to be pursued
with respect to the Philippines.[59] While the sincerity of President McKinley's personal misgivings is evident in the records,
it cannot be denied that powerful groups in the official world
and outside regarded the annexation of the Philippines as a
desirable consummation of ardent labors extending over a long
period of history. The chain of connections is too close and
too strong to be broken by emphasis on the uncertainties and
hesitancy prevalent in many circles during the summer of 1898.

Nor did President McKinley himself, while laying stress on
the element of moral obligation, overlook the force of practical
interest connected with the historical development of American
commerce in the Orient. Although the peace protocol left the
issue of the Philippines open and President McKinley informed the mediator, M. Jules Cambon, that the peace negotiators were to determine it, he ordered the American commissioners, in his opening instructions to them, to demand the cession of the Island of Luzon in full right and sovereignty and
equal favors for American ships and merchandise in the ports
left to Spain. In support of this demand, the President said,
"Incidental to our tenure in the Philippines is the commercial
opportunity to which American statesmanship cannot be indifferent. It is just to use every legitimate means for the enlargement of American trade; but we seek no advantages in the Orient which are not common to all. Asking only the open door for
ourselves we are ready to accord the open door to others. The
commercial opportunity which is naturally and inevitably as-

[58] *Autobiography of Seventy Years,* Vol. II, p. 312.
[59] Tyler Dennett, *Americans in Eastern Asia,* p. 623.

sociated with this new opening depends less on large territorial possessions than upon an adequate commercial basis and upon broad and equal privileges." Yet, Tyler Dennett remarks, "a fortuitous concurrence of events had brought within American grasp the very expedient which Commodore Perry and Dr. Peter Parker had urged in 1853 and 1857. Manila might become the equivalent for Hong Kong and the leased ports of China, for the lack of which American trade and interests in the Far East were, in the summer of 1898, in serious prospective if not present embarrassment." [60] A long series of commercial and naval efforts, deliberately conceived in terms of interest and far from accidental in character, had produced a desired result. No apparently fortuitous aspects could obscure the long-sustained purpose which had at last borne fruit.

Moreover, there were not wanting in the naval and military circles of the United States leaders now eager to take advantage of another apparently "providential circumstance" to secure additional territorial holdings in the general neighborhood—on the continent of Asia. Although hints of this fact were later given in the papers of John Hay, the fact itself was not made known until long afterward, with the publication of *Foreign Relations* for 1915, after reference had been made to the episode by the government of Japan. From the record it now appears that the commander of the American contingent in China, General Chaffee, proposed to the General Staff, on the basis of his experience, that the United States follow the other powers in the acquisition of Chinese territory, and American naval authorities proposed at the same time the acquisition of a naval base at Samsa Bay, north of Foochow. Elihu Root, Secretary of War, approved the army suggestion. John Hay, Secretary of State, let the American minister to China, Conger, know that the Navy was "anxious" to get the naval station and asked him to do "what you can to arrange this and if not feasible at present be on your guard against any preëmption by another power."

On demand of the Secretary of the Navy, Conger was again instructed "to obtain for the United States free and exclusive use of Samsa Bay as a proposed port, with the additional

[60] *Americans in Eastern Asia*, p. 622.

pledge that a circular zone 20 miles in radius with its center at the eastern point of Crag Island shall not be in future alienated, to be controlled or used by any other power or any fortification be erected thereon by the Chinese Government." The business was delicate. Secretary Hay, therefore, sounded Tokyo. The Japanese foreign office replied that it had, with satisfaction, taken note of the repeated declarations of Secretary Hay respecting the preservation of the territorial entity of China, and that the desirable end might best be gained if the respective powers refrained from excepting any advantages which would give other powers a pretext for making territorial demands. The hint from Tokyo to Washington was fully appreciated, no doubt. At all events, the United States did not at once acquire more territory, this time in China, "by the accidents of history." [61]

If such things are "accidents," then politics and statecraft are meaningless frivolities. If these are "accidents" what are deliberate determinations of policy?

SUMMARY

Under these two distinct types of territorial expansion, the total area under American dominion increased from an estimated 400,000 square miles in 1776 to an approximate 3,738,393 square miles in 1934. The continental domain covered 3,026,789 square miles, and the outlying territories and possessions 711,604 square miles more.[62] In this bare record of American territorial expansion certain facts stand out with the stubbornness of mountains rising from a plain. Both types of expansion —for land and for trade—represented and reflected a conflict of interests within the United States. At no time was there anything approaching a united front, except after the country had become involved in war. Each type of expansion was pushed by one group of interests and resisted by another, although within each group there were heterogeneous elements, united often only by compromises between them on sub-

[61] *Foreign Relations* (1915), pp. 113ff.

[62] Ernest L. Bogart, *Economic History of the American People,* p. 746, where there is also a chronological table of territorial expansion to 1917, the date of the last acquisition, the Virgin Islands.

sidiary interests. Both were connected with the maintenance of partisan supremacy in domestic politics—with control over the Government of the United States, its policies, measures, acts, and engines of power.

Each type of expansion associated with itself a certain philosophy of civilization carrying with it international implications. Jefferson was a nationalist in a narrow and racial sense,[63] and looked to the development, on this continent, of a homogeneous people primarily engaged in agriculture—a society of people speaking a common language, knit together by ties of blood and language, capable of self-government, and so placed in a strategic geographical position as to be easily defended without large military and naval establishments—those historic menaces to liberty. This American society, in Jefferson's view, was to be, in the main, self-sufficient economically, independent of the caprices and casualties of distant customers. It is true that under the leadership of planters Jefferson's conception was given a peculiar turn; if they had had their way America might have been a nation of Negro slaves dominated and exploited by a minority of whites; but climate, soil, technical progress, and the census returns made impossible the consummation of that dream. In the end, most of the soil acquired on this continent was tilled by Jefferson's upstanding farmers, and for a brief moment in universal history his conception of nationality came close to realization.

With a high degree of consistency, the Jeffersonian party long clung to its original position with reference to national interest in territorial expansion. As we have seen, it did not oppose any territorial acquisition which brought land for American farmers to till, or which embraced other peoples capable of easy assimilation; but it did resist the conquest and annexation of distant lands already occupied by other races and nationalities. Loyal to his party tradition, Senator George Gray, the only Democratic member of the commission which negotiated peace with Spain in 1898, objected to the addition of the Philippines to the territorial domain of the United States. Annexation of the Islands in whole or in part,

[63] Jefferson, it is well known, was opposed to miscellaneous immigration and in favor of a discrimination calculated to support the original stock.

he contended in a cable to President McKinley, "would be to reverse accepted continental policy of the country, declared and acted upon throughout our history. Propinquity governs the case of Cuba and Porto Rico. Policy proposed [annexation] introduces us into European politics and the entangling alliances against which Washington and all American statesmen have protested. It will make necessary a navy equal to the largest of powers; a greatly increased military establishment; immense sums for fortifications and harbors; multiply occasions for dangerous complications with foreign nations; and increase burdens of taxation. Will receive in compensation no outlet for American labor in labor market already overcrowded and cheap; no area for homes for American citizens; climate and social conditions demoralizing to character of American youth; new and disturbing questions introduced into our politics." [64]

The other school of territorial expansionists, associated with the names of Seward and McKinley, took no such view of American nationality. Its progenitors, the Federalists and Whigs, had, with a certain degree of consistency, opposed the annexation of western territories and their organization into states, through the fear that such a development would lead to agrarian supremacy in the Government of the United States, but it accepted the verdict of history respecting the continental domain. Then it looked beyond these shores. Making commerce the center of its concern in foreign relations—the export of American raw materials and manufactured products— it rejected the Jeffersonian concept of nationality and strategic defense. It was, therefore, prepared to annex new territories with little or no vacant land to be tilled by American farmers —territories inhabited by other races, speaking different tongues, bearing a different heritage, and civilized, so far as civilized at all, under different institutions. It proposed, officially at all events, "to educate, uplift, and Christianize" the new American subjects, and to bestow upon them "the benefits of American civilization," apparently on the assumption that this process was wholly feasible. And at the very moment when the United States, convinced that the melting pot had not

[64] G. F. Hoar, *Autobiography of Seventy Years,* Vol. II, p. 313.

operated as expected, was preparing to close the gates against races not readily assimilable to the original strains, advocates of territorial expansion for commercial purposes threw open the doors to migration from the new possessions and dependencies, bringing in immigrants still less adapted to the national heritage than many races later excluded by law, thus adding to the confusion of peoples, the babel of tongues, and problems of assimilation and association already existing in the country.

It is clear then, that, while both schools of territorial expansionists operated on a thesis of national interest, the Jeffersonian party had a more positive and limited view of nationality —a nationality fairly homogeneous in race, confined to this continent, and defended by small military and naval establishments. It was essentially isolationist in outlook and opposed to territorial adventures which brought the United States into economic rivalry with the imperialist powers of Europe and hence into the diplomatic entanglements inevitably associated with it.

The Republican party, on the other hand, in embarking upon overseas expansion and in throwing open the gates to immigration from the new possessions, eagerly assumed what it characterized as "international responsibilities," creating a strategic situation which called for a huge naval establishment. It was long inclined to treat the United States as "the asylum for the oppressed of all lands," without regard to race, color, or previous condition of servitude, thus submerging the racial concept of nationality in a cosmopolitan perspective—in short, emphasizing *interest* rather than *nationality* in its foreign policies.

Although, of course, the two parties did not absolutely divide the country on these lines, although neither of them maintained perfect consistency in program and measures, such were the fundamental principles and implications involved in the expansionist policies which they respectively pursued in the name of national interest—with fateful significance for the course of American civilization. While the historical circumstances in which these processes of territorial expansion were carried out can never be repeated, the two conceptions of national interest inherent in them yet remain as positive points of reference with which to relate future policies. Each of them calls for a definition of the terms nation and interest. Each of them has associated with it issues of security and defense. One places the center of gravity of state reason in the heart of the continental domain; the other moves it toward the periphery of the trade empire, with all the entanglements of international connections that must inevitably accompany it. Both reflect deep divisions of domestic politics and interests and are affected by the oscillations and movements of economic power within the country. Neither stands out as a transcendent commitment of the nation beyond the reach of controversy and diversity of opinion.

CHAPTER IV

NATIONAL INTEREST IN COMMERCIAL
EXPANSION—FIRST PHASE

FROM the survey of the things and patterns of conduct coming under the head of national interest as formulated by leaders among the founders of the American Republic, it is evident that recent expressions characterizing the United States as a "world power," as "coming of age," and as suddenly adopting a policy of "dollar diplomacy" reveal a superficial knowledge of American history. Coming from publicists and politicians, whose acquaintance with the long past is usually slight, such expressions may be pardoned, perhaps, but they obscure the true nature of events in course of development. They give a false perspective to recent and contemporary occurrences. They magnify the importance of these occurrences until the latter appear to constitute new principles in themselves, instead of merely illustrating long established traditions and principles. They break the continuity of history. They mislead the public and statesmen and distort all mature considerations of policy.

It is, of course, not difficult to see how publicists, writing from their memories of day before yesterday, arrived at the conclusion, during the latter years of the nineteenth century, that *Machtpolitik* in the national interest was a new phase of American development. Soon after the adoption of the Constitution, the Government of the United States fell into the hands of an agrarian party which selected every president, except two, between the retirement of John Adams and the inauguration of Lincoln, and devoted itself zealously to the acquisition of more land for farmers and planters, until the Pacific Ocean was reached at last. In this process, the balance of powers—agrarian and commercial—existing at the time the

Constitution went into effect was upset in politics and economics, especially the former. Yet, all during those years, commerce and industry were steadily growing, and after the final blow to planting leadership in 1865 their place in the balance of power was more than restored, making the old philosophy of national interest expounded by the Fathers again valid in fact, though long obscured by the verbiage of partisan debate. What the makers of the new phrases—world power, sea power, coming of age, new era, and dollar diplomacy—really did was to capture the popular ear without re-discovering the profound and systematic thought of the Fathers who had established the Republic.

CONTINUOUS INTEREST IN FOREIGN TRADE

If the phrase-makers of the new era had made even a superficial examination of American economic development, they would have discovered that their thought had been anticipated and that foreign relations and foreign trade, with all their implications of world power, engaged the energies of statecraft at the very beginning of the Republic.[1] In truth, speaking relatively, the United States, despite a crude self-sufficiency, was more dependent on foreign nations and foreign trade in the early years of its history than it is today. Scarcely established in a virgin territory, Americans needed many fundamental products of industry, capital to develop their latent resources, and most of the articles of trade constituting the refinements of civilization. Such needs could only be filled by foreign countries and through the aggressive pursuit of foreign commerce. Appreciation of the economic situation, if not acquaintance with the writings of the Fathers, should, therefore, dispel the notion that national interest in commercial expansion is a new element, marks a new era in the development of the country.

Both parties in the domestic scene were deeply involved in foreign commerce. Farmers and planters who rallied under

---

[1] It took a long time to overcome the handicaps of physical environment which made it easier for the states to trade by water, including overseas routes, than by land routes within the country. E. L. Bogart, *Economic History of the American People,* Chapter VII.

Jefferson's banner turned to Europe for the sale of their produce and the purchase of implements, textiles,. ironware, and other commodities requisite to their standard of living. If, for a short period after their foreign outlets had been closed by the Napoleonic wars and the War of 1812, when they saw their produce rotting in warehouses, they reluctantly adopted a protective tariff with a view to developing home markets, they later reversed themselves. During the long peace which followed the settlement of 1815, when British sails whitened the seas again, their produce found free vent abroad and they went over to the low tariff doctrine. In so doing they acknowledged their dependence on foreign trade, if not for a bare subsistence, at least for a fair standard of life.

On the other side the commercial and manufacturing interests, early marshalled under Hamilton's banner, were also deeply concerned with foreign trade. Facing the sea, skilled in the art of discovering opportunities to exploit their ingenuity, needing capital to develop their industries, and finding the carrying business profitable, they looked abroad in the prosecution of their enterprises. Turning from the stony soil and uninviting lands of their ancestors, the sons of New England had early set sail in ships. Soon they were, to use Burke's imagery, running the harpoon under the torrid heat of the equator and in the frozen regions of the Arctic, scouring the Atlantic and Pacific, visiting the ports of the Mediterranean, trading in the harbors of India and China, skirting the coasts of Africa, searching for opportunities to buy and sell. All through the nineteenth century these extensive and intensive activities were carried on with unremitting zeal, though sometimes obscured by the smoke of domestic politics and the dust of the westward migration across the continent. Even the acquisition of California was made palatable to many Whigs who had opposed the war on Mexico, because it suggested the opening of an overland route to Pacific ports facing the Orient which seemed to offer unlimited riches to traders. While Webster and Calhoun were debating the abstractions of state's rights, American merchants and naval officers were searching in distant places for markets and naval supports for commercial expansion. Southern planters rejoiced to hear that the Chinese might be induced to give up opium for tobacco and take millions of bales of the mollifying leaf grown on their own broad acres.

This energetic expansion of commerce was intensified when, in the course of time, American manufacturing had grown powerful enough to saturate the domestic market and when events and the accumulation of sufficient capital transformed the country from a debtor into a creditor nation. There was no break in the continuity of foreign trade, only changes in tempo and an increased diversity of interests through a shift in the economic base upon which the structure of foreign commerce rested. Where American merchants once carried fish to Spain they now carry radios, telephones, typewriters, and razor blades. Instead of ice they now ship the products of mill and factory to Calcutta. Where they once coveted the privilege of exchanging furs, ginseng, and tobacco in China for tea and silk, they later sought to construct railways and opportunities to make profitable loans of capital. While they no longer skirt the shores of Africa for human cargoes to be transported to the Americas, they establish rubber plantations in Liberia to supply factories in Ohio. While the area of operations widened, especially in Canada, Latin America, and the Far East, the range of commodities exchanged broadened, and financial activities came to be included, emphasis on the fundamental importance of commercial expansion remained unchanged. A new element—the export of the machines, technical processes, and managerial skill, sent abroad in the form of branch factories, patent pools, licensing arrangements, and the like—has been added to increase the volume and alter the character of commercial expansion.[2]

COMMERCIAL POLICY OF DEMOCRATIC ADMINISTRATIONS

To all phases of this development the policies of the United States Government have borne a positive relation; and the conflict of domestic interests, which marked the course of terri-

[2] See the further discussion in Chapter VII, on "The American Stake Abroad."

torial expansion and its covering philosophy, has likewise appeared in policies pertaining to the expansion of commerce. Here, too, there has been a striking continuity in the conception of national interest. Jefferson, as we saw, wanted to make America a nation of farmers, to keep workshop laborers in Europe, to exchange the produce of farms for the commodities turned out by factories, to let this exchange of goods take "a free and normal course," and to avoid what he regarded as the menace of a great navy.[3] Frightened by the agricultural havoc wrought by the Napoleonic wars, Jefferson's party veered for a time in the direction of protection for the purpose of providing home markets for agricultural produce, but later it turned toward the original course.

In conformity with its agrarian pattern of national interest and statecraft, the Jeffersonian party from its triumph in 1800 to the retirement of Buchanan in 1861 rejected the great measures of government policy designed to promote American shipping and overseas commerce. It reduced the navy which the Federalists had built. By a series of measures extending from 1815 to 1828 it swept away the discriminating tonnage duties which gave American ships a decided advantage in the carrying trade, and substituted the principle of "reciprocity," granting foreign carriers equality of privileges. Speaking of this new policy a member of Congress revealed the agrarian motive behind it: "The primary and highest consideration, which led to its adoption, was the desire to promote the interests of agriculture. To seek, if possible, in an unrestricted intercourse with foreign nations new and better markets for our produce. In this great national policy, navigation was but a secondary consideration, and was put to hazard for the public good."[4] On the eve of the Civil War, with cotton planters dominant in its councils, the Jeffersonian party reduced the tariff to a level designed mainly for revenue, and for many years it adhered to that principle, in theory, if not always in practice. In the

[3] "I am not," Jefferson wrote Elbridge Gerry during his first campaign for election, "for a standing army in time of peace, which may overawe public sentiment; nor for a navy which, by its own expenses and the eternal wars in which it will implicate us, will grind us with public burdens and sink us under them." Curtis, *The True Thomas Jefferson*, p. 290.

[4] W. H. Bates, *American Navigation*, pp. 287, 172–289.

administration of Buchanan, the mail subsidies intended to develop steam navigation, inaugurated under the Whigs, were abolished and that branch of enterprise was thrown into the arena of foreign competition.[5] In the same spirit Democratic administrations refused to support the proposals of American naval officers to secure bases of operation in the Oriental trade.[6]

In the later period of American history the Jeffersonian party maintained a fair degree of consistency, save under exceptional circumstances. President Cleveland rejected the annexation of Hawaii as a stepping stone to commercial dominion in the Far East and opposed the war on Spain with which commercial motives were closely entwined. His party took a stand against the conquest and annexation of the Philippines (above, p. 59) which furnished a base for bringing naval pressure in the Orient on behalf of American commercial interests.

Coming to power under its auspices, President Wilson broke the consortium through which American bankers were to participate in the "reconstruction" of China and open opportunities for the sale of American goods. He likewise failed to support the intensive commercial activities of his minister to Peking, Paul S. Reinsch, at least to the satisfaction of the latter. He came to an understanding with Japan, recognizing the special interests of that country in China; and he prepared the way for withdrawal from the Philippines.

During his administration the tariff was again substantially revised downward; and the party committed itself to a program of commodity exchange highly favorable to agriculture. If President Wilson bought the Virgin Islands and bore down heavily in the Caribbean, his action ran contrary to his declarations of policy in his famous Mobile speech and could be attributed to reasons of defensive strategy rather than commercial promotion. If, during his administration, government aid was given to shipping, this shift in policy could be largely attributed to the circumstances of the European war which curtailed the number of available bottoms for carrying American agricultural produce across the Atlantic. If he also declared

[5] *Ibid.*, pp. 344–350.
[6] Above, p. 62.

in favor of a superior navy, his declaration came late in his régime and was the outcome of his unusual experiences in dealing with the maritime powers in the course of the war. Only later when eastern influences became especially powerful in its management, and only after economic conditions raised serious paradoxes, did the Democratic party approve the idea of protection for a brief period. Then again in 1932, under southern and western auspices, it endorsed "a competitive tariff for revenue," omitting the significant word "only" and implying a continuance of the increasing uncertainty which had been impairing the validity of the original doctrines. In interpreting the party platform in one of his campaign speeches, Franklin D. Roosevelt declared that "Tariffs should be high enough to maintain the living standards which we set for ourselves." Relations with other nations should be arranged by means of "reciprocal tariff agreements" and the United States should participate in "an international economic conference designed to restore international trade and facilitate exchange." [7]

THE FEDERALIST-WHIG PROGRAM

On the other side, the Federalist-Whig-Republican succession displayed a fairly consistent record in employing the engines of government for the promotion of shipping and overseas commerce as contemplated by the leaders in the making of the Constitution. During the Federalist supremacy under President Washington, laws were enacted giving aid to American shipping in the form of discriminatory tonnage duties, establishing the principle of protection for American manufactures, and conferring special advantages on American enterprise engaged in trade with the Far East—then the most promising area of expansion. It was under the Whig President, Tyler, that the act of March 3, 1845, was passed authorizing "the making of contracts for the building and running of Mail and Naval steamers upon proposals satisfactory to the Navy

[7] *New York Times*, July 31, 1932, item "Governor Roosevelt's Radio Speech Interpreting Party Platform." For practice, as distinguished from words, see below, Chapter X.

Department," with the aid of mail subsidies under the direction of the Postmaster-General.[8] It was during Whig administrations, with Daniel Webster in the State Department, that steps were taken to open China to American trade, to break down the barred gates of Japan, and to establish American naval power in the Far Pacific. It was a Whig leader, W. H. Seward, who first formulated a systematic policy for extending American commerce and empire in the Orient, at the expense of a war with Russia, if need be. Had the Civil War and reconstruction, followed by the settlement of the great West, not intervened, the dénouement brought to pass by Dewey at Manila Bay might well have come many years earlier.

The substantial character of this generality may be illustrated by a few concrete passages from history. Sometime during the first half of the nineteenth century, United States navy officers, as a result of their cruises and reflection, reached the conclusion that the Orient offered almost unlimited opportunities for commercial expansion and that this expansion could only be secured by seizing one or more naval bases, to serve as points of support in defending American trade against local disturbances and preventing a monopoly by any European power. Just when the idea first took form it is difficult to say, but by the middle of the century it had become a positive creed in informed naval circles. In 1851, Commander James Glynn, of the *Preble*, who had seen long and practical service in Eastern waters, made a report to the President on Japan, where he had discovered at first hand the mistreatment of American shipwrecked sailors. In urging the importance of a commercial treaty with Japan, Commander Glynn dwelt upon the necessity of having a port in that country, especially for the proposed line of steamers, and insisted that the port should be secured, "if not peaceably, then by force." Although laying stress upon the utility of conciliatory methods, he added: "It may be desirable on some future occasion to justify ourselves before the world in the measures used toward Japan besides mere argument or entreaty." [9]

The policy at which Commander Glynn hinted in pointed

[8] W. H. Bates, *op. cit.*
[9] Dennett, *op. cit.*, p. 257.

terms was given elaborate form by Commodore Matthew C. Perry, commander of the expedition that opened Japan. In his writings and reports is revealed a restatement of the doctrine of *Machtpolitik* expounded by the authors of the *Federalist* (above, p. 33), and a concrete application of it to the Pacific. His leadership was unquestionable. Not without some show of propriety did he claim to have brought about the immediate effort to open Japan, by avowing his belief in the feasibility of the project "to several of his brother officers, as well as to some of the dignitaries of the government and prominent citizens long before the subject was publicly discussed, and the expedition resolved upon." [10]

Commodore Perry's program included several points, particular and general, touching the establishment of American power in the Pacific. In his letter to the Secretary of the Navy, December 14, 1852, he referred to the necessity of securing ports of refuge and supply in Japan, if possible without the use of force, and in the Lew Chew Islands at all events. "It strikes me," he said, "that the occupation of the principal ports of these islands for the accommodation of our ships of war, and for the safe resort of merchant vessels of whatever nation, would be a measure not only justified by the strictest rules of moral law, but is also to be considered by the laws of stern necessity."

Beyond the opening of Japan to American commerce lay a possible contest with Great Britain for supremacy in the Far East. "Success may be commanded by our government, and it should be, under whatever circumstances, accomplished. The honor of the nation calls for it, and the interest of commerce demands it. When we look at the possessions in the East of our great maritime rival, England, and the constant and rapid increase of their fortified ports, we should be admonished of the necessity of prompt measures on our part." After calling attention to the fact that Great Britain was so intrenched that she could control at will the trade of the China seas, Commodore Perry concluded: "Fortunately the Japanese and many other islands of the Pacific are still untouched by this 'annexing'

[10] F. L. Hawks, *Narrative of the Expedition of the American Squadron to the China Seas and Japan*, p. 97.

government; and, as some of them lay in the route of a commerce which is destined to be of great importance to the United States, no time should be lost in adopting active measures to secure a sufficient number of ports of refuge."[11] Here Perry was anticipating history.

Reinforcing this position, Perry later declared: "It is idle to suppose that because the policy of the United States has hitherto been to avoid by all means possible any coalition, or even connection with the political acts of other nations, we can always escape from the responsibilities which our growing wealth and power must inevitably fasten upon us. The duty of protecting our vast and growing commerce will make it not only a measure of wisdom but of positive necessity, to provide timely preparation for events which must, in the ordinary course of things, transpire in the East. In the development of the future, the destinies of our nation must assume conspicuous attitudes; we cannot expect to be free from the ambitious longings of increased power, which are the natural concomitants of national success." Giving point to this assertion of fact and theory, Perry expressed the opinion that trading settlements in the Pacific and in Asia would be "vitally necessary to the continued success of our commerce in those regions." Hence he urged "the expediency of establishing a foothold in this quarter of the globe, as a measure of positive necessity to the sustainment of our maritime rights in the east."[12] As a demonstration of his policy, Perry seized a naval base in the Bonin Islands, proposed a protectorate over Formosa, and would have occupied the island of Great Lew Chew if the President of the United States had approved it (above, p. 61).[13]

While Perry justified the proposal to seize Great Lew Chew on the ground of "stern necessity," if Japan did not yield to his demands, and insisted that "the argument may be further strengthened by the certain consequences of the amelioration of the condition of the natives although the vices of civilization may be entailed upon them," he confessed that he was

[11] *Ibid.*, p. 107.
[12] Dennett, *op. cit.*, p. 272.
[13] *Ibid.*, pp. 274 and 275.

acting upon motives of interest. "Of the selfishness of our motives we readily admit that we sought commercial intercourse with Japan because we supposed it would be advantageous. Such, we believe, is the motive of all intelligent nations in establishing friendly relations with others. We can only smile at the simplicity of those who expect to deceive the world by profession of pure, disinterested friendship from one nation toward another, irrespective of all considerations of national benefit. We think that every nation which has sought intercourse with Japan has supposed that such intercourse would prove advantageous to the seeker; nor are we aware that there is anything very criminal or selfish in the desire that advantage may result from the communication. But it is quite possible to believe that benefit to *both* nations may result from the intercourse we would establish, and such benefit may be honestly desired, even while we seek our own interest. This is not selfishness." [14]

HISTORIC POLICY UNDER REPUBLICAN AUSPICES—COMMERCIAL EMPIRE

For a brief period, during the Civil War, the Republican administration at Washington, successor in interest to the Whig party, was primarily occupied with the conflict in which the dominance of the planters in American politics was finally broken; but it was not unmindful of the old program of commercial expansion in the Orient. Anson Burlingame, a good Republican, was appointed by President Lincoln as minister to Peking, the first American diplomatic representative to reside in that ancient city. Robert H. Pruyn, a leader in Whig politics in New York and a protégé of Seward, the Secretary of State, was sent to Japan to succeed Townsend Harris. When Pruyn set out Seward warned him that Japan, having been "gently coerced" into opening her doors to American trade, might take advantage of the state of American affairs to "underrate our power," and "disregard our rights." Seward then added that he expected the day to come when "our domestic differences being ended, we are able once more to demonstrate

---

[14] Hawks, *op. cit.*, p. 93.

our power in the East and establish our commerce there on a secure foundation." [15]

Yet the Civil War and the turmoil of reconstruction did not prevent an occasional display of official force in the promotion of American interests in the Orient. In 1863 an American war vessel bombarded the seat of a recalcitrant Japanese prince at Shimoneseki and the following year another ship joined with certain foreign craft in a bombardment in the same theater of trouble. In 1866 an arrangement was proposed for a joint action of the United States and Japan in coercing Korea into opening her doors. Two years later Seward initiated the movement to break down Korean exclusion which, as Tyler Dennett explains, "was the most important political action undertaken by the United States in Asia until the occupation of the Philippines in 1898." [16]

In 1871, after prolonged negotiations in Peking, Admiral John Rogers was dispatched to Korea in the hope that he might repeat the operation of Commodore Perry in Japan nearly twenty years before; but the Koreans were stubborn. They fired upon a landing party, wounding two Americans, and Admiral Rogers retaliated by a bombardment in which five forts were destroyed and three hundred and fifty Koreans were killed [17]—without obtaining his objective in the end. Two years later Admiral Meade, on his own motion, acquired a naval base in the Samoan Islands—a stroke of no particular significance, except as an illustration of the continuity of historic policy among naval officers and as an indication of measures to come.

Then followed a lull in official activities on behalf of commercial expansion, which is to be explained largely in terms of domestic economics and politics. Under the protective tariff policy re-instituted after the Republican victory in 1860, American capital was intensely pre-occupied with the construction of railways and the development of industry on a national scale. The pressure for foreign commerce subsided. Problems of reconstruction engaged the energies of statesmen and politi-

---

[15] Tyler Dennett, *Americans in Eastern Asia,* pp. 391, 414.

[16] Dennett, *op. cit.,* p. 450.

[17] *Ibid.,* p. 453.

cians. Moreover the agrarian wing of the Republican party, which had been attached during the war on the planters, partly on account of the promise of free land made good in the Homestead Act of 1862, was true to the Jeffersonian tradition and displayed no active interest in such projects as the renewal of ship subsidies, the rebuilding of the navy, and similar measures conceived in the commercial interest. In addition, the Democrats, laid low during the Civil War, soon displayed amazing vitality. They got possession of the House of Representatives in 1873 and held one or both houses of Congress during most of the time until the great Republican victory of 1896. In these circumstances, with capitalists busy developing domestic resources and industries, and with agrarians waging war on the Republican leadership, the navy was neglected, subsidies for shipping were defeated, and the systematic program of commercial support, foreshadowed by Hamilton and envisaged and actively attempted by Seward, was momentarily shattered.

Beneath the surface of affairs, however, the way was being prepared for the great renewal of commercial policy. With amazing rapidity business enterprise spread across the continent, saturated [18] the domestic market, accumulated capital, and began to look abroad for outlets for goods and investments. In the administration of Garfield and Arthur the beginnings of a new navy were laid and the work was steadily continued, even under Democratic as well as Republican auspices. In 1890 Captain Alfred Thayer Mahan published the first of his epoch-marking works on the sea power, restoring the pattern of *Machtpolitik* outlined in the *Federalist* (above p. 33) and furnishing both instruction and inspiration for a commercial program and its inevitable concomitant, an enlarged navy. Six years later the Republicans, under the direction of William McKinley, girded themselves for the struggle with the agrarians led by William Jennings Bryan and in the ensuing election won a crushing victory.[19] Mean-

[18] In the "extensive" sense, and "at a price," two qualifications which must always be borne in mind when speaking of capitalist economics.

[19] For an interesting account of the popularity of the "new era" of commercial expansion and the "march of empire," see the early activities of Albert J. Beveridge in Claude Bowers, *Beveridge and the Progressive Era.*

while the revolt against Spain was dragging its weary and cruel way through the neighboring island of Cuba, ruining American commerce in that province of the Spanish empire, horrifying the American people of every class and opinion, and affording a golden opportunity for a war that could be won easily and which would at the same time afford an opportunity to popularize the navy and make commercial advances in the Caribbean and the Far East. And adding attractive embroidery to the bare structure of commercial policy erected by Hamilton and re-dedicated by Seward, Rudyard Kipling wrote a pæan in honor of "the White Man's Burden." The stage was set for a re-crystallization of the Federalist-Whig conception of national interest on a large scale and with more powerful support in the country.

Under President McKinley the first war of commercial empire was waged, not as such in any official thesis, but in upshot, outcome, and realization. Despite the pledge of inde-pendence contained in the declaration of war on Spain, Cuba was made a protectorate and a naval base was acquired within her domain. Porto Rico was seized and transformed into a dependency. The Philippines were annexed outright, with full recognition on the part of the President that they would afford the long-sought base for the expansion of commercial activities in the Far East (above, p. 83). In the State Department John Hay was installed as the director of diplomacy. Though by profession a man of letters and a publicist, Hay was affili-ated with business enterprise through his wife's fortune and had already demonstrated in an anonymous novel, *The Bread-winners*, just where his philosophy of statecraft and his sympa-thies lay. With the Philippines secure, he faced France, Great Britain, Germany, Japan, and Russia actively engaged in carving the Chinese Empire into spheres of influence and monopolies, and he perilously proclaimed the American atti-tude in the policy of "the open door," meaning an equal oppor-tunity for American commerce in that tempestuous area.

No other alternative seemed possible to Hay at the moment. The American public, he said, would not support the United States Government in joining in the scramble of the greedy powers for territory and special privileges; and yet, if American commercial enterprise was to make the expected gains, some kind of a wedge would have to be driven into the Chinese situation. Some sort of a compromise was necessary. Hay found it in the "open door" policy. With the Philippines in the rear, Hay forced open the door—to a house aflame; and, fortunately for him, the jealousies of his opponents enabled him to secure verbal adherence to his proposal, reserving all vested rights already acquired.

In the quest for commercial empire, the United States had thrust itself into the European balance of power in the Far East as well as in Latin America, for the great states operating in Asia, save Japan alone, were European. Well aware of the obligations thus created, President Roosevelt took a positive interest in the Russo-Japanese war; and at the proper moment, to prevent the complete triumph of either contestant in the conflict, he intervened to bring them together in a peace conference at Portsmouth. With that out of the way, he approached Great Britain with a view to friendly coöperation in international politics. Then he came to a secret understanding with Japan and Great Britain to preserve the *status quo* in the division of spoils in the Far East, winning from Japan recognition of the American position in the Philippines in part return for according supremacy to her in Korea. Meanwhile he devoted great energies to building up the navy and sent a fleet of battleships "on a good-will tour" around the world, demonstrating, so to speak, that the man with a soft voice carried "a big stick."

Yet, owing to his temperamental qualities, his colorful imagination, and the implications of a certain social sense faintly reminiscent of a benevolent despot, President Roosevelt did not restore and make official the exact pattern of commercial expansion which Hamilton had created, and which Seward had refashioned after the great agrarian upheaval of the Jacksonian era. That was left to his successor, President Taft, who had been a member of the Roosevelt cabinet and who was well-prepared for the task by his experience as governor-general of the Philippines. Moreover he had been the emissary who negotiated the secret understanding with Japan. These experiences and the logical discipline of legal training admirably fitted him to appreciate the realities and requirements of the national interest in commercial expansion.

In keeping with his practical outlook upon the promotion of American interests abroad, President Taft selected as Secretary of State Philander C. Knox, of Pennsylvania, long an associate of large business enterprises. And in the Department, Mr. Knox was ably fortified by F. M. Huntington Wilson, Assistant Secretary of State, who had seen service in many diplomatic posts and who sought to construct out of the tough facts of the daily grind a fairly consistent philosophy of national interest. The language of diplomatic documents and state papers now became more austere. High sounding phrases were studiously avoided. After he had been keenly disappointed in an effort to neutralize the Chinese Eastern Railway and force an American wedge between Russia and Japan in Manchuria—an adventure which drove the two powers into a secret alliance directed in fact against the United States—Secretary Knox sought coöperation in the China sphere and concentrated his efforts principally in the Caribbean as a region beyond dispute and most likely to bear fruit in economic advantage.[20]

NATIONAL INTEREST FORMULATED IN
DOLLAR DIPLOMACY

Throughout his administration, President Taft, duly instructed by the State Department, emphasized the fact that "modern diplomacy is commercial." It was accompanied, to be sure, by "idealistic humanitarian sentiments" and moral obligations, but there was no doubt about the main business in hand. "The diplomacy of the present administration," he said in his message of December 3, 1912, "has sought to respond to modern ideas of commercial intercourse. This policy has been characterized as substituting dollars for bullets. . . . It is an effort frankly directed to the increase of American trade upon the axiomatic principle that the Government of the United States shall extend all proper support to every legiti-

[20] Siebert and Schreiner, *Entente Diplomacy and the World*, pp. 3–40. L. Pasvolsky, *Russia in the Far East*, p. 165.

mate and beneficial American enterprise abroad. How great have been the benefits of this diplomacy, coupled with the maximum and minimum provision of the tariff law, will be seen by some consideration of the wonderful increase in the export trade of the United States."

In the realization of this policy, the State Department was reorganized to handle more effectively the "mass of intricate business vital to American interests in every country of the world." Through the establishment of regional divisions in the Department, "American interests in every quarter of the globe are being cultivated with equal assiduity." Foreign trade advisers were added to "coöperate with the diplomatic and consular bureaus and the politico-geographical divisions in innumerable matters where commercial diplomacy or consular work calls for such special knowledge." The merit system was strengthened in the State Department to guarantee continuity of service and greater technical competence; and "in order to assure to the business and other interests of the United States a continuance of the resulting benefits of this reform," additional legislation was requested from Congress.

Much had been done to advance American interests abroad, the message continued; but a greater consolidation of forces and more ingenuity were necessary: "If this Government is really to preserve to the American people that free opportunity in foreign markets which will soon be indispensable to our prosperity, even greater efforts must be made. Otherwise the American merchant, manufacturer, and exporter will find many a field in which American trade should logically predominate preëmpted through the more energetic efforts of other governments and other commercial nations. There are many ways in which through hearty coöperation the legislative and executive branches of this Government can do much. The absolute essential is the spirit of united effort and singleness of purpose. I will allude only to a very few specific examples of action which ought then to result. America cannot take its proper place in the most important fields for its commercial activity and enterprise unless we have a merchant marine. American commerce and enterprise cannot be effectively fostered in those fields unless we have good American banks in the countries referred to. We need American newspapers in those countries and proper means for public information about them. We need to assure the permanency of a trained foreign service. We need legislation enabling the members of the foreign service to be systematically brought into direct contact with the industrial, manufacturing, and exporting interests of this country in order that American business men may enter the foreign field with a clear perception of the exact conditions to be dealt with and the officers themselves may prosecute their work with a clear idea of what American industrial and manufacturing interests may require." [21]

In other words, President Taft believed he saw the dawn of a "new age" in American diplomacy; although what he beheld seemed very much like the fires of Federalist *Machtpolitik* kept glowing through the years, especially by the navy, and fanned into flame by the economic intensities of the twentieth century. "We have emerged full grown as a peer in the great concourse of nations. We have passed through various formative periods. We have been self-centered in the struggle to develop our domestic resources and deal with our domestic questions. The Nation is now too mature to continue in its foreign relations those temporary expedients natural to a people whose domestic affairs are the sole concern. In the past our diplomacy has often consisted, in normal times, in a mere assertion of the right to international existence. We are now in a larger relation with broader rights of our own and obligations to others than ourselves. . . . The successful conduct of our foreign relations demands a broad and modern view. We cannot meet new questions nor build for the future if we confine ourselves to outworn dogmas of the past and to the perspective appropriate to our emergence from colonial times and conditions. . . . We must not wait for events to overtake us unawares." To this conclusion the President had come, and now "Congress should fully realize the conditions which obtain in the world as we find ourselves at the threshold of our middle age as a Nation." By 1912, the Executive Department of the Federal Government had taken on the doctrines

[21] Taft, Message, December 3, 1912, *Messages and Papers of the Presidents,* Vol. XVI, pp. 7789–7790.

of *Realpolitik* which Germany had already begun to pursue in an effort to secure "free opportunity in foreign markets," to push "legitimate economic interest," and to find "a place in the sun"; but American policy was accompanied by a special emphasis on moral obligations and "idealistic humanitarian sentiments."

Here, then, is the "new" *Realpolitik*. A free opportunity for expansion in foreign markets is indispensable to the prosperity of American business. Modern diplomacy is commercial. Its chief concern is with the promotion of economic interests abroad. Possession or control of the sources of raw materials and freedom to trade in the existing old markets and to exploit the new are essential to the progress of the country. These things must be actively fostered by the Government and the preëmption of them by competitors under the protection of rival governments must be prevented. The Government of the United States can do much in this direction and must have the united support of the country in such foreign relations. These objectives and the process by which they are to be obtained require a large navy, a merchant marine, American banking houses in foreign countries, American newspapers abroad to convey information and counter the propaganda of rival sheets, a larger and more efficient consular and commercial service, and systematic efforts to establish direct and intimate connections between the government officials engaged in commercial promotion on the one side, and industrial, manufacturing, and exporting interests in the United States on the other. Such were the instrumentalities and implications of dollar diplomacy by which the national interest was to be actively fostered and achieved.

At length a philosophy was attempted. As described by F. M. Huntington Wilson, Under Secretary of State, after his retirement from the Department, dollar diplomacy, like the diplomacy of Europe, was a more or less discreet combination of politics and economics.[22] It was not a policy to be attained by haphazard methods. Nor was it supposed to rest upon

[22] "The Relation of Government to Foreign Investment." *Annals of the American Academy of Political and Social Science*. Vol. LXVIII, November, 1916.

vagaries. Dollar diplomacy, according to Mr. Wilson, is common-sense diplomacy. It is "determined by the application of scientific principles and sound thinking to plain facts studied and understood as they really are; a diplomacy preferring to build for the long future, rather than to dogmatize for the moment's expediency; preferring the truth to a beautiful idealization not resting upon the truth." [23]

The aim of dollar diplomacy was political and economic advantage for the nation. Its purpose was not charity abroad. "Service to humanity" wrote Mr. Wilson, "is not mentioned separately because charity begins at home; because it is America's first duty to serve America; because America, as a government, can amply serve humanity in spheres and in ways in which America also serves itself; and because if it does that, the service of humanity may be considered by diplomacy, which is not, by the way, an eleemosynary institution, as merged in service to America, that is America's political advantage. Those who dissent from this view and yield to our national foible for grandiloquent sentimentality ought to reflect that a trustee, however admirable his private charities, would be put in jail if he used trust funds for benefactions, . . . an American executive defrauds the nation if he uses its prestige and power in a diplomacy directed by sentimentality to the service of humanity in general, instead of a diplomacy seeking the political and economic advantage of the American taxpayer, the American nation."

The political advantages of foreign operations in dollar diplomacy, which are vitally associated with national defense and security, consist, according to Mr. Wilson, of the following:

> (a) strengthening American influence in spheres where it ought to predominate over any other foreign influence on account of reasons of fundamental policy, like the Monroe Doctrine, or of military strategy or of neighborhood. Such a sphere is "Latin America." . . . In this category falls also, for example, the discharge of our historic obligation to Liberia (for benefits to commerce and emigration of Negroes). . . .
> (b) the maintenance of a traditional position favorable to our trade where trade may go by political favor, as in the Chinese Empire,

[23] *Ibid.*

(c) the strengthening of our friendship with other great powers, (such as the English-speaking peoples),

(d) with countries where it is wise to preëmpt a share in a dawning development, like Turkey,

(e) with countries whose markets are especially valuable.[24]

Among the economic advantages there are:

(a) those investments or enterprises which most promote vital political interest. . . .

(b) foreign investments or enterprises which establish permanent and valuable markets for trade while at the same time subserving political strength where the policy of this country demands that it be strong if we are to have security and tranquillity. . . .

(c) investments or enterprises which have these same purely material advantages while carrying with them some political advantages as well, as, for example, in safeguarding our Chinese trade;

(d) those investments or enterprises which serve in giving us a commercial standing in some valuable market where development may be preëmpted by others if a footing be not early obtained (like Turkey);

(e) in cementing friendship with our natural allies, as Canada and the English-speaking peoples generally;

(f) in bringing profit and employment to the American people in general.[25]

Dollar diplomacy was thus economic and political in its objectives and associations. The two were welded into a single unity by which the nation expressed itself. "The value of our foreign investments rests, in the last resort, upon our diplomacy, the conduct of our foreign policy. The efficacy of these depends upon our prestige and our military power, and these last are the possession of the nation." [26] As expounded in official statements and as exemplified in practice, dollar diplomacy was highly particularistic in substance and methods; but it was not to be a policy responding automatically to the pressures of private interests without due regard to circumstances or geographical considerations. It was not intended to throw the whole support of the nation behind every form of American business enterprise abroad. There was an attempt to

[24] *Ibid.*
[25] *Ibid.*
[26] *Ibid.*

transcend particularity and to rise to a broader conception of the substance, meaning, and advancement of national interest. On occasion the Government might blow hot or blow cold, adopt an aggressive initiative or remain passive as the circumstances might warrant.

Where we have no strong influence or where we have very little economic interest, an equitable adjustment, doing justice in a general way to our citizens, would be a proper policy. Such a course was followed when American advisers were forced out of Persia by Russia and England. But "If, on the other hand, those advisers had been in a country where American influence was of national importance, the American government must have resisted their dismissal and insisted upon specific performance, although the contracts were no more binding in one case than in the other." [27]

In the relation of the Government to foreign investments, dollar diplomacy recognized a general obligation on the part of the Government to protect the citizen's rights; but also the authority to control the citizen's course by giving great or little protection, or none at all. "The Department of State will give all proper support to legitimate and beneficial enterprises in foreign countries." But the measure of that support is "limited by its variant authority or power, expressed in terms of action, diplomatic, or in the last resort warlike." A balance must be struck between the Government's "duty to the citizen plus or minus the sum of the political and economic national advantage." [28] Explaining this somewhat cryptic utterance, Huntington Wilson said: "A legitimate enterprise must be honest and fair, and just to the foreigners concerned. But it may be legitimate so far as the interested American is concerned and beneficial to him individually, while not beneficial to the nation. Such would be the case if the dangers of seriously involving this country in fresh obligations outweighed any national advantage; if the investment diverted from channels of real national advantage money that might otherwise serve that advantage either abroad or at home; or if the project offended a valued friend among the nations. To merit the

[27] *Ibid.*
[28] *Ibid.*

strongest governmental support the foreign investment or enterprise must be really beneficial to the nation." [29]

Again, on occasion, the Government might legitimately take the initiative and pursue some interests aggressively. Furthermore, it might make use of its own citizens and their interests to advance the national interest. In the Caribbean and Central America, and with respect to the loan policy in China, for example, the foreign investments involved are "of such great and unquestionable national advantage that the Government was an active participant in them; and, by urging on the investors to lend themselves as instrumentalities of foreign policy, the government clothed those investors with rights to protection of especial dignity." [30] In balancing the American national interest against the interests of other nations, the United States should keep out of the spheres of interest held by other countries, such as in Korea and Manchuria, Persia and Siam; but in turn, should "crowd out from our own sphere of interest foreign interests whenever they are predominant to an uncomfortable extent. . . ." [31]

Dollar diplomacy thus resembled in many respects the philosophy of policy expounded by leaders in the establishment of the American Republic (Chapter II), although it was lacking in their precision of thought and realism; nor in practice did it differ much from the tactics employed by European powers in the Near East, Africa, and the Orient during the half century preceding the World War.[32] Like Hamilton, its sponsors rejected sentimentality and generosity in diplomacy and permitted the exercise of beneficence only where the exercise coincided with American interest. But unlike Hamilton they did not make the rule universal, for they spoke of the "traditional friendship of the English-speaking peoples"—a sentiment which could be indulged in safely only where there was no evident conflict of interests and inexorable competition in commerce. Like Hamilton they were prepared to use all engines of the Government and naval power to protect Ameri-

[29] *Ibid.*
[30] *Ibid.*
[31] *Ibid.*
[32] Herbert Feis, *Europe the World's Banker;* G. Lowes Dickinson, *The International Anarchy, 1904–1914.*

can interests; but unlike him they took within the scope of their naval diplomacy distant places, like Liberia, China, and Turkey, where no adequate or effective naval control could be applied. In other words, dollar diplomacy, like Federalist philosophy, was directed to practical ends.

RELATION OF POLICY TO ECONOMIC REALITIES

From this review of American commercial expansion it is clear that politics and economics, facts and formulas, evolved together in developing the doctrine of national interest expressed in dollar diplomacy—the diplomacy of economic promotion restrained here and there by political considerations. Public policies, as Secretary Hughes pointedly remarked, are not abstractions. They are not manufactured in the Department of State by phantoms. They are the products of concrete experiences with concrete economic phenomena, such as the production and exchange of American commodities, the acquisition of material sources and markets abroad, the performance of services, the barriers (governmental and private) to trade, the action of external forces upon opportunities for enterprise, the pursuit, gain or loss of profits, and the infinite variety of domestic and foreign influences upon the occupations, the interests, and the welfare of the American people.

Nor are public authorities who make, continue, and develop policies, abstractions either—"library lawyers"—closeted within the four walls of official buildings, engaged in consulting manuals on the principles of international law and diplomacy and remaining monastically aloof from the realities of the outer world. They, too, have roots in the reality of experience. They spring from different sections of the country, from circles concerned with economic operations of infinite variety and degree; they have their spheres of associates, wide or narrow, as the case may be, but generally restricted by congeniality of social and economic outlook. Again, experiences in economic operations are continuous; they may be slowly or swiftly transformed, but they are seldom arbitrarily broken; the main currents sweep on irresistibly, whatever may be the outward signs of the political pageant. The personalities that formulate policies are not momentary appearances; they have a span of years; they are linked through parentage with the distant past and through children with the coming years. Brought up within a definite environment they acquire, develop, and transmit a heritage of policy, thought, and action.

These generalities may be given sharp point by practical illustrations. Take, for example, the policy of encouragement and assistance applied by the Federal Government in 1791 to the American trade in the Far East. Under this policy were included, among other measures, discriminations in the tonnage taxes, low duties on East Indian imports, exclusive rights in the importation of tea, and special favors in warehousing. This program was not adopted because some theorist in the State Department hit upon it in a moment of idle speculation. It was the outcome of specific demands by particular persons placed high in the scale of political influence. It had roots in widespread popular sentiments. At the close of the American revolution many privateering ships and other vessels were idle; commercial centers were suffering from depression; and the shipbuilders, owners, merchants, and sailors of New England in particular were eagerly searching, of necessity, for outlets into which to pour their capital, labor, and enterprise, with a view to lucrative returns. In fact, the ports of Massachusetts, Rhode Island, Connecticut, New York, Pennsylvania, Maryland, and to some extent Virginia, were without business sufficient to absorb their actual and potential energies. It was not unnatural that their search for relief should disclose immense opportunities in the Oriental, or as it was popularly called, "the East India trade."

It was no accident that the leaders in the commercial centers during the early days of the American republic were men of large influence in political affairs. It was inevitable that they should seek the most effective ways of developing the potential trade and the kind of governmental policies and discriminations necessary to promote their commercial activities. To come down to concrete cases, John Ledyard, of Connecticut, on a world voyage with Captain Cook, discovered the rich possibilities of Oriental trade; to be specific, he found that furs bought at six pence apiece on the Northwest Coast could be sold in China for $100, and, as Mr. Dennett precisely puts it, Ledyard "ordained himself a missionary to American merchants to convert them to the limitless possibilities" of the Far Eastern traffic. The first American ship to make the China venture, the *Empress of China*, was sent out in 1784 by New York and Philadelphia merchants. The leader of the latter group was Robert Morris, a merchant prince, who later served as a member of the convention that drafted the Constitution of the United States, and was a United States Senator from Pennsylvania at the time the Federal Government adopted the policy of encouraging and supporting the China trade.[33] Among the other men prominently interested in East India commerce was Rufus King, born in Massachusetts, also a former member of the constitutional convention, and later a representative of New York in the United States Senate. It was understood at the time the Constitution was drafted, and the *Federalist* made it doubly clear (p. 37), that its adoption meant the regulation of foreign commerce in American interests. The seaport towns were overwhelmingly in favor of ratification. In other words, the men who drafted the Constitution, voted for it, and set up the new government under it, understood the realities of economic operations and the relations of public policies to economic advancement.[34]

Again, toward the middle of the nineteenth century, there arose the question of opening formal relations between the Government of the United States and China. The immediate impulse came early in 1840 when a memorial was presented to Congress from American merchants at Canton, "asking for naval protection and the appointment of a commissioner to negotiate a treaty." This memorial was presented by Abbott Lawrence, a Whig member of the House of Representatives from Massachusetts, a great leader in the textile industry of the country. The message of President Tyler to Congress on December 30, 1842, urging action, was written by Daniel Webster, of Massachusetts, then Secretary of State; and the

[33] For an account of the interests of Robert Morris and other men influential in the Government of the United States when its early policies were formulated, see C. A. Beard, *Economic Interpretation of the Constitution.*

[34] For instance, see S. E. Morison, *Maritime Massachusetts*, Chapter III.

head of the commission sent out to negotiate with the Chinese government was Caleb Cushing, of Massachusetts, the son of a Newburyport shipowner, a man thoroughly acquainted with the economic realities of the Oriental trade. Incidentally Webster's son, Fletcher, was made secretary of the commission. It is scarcely necessary to demonstrate the realities and the implications of such an intimate association of private interests and public policies.

A few years later when the decision was made to open the barred gates of Japan to American commerce by a delicate combination of negotiation and naval display, Daniel Webster of Massachusetts was once more Secretary of State. The original set of instructions for this expedition was drafted by Webster. Owing to his illness, however, the final revision fell into other hands; indeed, into the hands of the naval officer in charge of the mission, Commodore Matthew C. Perry. Commodore Perry, it is appropriate to note, was born in the commercial state of Rhode Island and had seen more than forty years' service in the United States Navy where, as his reports reveal, he acquired by experience an exact knowledge of the naval policy expounded in the *Federalist* and steadily developed and applied on occasion by commanding naval officers (above, p. 97). Although this officer who drafted his own instruction adopted a tone more peremptory than that employed in the original instrument, he left the practical objects of the expedition substantially as Webster had formulated them. Distressed American sailors were to be protected by the Japanese, one or more ports were to be opened for trade, and the right to buy coal was to be clearly established. In fine, a beginning was to be made in breaking down Japanese exclusiveness, by a display of force if necessary; and the public policy which this action represented had been formulated by the Massachusetts Secretary of State in line with the heritage of a policy that had been growing up with the expansion of American trade.

An examination of the documents and papers bearing on the later period of commercial expansion also reveals a close connection between government and private initiative and action, in the development of the theory as well as in the practice of

national interest in diplomacy. Although President Taft intimated in his messages that, before his time, the State Department had operated on outworn dogmas and had possessed
neither the desire nor the equipment for aggressive action in
promoting foreign trade for American business and industrial
concerns, the imputation was somewhat exaggerated and betrayed a neglect of the clear-cut philosophy of *Machtpolitik*
enunciated in the *Federalist*. Despite fluctuations in policy,
particularly when agrarian Democrats were in control of the
Government, the State Department had often been solicitous
in supporting American interests abroad, and it had not always
waited on the initiative of others. The consolidation of forces
and the sharpening of policy between 1897 and 1913 merely
marked an integration and an intensification rather than a
radical departure from earlier conceptions.

In this there was nothing strange. The Government is not
now and never has been an independent engine operating in
a vacuum under its own momentum. Those who direct it are
members of a political party and derive ideas and impetus
from that source. For the election of presidents in the later
period, as in earlier times, campaign funds were collected, generally in large individual sums. Those who contributed these
funds sought, in some cases, particular favors; but more commonly they expected pursuit of policies favorable to their
interests. The promotion of export business in manufactured
commodities was a policy as definite as the protection of domestic industry against foreign competition by high tariffs.
The growth of this export business had proceeded contempo-
raneously with changes in the direction of policy. Men in
politics and outside were aware of the tendency and its requirements. The promotion of export business by the Government, whether it proceeded on theories or with reference
to practical exigencies, was in fact a bid for political support
at home. Presidential messages were not academic essays;
they were political documents written with an eye to gaining
strength for the administration in power at the moment and for
the party which it represented. In short, domestic politics and
economics enter into foreign policy and influence its course.

Moreover, private citizens entering the service of the Government do not pass through a personal metamorphosis. A banker, called to serve in the Treasury Department from his post in a private banking house engaged in the flotation of foreign loans, cannot be expected to divest himself of the customs and policies, the conception of interests and the tactics of the banking fraternity in which he has been trained. Nor can he be expected to shake off the personal associations he has made there, or turn a deaf ear to the importunities of friends when the occasion arises. The same is quite true of men called from any particular station in life. They are bound to bring with them the thoughts, practices, and sympathies of the group in which they have moved in a private capacity. It is a natural phenomenon and easy to understand.[35]

There is also the pattern of thought which comes almost naturally to stamp itself upon government policy and action. The Government is not an abstraction. It can only act at the behest, upon the advice, and through the agency, of specific individuals. The more prominent these individuals are, the more weight their requests, their opinions and advice, will bear in the governmental policy and decisions. The more prominent they are the greater is the chance of their selection as consultants, envoys, spokesmen, negotiators. Furthermore, it is a common occurrence for men, even when wholly confining themselves to private affairs, to write, telephone, telegraph to, or effect personal contact with, government officials and agencies on their own initiative whenever a situation arises wherein the Government must act upon matters either directly or indirectly affecting private business.[36] Here also, the more prominent these men are the more value and respect are ac-

[35] For a wealth of informative and illustrative detail on this point see the *Hearings on Sen. Res. 84 and 239*, 72d Cong., 2d Sess., and continuations thereof into the 73d Cong., 1st Sess., particularly those parts dealing with the investigation of private banking institutions and practices.

[36] Instances of this are unlimited. For a specific example in an actual controversy, see the telegram sent by ex-Governor Harry F. Byrd to John W. Fishburne, Congressman from Virginia, and by him read into the record at the Hearings concerning the competition between the Baltimore Mail Line and the America-France Line which involved questions of merchant marine policy and practices. *Hearings before House Committee on Merchant Marine, Radio, and Fisheries*. 72d Cong., 1st Sess. (February 2, 1932), pp. 199–200. Washington, Govt. Printing Office. 1932.

corded their opinions, advice, wishes, and demands. So that a situation is reached ultimately in the major routine business of the Government, and often in matters of great moment to the country as well, wherein the Government comes to lean very heavily upon a rather distinct body of men, drawn from private life and often spoken of as men "of affairs and position." [37]

In these circumstances advice given, demands made, policies formed, and choices of action made, by or under the influence of men "of affairs and position," moving in the same environment and associated by ties of friendship, favor, family, class, and business relationship, are bound to conform to a recognizable frame, which displays, above all minor deflections, a consistent unity, a set of defined characteristics and an unmistakable bias, which is naturally representative and favorable to the group from which these men, giving the advice, voicing the demands, and making the decisions, have come. Add to it the fact that the whole operates within a profit economy characterized by intense competition for advantage, for raw materials and for markets, and for legislation, administration, and domestic and foreign actions of public bodies favorable to such an economy; that men are scarcely actuated in their practical, private affairs by any other philosophy of public welfare or private advancement than that implied by such an economy; and there is but little question that a distinct pattern of social, political, and economic thought and action is bound to emerge.

Nor is the immense official bureaucracy in the Departments of State and Commerce and other federal establishments, engaged in giving government support to "every legitimate and beneficial American enterprise abroad," entirely free of the imputation of interest. Once created, it becomes a special interest itself, naturally attentive to the enlargement of powers

---

[37] A phrase used by Mr. J. P. Morgan in describing the list of private subscribers of his banking institution. New York *Times,* June 10, 1933, item, "J. P. Morgan's Statement on Senate Banking Inquiry." The hearings of the Senate Committee brought out many notable instances where men on these lists of private subscribers of private banking houses were also prominent either officially or through their private activities in affairs of the Government. See *Hearings, Sen. Res. 84* and *239,* etc., *op. cit.*

and an increase of emoluments. Its prime concern then is to convince business men that it does serve their interests; and the country, that it promotes a general interest. If political support is withdrawn by the President and Congress, the bureaucracy suffers. To maintain itself, it must be active, must take the initiative, must encourage industrialists to seek foreign markets, must lend official support to every kind of "legitimate," that is, not illegal, business abroad. Thus political institutions and practices become inextricably involved in private institutions and practices until it is impossible to tell where one begins and another ends, or whether economic forces outside the Government are driving it or political forces within the Government are stirring up and enlisting business support for foreign policies. The fact that these things are done on the theory that national interest is the sum of all special interests does not transform the theory into a mathematical axiom, obscure the political aspects of the transactions, or authorize the assumption that patriotism requires "a united front" in support of them. The matter is not as simple as the official formulas of presidential messages seem to imply.

It is true that efforts have been made to represent commercial expansion as a national interest and to demonstrate that a united front must be presented in support of any decisions that may be made in the field of foreign relations. In his message of December 3, 1912, President Taft declared: "The fundamental foreign policies of the United States should be raised high above the conflict of partisanship and wholly disassociated from differences as to domestic policy. In its foreign affairs the United States should present to the world a united front. The intellectual, financial, and industrial interests and the publicist, the wage earner, the farmer, and citizen of whatever occupation must coöperate in a spirit of high patriotism to promote that national solidarity which is indispensable to national efficiency and to the attainment of national ideals."

While this may be accepted "in principle," as diplomats say, practice in concrete cases (and it forms the substance of policy) assures no such ideal solidarity. Nor could it be said that the policy of creating new agencies and concentrating great energies on the promotion of export trade was "a fundamental foreign policy" on which the country had solemnly resolved with a practical unanimity approaching solidarity. The fact is that President Taft, as head of a Republican administration, gave all the appearance of laboring hard by his messages to educate Congress and the electorate into believing that it should be united and that realistic exigencies demanded unity. He was trying to make it fundamental against some opposition and much indifference.

Later, a unity sought by President Wilson was repudiated by ex-President Roosevelt in announcing to the world after the congressional elections of 1918 that President Wilson had no right to speak for the country on fundamental matters of foreign policy; and by Senator Lodge in preparing a note against President Wilson's policy for Henry White, an official delegate at the Paris peace conference, to be shown "in strict confidence" to Balfour, Clemenceau, and Nitti, representatives of foreign governments at the same assembly.[38] In fact, President Taft's call for national solidarity in the enforcement of national interest and a similar appeal by President Coolidge in later years were demands for support for their particular interpretations of that interest, and had no higher or greater claim upon the nation than President Wilson's insistence on his League of Nations program. A claim to higher validity is an assertion, not an axiom.

[38] Fleming, *The United States and the League of Nations*, p. 64.

CHAPTER V

NATIONAL INTEREST IN COMMERCIAL
EXPANSION—SECOND PHASE

JUST at the moment when the conception of national interest represented by dollar diplomacy seemed triumphant beyond question, a domestic explosion, within the ranks of the Republican party, brought about a interregnum in national affairs extending from 1913 to 1921—eight long and crowded years. Then, after this hiatus, which was largely due to historical "accidents," including the defection of Theodore Roosevelt and the World War, came a restoration, a "return to normalcy," the pursuit of national interest by traditional methods.

THE PROGRAM OF PRESIDENT WILSON AND ITS FATE

In the main, the policies of President Wilson, both domestic and foreign, ran counter to corporate development and to commercial expansion under the impulse of dollar diplomacy, with their accompanying interpretations of national interest. During his administrations the tariff was lowered materially, for the first time since the Civil War, heavy duties were imposed on corporate and individual incomes, war was declared on industrial combinations under the Clayton Anti-trust Law, and agriculture especially favored by the Farm Loan Act. Not without justification was the complaint made that President Wilson turned a cold shoulder to the great economic interests which, he declared, had dominated the country during the administrations of his immediate predecessors [1]—the great interests which had, on the whole, supported and benefited by dollar diplomacy.[2]

---

[1] *The New Freedom; Intimate Papers of Colonel House,* Vol. I, pp. 132–133.
[2] Yet it must not be overlooked that it was under William C. Redfield, Wilson's Secretary of Commerce, that the preparation of the Commerce De-

In foreign affairs, President Wilson's program and activities, excepting naval expansion and war on Germany, which incidentally brought enormous profits to American industries and prepared the way for a swift renewal of commercial expansion, cut across the old course and its official connotations. Independence was formally promised to the Philippines by the Jones Act of 1916; a special position was accorded to Japan in the Orient by the Lansing-Ishii agreement; the first consortium in China was repudiated; opportunities to push trade and investments in that country were neglected; and Japan took advantage of the occasion to disregard the open door doctrine by forcing her twenty-one demands upon Peking. While the policy inaugurated by President McKinley had been continued in the Caribbean, despite much twisting and turning, efforts of Republican leaders to bring about a war on Mexico for the protection of American interests there were defeated by "watchful waiting," by a policy of masterly inactivity in that direction.

The wider international policies of President Wilson likewise ran against the Federalist-Whig-Republican tradition, as their rejection by the Senate under the management of Senator Lodge conclusively demonstrated. These policies included freedom of the seas, except as restricted under an international covenant, the removal, so far as possible, of trade barriers, the establishment of an equality of trade conditions among all nations consenting to the peace and associating themselves for its maintenance, the renunciation of annexations, the substitution of the mandate system for imperialist exploitation, a drastic reduction of armaments on land and sea, the renunciation of war as an instrument of commerce and expansion, and a League of Nations to reorganize the "world community" along new lines and to stabilize the existing political distribution of the earth's backward places and peoples.

In all this there was little fortuitous. That his foreign policies cut across the measures of the Federalist-Whig-Republican tradition and reflected a divergence of views made

partment for advancing foreign trade vigorously was carried forward; and also that it was in 1918, while Wilson was still in office, that the Webb Export Act, aiding corporations in foreign trade, was passed.

manifest in the conflict of domestic politics, President Wilson clearly recognized from the beginning of his first administration. During the campaign for election, he had portrayed the domestic scene as a struggle between "the plain people" and the "great special interests" which had long dictated terms to the Government of the United States; and in his inaugural address he conceived his duty to be "to cleanse, reconsider, and restore." He had waged a political war against "a trusteeship of the powerful interests that controlled the trusts, the railroads, the banks, the industries of the nation." [3] He had not given much attention to foreign affairs, either in his earlier studies or during his campaign, but on coming face to face with their stubborn exigencies at the opening of his administration, he discerned, or thought he discerned, the domestic division in a new guise.

"What Wilson saw vividly, therefore," says his biographer, R. S. Baker, "when unexpected foreign problems confronted him, was that the same forces were arrayed against him in the foreign field as at home. The very same men! He had attacked in his campaign the 'interlocking directorates' of the great bankers and capitalists which controlled the trusts, the railroads, public utilities. He had only to scratch the surface of the situation in Mexico and China to discover the same forces at work. Five days after he had been elected to office, representatives of J. P. Morgan appeared at Washington to inquire if Wilson would continue the policy of the Taft administration and smile upon the great financial venture into China known as the 'Six Power Loan.'" On what basis did President Wilson rest his decision in the case? "He knew painfully little at that time about actual conditions in Mexico or China, or any other foreign nation, but he had the essential knowledge that the real fighter needs. He knew the enemy! And he hit instantly, before the opposition had fairly waked up." [4] Thus his foreign policy had the same popular appeal as the domestic policy of which it was the corollary.

In the contest between moral obligation and material interest, Woodrow Wilson, as a scholar, saw interest usually emerging

[3] R. S. Baker, *Woodrow Wilson: Life and Letters,* Vol. IV, p. 60.
[4] Baker, *op. cit.,* Vol. IV, p. 60.

triumphant, though not always supreme. "We have become confirmed," he said, ". . . in the habit of acting under an odd mixture of selfish and altruistic motives. . . . We have sympathized with freedom everywhere, have pressed handsome principles of equity in international dealings. . . . And yet, when issues of our own interest arose, we have not been unselfish. We have shown ourselves kin to all the world, when it came to pushing an advantage. . . . Our action against Spain in the Floridas, and against Mexico on the coasts of the Pacific, and then the French, with regard to the control of the Mississippi; the unpitying force with which we thrust the Indians to the wall, wherever they have stood in the way, have suited our professions of peacefulness and justice no more than the aggressions of other nations that were strong and not to be gainsaid." To this double passion he referred on another occasion: "We have great ardor for gain; but we have a deep passion for the rights of man." [5]

But, having come into office after waging a fierce verbal battle against powerful economic interests in the United States, cherishing in his mind traditional conceptions of American democracy, committed to *"a priori* or moral principles," [6] President Wilson chose to challenge "every aspect of 'dollar diplomacy,'" in an effort "to assert and apply the old democratic and moral principles." [7] In one of the first pronouncements of his administration, he exposed his philosophy of diplomacy, in a statement on Latin American affairs released to the press on March 12, 1913. For coercion he proposed to substitute coöperation, and promised to "promote in every honorable and proper way the interests [8] which are common to the people of the two continents." Yet, he pointed out, such coöperation must rest upon "the orderly processes of just government based upon law, not upon arbitrary or irregular force." His idealized picture of a workable situation was a world of democracies founded on the principles of constitutional regularity, orderly procedure, popular consent, and respect for persons and prop-

[5] *Ibid.*, pp. 423–424.
[6] *Ibid.*, p. 76.
[7] *Ibid.*, p. 61.
[8] In President Wilson's original draft the words "material and political" appear; *ibid.*, p. 65.

erty as exemplified in the United States—at least as he hoped his country would appear after his operations of cleansing and restoration. In other words, his emphasis was upon democratic theories and procedures rather than upon the use of government to advance economic interests in accordance with the methods of economic imperialism, to which he was strongly opposed. Thus he deliberately sought to break with the dollar diplomacy of his predecessor and to follow a course calculated to promote the spread of republican and democratic practices in government, trusting that commercial intercourse would naturally follow peace and stability.

With a brusqueness uncommon to the management of foreign affairs President Wilson attempted to apply this framework of principles to the conduct of diplomacy. Indeed he acted with such slight consideration for the conceptions of the State Department that the Under Secretary of State, F. M. Huntington Wilson, who had been chiefly instrumental in bringing dollar diplomacy to a reasoned formulation, felt compelled to resign at once in protest against the reversal of policy "with such quite unnecessary haste and in so unusual a manner." [9] Having attempted to break with the past, the President went on in the course which he had laid out for himself and followed it as best he could, making concessions when he discovered that "republican and democratic principles" did not work out as anticipated in many places—Mexico, China, and Nicaragua, for instance. Other Presidents had expected the example of the American republic to exert a profound influence on the course of world history; President Wilson tried, within limits, to make American principles of popular government prevail generally through the uses of diplomacy. His failures, if such they were, did not prove the superiority of the diplomacy which he superseded, but they illustrated again the difficulties confronting all leaders who attempt to make the tough facts of human development conform to any consistent and logical pattern. Whatever their forms and restrictions in practice, however, his measures and policies in gross, if not always in detail, traversed those which had long prevailed in the conduct of American foreign affairs.

[9] Baker, *op. cit.*, p. 72.

Since these measures and policies broke in upon the course of commercial and territorial expansion pursued under Federalist-Whig-Republican auspices, it was natural that leadership in defeating President Wilson's program should be taken by Senator Lodge, early formulator of the imperial program finally adopted by President McKinley, opponent of Philippine independence, high-tariff advocate, and confidant of Admiral Mahan, the author of *Machtpolitik* on the high seas. Nor was it an accident that a large part of the money which financed the campaign to defeat the League of Nations was furnished by two great Republican industrialists—Henry C. Frick and Andrew D. Mellon—the latter on the solicitation of Senator Knox, the exponent of dollar diplomacy.[10] Something more than the abstractions of peace were at stake in the formulas of the League of Nations Covenant.

THE NEW ECONOMIC SCENE AFTER THE WORLD WAR

With the League of Nations rejected, and the party of President Wilson more thoroughly defeated than in 1860, the party of dollar diplomacy found economic conditions at home and abroad favorable to the renewal of commercial promotion on a large scale. Owing to the enormous sale of commodities at high prices to the Allied Powers of Europe, the United States had been transformed from a debtor province into a creditor nation, a cosmopolitan, lending nation. Huge profits accumulated during the war were now available for investment in plant extension at home and in enterprise abroad. According to Professor Davis R. Dewey, "Tax returns showed that all corporations in the United States between January 1, 1916 and July 1, 1921, made net profits of $47,000,000,000 and that after paying all federal taxes, income taxes, excess-profits, and war taxes, they had a clear profit of $38,000,000,000, of which more than one half was made by about a thousand corporations." [11] Owing to the high prices of farm produce and the general rise in wages, farmers, industrial workers, and the lower

[10] George Harvey, *Henry Clay Frick the Man*, pp. 325–326, 329–330; Fleming, *The United States and the League of Nations*, pp. 209ff.

[11] *Financial History of the United States*, p. 513.

middle class had savings on hand to combine with the accumulations of industrial profits in buying foreign stocks and bonds; and the Liberty Loan drives had "educated" them into "investment habits" without inculcating any special powers of discrimination. Thus a swollen pool of liquid capital was pressing its banks for profitable outlets—anywhere in the world.

In the meantime, owing to the feverish demands of the war period, there had been a wide extension of industrial and agricultural plants. The banking system of the country was operating in such a way as to favor the expansion of credit for production as against credit for buying power.[12] As the swelling streams of commodities flowed from mills and farms, the demand for markets increased. Selling became the great national pre-occupation on which amazing engines of ingenuity were concentrated. From the domestic field American interest in this activity spread to the uttermost parts of the earth, creating new forms of national interest and carrying them to all quarters of the globe with a zeal and success which the authors of the *Federalist* could not have imagined in their highest moments of divination. From London to Prague, from Budapest to Athens, from Istanbul to Rangoon, from Saigon to Tokyo, American sales agents expanded their enterprise, scattering American goods and money with an astounding profusion.

The extension of the producing and selling process was facilitated by the rapid growth of manufacturing and exporting corporations. Despite the dire threats of the Clayton Anti-trust Act, the concentration of industrial and commercial wealth had proceeded with impressive rapidity. By 1930, it was estimated, nearly half the business wealth of the country had been centralized in the hands of approximately two hundred corporations.[13] In control of matchless productive facilities, having access to an ample supply of raw materials and of highly skilled labor, equipped with abundant capital, possessing highly developed engineering talents and compact selling organiza-

[12] Paul Mazur, *New Roads to Prosperity.* Viking Press, New York, 1931.
[13] Harry W. Laidler, *Concentration of Control in American Business.* Also A. A. Berle and Gardiner C. Means, *The Modern Corporation and Private Property.* Macmillan, New York, 1933.

tions, many corporations—especially "the Big Thirty," as they are known in South America—set out to extend American economic interests in every direction with an energy and skill far beyond the command of the historic private traders. Almost if not quite as strong as the state, unhampered by the formalities and niceties of diplomacy, and yet always able to summon diplomacy to their aid in an emergency, these economic giants in seven-league boots took over a lion's share of the economic operations which constituted the substance of American interest in foreign countries and on the high seas.

At the very moment when this transformation of the American economic scene began, the condition of other countries was favorable to the rapid growth of American trade and investments. Central and Eastern Europe was shattered by the war; its railways, bridges, public works, and industrial plants were either depleted or adapted to war purposes. Hence there was an enormous demand for American capital and commodities to fill the vacuum created by years of armed conflict. During that struggle German banks and selling agencies in the Orient and Latin America had been cut off from support at home, and at the peace table Germany was stripped of her shipping and overseas establishments. On account of their pre-occupation with fighting, Great Britain, France, and Italy had been unable to press their selling enterprises in their former markets or to make the loans necessary for the promotion of their commerce. Moreover, under the enormous demands for goods created by the war, American industrial technique and facilities had been brought to a high point of perfection which continued to improve, even with increasing rapidity, in the subsequent years. In these advantageous circumstances, American capitalists made heavy inroads upon the foreign markets of European industrial countries, particularly in Latin America, and planted American interests in fields never before successfully cultivated.[14]

Meanwhile the parochialism of American banking was cast off. Previous experience in foreign financing, in Mexico, the Caribbean, and Japan, was now supplemented by loans to the Allies, with the Anglo-French loan of $500,000,000 as an in-

[14] Normano, *The Struggle for South America.*

dex to the future. President Taft's suggestion respecting the establishment of branch banks abroad was heeded and soon a network of American financial agencies spread around the world. With capital accumulated from war profits and savings, with the monetary system and the mechanics of corporate financing holding out almost unlimited possibilities of creating additional "capital," and the field ripe for the harvest, American bankers began to float loans for foreign governments and business enterprises with all the zest of young soldiers setting out to war. Instead of waiting sedately in their counting houses for customers, they sent agents into the highways and byways offering American dollars with a lavish hand, at a high rate of interest and on generous commissions—the more impecunious the borrower and the more insecure the loan the richer the reward, it seemed, for the lenders and the middlemen. With accelerating speed the process went on until by 1929 the foreign investments of the American people, exclusive of the war debts, totalled fourteen billion dollars in round numbers.[15] American interests in the form of money lent or credit advanced ran into the most remote places of the earth and were connected by economic ties with thousands of investors in all parts of the United States.[16]

RESTORATION IN OFFICIAL POLICY

It was amid such circumstances that the party of "normalcy" set to work in 1921 to restore the conception of national interest formulated under the head of dollar diplomacy, with the possibilities of American commercial and naval supremacy in sight. It repudiated the low-tariff policy embodied in the law of 1913 and by successive acts raised the duties to the highest general levels in the history of the country. It revived and sharpened the instruments of protection and discrimination. Defeated in its efforts to subsidize the merchant marine directly, despite the recommendations of President Harding and President Coolidge, owing to agrarian opposition in Congress,

[15] See the Appendix.
[16] Dwight Morrow, "Who Buys Foreign Bonds?" *Foreign Affairs,* January, 1927.

it finally accomplished the same end indirectly by authorizing lucrative mail contracts to ship operators and loans to ship builders at low rates of interest. It continued the naval program which had been enlarged during the war, until at last the United States was in sight of supremacy on the seas and would have gained that goal if caution had not led civilians to compromise at the Washington conference in 1922.

With the stage set at home, the Government intensified its commercial activities abroad. Under the direction of Secretary Herbert Hoover, the Department of Commerce was enlarged to gigantic proportions. New divisions and thousands of employees were added. A palatial building was planned and erected in Washington. The searching and propaganda work carried on by consular officers under the auspices of the Department of State was supplemented—and to a large extent duplicated—by the creation of special commercial agents authorized to scour the world in quest of outlets. The United States was laid out into regional and industrial units; local agencies of the Department were set up in strategic centers; contacts were formed with merchants and industrialists in every important branch of economic life; continuous efforts were made to arouse a zeal for foreign trade and to consolidate the commercial interests of the country for the conquest of the world's markets, for the "economic war after the war." The Secretary and his assistants threw the whole weight of the Department, supplied with millions of dollars annually by Congress, into the struggle for selling and investment opportunities, and sought, by speeches, articles, press releases, and letters, to convert the whole country to the creed formulated by President Taft, namely, that an increasing expansion of foreign trade is possible and indispensable to the prosperity of American business.

The philosophy of the new promotion program is expressed in numerous statements scattered through the publications of the Department of Commerce. It was briefly summed up by Secretary Hoover in an address before the Export Managers' Club of New York in 1926. "Foreign trade," he said, "has become a vital part of the whole modern economic system. . . . In peace time our exports and imports are the margins upon which our well-being depends. The export of our surplus enables us to use in full our resources and energy. . . . The great problem in our foreign trade, however, is the export of goods in which we compete with other nations—but if we are intelligent we should be able to command our share of them. Our most competitive group is that of manufactured goods, and expansion of the exports of our manufactured goods is of the utmost importance to us. As our population increases we shall consume more of our foodstuffs, and this important item in our exports will tend to decrease because our easily cultivable land is now well occupied. . . . If we are to maintain the total volume of our exports and consequently our buying power for imports, it must be by steady pushing of our manufactured goods. . . . The making of loans to foreign countries for productive purposes not only increases our direct exports but builds up the prosperity of foreign countries and is a blessing to both sides of the transaction." [17] Though by no means oblivious to the non-competitive aspects of foreign commerce, Mr. Hoover impressed upon his audience the importance of promoting actively the sale of manufactures abroad.

In supporting this general thesis, the Assistant Secretary of Commerce, Julius Klein, restated the argument in more picturesque, if not less emphatic, language. Foreign trade, he declared in 1929, "has become a modest but invaluable part of our whole economic system. It has served again and again as a stabilizer of our domestic position and as an indicator of the general trend of our commercial and industrial growth. Because of its far-flung variety of contacts and of its innumerable participating industries, it is no longer likely to suffer hectic gyrations due to the whims and shifting plans of a few participants, as was the case in pre-war years. Even though it may not contribute more than perhaps 10 or 11 per cent of our total commercial life, that modest margin has frequently saved more than one major industry from distress." Thus in addition to being the margin upon which our welfare depends, foreign trade is a stabilizer of American business, a source of outlet in times of stress, something of a "compensator" or balance wheel. Though treated as modest, this trade

[17] *The Future of Our Foreign Trade*, pp. 1–13.

is, in fact immense: "Our total dealings with foreigners in 1927 amounted to more than eighteen billion dollars. This is our 'international turnover'—about $152 for every man, woman, and child in the Republic; and if you will count that up for the circle of your family, you will realize what a stake each one of us has in this matter." [18]

The export of American capital, it also appears, contributes to the prosperity of the United States. "The total of our private loans in foreign countries is at present [1929] about thirteen or fourteen billion dollars. In other words, every man, woman, and child in the country has a stake of $120 in these overseas interests, which is about six times the per capita amount in 1914. . . . Our fourteen billions of overseas investments are owned, not in concentrated blocks by a few large bankers, but by tens of thousands of small investors scattered all over this broad land. . . . This vast capital, which we are pouring into the pool of the world's business at the rate of four or five million dollars a day, is an invaluable contribution to prosperity in general. Any prosperity anywhere is 'all to the good.' . . . It is greatly to our interest in cold dollars and cents to have business booming in all parts of the world, to find ourselves surrounded by contented and busy neighbors." All this is being done by American loans abroad without bringing to pass any shortage of capital for domestic purposes. [19]

With the pressure for the extension of commerce went an expansion of the conception of national defense to cover all the realities involved in economic transactions. This expansion reached its limits under the administration of President Coolidge. He himself took the position that American citizens and property abroad were as much a part of the national domain as citizens and property within the jurisdiction of the United States. [20] His Secretary of the Navy, Curtis D. Wilbur, gave more minute specifications; he enumerated the American ships and goods on the high seas, American investments and holdings abroad, the various forms of American property in foreign countries, and then declared that defense of all these things

---

[18] Julius Klein, *Frontiers of Trade,* pp. 141, 182.

[19] *Ibid.,* pp. xi, 159, 175–176.

[20] Below, Chapter VII.

was an obligation of the United States Government.[21] They did not explain how it would be possible to have an army and navy large enough to accomplish this purpose against any power or combination of powers, but they sought to commit the nation to this conception of defense.

In the field of diplomacy, the restoration of 1921 meant the rejection of the League of Nations and a return to what was called "isolation." Instead of relying upon the opinions and decisions of an international council and assembly, the United States was to define its own rights and interests and enforce them by its own methods. No shred of sovereignty was to be surrendered. The plenary power of the United States to operate in the Western Hemisphere under its own conception of interests was to be preserved. "The Monroe Doctrine," said Senator Lodge in opposing the League, "has expanded. A resolution was passed unanimously in the Senate a few years ago stating that the United States would regard it as an act of hostility for any corporation or association of any other nation to take possession of Magdalena Bay, being a post of great strategic, naval, and military advantage. That did not rest on the Monroe Doctrine. It rested on something deeper than that. It rested on the basis of the Monroe Doctrine, the great law of self-preservation." The United States was not to endure any interference with its right to compose difficulties in Latin America. "I believe," continued Senator Lodge, "the people of the United States are just as humane, just as anxious to do right to others, as any nation in the world. We have cared for three of those states . . . Santo Domingo, Haiti, and Nicaragua. In every instance war has been stopped and civilization and peace have progressed."[22]

With respect to the rest of the world, the Government of the United States must have a free hand. It would not attempt to take part in composing quarrels in the Old World through co-operating with the League of Nations, but, as Senator Knox explained, "if, unlikely as it may be, the cause of humanity ever should beckon us to give assistance to the peoples of the Old World, that assistance can be given when the time comes as

[21] Below, Chapter VII.
[22] *The Lowell-Lodge Debate on the Proposed League of Nations,* pp. 16, 48.

readily and strongly as it has been done in the past." [23]   In the Far East the course mapped out in the nineteenth century, pursued by McKinley, and followed by Roosevelt, was to be renewed. The open door was to be kept open and the right of the United States to choose the time, circumstances, and manner of operation and intervention was to be kept unimpaired. "We would have our country strong enough to resist a peril from the West," exclaimed Senator Lodge, who was deeply moved by the Shantung question, "as she has flung back the German menace from the East." [24]   The United States would not submit the determination of its interests to any association of nations or any world tribunal. The diplomatic implications of the decision were clear and unmistakable.

With Charles E. Hughes installed in the State Department, the idea of national interest as the controlling principle of diplomacy was reëstablished. It was he who announced the doctrine with which the first page of this book opens. His statement deserves fuller quotation: "Foreign policies are not built upon abstractions. They are the result of practical conceptions of national interest arising from some immediate exigency or standing out vividly in historical perspective. When long maintained, they express the hopes and fears, the aims of security and aggrandizement, which have become dominant in the national consciousness and thus transcend party divisions and make negligible such opposition as may come from particular groups. They inevitably control the machinery of international accord which works only within the narrow field not closed by divergent national ambitions or as interest yields to apprehension or obtains compensation through give and take. Statesmen who carry the burdens of empire do not for a moment lose sight of imperial purposes and requirements." [25]   Although the term, "dollar diplomacy," does not appear in this formulation, its substance is implicit, and the practice of Secretary Hughes conformed to that conception of policy and action.

[23] For Republican policy, see Fleming, *The United States and the League of Nations.*

[24] *Ibid.*, p. 307.

[25] Address at Philadelphia, November 30, 1923, reprinted in *The Pathway of Peace*, p. 142.

In its application to Europe this doctrine meant no official participation in the collective efforts to clear up the wreckage of the war and smooth out the rivalries of that continent which had so deeply affected American interests in the past—in Europe and in the Pacific. Secretary Hughes said finally: "Europe still has 'a set of primary interests' which are not ours," and "we had better bear those ills than suffer the greater evils which would follow the sacrifice of our independent position." [26] In keeping with this rule he refused at the outset to reply to formal notes directed to his Department by the Secretariat of the League of Nations. The debts owed to the Government of the United States were settled on the hypothesis that they were bona fide obligations; the terms of settlement were generous enough, no doubt, but the plea for abrogation on the ground that the war had been a common moral crusade was firmly rejected. Invitations to take part in the councils of Europe were declined, but European decisions pertaining to oil and other substantial interests were controverted when they were deemed contrary to American rights and to the doctrine of the open door for American business enterprise.[27]

When the question of Russia was raised in 1923, Secretary Hughes based his refusal to recognize the government of that country on grounds of substantial interest and implied that the way to recognition lay clearly before the Soviet state. "If the Soviet authorities," he stated, "are ready to restore the confiscated property of American citizens or make effective compensation, they can do so. If the Soviet authorities are ready to repeal their decree repudiating Russia's obligations to this country and appropriately recognize them, they can do so. It requires no conference or negotiations to accomplish these results which can and should be achieved at Moscow as evidence of good faith. The American Government has not incurred liabilities to Russia or repudiated obligations." [28] On another occasion he said: "Of what avail is it to speak of assurance, if

---

[26] *Ibid.*, pp. 151–152.

[27] Discussed generally in Anton Mohr, *The Oil War*, Harcourt, Brace & Co., 1926, particularly, pp. 224–232.

[28] Hyde, *American Secretaries of State and Their Diplomacy*, Vol. X, p. 286.

valid obligations and rights are repudiated and property is confiscated?" [29] In upshot this seemed to mean that the prime consideration at stake was the fulfillment on the part of Russia of economic obligations to the United States and its citizens.

With respect to the Caribbean and Latin America generally, Secretary Hughes continued the policy pursued by Secretary Knox. The idea of conquest and aggression for the sake of conquest and aggression was distinctly repudiated, as it had been repeatedly in previous years, but action was taken along earlier lines wherever and whenever American interests were threatened. In an address on the Monroe Doctrine, Mr. Hughes informed the Latin American countries that "States have duties as well as rights. Every state on being received into the family of nations accepts the obligations which are the essential conditions of international intercourse. Among these obligations is the duty of each state to respect the rights of citizens of other states which have been acquired within its jurisdiction in accordance with its laws. A confiscatory policy strikes not only at the interest of particular individuals but at the foundations of international intercourse." Where intervention was deemed necessary, no infringement of sovereignty was intended: "In promoting stability we do not threaten independence but seek to conserve it. We are not aiming at control but endeavoring to establish self-control." [30] Again: "We are not aiming to exploit but to aid; not to subvert, but to help in laying the foundations for sound, stable, and independent government. Our interest does not lie in controlling foreign peoples. . . . Our interest is in having them prosperous, peaceful, and law-abiding neighbors, with whom we can coöperate to mutual advantage." [31]

In action this doctrine meant a continuance of American authority over Santo Domingo until 1924 when the establishment of a local government under American auspices and arrangements guaranteeing life and property made withdrawal possible. In announcing this outcome, Secretary Hughes stated: "Of course we could have remained in control had we desired, but instead of doing so we have been solicitous to aid in the es-

---

[29] In *The Pathway of Peace*, p. 62.
[30] *Ibid.*, pp. 151–161.
[31] *Ibid.*, p. 137.

tablishment of an independent government so that we could withdraw and, such a government having been established through our efforts, we have withdrawn." [32] Similar steps were taken to create a government in Haiti satisfactory to the United States and to permit a restoration of local authority with adequate safeguards for American interests in that republic, but no settlement on such terms could be reached. Nor could adjustments be made in Nicaragua which would sanction a complete abrogation of American tutelage. With the installation of a new president there in 1925, it was thought that an end could be made to American supervision, but civil strife with both liberals and conservatives seeking to control the government became so disruptive that Secretary Hughes had to announce that "the newly elected president has besought us in the interest of peace and order to permit it [the American guard] to remain until a constabulary or local police can be provided." [33] As things turned out the expected day was a long time arriving. The United States marines remained in Nicaragua "at the request of that government," and undoubtedly under the pressure of events as well, to supervise the elections there in 1928 and 1930. It was not until February 13, 1931, that the State Department announced that conditions were paving the way "for the ultimate removal of all the Marine forces from Nicaragua after the election of 1932." [34] In his annual message of December 9, 1931, President Hoover declared: "We have continued our policy of withdrawing our marines from Haiti and Nicaragua." Practically all the marines, except the customary legation guard, were withdrawn before Franklin D. Roosevelt assumed the presidency in 1933.

With regard to Mexico, Secretary Hughes inherited a statement of American interests in that country, which had been formulated under Republican leadership in the Senate and presented to the country in a report on Mexican affairs drafted by the subcommittee of the Senate Committee on Foreign Re-

[32] C. C. Hyde, *American Secretaries of State and Their Diplomacy,* Vol. X, pp. 339–340.

[33] *Ibid.,* p. 340. For an account of the situation, see *The United States and Nicaragua;* Department of State; Latin American Series No. 6; Washington, 1932; particularly, pp. 64–69 and 107–108.

[34] *The United States and Nicaragua,* p. 107.

lations under the direction of Albert B. Fall as chairman.[35]
This document contained a pointed bill of particulars. In
general, as far as American interests were concerned, it declared that any government in Mexico before receiving recognition, must show a capacity and a disposition "to comply with
the rules of international comity and the obligations of treaties."
In this connection everyone who assumes to exercise authority
in Mexico must be informed "in the most unequivocal way that
we shall vigilantly watch the fortunes of those Americans who
can not get away, and shall hold those responsible for their
sufferings and losses to a definite reckoning."

This broad statement is followed by specific items. The Report attacks Article 130 of the Mexican Constitution of 1917
imposing restraints on religious teaching and providing that no
one except a Mexican by birth may be a minister of any
religious creed in Mexico. It flatly declares that the Article in
question "shall not apply to American missionaries, preachers,
ministers, teachers, American schools, nor to American peri-
odicals"; and insists "that American missionaries, ministers,
and teachers shall be allowed freely to enter, pass through,
and reside in Mexico, there to freely reside, preach, teach, and
write, and hold property, and conduct schools without interference by the authorities so long as such ministers, teachers,
or missionaries do not participate in Mexican politics or revolutions." Article 3 of the Mexican Constitution forbidding
ministers and religious corporations to establish or direct primary schools of instruction is likewise brought under the ban
of the subcommittee. Its Report announces that this Article
"shall not apply to any Americans teaching or conducting primary schools." The provision of Article 27 making religious
property liable to confiscation, the Report continues, "shall
not apply to the church properties or Episcopal residences, rec-
tories, seminaries, orphan asylums, or collegiate establishments
or religious institutions or schools held or owned by Americans." In other words, American interests seem to demand the
right of American citizens to engage in missionary and educa-

---

[35] See *Preliminary Report and Hearings of the Committee on Foreign Relations of the Senate,* pursuant to S. Res. 106, 66th Cong., 2d Sess., Doc. No. 285,
2 Vols., Washington, 1920.

tional work in foreign countries and to hold property in connection with their enterprises.

Coming specifically to the rights of property employed in economic undertakings, the Report declares "that none of the provisions of Article 27 of said constitution with reference to limitations upon rights of property heretofore acquired by Americans, or which may hereafter be acquired, shall apply to Americans except where the limitation is written in the deed, lease, or other instrument of title." It particularly emphasizes the provision nationalizing subsoil products other than metalliferous minerals, and insists that such provision shall not apply to the property of American citizens acquired in Mexico, unless reservation of the subsoil is written in the original instrument of conveyance. Furthermore "the prohibition against the ownership of property in lands, waters, or their appurtenances, or against the concessions for the development of mines, waters, or mineral fuels in the Republic to foreigners shall not apply to American citizens." Neither shall the provisions for nationalizing certain lands and offering in compensation "agrarian bonds," asserted to be "entirely worthless," apply "to the property of any Americans now owned under whatsoever title or which may hereafter be acquired," except where such reservations and limitations are clearly set forth in the instrument of transfer.

Rights of person are also to be safeguarded. The Report emphatically declares that the provision of the Mexican constitution conferring on the President the power to expel from the Republic "forthwith and without judicial process any foreigner whose presence he may deem inexpedient," shall not apply "to any American citizens, who shall, when they so demand, have access to their consulate or consular agent or diplomatic representative and have the right to avail themselves of the assistance of such officials, and until after due judicial proceedings upon application of such Americans." Finally, agreement must be made for a mixed commission to hear and decide all claims for damages to Americans in Mexico or upon its boundaries, and its decisions must be carried out by the payment of damages awarded.

Taking this difficult situation in hand, the State Department declared that Mexican legislation affecting subsoil rights was "retroactive, confiscatory, and contrary to the principles of international law and equity." On its part the Mexican government claimed that the legislation in controversy was purely domestic in character and enacted in "pursuance of full sovereignty." By firm insistence the Government of the United States secured a convention with Mexico in 1923 which guaranteed a recognition of the rights of American nationals to subsoil in all cases in which, prior to the promulgation of the constitution of 1917, the owners of the surface had performed positive acts indicating a desire to use the subsoil. After this settlement had been effected, the Government of the United States sold arms to the government of Mexico and supported it in its efforts to suppress a revolution which flared up under the leadership of Huerta.[36] Yet in point of fact, there were numerous vested interests of American citizens in Mexican mines, franchises, landed property, and oil wells which were not realized under the policy of the restoration. Doubtless the appearance of salt water in oil wells and the general slump in the oil business relaxed the pressure on the Government of the United States for more active interference but, in any event, it chose a course of negotiation, not that of armed intervention.

In the Far East the diplomacy of the restoration was true to the tradition. General Leonard Wood was sent out as governor general of the Philippines and the policies of his predecessor were reversed with a view to stricter control. On the basis of a report by a special commissioner, President Coolidge let it be known that the independence promised by the Jones Act was to be indefinitely postponed, meaning in effect a renewal of the commercial and investment program inaugurated by President McKinley. When the issue was again pressed, President Hoover and his Secretary of State, Henry L. Stimson, took a decided stand against it and stoutly resisted withdrawal from the Islands, on historic grounds. Moreover the ultimate use of the Philippines as a fulcrum of American naval power in the East was assumed in the naval policy formulated by the Navy Department in 1922, advocated in the testimony of naval officers at the hearings of various congressional committees, im-

[36] Hyde, *op. cit.*, p. 309.

plied in the threat conveyed to Japan by Secretary Stimson in a letter to Senator Borah, and confirmed by the reservation of naval bases in the resolution granting independence laid before Congress in 1932, and finally safeguarded in the Independence Bill passed in January, 1933. If there was to be any retreat, the foundation of naval power in the Orient was to be retained at all costs, for eventualities, should they arise.

During negotiations with China and Japan, the policy of the restoration reversed the measures of the interregnum and returned to the original course. Traditional friendship for China, with the commercial implications inherent in it, was revived in the State Department. In due time Japan was "gently coerced" into surrendering Shantung, which President Wilson had permitted her to retain against the violent protests of Senator Lodge and other opponents of "Japanese imperialism." The Lansing-Ishii agreement conceding Japan a special position on the mainland was cancelled and the *status quo ante* restored. Taking a step in advance, Secretary Hughes managed to dissolve the Anglo-Japanese alliance, at least formally, and thus broke up a combination possessing spheres of influence in China. Then, to crown it all, he reasserted the doctrine of the open door, although the house was clearly on fire by this time, and induced the great powers to proclaim once more their adherence to this interpretation of American interest. To be sure, a significant price in naval reduction and in the curtailment of American power in the Pacific through restrictions upon armaments in the Philippines was paid for the concessions received from Great Britain and Japan—a price which made the restoration fall short of the position promised in 1921.

COMPROMISE IN "MACHTPOLITIK"

In fact, a balance sheet struck at the end of ten years revealed some fundamental losses in the paraphernalia of dollar diplomacy, serious failures in the realization of hopes, and signs of retreat in various directions. At the close of the World War, with enormous capital accumulations on hand, with industrial plants widely extended, with naval supremacy in sight, the United States might have carried the conception of national interest as commercial expansion into effect on a gigantic scale. It was true that the American public was saturated with the internationalism of President Wilson and that the agrarian wings of both parties put obstacles in the way of imperial enterprises in the Caribbean, but the ease with which money was raised to pay for the propaganda against the League of Nations and the success of the counter agitation indicated that courage and campaign funds might go far in re-educating the country and establishing the commercial and naval supremacy of the United States throughout the world. The economic power was here. The navy was in process of building. All that was needed was more of the kind of daring displayed by Theodore Roosevelt, Henry Cabot Lodge, and William McKinley a generation before. Why did the leadership fail to appear? Why did the greatest economic power on earth refuse to grasp the trident of the seas and the scepter of world trade?

The lack of logical consistency in the official thesis of national interest, the presence of contradictions, limitations, and opposing variables, is to be explained by reference to the conflicts of domestic politics and the historical circumstances of American commercial expansion. In its genuine form, the doctrine of *Machtpolitik* contains certain inevitable elements. It includes the pursuit of economic interests abroad with full preparations for the utmost consequences, the maintenance of a navy, not second to none, but clearly superior to the nearest competitor, and willingness to employ the ultimate arbiter, force, to break down resistance to the march of the economic conquest. Such a pure and self-consistent policy was possible for the government of Great Britain during a brief period of history, when the industrialists had triumphed completely over agriculture and had either subdued or absorbed the old landed aristocracy. It appeared to be possible in Germany where a large part of agriculture was in the hands of powerful landlords who, instead of courting ruin, compromised with the great industrialists, granting them a free hand upon the sea in exchange for tariffs on grain and other concessions.[37] If national interest, as currently conceived, was to be consolidated and

[37] E. Kehr, *Schlachtflottenbau und Parteipolitik, 1894–1901.*

pursued with relentless might, then Reventlow was right when he said that the choice lay between world power and downfall.

In the United States, on the other hand, no such solid fusion of industry and agriculture behind national interest proved to be possible. It was contemplated for a brief moment by the Northern Whigs and the conservative planters of the South, but the conflict of their immediate interests defeated the program. The agriculturalists, under planting leadership, swung over to violent opposition to protective tariffs, ship subsidies, discriminating duties against foreign shipping, efforts at building up a great naval power, and similar features of *Machtpolitik*. Even after planting leadership was destroyed in the Civil War, and industrial enterprise overtopped agriculture in the amount of capital engaged and the number of people employed, it did not gain unhampered dominance in politics, as in Great Britain and Germany. Its chief exponent in the political sphere, the Republican party, from the beginning, had a huge agrarian wing, inherited from the compromise at Chicago in 1860 when free homesteads were exchanged for a protective tariff. Hence from the outset, industrial leadership in the pursuit of *Machtpolitik* was restrained, deflected, and forced to accept halfway measures by the agrarian elements in both political parties. It got a navy, but not naval supremacy. It secured subsidies for shipping, but not enough and too late. It could take naval bases in distant places, but too few and always with the hampering sentiments of moral obligation. It could interfere in China, for example, but, as John Hay pointed out, it could not win popular support for an open and unashamed participation in the division and spoliation of China according to the French-British-German-Russian-Japanese program of action, for the simple reason that a large section of the population, especially, the agrarian wing of the Republican party and the agrarian Democrats under Bryan, would not lend whole-hearted allegiance.

Then at the fateful moment in world history, at the close of the World War, when Germany was prostrate and Great Britain staggering under debts, when the United States Navy was just on the point of wresting supremacy from the British at sea, on account of the fever of national solidarity raised

during the war, the opportunity to grasp the trident of commerce was allowed to pass. For a moment the world was
weary of the fruits of empire. Victors and vanquished were
shattered and bewildered. Under President Wilson, the leader
of Jefferson's old party, an opponent of the Federalist-Whig-
Republican tradition, other conceptions of international relations had been everywhere accepted, in many quarters with a
wry face, as a price of money and guns. Although the Republican party swept into power in 1920 promising a return to
"normalcy," it came back with the old agrarian wing still tearing at its flanks and had to march carefully, with a farm-bloc
powerful in both houses and with the left wing of the Democratic party, though defeated, still militant. With mankind still
reeking in the blood of the World War and torn by a revolutionary sentiment which had upset Tsarism, with the old conflict of American domestic politics renewed, with the American
people disillusioned by the impact of "secret treaties" and by
the unreality of such slogans as "making the world safe for
democracy" and "the war to end war," compromise seemed
necessary; and it was reached in a series of agreements at the
Washington and London conferences which made dangerous
the ruthless pursuit of *Machtpolitik* by any of the participating powers.

It is possible, of course, that an uncompromising choice
might have been made by Republican leadership in the United
States, as the directors of the Navy League and perhaps a
majority of the naval officers ardently desired. Supremacy over
Great Britain and Japan at sea might have been grasped and
held. But the character of American leadership precluded that
outcome. Businessmen, lawyers, and politicians were not cast
in the mold of Cæsar. There was no landed aristocracy in the
United States to furnish the requisite military direction and the
war had produced no great captains of dictatorial capacity.
The American naval bureaucracy was at sea, both in fact
and in theory, and had no powerful roots in the soil of American politics. Had the iron will been available, advantage might
have been taken of the occasion to subdue England and Japan;
and the glory of the adventure, if successful, might have closed
all opposition in the country. But the fateful hour passed and

a limited and inconsistent *Machtpolitik* was accepted, one so hedged about by naval restraints that it could only operate timidly and without assurance. Perhaps, after all, a new stage had been set for the manipulation of world affairs. The old order seemed dead and the new powerless to be born.

This uncertainty of policy—this hovering between the desires and the dictates of the official thesis, or dollar diplomacy, and the necessity of framing different and contrary policies under the pressure of new situations, continued to the end of the Republican régime. The indecision was further intensified, and thus became more apparent, in the economic holocaust that swept the country and the world after 1929. Before that set in, however, President Hoover, Secretary Stimson and the other leaders of the Republican administration restated many of the old formulas in the hope apparently that the traditional principles would either control the new and unfamiliar circumstances, or at least limit to a minimum any ground that would have to be yielded.

In dealing with the Philippines [38] President Hoover enlarged America's moral duty and found sufficient reason in the larger conception for vetoing the independence act passed by the Congress. "In securing this spiritual boon [separate nationality] to the 13,000,000 people in these islands," he asserted, "the United States has a triple responsibility. That is, responsibility to the Philippine people, responsibility to the American people, and responsibility to the world at large." [39] As to the Philippine people, our responsibility is, "that in finding a method by which we consummate their aspiration we do not project them into economic and social chaos, with the probability of breakdown in government, with its consequences in degeneration of a rising liberty . . . so carefully nurtured by the United States at the cost of thousands of American lives and hundreds of millions of money." To the American people we owe the duty of accomplishing Philippine separation "without endangering ourselves in military action hereafter to maintain internal or-

[38] Below, Chapter XII.

[39] New York *Times*, January 14, 1933, item: "Text of President Hoover's Message Vetoing the Philippine Bill." Other extracts which follow on this subject are also quoted from the same message unless otherwise noted.

der or to protect the Philippines from encroachment by others. . . ." Having undertaken to develop and to perfect freedom for the Philippine people, we owe a duty to the world that "we shall not by our course project more chaos into a world already sorely beset by instability."

"The present bill," Mr. Hoover concluded, "fails to fulfill these responsibilities. It unites all these dangers. It does not fulfill the idealism with which this task in human liberation was undertaken." The ten year period during which the Philippine people are to adjust their affairs is "too short, too violent" and "the American Government will be faced after projection of these events with years of military occupation among a degenerating economic and social life. . . ." Touching upon the motivation for the passage of the bill—"presumed relief to certain American agricultural industries," he remarked, "We are trustees for these people and we must not let our selfish interest dominate that trust. However, from our agricultural point of view, during the first period of presumably two years it gives no protection of any kind. During the following five years it gives no effective protection. . . ." During the period of intermediate government, the United States will have grave responsibilities "without adequate authority." The Philippines will be subjected to the infiltration of races "more devoted to commercial activities than the population of the islands," a condition "fraught with friction." "Nor has the spirit of imperialism and the exploitation of peoples of other races departed from the earth."

Before these dangers, greatly increased by the political instability of the Orient, the Filipino people alone will be helpless. Neither is the American mission in the Philippines fulfilled, nor are the Filipinos prepared for self-government; but "we must undertake further steps . . . based upon a plebiscite to be taken fifteen or twenty years hence." In the meantime "we should develop . . . a larger importance to their own officials . . . with a full reserve of authority to our representatives. Immigration should be restricted at once." And then after all these things are done and before the Philippine people hold the plebiscite ("fifteen or twenty years hence") the United States should announce "whether (a) it will make absolute and complete withdrawal from all military and naval bases; and from every moral or other commitment to maintain their independence, or (*b*) the conditions as to authority and rights within the islands under which we will continue that protection." Although the message was directed to a specific bill, the attitude taken was a broad one interpreting the content of American "trusteeship," in wider terms apparently than had been asserted before in the official thesis of dollar diplomacy and national interest.

With respect to Latin America, Secretary Stimson carried the traditional principles through the final years of the restoration.[40] Standing upon the policy that "from the beginning we have made the preservation of individual independence of these nations correspond with our own interest" which "has coincided with the basic conception of international law, namely, the equal rights of each nation in the family of nations . . . [which is] . . . the chief protection of weak nations against oppression," Secretary Stimson maintained, as had Mr. Hughes, that "independence imposes duties as well as rights." The Latin American states, especially those republics located in the region "which nature has decreed to be most vital to our national safety, not to mention our prosperity" have afforded us, in the hundred years which have ensued since the announcement of our policy, "recurring evidence of how slow is the progress of mankind along that difficult highway which leads to national maturity and how difficult is the art of popular self-government." On occasion necessity compelled "temporary intrusions into the domestic affairs of some of those countries." Except for slight departures, the recognition policy of the United States had been substantially uniform from 1792 to 1913. It was based upon the *de facto* capacity of a government to fulfill its obligations as a member of the family of nations. President Wilson's administration, Mr. Stimson asserted, "radically departed" from this policy with respect to Mexico "in seeking actively to propagate . . . [constitutional institutions] . . . in a foreign country by the direct influence of this Government and to do this against the desire

[40] "Address before the Council on Foreign Relations," New York, February 6, 1931. Publication No. 156, Dept. of State. Latin American Series No. 4.

of the authorities and people of Mexico." Except in the case of the five Central American republics, which is covered by treaty, "the present administration has refused to follow the policy of Mr. Wilson," but has "followed consistently the former practice of this Government since the days of Jefferson."

In the matter of the export of arms and munitions, the Government, when insurrection broke out in Mexico in March, 1929, maintained an embargo upon arms "which might reach the rebels" and at the same time "permitted the sale and itself sold arms . . . to the established government of Mexico." In three months the insurrection was suppressed and the relations of the two countries, hostile "ever since the intervention of President Wilson against Huerta in 1913 . . . became friendly and cordial."

Again, in October, 1930, the United States, making reference to the embargo resolution of Congress, of 1922, as well as the compulsion [41] of a treaty between the United States and twenty Latin American Republics, attempted to perform a similar service for the Government of Brazil when a rebellion broke out in that country. Notwithstanding this aid, the rebellion succeeded, much to the embarrassment of the United States which had been "criticised for 'taking sides in that civil strife' as if we had been under the duty to maintain neutrality between the Brazilian Government and the rebels who were seeking to overthrow it"; the United States was pursuing strictly the precepts of international law. Mr. Stimson implied, though he did not say so, that the situation was clearly only an embarrassment of fact and not of law. In closing his address, he gave full approval to the congressional joint resolution of 1912, enlarged as to its area of operation by the resolution of 1922, placing the right to prohibit the export of arms in the discretionary power of the American President.

With respect to Manchuria, the Hoover administration, in seeking to maintain in substance the open door policy, embracing the territorial integrity and political independence of China,

---

[41] Secretary Stimson used the expression "Between its signatories it [the treaty] rendered compulsory the policy of protecting our Latin American sister republics against the traffic in arms and war material carried on by our nationals. . . ." Address, *op. cit.*

had to face the establishment and stubborn maintenance of the Manchukuo state by the Japanese. The necessity of coöperating with the League of Nations had to be squared with the traditional attitudes of "isolation." So the Paris Pact, renouncing war, became the vehicle for whatever compromises were demanded. To safeguard the open door policy with its implications of respect for the territorial and administrative integrity of China, Mr. Stimson promulgated the "Hoover Doctrine." Serving notice upon both China and Japan, although intended evidently for Japan alone, the American Government took the position that "it can not admit the legality of any situation *de facto* nor does it intend to recognize any treaty or agreement . . . which may impair the treaty rights of the United States . . . including those which relate to the territorial and administrative integrity of the Republic of China, or to the international policy relative to China, commonly known as the open-door policy. . . ." [42] In practice this meant the refusal to recognize the government of Manchukuo.[43]

To justify this "international coöperation" while at the same time "conforming strictly to the American views against foreign entanglements and the use of force to promote peace . . . ," [44] Mr. Stimson, in his address before the conference of the Methodist Episcopal Church at Pittsburgh, held the Paris Pact to mean that "wherever a breach of the treaty is threatened by approaching hostilities, it implies a duty of

[42] For the full course of the diplomatic exchanges during the Sino-Japanese controversy, see *Conditions in Manchuria*, Senate Document No. 55, 72d Cong., 1st Sess. (January 26, 1932)

[43] With this, the United States was actually maintaining three distinct recognition policies as follows: (1) The traditional *de facto* policy; (2) The policy confined by treaty to the five Central American republics under which the parties "shall not recognize any other government which may come into power . . . as a consequence of a *coup d'état,* or of a revolution against the recognized government . . ."; and (3) The "Hoover Doctrine" by which the United State "does not intend to recognize any situation, treaty or agreement which may be brought about by means contrary to the covenants and obligations of the Pact of Paris of August 27, 1928." See *Sen. Doc., ibid.,* p. 54. In view of the moral element involved in the Pact of Paris, the "Hoover Doctrine" does not appear to be very different in substance from the Wilson recognition policy which Mr. Stimson had declared was repudiated by the Republican party.

[44] A position explained by Mr. Stimson in "Bases of American Foreign Policy during the Last Four Years," *Foreign Affairs* (April 1933), Vol. XI, No. 3, pp. 383–396.

consultation among the other parties in order that public opinion may be mobilized against the impending disaster of war." [45]   A few months before, in his speech accepting the nomination, President Hoover had taken the same position. "We shall," he declared, "under the spirit of that pact, consult with other nations in times of emergency to promote world peace." But he immediately added: "We shall enter no agreements committing us to any future course of action or which call for use of force to preserve peace." [46]

The compromises were made not alone in the political field. They appeared in the economic field as well where the desire to follow the official thesis was found to be incompatible with conditions and events. Such views as the following were vigorously reasserted: "We are more economically self-contained than any other great nation . . . [and] . . . we can and will make a large measure of recovery irrespective of the rest of the world." [47] "I am squarely for a protective tariff. . . . I am against . . . proposals to destroy the usefulness of the bipartisan tariff commission. . . ." [48] The war debts "must not be canceled or the burdens transferred to our people." [49] "We have defended the country from being forced off the gold standard. . . ." [50] On the other hand, qualifying sentiments crept into words and deeds. Thus, "we are part of the world, the disturbance of whose remotest populations affects our financial systems, our employment, our markets and prices of our farm products," and ". . . we have joined in the development of a world economic conference to bulwark the whole international fabric of finance, monetary values, and the expansion of world commerce." [51]

After the election was over, President Hoover declared: "We cannot isolate ourselves. During the past two years the crash

---

[45] For the text of the address, see New York *Times*, October 27, 1932, item: "Stimson's Pittsburgh Speech, Hailing Our Aid to Peace."

[46] New York *Times*, August 12, 1932.

[47] President Hoover's Address before the Indiana Republican Editorial Association. Indianapolis. New York *Times*, June 16, 1931.

[48] Acceptance speech.

[49] *Ibid.*

[50] President Hoover's Des Moines address. New York *Times*, October 5, 1932.

[51] Acceptance speech.

of one foreign nation after another . . . has dominated the whole economic life of our country." [52] In the economic war that is now going on, "We will be ourselves forced to defensive action [on tariffs, trade restrictions and currency depreciation] to protect ourselves unless this mad race is stopped." The first point of attack "is to secure assured greater stability in the currencies of the important commercial nations." Some way must be found quickly to bring about the "reëstablishment of gold standards among important nations," and some part of the debt payments due to us might be set aside for temporary use in effecting this purpose.[53] Earlier he had said that the war debts might be reduced if the American people were offered "some other tangible compensation such as the expansion of markets for American agriculture and labor." [54]

Thus, side by side with the attempt to reinstate the old policies of the party of the restoration, there was the attempt to gauge and meet the forces of newer situations. But no policy appeared to rise high enough above the cross currents to contain within itself a consistent, workable, and effective philosophy or program for future guidance. The spirit of uncertainty, commencing with the restoration after Wilson, continued, becoming increasingly more marked as the years passed and as the country was plunged into the economic dislocation that engulfed the world.

In these circumstances, as already indicated, the party of restoration paid a heavy price in the form of concessions for its success in reinstating dollar diplomacy and "isolation" as national interest. As a reward to Japan for her apparent relinquishment of supremacy in China, the United States, at the Washington and London conferences, agreed to naval restrictions which made the Japanese navy supreme in its own waters, and, besides, bound itself not to proceed with the construction of impregnable fortifications in the Philippine Islands. In addition, the United States relinquished the possibility of complete naval superiority over Great Britain and accepted

---

[52] Address at Lincoln Day Dinner of the National Republican Club, New York City. Text in New York *Times,* February 14, 1933.

[53] *Ibid.*

[54] Acceptance Speech.

an equality in ships which left that imperial power dominant in all waters outside the American Hemisphere and the Sea of Japan. To make the surrender of sea power more complete, the Government of the United States failed to build up to the naval ratio established, partly on account of agrarian opposition in Congress. Then under the pressure of peace advocates, it renounced war as an instrument of national policy, agreed to the peaceful settlement of all international disputes, and thus tied its hands by treaty against excursions in commercial expansion, such as the Spanish war, apparently on the assumption that Japan, to take one example of any number, would observe her pledges and abstain from carrying out her designs of dominion in China.

CHANGING CONDITIONS OF COMMERCIAL EXPANSION

In this survey of American commercial expansion and its associated policies [55] the subject has been treated as if no alterations took place in the conditions and processes of international trade, but as a matter of fact both were undergoing revolutionary changes as time passed. Obvious as this should be to everyone, it is necessary to emphasize the point, for there have been so many references to a "world order" and a "system" of international trade that the impression has become quite common that the world political structure is built upon a fixed, stable, or normal condition of ordered economy. Such references are usually accompanied by long discussions about the "recovery" of former conditions, a "return" to "normal" arrangements, or a "re-establishment" of "stability." But the conception of the world as an "order," with its implications of fixity and stability, is not in accord with the facts of social evolution. Viewed in a larger perspective "the world order" is often a world disorder, and speaking of the "system" of international trade does constant violence to the common definition of the word. At best social relationships are in constant flux, in process of evolution, forever becoming something else. In specific conditions and in limited spheres the economies of commerce seem to exhibit and respond to

[55] The last Chapter continues this survey.

certain laws, but these laws are relative and pertinent to the movement of things. When not actually destroyed by realities, the validity of these laws is constantly in doubt.

When the American Republic was established, international commerce was carried on principally among civilized countries dominated by relatively stable governments. Apart from the quest of gold and silver, there was little searching for mineral resources in backward places. Manufacturing economy was, after all, limited to a relatively few commodities; and these consisted chiefly of goods ready for consumption. Competition was severely circumscribed by the mode of production and the character of commodity exchange. With a certain foundation in fact and reason, economists could speak of "the natural course of trade" because the exchange of commodities did consist of goods produced by the private citizens of the participating countries out of the resources found principally within the borders of their own territories and worked up mainly through the labor and skill of the native population.

In the circumstances, national interest, just beginning to emerge as a distinct conception, seemed to demand only "fair" or "equal" trading privileges—privileges which in a large measure were obtained by negotiation and barter in the "natural course of trade," or secured under the pressure of discriminating tariff duties, tonnage rates, and similar measures. There was little occasion for forcible intervention in the domestic concerns of the participating states, such as the blockading of ports in time of peace and the landing of troops to enforce commercial rights, protect property, and maintain order. There was, to be sure, a considerable amount of dislocation in commercial relations on account of incessant wars and internal revolutions, but these dislocations were not continuing obstacles to trade. Moreover, interruptions in the stability of intercourse between state and state were offset by the practice of requiring successor governments to assume the obligations of their predecessors. For a time during the nineteenth century, it looked as if the ancient restrictions on commerce were to be relaxed in favor of a full reciprocity and a generous freedom of commercial relations.

During the early decades of the American Republic, conditions were favorable for the development of this "natural course" economy over a large part of the earth's surface. The state system of Europe was highly developed. The United States was well launched in the way of law and order. Though closed for a long time to foreign commerce, the governments of Japan and China were accounted among the powerful institutions of the world. Within this vast area international traffic could be carried on with a high degree of safety, and discriminations could be combated ordinarily by counter measures of policy, without resort to force. To be sure, the imperial powers of Europe had long been and were continually engaged in military and naval enterprises in backward places, conquering weaker peoples, annexing territories, and monopolizing trading advantages; but there was a span of years extending well beyond the middle of the nineteenth century when there was an unmistakable lull in these activities, and when the wisdom and profit of engaging in them was distinctly in doubt. The United States, just launched on a national career and with an immense continent to win and develop, was not prepared by its intellectual heritage or by the stage of its economy for extensive undertakings in the realm of overseas conquests and annexations. Those goods which it had to turn into the stream of international trade flowed with relative ease to ready markets. It did not have a vast surplus of manufactures to export; and it was a borrowing, not a lending, country.

For a long time the foreign trade of the United States was largely confined to the reasonably well settled places of the earth where stable governments afforded a fair degree of protection to persons and property engaged in mercantile transactions.[56] It was seldom necessary to clothe acts of policy involving national interest in the forms of force and violence. Although leaders in the early days of our Republic well understood the rôle of force, potential and actual, in executing policies of national interest, the occasions for applying the doctrine were not frequent. Had it not been for the preoccupation of the people and capital with the westward expansion and with

---

[56] Even as late as the period 1876–1880, of the total United States trade with all foreign countries, 83.1 per cent of its exports and 50.3 per cent of its general imports were transactions with the countries of the Old World.

development on this continent, the occasions would have multiplied rapidly as the nineteenth century advanced; but that
preoccupation was a fact of immense significance in determining America's trade with the rest of the world. So it turned
out that for many years American overseas commerce followed
with a high degree of regularity the "natural" course. There
were, to be sure, Mediterranean pirates to be suppressed and
brushes now and then on the coasts of Africa and in distant
islands, but they were unhappy incidents in commercial expansion rather than the fruits of any large policy of national
interest, deliberately framed and pursued with minute calculation.[57]

Until near the middle of the nineteenth century, and in many
regions until long afterward, the countries participating in
international commerce were predominantly agricultural in
economy and ruled by agricultural classes with an eye to their
own interest. The production of manufactured commodities
was a minor concern and in a primitive state, even in England
for a long time after the beginnings of the first mechanical
revolution. The idea of trade was a fair exchange of reciprocally useful commodities. It was clearly and effectively
stated by Benjamin Franklin: "Fair commerce is where equal
values are exchanged for equal values, the expense of transportation included. Thus if it cost A in England as much labor
and charge to raise a bushel of wheat as it costs B in France
to produce four gallons of wine, then are four gallons of wine
the fair exchange for a bushel of wheat; A and B meeting at
half-distance with their commodities to make the exchange.
The advantage of fair commerce is, that each party increases
the number of his enjoyments, having, instead of wheat alone,
or wine alone, the use of both wheat and wine." Thus the
dominating conception was a simple exchange of values, expressed in mutually desired commodities which neither coun-

---

[57] The story of the Barbary pirates is well known and needs no mention
here. After the natives of Quallah Battoo in Sumatra, angered by American
trading methods, attacked the *Friendship* of Salem, Massachusetts, in 1830,
they were severely punished by the United States Frigate *Potomac*, dispatched
to exact reparations. Dennett, *op. cit.*, p. 31. Commodore Perry relates
(1852) that in the course of duty off the coasts of Mexico and Africa it fell
to his lot "to subjugate many towns and communities." Hawks, *op. cit.*, p. 106.

try alone possessed, and not the accumulation of profits in the hands of operators and promoters.

Under the handicraft system and even the early mechanical system, mass production in a huge and swelling volume was out of the question. Differences in climate, soil, and stages of economic development gave to the several countries many positive differences in requirements and products, which made exchange of mutual advantage and justified economists in speaking of "the natural course" of commerce. In every case the volume of goods to be offered in foreign markets was small in comparison with the total domestic trade. Raw materials and innumerable products now indispensable to machine and chemical industry were unknown. Production did not rise swiftly under the pressure of technology and profit-making enterprises, but rose so slowly, in comparison with the sheer want of material goods, that exchange could easily maintain a fairly even balance. The imperial practice of conquering backward peoples wholesale, exploiting their natural resources, and raising their standards of life was as yet an idea in embryo and its enormous potentialities were but dimly foreshadowed. Such were the primitive and relatively stable conditions under which the expansion of American commerce began.

But in the long course of this commercial expansion, the conditions of exchange and production were revolutionized. Regions, such as China, where social order was once maintained under strong government, and even large parts of South America, were Balkanized and were broken down into contending and unstable factions. Elsewhere, as in Africa, large areas formerly under little control other than tribal power were brought within the orbit of what is termed "western civilization." Territories pursuing a course of native exclusiveness— "isolation"—were "opened up" to trade and commerce. Spheres of interest and of influence and other monopolies were staked out by governments acting in the interests of their nationals. Invention and the changing character of productive processes and enterprise transformed the industrial arts. Where individuals once owned the means of production and managed the processes of exchange, powerful corporations, anomalous entities within the state, rendered truly prodigious by forms of concentration, began to operate on a large scale, bringing pressure to bear upon foreign governments, within whose jurisdiction they carried on business, and upon their own governments at home. In these later stages of commercial expansion also, the banker and finance capitalist entered the scene. They made loans to foreign governments and political subdivisions and invested in foreign industrial and commercial undertakings. Vast political and social changes both within and between governments also contributed to affect commodity exchange and production.

Along with the activities of bankers and the growth of corporate enterprise in commercial expansion, the business of commodity exchange was supplemented by control practices. American companies, for example, which once had all their plants inside the United States, extended their operations to foreign countries directly by acquiring vast natural properties, buying up or building productive plants, operating in and developing markets. A veritable revolution in the substance and practice of foreign trade took place, requiring adjustments in policy.

In establishing the plants abroad themselves instead of confining their productive activities to industrial plants within the United States and shipping the products abroad, American economic enterprises "exported" not consumption products so much as the equipment, the production technique, and the managerial skill of an industrial process that had reached a high stage of development in the United States. This phenomenon, sometimes referred to as the "branch factory movement," and as "the new export technique," was different, therefore, in two important respects from the historic conception of export: (1) It was not primarily concerned with the export of goods for ultimate consumption—"consumers' goods"; and (2) the control and utilization of that which was "exported" remained largely in American hands after reaching the countries of destination. With some exceptions, it was a movement such as the removal of a Massachusetts textile plant to Georgia rather than a shipment of cotton fabrics from a factory in Lawrence to a department store in Atlanta. In the one case the "producers' goods" move once and for all;

in the other, there is a continuing relation in the trade of "consumers' goods."

Besides interest in control, other considerations were involved in this phenomenon.[58] The broad reasons for that extraordinary activity, aside from the continuous element of profit-seeking, appear to be chiefly a desire to insure a supply and full control of raw materials, an effort to retain or exploit foreign markets, a struggle for lower costs of production, and the constant tendency toward greater productive efficiency.

This form of expansion has gone through several phases, dating approximately from the last quarter of the nineteenth century. Activity on the part of American interests in this field since 1900 has been particularly broad and increasingly world-wide, especially marked in Canada, South America, and even in some of the most advanced industrial countries in Europe. There has been considerable discussion of the effect of the movement on the "home" economy; and there are many individuals, speaking from some conception of the national interest, who declare that the movement is beneficial, while others, having different conceptions of the national interest, maintain that the movement is detrimental. No detailed or complete study of the phenomenon has been made. To come to any reliable judgment on the subject a careful analysis and a complicated balance-sheet would have to be made. The purpose in mentioning the movement here is not to determine its true relation to any particular conception of national interest, but to note the existence of the phenomenon within the changing structure of economic activities.[59]

All these conditions of commodity exchange and production were accompanied by other phenomena which made the "normal" or "natural" course of exchange increasingly difficult, if not completely impossible. A practice of active intervention in the affairs of other countries, involving the employment of political, military, and naval power, was entered upon by

[58] These effects are suggested but not discussed in a governmental study of the movement. See *American Branch Factories Abroad,* Sen. Doc. 258, 71st Cong., 3d Sess. (1931) Washington Printing Office.

[59] For further information on this subject, see the material in the Appendix below.

governments on behalf of the lives, property interests, and trade of their nationals. The rivalry of trade often became a rivalry of governments, of peoples, and of factions, with frequent wars, domestic and foreign, as something of an inevitable consequence. An economy of profit-accumulation seemed to supplant an economy of use, so that the face of the earth was transformed and the conditions and processes on which international trade was once predicated were simply turned upside down and inside out.

Finally we come to the last phase of commercial evolution, the internationalization of capitalist undertakings. All competent students of capital investment agree that it is now extremely difficult, if not impossible, to discover with mathematical accuracy just how extensive are American interests in foreign countries. Although a minute study of a particular issue of stock and bonds may disclose the exact distribution of holdings at a given moment, few such studies have been made; indeed the data for them are difficult to disclose; and at best they are only valid for a specified hour. The stocks and bonds of the world's great capitalistic concerns are continuously traded on all the leading exchanges. Even though an issue floated by an American concern may be all sold to American citizens, it is likely to be speedily broken up and scattered far and wide among the investors of foreign countries. On the other hand, American capitalists invest in the internal bonds of foreign governments and in the stocks and bonds of foreign concerns. The best that can be done to ascertain or appraise what may be termed the American "stake" abroad amounts to little more than an estimate which must be highly tentative, and even then taken broadly and with a considerable allowance for error.

In short, a movement of forces invalidated the simple theory of international trade which was formulated with reference to differences among countries in respect of climate, soil, crude natural resources, and inherited crafts. Governments which were once thought to be stable were found to be crumbling structures. Countries which were supposed to be destined primarily to agriculture and to produce food stuffs and raw materials for manufacturing nations went into manufacturing themselves. The stability of international exchange based on climate, soil, materials, and native skill was destroyed by the spread and redistribution of industry and productive power. The mutuality of interest arising from the exchange of commodities of reciprocal advantage was transformed into a bitter struggle for outlets and profits. All civilized countries showed a tendency, swift or slow, to become industrial countries, to engage in manufacturing and selling the same standardized products of the machine. For the low productive capacity of early industry, which kept exchange on a fairly even basis, was substituted unlimited mass production, which expanded with feverish rapidity, violently upsetting the course of reciprocal commodity exchange and making a return to primitive stability on the old terms entirely out of the question. And from private enterprise, the fever of expansion was communicated to politicians and governments, dragging all the engines of state into a world of swelling, tossing, and clashing commercial interests.

Only within severe limits, therefore, is the theory of the "natural course" any longer sound. Climate remains fairly fixed; Sweden is not likely to engage in growing oranges on a large scale. The distribution of basic materials—coal, iron, oil, and platinum, for example—does not conform to national boundaries; some countries are rich in them; others are poor, indeed utterly devoid of them. Yet with reference to the broad hypothesis of the "natural course," science and technology have made a fundamental revolution. They provide substitutes for basic raw materials by the manufacture of artificial silk or the supply of nitrogen through the fixation processes which make the world independent, if need be, of the natural nitrates of Chile. Technological knowledge and managerial skill, unlike historic handicrafts, are not monopolies or "mysteries," as the old crafts were called; they may be readily acquired by peoples long accustomed to primitive economy. The spinning mills of India, China, and Japan, if not as efficient as the best mills of the West, are efficient enough to supply the markets of their respective areas. The moist atmosphere of Manchester, so favorable to fine spinning, can be artificially reproduced; indeed can be steadied and improved upon by scientific methods. Even "native skill" itself, equally important with natural resources and supposedly an established factor in determining the economic status and trade advantages of particular countries, has begun to yield its superiority to science, invention, and modern technology. If in many cases the costs of artificial stimulus are high, they are often felt to be more than offset by the savings in the high costs of long-distance transportation, more effective control, and similar compensating factors.

Again, technology and science, which are merely at the beginning of their voyage of discovery, are inescapably international in their operations. Their findings are described in the language of mathematics and precision, which is a universal language, and are spread with lightning rapidity to the four corners of the earth. Particular "trade secrets," protected by patents, may indeed be safeguarded and exploited for a time in some particular community. But the vast body of scientific literature is open to the scientists of the whole world. The problems of science are known to the scientists of every civilized nation and a discovery in one place may be independently duplicated in a distant laboratory at any moment. In other words, this new and revolutionary element in international economic relations, like the general body of knowledge and ideas which is today spread rapidly and widely throughout the world, utterly ignores state boundaries.

Even if science and technology were parochial in nature, international capitalism would operate to destroy their provincialism; the capitalists of industrial countries sell to potential competitors the perfected machinery which enables the latter to undo any monopoly enjoyed by the former. American capitalists sell machinery to communist Russia, send technologists to build and operate industries for the service of the latter. Hence there can be no doubt that science and technology have introduced revolutionary elements into the field of international commercial exchange—elements which counteract and break down the simple factors of "natural" differences in economy upon which the "natural course of trade" was predicated in the early years of the nineteenth century.

Theories of state interest and progress, based upon a given superiority at a particular moment in certain resources and industrial skills, are no longer adequate, no longer correspond to the realities of the economic world. That theory of national interest, for example, which requires the country adopting it to safeguard its superiorities by various engines of state, to push vigorously in all parts of the world the commerce founded upon its superiorities, and to hold down or beat back rising competitors who threaten its quasi-monopolistic position, is severely strained, if not completely invalidated, by these stubborn realities. In the early stages of the industrial revolution, England was able to proceed on this course with a high degree of success—a success which deluded other countries into the belief that a particular rule might become universal. But the value of England's natural resources has been sharply discounted, and her technological superiority is lost; while the very attempt to build up and maintain her position has raised up a host of emulators, each aggressively seeking the same ends, using much the same methods, and each apparently checkmating the efforts of the others, with the action of them all doubling back not only to restrain England's course, but also to slow down the very system in which all operate.

The great managerial outcome of science, technology, and mass production—planning—introduces disturbing factors into the international exchange of material goods. Conceivably a highly-developed country, such as the United States, could by a closely integrated system of economy produce most of the standard commodities of the world's use at a cost so low that nothing short of tariff prohibitions could prevent it from ruining the industries of other countries not so favorably situated with respect to resources and domestic markets. Scientific management and its logical outcome, planned economy, whether state or corporate, are operating forces of immense potentiality destined to make the theory of national interest in the "natural" course of trade look almost as unreal as the Ptolemaic conception of the physical universe. Although particularity and exclusiveness in natural resources, in other physical conditions, and in native skill, are not wholly levelled down or eliminated—Germany, for example, may maintain for years a preëminence in dyestuffs and optical instruments and the United States in typewriters, office appliances, and the like—

the trend of trade according to the "natural course" has moved far from the simple circumstances of its origin, and economics has not yet revealed a synthesis capable of forming a new foundation for international economic relations.

CHANGING THEORIES OF ECONOMY AND STATECRAFT

The evolution of theories of political economy and statecraft has followed roughly the course of economic movement. Broadly speaking the policies of Western governments with respect to commercial expansion fall into five stages. The first, practised somewhat as early as the fourteenth century, but formulated and widely influential from the sixteenth through the eighteenth century, may be characterized as mercantilism. Assuming the utility of possessing the precious metals, and emphasizing foreign as against domestic trade, it meant government interference in manufacturing and shipping for the purpose of promoting trade to gain national advantages. This policy is best exemplified in the program elaborated under Richelieu, Mazarin, and Colbert in France and in the British colonial system, against which the American revolution was a violent protest.

The second stage, far less universal, in fact largely confined to Great Britain, was characterized by *laissez faire* in domestic economy and free trade in world markets. Espoused by Adam Smith and spread largely by the Manchester school of economists, the doctrine upon which it was founded, though never carried to its logical limits and constantly violated by the use of the British navy to control "the natural course of free trade," for a long time widely dominated economic thinking and influenced economic practice and political policy. Intended at first to be applied specifically to trade, it was carried into every aspect of economic activity. Maintaining not only that the individual has a right to an unrestricted range of economic enterprise, but also that such freedom is the best method of promoting the prosperity and advancement of the nation, advocates of the doctrine sought the removal of all governmental interference and the confinement of political action and public regulation to the simple maintenance of law and order. Hope for a final and "natural course of trade" took its rise and found favorable conditions for a time under the sway of *laissez faire*. Even in the United States, where the creed was never fully adopted, it exerted a profound influence on economic speculation.

The third stage of commercial policy was marked by an increasing use of political agencies to stimulate, promote, and protect industrial and trading operations at home and abroad. It was to some extent a combination of mercantilism and *laissez faire*, having a number of the characteristics of each but neither wholly the one nor the other. Its signs were tariffs, subsidies, bounties and other aids to industry and shipping, the use of consular and commercial agents to push commodities in foreign markets, the employment of diplomatic intervention in the interest of nationals to gain markets, contracts, and concessions, and the use of navies in backward places to protect merchants and compel compliance on the part of local authorities to economic demands. During this period of historical development it was deemed proper to employ war as an instrument of national policy in acquiring imperial possessions, concessions, and protectorates, with a view to more or less exclusive national advantages in the markets thus conquered by arms. In other words, all the engines of taxation, privileges, financial aid, diplomatic intervention, and physical violence were thrown on the side of manufacturers and merchants, on the assumption that national interest was thereby substantially served. Thus the pecuniary advantages of their nationals were made the interests of governments, and the conflicts of private persons became the conflicts of states.

Before the third phase in the evolution of governmental policy with respect to commercial expansion had been fairly perfected, emphasis on a new factor in international economy, namely, investment promotion, reached such a point of command as to mark a fourth stage in political economy. In this new régime, governments not only intervened to secure investment opportunities for their nationals, but began to make promises and commitments in behalf of loans and advances of money which took on the nature of state guarantees, in fact, if not in theory. It is true that no definite date marks the transition, but the identification of government with investment enterprise became so great that the multiplication of departures from ancient practices constituted an epoch in commercial expansion and state theory.

With the growing involution of economics and politics, a fifth stage in the development of policy was reached as the twentieth century wore on—the beginning of planned economy and controlled international exchange. The origins of this system of thought may be traced far back into the nineteenth century, to the writings of Charles Babbage; and its unfolding runs through the limited system of scientific management associated with the name of Frederick Winslow Taylor, through the *Planwirtschaft* of Rathenau devised in Germany during the World War, through the War Industries Board in the United States, through the efforts at wholesale national planning attempted in Soviet Russia, and into the administration of the National Industrial Recovery Act. As governments, through their banking and financial affiliations, through their loans, stock purchases, and other activities, and through their attempts to uphold capitalist structures during the crisis which followed the World War, became more and more deeply entangled in their respective social orders, integration and supervision in economy were made increasingly necessary. From domestic economy, control spread to foreign trade through elaborate forms of licensing and quota systems and specific agreements for commodity exchange, such as were formulated at the British imperial conference at Ottawa in the summer of 1932; and to forms of monetary stabilization and control such as the equalization fund of the Bank of England.

Thus efforts to formulate conceptions of national interest upon an assumption that world economy is an "order" or "system" in which international economic and political relationships operate in a fixed, schematic framework were countered by disruptive forces and evolving forms as real, as "natural" and as "normal," as "normalcy" itself. It is not necessary to go all the way back to Heraclitus and declare the universe to be nothing except flux, but a survey of commercial expansion and its shadowing policies inexorably establishes the fact that conceptions of national interest in detail were being continuously challenged by events in the course of world economic development.

SUMMARY

Notwithstanding the popular belief that events during the closing years of the nineteenth century marked a "new era"—the rise of the United States as a world power—the facts in the case warrant no such arbitrary break in the history of the country. Commercial expansion, accompanied by appropriate diplomatic and naval policies, formed one of the prime considerations of national interest as conceived by founders of the Republic. And after the Constitution was put into effect, the course of commercial expansion was firmly pursued by the Federal Government.

On the importance of commerce as a phase of national interest both political parties were agreed. Their difference pertained to the content of that commerce and the policies to be applied in connection with it. The Jeffersonians, as agrarians, were long primarily concerned with obtaining markets for their agricultural produce and securing manufactured products at the lowest cost. Despite fluctuations due to peculiar circumstances, they displayed a strong aversion to purely commercial undertakings, aids to shipping, banking affiliations, obstructions placed by tariffs and other measures in the way of "natural" trade, the upbuilding of a powerful navy, and the acquisition of distant territories as supports for overseas trade. The Federalist-Whig-Republican succession, on the other hand, sought to change the structure of internal economy by affording protection to manufacturing, and openly espoused the vigorous promotion of commercial expansion by lending aid to shipping, the construction and use of an effective navy, the acquisition of naval bases and points of trade support, the creation of special agencies of diplomacy and commercial pressure, the use of force in distant places as well as nearer home in aid of private enterprise, and a frank recognition of the system later known as "dollar diplomacy."

In the course of this commercial expansion, the Government of the United States appears at times as an agent responding to the demands and importunities of private interests and at times as a director bidding for the support of private interests by making tenders of assistance and lending aid to particular individuals and concerns. So involved were these relations of Government and Economy that it is difficult to discover where one began and the other ended, whether the initiative came from the one side or the other. But whatever the source or origin of government action on behalf of commercial expansion, such action was justified on the ground of "national interest."

In the official papers which accompanied this development of policy in connection with commercial expansion, there appears no comprehensive statement covering the meaning of national interest as the term is employed. Nowhere is there a reasoned analysis of the content of the conception, except in respect of the broad antagonism between agricultural and commercial interests. At no point was a transcendent philosophy of national interest set up as the supreme benchmark for determining the relation of lesser and particular interests to the whole, unless *laissez faire* and dollar diplomacy may be so dignified.

The conception of national interest revealed in the state papers is an aggregation of particularities assembled like eggs in a basket. Markets for agricultural produce were in the national interest; markets for industrial commodities were in the national interest; naval bases, territorial acquisitions for commercial support, an enlarged consular and diplomatic service, an increased navy and merchant marine, and occasional wars were all in the national interest. These contentions were not proved; they were asserted as axioms, apparently regarded as so obvious as to call for no demonstration.

In the background, through the years, ran swift changes in the economy on which commercial expansion rested and the world conditions in which it operated. In the early years, the countries involved were what Erich Zimmermann calls "vegetable civilizations" in contrast with "mineral civilizations"; they were mainly engaged in producing and shipping biological products, more or less refashioned by machinery and labor. Trade consisted principally in the exchange of reciprocally useful commodities produced by countries having differences of climate, soil, and skills. Trade did follow a certain "natural" course. But in due time science and technology worked a revolution in "natural" industry. New inventions, new processes, new commodities, new agencies of economic administration, especially the corporation, and new methods of organizing, financing, and carrying on business appeared at an increasing tempo. To trade was added the quest for privileges, investment opportunities, concessions, and special rights—accompanied by active intervention, by political, military, and naval aids to private enterprise, by ever sharpening rivalries of governments over economic advantage, with consequent wars and internal dislocations. But all these shifts in the nature of the things and patterns of conduct covered by the conception of national interest made little or no difference in the use and application of the term. It still remained the chief formula of diplomacy.

CHAPTER VI

ILLUSTRATIONS OF NATIONAL INTEREST IN ACTION

THE broad outlines of national interest in commercial expansion previously drawn, even if accurate and precise, do not go far in presenting the actualities of policy or the mechanics of its execution. Here as elsewhere generalizations have meaning only when they are illuminated by reference to concrete events embedded in their underlying content. In a strict sense, therefore, it is only when the ultimate realities of the particular cases constituting the sum of national interest in official practice are brought within the circle of minute examination and viewed in the order of their inherent relations that the nature of the dogma can be discovered and made to stand forth as objective occurrence and experience. This much may be said with safety, even though Berkeley's denial of abstractions be rejected by philosophers.[1]

Yet the task here suggested is obviously impossible of practical performance. The pursuit of national interest has involved innumerable private activities—negotiations for concessions, commercial privileges, investment opportunities, and other economic advantages. It has likewise included innumerable official conversations, promises, demands, and orders. The influence of an immense number and variety of forces of a kind difficult to perceive, impossible to measure or describe, and soon obliterated by time, enters into the relevant situations and shapes the course of events. Of many operations, even those highly important in nature, no record was made and little or nothing can be known about them. Where documentary evidence of specific events has been kept, it is seldom complete and by no means always open to the scrutiny of a mere scien-

[1] Bertrand Russell, *The Nature of Intelligence,* p. 214.

tific inquirer, whether in private or public archives. It is an old story: all the relevant data of the whole problem or any partial aspect cannot be assembled or known. Obviously, then, the only recourse left open is the illustration of national interest as officially conceived by a minute description of some narrow area or areas of operations concerning which authentic and plentiful material is available.

THE DIPLOMACY OF NATIONAL INTEREST IN NICARAGUA
(1909–1912)

Of all such limited areas perhaps the best for purposes of illustration is that of American procedure in, and with reference to, Nicaragua from 1909 to 1912. Voluminous papers bearing on the subject have been published by the Department of State. Contests in Congress over executive and naval actions have led to investigations and have developed detailed testimony respecting the primary things and occurrences of the total situation in the chosen area of time and space. In other words, it is possible to secure a minute and fairly accurate picture of the realities of national interest as pursued by citizens and the Government of the United States in Nicaragua during this particular period.

The background of the scene is Nicaragua in 1909. It was at that time an independent country about the size of the state of New York, inhabited mainly by Indians, Negroes, and mixed races, with a white population amounting to approximately one-eighth of the total.[2] Primitive in economy, its immigration from Europe and the United States was almost negligible. Most of its roads were mere trails, and communication between the different sections was slow and hazardous. Managua, the capital city, had an estimated population slightly in excess of 30,000. The population of Bluefields, one of the principal Atlantic (or Caribbean) seaports, was placed at 5,000.[3] Its industries were few in number and unimportant.

---

[2] Estimates of the population placed the total in 1905 at 550,000; and in 1913, at 689,891.

[3] The importance of Bluefields did not depend upon the size or population of the city, but upon its location in relation to water-borne commerce, and especially upon the deep water facilities of the port and the surrounding area.

Mineral and timber resources, though abundant, were in a low state of development. Agriculture was the chief occupation of the people, and while for the most part primitive in character it supplied coffee, sugar, cocoa, and fruits for which the United States provided a favorable market. In effect, the government of Nicaragua, if nominally constitutional, was a dictatorship under the direction of José Santos Zelaya who, as a student of Caribbean affairs has said, sold concessions "for almost any privilege, which international-gambler investors would buy, censored the press, and imposed heavy and oppressive taxes on both exports and imports," thus interfering arbitrarily with the course of foreign trade.[4]

AMERICAN INTEREST IN NICARAGUA

In 1909 the American private economic interests in Nicaragua fell into certain broad classes.

The first included individuals and concerns engaged in operating plantations. In the field of industry and commerce there were a number of American concerns actively interested in Nicaraguan affairs. Prominent among them was the George D. Emery Company which had secured from Zelaya a lumber concession. According to the specifications of the original contract the Company paid $30,000 flat for its rights, and agreed to pay $10,000 a year plus additional sums in the nature of a royalty of $1.00 for each log cut in the course of its operations. In addition, it obligated itself to plant two trees for every one cut within its area of exploitation. After the Company had

Its possibilities to the American fruit industry and other enterprises were evident even as early as 1910. Inhabited principally by the Mosquito Indians, the extent of its population in 1909 was evidently considered to be of such relative insignificance as to be treated by "estimates" rather than exact calculations in many compendiums of facts and even in official reports and geographical studies. Thus in W. H. Koebel, *Central America*, p. 216, it is written of Bluefields: ". . . its population . . . probably does not exceed 6,000." Latest census figures give the population a total of 4,706. The point is of no special importance except as to the many inferences which may be drawn from the relation between commercial and political exploitation and "backward" places and peoples.

[4] C. L. Jones, *Caribbean Interests of the United States*, p. 176. See also *The United States and Nicaragua*, Publication of the United States Department of State, Latin American Series No. 6, Washington, D. C., 1932, p. 6.

been under way for some time it fell into a dispute with Zelaya. He claimed that it was not planting trees as required by the contract, and it insisted that its obligations in that respect were being duly observed. After some controversy, the government of Nicaragua cancelled the concession and the Company, which had been making an annual profit ranging from $170,000 to $180,000, filed claims for damages amounting, it appears, to $100,000.[5]

On the assumption of national interest, the Government of the United States took up the claim of the Emery Company against Nicaragua and pressed for a settlement. After prolix negotiations, the Secretary of State, Philander C. Knox, secured a treaty with Nicaragua on May 25, 1909, in which an agreement was reached to submit the dispute to arbitration by a special tribunal, the expenses of which were to be equally shared by the two governments.[6] The tribunal was duly appointed and rendered a verdict on September 18, 1909, awarding to the United States of America "for and in behalf of the George D. Emery Company" the sum of $600,000 gold, to be paid in installments, in return for a complete release of all its claims against Nicaragua.[7] But before the transaction was completed by payment, revolution broke out in Nicaragua, leaving this claim as one of the vested interests considered in the diplomacy which accompanied and followed the upheaval.

A second American interest in Nicaragua was "the United States-Nicaragua Concession," held by a Pittsburgh concern. So far as later claims against Nicaragua were concerned this seems to have been the most important American interest in that country. It was a mining concession covering 6,000 square miles and operated on a royalty basis.[8] Important American citizens were connected with it, including the Fletcher family; [9] and Philander C. Knox, in his capacity as

---

[5] *Hearings before the Subcommittee of the Committee on Foreign Relations. . . . Pursuant to S. Con. Res. 15* (1927), p. 26, hereinafter cited as *Hearings, Senate For. Rels. Com.* (1927).

[6] *Foreign Relations of the United States* (1909), p. 460, hereinafter cited as *Foreign Relations* with the appropriate year in parenthesis.

[7] *Foreign Relations* (1909), p. 465.

[8] *Hearings, Sen. For. Rels. Com.* (1927), p. 43.

[9] *Ibid.*, p. 43.

a lawyer, had formerly served as counsel for the Company and had passed upon the validity of the original agreement.[10] Like the Emery Company, the United States-Nicaragua concern became involved in difficulties with Zelaya who insisted that the grant was objectionable and wished to cancel it, in the hope, it was asserted, of re-selling the concession on more favorable terms.[11] This dispute was also pending when the revolution against Zelaya broke out and the American rights asserted under the concession constituted the largest claim to be settled after Zelaya was overthrown by arms.[12] In fact, the American consul at Bluefields during the disturbance, Thomas P. Moffat, declared at a Senate committee hearing that this claim was "the cause of the desire to eliminate Zelaya." [13]

A closely related American interest in Nicaragua was the La Luz and Los Angeles Mining Company (engaged in operating the United States-Nicaragua concession). If the testimony of the United States consul in Bluefields at the time is to be accepted, the Company was "under the control of the Fletcher family" and the Knox "interests." [14] At all events, John Martin, the husband of the former Miss Fletcher, was resident manager of the Company in Bluefields. During the revolution in Nicaragua, he advised installing the local secretary of the Company, Adolfo Diaz, in the presidency of the Republic, and told the American consul that his future promotion would be assured if he would "put Adolfo over the line there." [15]

Such was the situation in Nicaragua in 1909 when diplomacy in defense of American interests was put into active operation by the Secretary of State, Philander C. Knox. American citizens and business concerns had large outstanding claims against the Nicaraguan government; their operations were subjected to adverse interference on the part of Zelaya; losses had been incurred, and prospective profits had been seriously endangered. No satisfactory headway could be made while he

[10] *Ibid.*, p. 62.
[11] *Ibid.*, p. 43.
[12] *Ibid.*, p. 42.
[13] *Ibid.*, p. 42.
[14] *Ibid.*, p. 35.
[15] *Ibid.*, p. 36.

remained in power. Here were substantial, measurable reasons why American interests desired a change in political affairs and the establishment of a government in Nicaragua more compliant with American claims and demands. And as constantly happens in certain Latin-American regions, there was a great deal of discontent among the natives, civilian and military, which furnished the fuel for a quick revolutionary outburst.

In October, 1909 the revolution came. Early in the month the American consul at Bluefields informed the State Department in Washington that he had received secret information on the subject, that in his opinion a revolution would start in Bluefields on the 8th, that a provisional government would be set up, and that appeal for recognition would be made immediately to Washington. A few days later the consul announced the revolution as a fact and stated that the new government was "friendly to American interests," that the tariff was to be reduced, that all concessions not owned by foreigners were to be cancelled, and that "the foreign business interests are jubilant." [16]

During the struggle which ensued between President Zelaya and the revolutionary government set up at Bluefields under the provisional presidency of Juan J. Estrada, Secretary Knox wrote a sharp note on Zelaya's policy and terminated official relations with his diplomatic representative in Washington.[17] In this attack on the President of Nicaragua, Secretary Knox accused him of keeping Central America in turmoil, putting an end to republican institutions in his own country, throttling the press and public opinion, rewarding with prison "any tendency to real patriotism," placing a blot on the history of his people, executing two American citizens in a barbarous manner, menacing the American consulate in Managua, and offering no promise of protection for "American interests." "The Government of the United States," the note asserted, "is convinced that the revolution represents the ideals and the will of a majority of the Nicaraguan people more faithfully than does the Government of President Zelaya, and that its peaceable

---

[16] *Foreign Relations* (1909), p. 454.
[17] *Ibid.*, (1909), pp. 455ff.

control is well-nigh as extensive as that hitherto so sternly attempted by the government at Managua." Having disposed of Zelaya in this summary fashion, Secretary Knox severed formal relations with his government. At the same time he informed the government of Nicaragua, as well as the leaders of the revolution, that the United States would hold it strictly accountable "for the protection of American life and property" and would take such steps as it deemed "wise and proper to protect American interest."

Long afterward the curtain was raised, by a Senate investigation and the publication of state papers, on the inner history of the revolution, and it was made known that American citizens and officials in Nicaragua had aided in fomenting and carrying through the uprising against President Zelaya. A former official of Nicaragua testified before the Senate committee that "this revolution was supplied with money and arms by Americans." Pressed for details, he named Bellanger and Company as one of the participants in the transaction, and declared that Adolfo Diaz, an employee of the La Luz and Los Angeles Company, an American concern, filed a claim for $600,000 against the Nicaraguan government for money furnished by himself to the revolution, when "in fact everybody knows in Nicaragua that it was supplied by American interests in the United States." [18]

This statement, which may be discounted as *ex parte* testimony in behalf of Nicaragua, is supplemented by other evidence. A number of diplomatic documents show that two American citizens, Le Roy Cannon and Leonard Groce, were active among the revolutionists as "dynamiters," and were captured and shot by Zelaya's forces.[19] The American consul at Bluefields, Thomas P. Moffat, later testified at a Senate investigation that shortly after his arrival at his post he heard intimations that American officials before him and naval officers had been suggesting to the people that they "get up and get rid of Zelaya" and had been making promises of some kind to them. He added that he had noticed Adolfo Diaz engaged in the conferences and discussions which preceded the

---

[18] *Hearings, Sen. For. Rels. Com.* (1927), p. 2.
[19] *Foreign Relations* (1909), pp. 452ff.

uprising.[20] Two revolutionary leaders, Estrada and Diaz, told Mr. Moffat "that some of our [American] naval officers had said, 'Now, some of the Americans at home are not satisfied with some of the concessions that are being interfered with, and Zelaya, they think, ought to be put out. They would be very glad to see him go out.' And Estrada said he asked, 'Well, what would be the attitude of the American Government? Would it [revolution] be supported or not?' They told him to go ahead: 'You will get the support.' " [21]

Whether these promises were made or not, official support for the revolution was certainly afforded by the Government of the United States soon after the uprising was started. When Zelaya's army approached Bluefields for the purpose of suppressing the insurrection there, General Estrada, in charge of the revolution in the city, told the American consul, Mr. Moffat, that he was unable to overcome the advancing troops with the forces at his command, and that they would loot the town, in case they entered it, because they "feel that the Americans have started this revolution." The consul replied that this would mean an enormous loss to the foreign interests, the Americans alone having about $2,000,000 worth of supplies in Bluefield, and that protection should be provided. Accordingly, the consul cabled the State Department and consulted "with different businessmen and they said, yes." [22] In due course American forces under Major Smedley Butler arrived on the scene and "the situation cleared up in Bluefields," that is, Zelaya's efforts to put down the revolution were checked by the appearance of American troops. In these circumstances the uprising was successful at the point of inception.

Stripped of authority in Bluefields, President Zelaya issued a manifesto to the National Assembly at Managua and tendered his resignation. In this message he ascribed the chief responsibility for the revolution to "the hostile attitude of a powerful nation which, against all right, intervened in our political affairs and publicly furnished the rebels with all the aid which they have asked for"—to employ his phrasing of the case. Ex-

[20] *Hearings, Sen. For. Rels. Com.* (1927), p. 33.
[21] *Ibid.*, p. 34.
[22] *Ibid.*, p. 34.

pressing a desire to contribute to the good of Nicaragua and the establishment of peace and to end "the hostility manifested by the American Government," he deposited his power with the Assembly and proposed the designation of a successor in conformity with the terms of the constitution.[23] Without any express objection on the part of the United States—a position which, President Taft declared, "equally implied no approval or acquiescence"—Zelaya found refuge on board a Mexican war vessel and was taken out of the country.

Zelaya's successor, Dr. José Madriz, unanimously designated by the Nicaraguan Congress, now proposed a truce with the revolutionary leaders and sought a settlement by conference; but the latter refused to abide by the action of the Congress and insisted on treating Madriz as a "usurper of the rights of the people." [24] Defeated in this attempt at pacification, Madriz for a time continued the unequal struggle. His government purchased at New Orleans a British vessel, loaded it with guns and ammunition, and, after fitting it out as a war ship at San Juan del Norte, tried to blockade the port of Bluefields with the design of preventing, as President Madriz put the case, "the revolution from continuing to receive, as before, arms, supplies, and funds from New Orleans." [25] After the troops of Madriz stormed the Bluff commanding Bluefields and his new war vessel prepared to blockade the harbor, the Government of the United States intervened, forbade fighting in Bluefields, kept the port open for supplies destined to the revolutionists, compelled the payment of customs to the latter, and informed the Madriz commander that a shot fired by his ship at any incoming American vessels would mean a declaration of war against the United States.[26] In other respects the Government of the United States took a position of neutrality in the conflict between the contending factions.

In such circumstances, Dr. Madriz was unable to make headway, and late in the summer of 1910 he too fled from Managua, while the troops which had been supporting him

---

[23] *Foreign Relations* (1909), p. 459.
[24] *Foreign Relations* (1910), p. 729.
[25] *Ibid.*, p. 751.
[26] *Ibid.*, pp. 743–757.

crumbled before the army of the revolution. Thereupon a provisional government headed by General Estrada was established at the capital, and the Secretary of State at Washington was informed that a general election would be held, a new constitution adopted, the aid of the Department of State sought in securing a loan to rehabilitate finances, and reparations made for the death of the two Americans shot as revolutionists by Zelaya.[27] Replying to such overtures, the Department of State ordered Thomas P. Dawson, minister to Panama, to proceed to Managua and, with the aid of the two American consuls, Moffat and Olivares, to facilitate a settlement. In its instructions to Mr. Dawson it suggested the following program as the basis for action: the election of a president at the earliest practicable date, the establishment of a liberal constitution containing "suitable guarantees for foreigners" and affirming the "inhibitions of commercial monopolies," the rehabilitation of finances, a loan to pay claims secured by customs receipts according to an agreement to be reached between the governments of the United States and Nicaragua, payment of claims already determined, adjustment of other claims arising out of the revolution by a commission created by convention to be drawn by the two governments, and reparation for the death of the two Americans executed by the Zelaya government.[28]

After extended negotiations with the revolutionary leaders, the minister of the United States was able to bring them into agreement on the principles proposed by the Department of State and the documents were signed on October 27, 1910.[29] An understanding was reached respecting the candidates— Estrada for president and Diaz for vice president; the Zelayistas were excluded from the government; elections were held late in November, 1910; the candidates suggested were unanimously elected; and the American consul reported "intense enthusiasm."[30]

But the program was soon disturbed by events. In February, 1911, the new American minister, Elliott Northcott,

[27] *Foreign Relations* (1910), p. 762.
[28] *Ibid.*, p. 763.
[29] *Foreign Relations* (1911), pp. 652ff.
[30] *Ibid.*, p. 767.

stated that Estrada saw no hope for Nicaragua except in "close alliance with the United States," that opinion in Central America was against such a step, that "the natural sentiment of an overwhelming majority of Nicaraguans is antagonistic to the United States," that even in Estrada's cabinet there was distrust of American motives, and that the Zelayistas were again active in stirring up opposition to the settlement.[31] A month later, the American minister added: "As the matter now looks to me, President Estrada is being maintained solely by the moral effect of our support and the belief that he would unquestionably have that support in case of trouble." [32]

Despite the apparent settlement, things were not running smoothly in fact. The American minister, therefore, informed President Estrada: "You have got to turn over the power and leave the country; otherwise my Government will not further recognize you." So Estrada, unsatisfactory to the American Government and yet attacked by the Nicaraguan National Assembly for his compliance with American requests, passed from the scene, and at last Adolfo Diaz, who had evidently been the principal American candidate from the beginning of the revolution, was installed in the presidency.[33] Then the American minister announced the news to the State Department and added that "a war vessel is necessary for the moral effect." [34] Acting Secretary Huntington Wilson replied: "Make suitable expression of this Government's satisfaction with the Diaz Government's assurance of its desire to continue with the program." [35] The American war vessel *Yorktown* was ordered from Panama to intercept a filibustering movement against Diaz engineered by an "anti-American party." [36] By way of supplement Secretary Knox instructed the American minister in Nicaragua to inform Diaz that the United States "renews assurances of support in assisting his government in so far as it properly may," and to warn the principal rival of Diaz, General Mena, that "since Diaz is the constitutional

[31] *Ibid.*, p. 655.
[32] *Ibid.*, p. 656.
[33] *Hearings, Sen. For. Rels. Com.* (1927), p. 38.
[34] *Ibid.*, p. 35.
[35] *Foreign Relations* (1911), p. 611.
[36] *Ibid.*, p. 662.

President, recognized by this Government as such," the General "must see it to be indispensable to his own interest that Diaz remain in office." The minister was also to let Diaz know that the *Yorktown* had been ordered from Panama "to watch for the reported filibuster." [37]

With a pliant President installed in Nicaragua the Department of State drew up a convention determining the issues of national interest at stake in the country. Although it deferred action on a proposal from Diaz that a treaty should be made, or the Nicaraguan constitution amended, with a view to permitting the United States to "intervene in our [Nicaragua's] internal affairs in order to maintain peace and the existence of lawful government," [38] it took steps to put the affairs of that country on a positive basis. In the convention signed on June 6, 1911,[39] Nicaragua agreed to make a contract providing for the refunding of the external debt, to settle all claims, and to establish its finances on "a sound and stable basis." It promised to make the refunding loan a first lien on its customs duties and not to alter charges affecting the import and export of goods without the approval of the Government of the United States. Full and detailed statements respecting fiscal operations under the contract were to be made periodically to the Department of State in Washington and at other times on request. The manager of the customs, "who need not be a Nicaraguan," was to be chosen with the approval of the President of the United States and afforded full protection in the discharge of his functions. As a precaution it was added: "The Government of the United States, should the circumstances require, will in turn afford such protection as it may find requisite." [40]

The program, of course, was realized largely through private operations.[41] Owing to the failure of the treaty to receive the consent of the Senate, Brown Bros. and Co. and J. & W. Selig-

[37] *Ibid.*, p. 662.

[38] *Ibid.*, p. 670.

[39] The Knox-Castrillo Convention. For the text, see *The United States and Nicaragua*, Appendix B., p. 126.

[40] *Foreign Relations* (1912), p. 1074.

[41] A summary of the financial arrangements is given in *The United States and Nicaragua*, pp. 13–15; 17–19.

man and Co., the bankers who were to lend $15,000,000 to Nicaragua upon the ratification of the treaty, entered into the Treasury Bills Agreement of September 1, 1911 with the Nicaraguan Government. Under this agreement the bankers obtained virtual control over the fiscal structure of the country. The bills issued under the agreement were to be a lien and charge upon the customs duties which were not to be altered without the agreement of the bankers. The collector general was to be nominated by the bankers, approved by the Secretary of State of the United States, and "appointed by the President of Nicaragua." Notwithstanding the fact that they had in President Diaz a man of their own choosing, the American interests were taking no chances. Mr. Clifford D. Ham, an American citizen, was for this reason chosen to serve as Collector General of Customs. He served in that capacity from December, 1911, until June, 1928. His successor, Mr. Irving A. Lindberg, had been Deputy Collector General since 1912. The bankers also were given an option to secure at par 51 per cent of the shares of a National Bank which was to be established under the Treasury Bills Agreement and the supplementary monetary law, enacted at the suggestion and under the supervision of the bankers in March, 1912. The bank, with a paid-in capital of $100,000, all subscribed by the Nicaraguan Government, was incorporated under the laws of Connecticut as the Banco Nacional de Nicaragua. It opened for business in August, 1912, with its management under the supervision of the bankers. How intimately associated this bank was with the fiscal structure of Nicaragua may be seen in the powers possessed by the bank. It had the exclusive right to issue notes which were legal tender; and it was made the fiscal and disbursing agent for the government and the depository of government funds.

The bankers also became the authorized agents of Nicaragua for the purpose of reaching a settlement with the Ethelburga Syndicate, prior creditors of the government; and under their authority settlements with the English and French bondholders were effected in June, 1912. Among other provisions of a supplementary loan agreement of March 26, 1912, the bankers secured further liens on customs duties, and an option to purchase 51 per cent of the stock of the Pacific Railway, together with its steamship lines, which was to be reorganized and incorporated in the United States with the management under the control of the bankers. Bankers' commissions and the customary interest charges were charged against all funds advanced.

Thus the foundations for the security of American interests in Nicaragua were firmly laid by diplomatic and naval action on the part of the United States Government. An official of an American mining company was established as President of Nicaragua. A constitution incorporating economic principles common to the conduct of business enterprise in the United States and appropriate legal methods for securing enforcement were adopted with the counsel and supervision of the State Department. Provisions were made for stabilizing Nicaraguan finances, introducing American investment bankers into the financial scene, guaranteeing the payment of American claims against the government of Nicaragua, and affording security for American citizens operating in Nicaragua. Customs duties on exports and imports were subjected to the control of the State Department. A tribunal, composed of one Nicaraguan and two Americans, was instituted to pass upon claims lodged against the government of Nicaragua by foreigners, including American citizens and concerns. Finally, the armed forces of the United States were employed on executive order to facilitate the transactions which led to the settlement satisfactory to the State Department. The fact that the Senate of the United States three times rejected the Loan Convention and refused to accept the final adjustment did not prevent the State Department and the President from realizing the major and more substantial portion of their program, in spite of many vicissitudes. Thus in a single case, relatively detailed but actually given in bare outline and limited to a brief time, is presented a concrete picture of national interest in commercial expansion, as conceived by the Department of State, and a description of the technique employed in its realization. For additional details showing the involution of private interests and the State Department, the student is referred to hundreds of pages in the documents cited above.

THE DIPLOMACY OF NATIONAL INTEREST IN CHINA
(1914–1921)

An equally intimate and authentic view of national interest in action is given in the memoir of Paul S. Reinsch, American minister to Peking under President Wilson.[42] Although he did not belong officially to the school of dollar diplomacy, Mr. Reinsch believed in its tenets, followed them closely in discharging his official duties, and resigned when he was convinced that adequate support for them was not forthcoming from the Democratic administration in Washington. From his full and frank description of his experiences and methods it is possible to draw a realistic picture of national interest as pursued in China during the period of his incumbency, to supplement the illustration afforded by the Nicaraguan episode.

Through the pages of Mr. Reinsch's book American business interests are seen operating in China. The ordinary merchants engaged in buying and selling—in transactions with private concerns—do not often appear, unless revolution or disturbances call for protection or indemnification. The normal process of commodity exchange makes little grist for the diplomatic mill. Other operations of private parties appear to be more or less haphazard. An American contractor, G. M. Gest, comes to Peking on a visit with his family, sees that the city has no street car lines, and is struck by the thought of securing a tramway franchise from the government.[43] On inquiry it is found that French interests had already foreclosed on this privilege. American selling agents pour into China, advertising automobiles and other commodities with great display and making a general onslaught in the local market. American promoters come, seeking concessions, contracts, and opportunities. American bankers occasionally take an interest, but Mr. Reinsch finds them "at this time still notoriously the most timid beings known to experience, when it came to the matter of foreign investments." [44] Although they are to be aggressive and reckless enough in later years, they are for the present

[42] Paul S. Reinsch, *An American Diplomat in China.*
[43] *Ibid.*, p. 90.
[44] *Ibid.*, p. 218.

diffident and skittish about money lending in China, much
to the chagrin of the minister bent on economic designs.

In other words, American economic interests in China were
at the moment unorganized, without policy or program. They
presented no united front anywhere. They brought no common
pressure upon the Government of the United States for support
and assistance. Individuals here and there sought aid and made
demands but there was no concerted drive on American official
agencies, calling for political action. American business men
apparently had no finished conception of the uses of government in promoting their enterprises. They did not understand
the system of dollar diplomacy.

Indeed, the American minister in Peking lamented that
American finance was "still too provincial to act independently"
without reference to other nations. Also, "it would approach
each piece of business as a separate unit, not ready to exert
itself in behalf of a loan in order to create a more favorable
situation for other transactions. European and Japanese combinations in China took a different view; they were organized
to represent a broad national interest in Chinese business.
While the attitude of individual American corporations cor-
responded to the individualism of our business, yet the national
commercial interest of America was bound to suffer because
an organization did not exist, which was broadly representative, which would look upon all parts of Chinese commerce and
finance in their interrelation, and gather from every individual
exertion favorable cumulative effects in other fields of enterprise. . . ." When Chinese officials complained about the ir-
regularities of American business methods, Mr. Reinsch pointed
out "that in the United States, capital, industry, and commerce are not mobilized for foreign enterprise as is the case
with the big foreign banking institutions of Europe. I tried to
encourage them to set American firms to doing constructive
work in China, and assured them that out of such relationships would naturally grow a readiness to afford financial
support." [45]

In some cases, however, American financial, as distinguished
from trading, interests operating in China took the initiative

[45] Reinsch, pp. 214–216.

in soliciting government support. For example, Mr. Gest, to whom reference has been made, on his return to the United States "took up the matter of a loan to China with American financial interests, but they hesitated to act until the American Government expressed its approval and willingness to give support. Mr. Gest thereupon laid siege to the Department of State." Despite Secretary Bryan's preoccupation with other affairs, Mr. Gest managed to secure from the Department a letter expressing gratification in seeing China receive fiscal aid of this character and adding that the Government "will, in accordance with its usual policy, give all proper diplomatic support to any legitimate enterprise of that character." [46]

Pursuing a similar line, Mr. Willard Straight, of J. P. Morgan and Company, wrote to Mr. Reinsch that American bankers could not create a market for a certain Chinese loan "without the active and intelligent support or at least the declared approval of the Government." President Wilson, by reversing the position of the preceding administration, had destroyed public confidence and had condemned "the only American banking group which had the enterprise, the courage, and the patience to enter and remain in the Chinese field and which, despite its unpopularity among certain yellow journals and a number of Western congressmen, stood for integrity, fair dealing, and sound business in the minds of the bond-purchasing public." Therefore, Mr. Straight continued, the public must be assured that the Government is behind the new loan plan if confidence is restored.[47] But in the main, the initiative in putting the Government behind American interests in China during Mr. Reinsch's régime came from the American legation, sometimes alone and sometimes in coöperation with the private parties involved.

Into this Chinese scene, where American interests were somewhat disorganized, where foreign governments were contending for position and vigorously supporting their respective national interests, where the native government was in process of disintegration, the American minister came with a general roving commission under which many things could be said and

[46] *Ibid.*, p. 101.
[47] *Ibid.*, p. 92.

done. His instructions from the President of the United States were moral rather than economic. From his conversations with President Wilson, Mr. Reinsch came to the conclusion that, since the United States had withdrawn from the consortium, the President felt "it was incumbent upon her to do her share independently and to give specific moral and financial assistance; in fact, I received the President's assurance of active support for constructive work in China." But the mandate was vague. "In his conversation he dwelt, however, more on the educational side and on the political example and moral encouragement, than on the matter of finance and commerce." [48]

As for Mr. Reinsch himself, his views were already fixed: "Having long been familiar with the underlying facts of the Far Eastern situation, I had entirely made up my mind on the primary importance of American participation in the industrial and economic development of China." He did not intend to enter into a scramble for concessions but he proposed to cast about for opportunities, to support Americans seeking commercial advantages, and to see that they were not defeated by opposition from any other powers. "To Americans," he said, "the idea of securing preëminence or predominance is foreign, but from the very nature of their purely economic interest they have to resist any attempt on the part of others to get any rights or a position of predominance, which could be utilized to restrict, or entirely extinguish, American opportunities." [49]

Committed personally to this view of his mission, whatever may have been the conceptions of his superior—the President of the United States, Mr. Reinsch began to look for openings and possibilities for American manufacturers, merchants, and financiers. He saw that China needed good roads, railways uniting its scattered provinces, and public works to control floods and redeem devastated regions. "It was impossible," he said after looking over the scene, "not to be fascinated by the prospects that were here unfolded. A country of vast resources in natural wealth, labor power, and even capital, was turning toward a new form of organization in which all these forces

[48] *Ibid.*, p. 63.
[49] *Ibid.*, p. 65.

were to be made to work in larger units, over greater areas and with more intensive methods than ever before. . . . The only disturbing thought was the question whether Americans were ready to appreciate the importance of the opportunity here offered." [50] Determined to overcome the hesitance of American economic concerns, Mr. Reinsch set to work with great energy to promote American enterprises already in process, to open new opportunities, to enlist a wider interest in China on the part of American businessmen, and to counteract interference by foreign governments with the extension of American activities.

Examples will illustrate his methods. Among the public works which, he thought, China needed was a system of canalization and dykes to protect the Hwai River valley from devastating floods. A flood there had recently caused a frightful famine during which the American Red Cross had rendered great services. Through the State Department, Mr. Reinsch asked whether the Red Cross would "take steps toward the choosing of a reputable and efficient American engineering firm and have this firm supported by American capitalists, who might lend the Chinese Government the funds to reclaim the rich Hwai River region?" [51] The Red Cross responded favorably. Mr. Reinsch then visited the Chinese minister in charge of the business and "got from him a definite agreement to entrust to the American Red Cross the selection of engineers and capitalists to carry out this great reform upon conditions laid down. The minister and I had frequent conferences. We discussed carefully the engineering contracts, the conditions of the loan, the security. Every sentence in the proposed agreement had been weighed, every word carefully chosen; finally on January 27, 1914, it was signed by Chang Chien as minister, and by myself in behalf of the American Red Cross." Thus a proposal offering decided economic advantages to China and American participants was confirmed. Preliminary steps were taken to realize the project, money was expended on surveys, but the loan could not be floated, the scheme lapsed, and American funds were lost in the operation.

[50] *Ibid.*, p. 76.
[51] *Ibid.*, p. 81.

A second project sponsored by the American minister at Peking was a railway concession. W. F. Carey, who had come to the country in connection with the Hwai River conservancy enterprise, thought he saw an opportunity for railway building and sought a contract from the Chinese government in that field. Mr. Reinsch gave him introductions to the various Chinese officials concerned and "from time to time supported his efforts, but did not take part in the details." The minister was, however, "careful to abstain from anything that could possibly savor of pressure, or a desire to take advantage of the difficult financial necessities of the Government." In due course the contract was signed and the Chinese government gave the American concern the right to build fifteen hundred miles of railway.[52] Mr. Carey sought a loan in the United States to initiate the work and finally turned the holding over to the American International Corporation which entered into negotiations with foreign banking interests and entangled the project in international affairs so that nothing came of the undertaking —much to the chagrin of the American minister over the failure of American interests to act courageously and unitedly in China.[53]

Turning to commercial affairs, the American minister found the American position lacking in efficiency and organization. "There were but few American commission houses. In most cases American-manufactured goods were handled by houses of other nationalities, who often gave scant attention to promoting American trade and used American products only when those of their own nation could not be obtained. It seemed worth while to establish additional trading companies, especially coöperative organizations among exporters, after the 'Representation for British Manufacturers, Ltd.' Further, I strongly urged the American Government to station a commercial attaché in China." The request for such an agent was granted and Julean Arnold, duly appointed to the post, began a vigorous campaign to arouse interest in the China trade on the part of American manufacturers and merchants by publishing alluring, and sometimes highly imaginative, pamphlets and

[52] Reinsch, p. 213.
[53] *Ibid.*, p. 214.

leaflets on the opportunities for trade and profits in that country.[54] Thus the Government of the United States, in addition to furnishing protection for trade already established, undertook an elaborate and organized propaganda to draw American manufacturers and merchants into that area of business opportunity.

Realizing that other countries had been pouring large quantities of capital into China in connection with their respective interests, Mr. Reinsch made a special point of discussing American loans to China and arousing American bankers to the importance of the supposed opportunities. As the official representative of a great power he had easy access to the officials of the Chinese government. It was, in fact, extremely easy because they were now in desperate straits and eager to get their hands on foreign money. Indeed, their government was actually sliding down hill to ruin, and foreign bankers who made loans to it lost huge sums of money in the débâcle; but Mr. Reinsch apparently thought that it might be saved and strengthened by American capital, with reciprocal advantages.

Accordingly he engaged in endless loan negotiations with Chinese officials. He made a special visit to the United States and, as he said, "conferred with members of the National City Bank; J. P. Morgan & Company; the Guaranty Trust Company of New York; Kuhn, Loeb & Company; the General Electric and American Locomotive companies; the Standard Oil Company of New York; the International Banking Corporation and the American International Corporation; the Chase National Bank; the Siems-Carey Company; the Pacific Development Corporation, and Continental and Commercial Bank of Chicago."[55] Seeing foreign banks in China "scooping off the cream of international commercial transactions and commercial operations,"[56] Mr. Reinsch earnestly sought to arouse interest at home in the development of American banking enterprise in China. But his efforts were not, on the whole, successful. After President Wilson's cavalier treatment of the consortium, American bankers were loath to press matters

---

[54] Reinsch, p. 103.
[55] *Ibid.*, p. 355.
[56] *Ibid.*, p. 102.

again. Although one or two loans were made during Mr. Reinsch's tenure, the results were not happy for American investors. He rejoiced in the Continental Commercial Bank loan to China [57]—which, in the end, proved to be an ill-advised transaction.

Such were, in brief, the American minister's conceptions of national interest and such was the substance of things desired under that head. A word may be said about the methods which he felt compelled to adopt in extreme cases. In 1917 the American International Corporation offered to float an issue of bonds to begin railway construction under the contract obtained by Mr. Carey.[58] Thereupon the vice-minister of communications in Peking, who had a Japanese wife and was supposed to be under Japanese influence, sought to block the transaction. Informed of the difficulty, Mr. Reinsch drew the attention of the Premier to the impasse. He even appealed to the President of China. In response to a suggestion from the Premier, he finally wrote a note "demanding" the execution of the contract. After some heated negotiations, the recalcitrant vice-minister formally accepted the offer of American funds. And yet after the exercise of all this official pressure, the arrangement came to nothing on account of the chaotic conditions prevailing in Peking and China generally.[59]

It is now necessary to look at the other side of the shield. Representatives of the Chinese government were as eager as Mr. Reinsch to enlist American interest in loans, concessions, trade, and other projects. They frequently visited him for the purpose of talking about the possibility of securing huge loans for various government enterprises, about the establishment of a Chinese commercial and industrial bank "in co-partnership with American capitalists." [60] They suggested the creation of a tobacco monopoly to produce increased revenue and to bring about a more efficient production of tobacco in China. After the Chinese government was induced, by strong diplomatic pressure, to break with Germany and declare war, its

[57] *Ibid.,* p. 22.
[58] Above, p. 188.
[59] Reinsch, pp. 225–227.
[60] *Ibid.,* pp. 70–75.

officials asked for financial help from the Government of the United States. Indeed, it seems that, not without reason, they were sure, when they took the fateful step, that aid would be forthcoming. Feeling under certain obligations to them, Mr. Reinsch appealed to Washington for money [61] and was deeply disappointed to find that the Government of the United States, after lending billions to the Allied and Associated powers, would not make any grants to China. As events turned out, if the American minister had been able to induce American financiers to heed the appeals of Chinese officials for loans, the American losses in that country would have run into the hundreds of millions.

Owing to the prevailing uncertainty of things, all these negotiations between the American minister and the government of China were carried on in a web of intrigue woven by the competing foreign representatives in Peking. Mr. Reinsch, according to his record, could not take a single important step in the direction of a concession or loan without encountering opposition on the part of France, Russia, Great Britain, or Japan, sometimes singly and sometimes in combination. When, for example, a coöperative arrangement was made with a British corporation for railway construction, "the British government objected. It would accept the principle of the international company only on condition that all the lines traversing the Yangtze Valley should be constructed by the British participant in the syndicate." [62] Against the Siems-Carey project for railway construction, Russia and France filed objections, claiming that it infringed their prior rights and privileges. [63] A concession to the Standard Oil Company in the provinces of Shensi and Chihli aroused the ire of Japan; [64] a contract with the Bethlehem Steel Company stirred up protests in the same quarter; [65] and other activities of the American minister in China were countered by the Japanese either directly on the ground or through representations in Washington. Indeed, irritated by finding every important economic advance on the

[61] *Ibid.*, p. 321.
[62] *Ibid.*, p. 101.
[63] *Ibid.*, pp. 219–221.
[64] *Ibid.*, p. 83.
[65] *Ibid.*, p. 84.

part of American interests stoutly resisted, Mr. Reinsch was finally moved to write a long and detailed memorandum to Washington on what he deemed Japan's secret, coercive, and corrupt interference with the legitimate rights of Americans in China.[66] In other words, behind the diplomatic façade, there was going on through these years a bitter rivalry that stirred up enmities and ill-will which, the American minister thought, were bound to culminate in war if not otherwise mitigated. And to add fuel to the fire the respective contestants maintained foreign newspapers in China, secretly subsidized, yet irresponsible, and constantly engaged in fanning the flames of hatred kindled by economic contests.

According to Mr. Reinsch's interpretation and record, the diplomatic agents of other powers were engaged in reprehensible and intolerable intrigues against his operations, and, according to their opinion, he was himself playing a game of bluff and hypocrisy.[67] The outstanding feature of the whole situation was not the aggressiveness of the private interests involved in the struggle, but the insistent and unremitting efforts of diplomatic representatives to consolidate their respective nationals and to use the power of their governments to promote private economic advantages.[68] Judging by Mr. Reinsch's statements, American capitalists were not belligerent but slow and negligent. Judging by the history of the first consortium [69] and by the policies of the Consortium Council,

[66] *Ibid.,* p. 335.

[67] *Ibid.,* p. 62.

[68] Writing of American holdings of Chinese Government obligations, C. F. Remer says of one of the first American proposals, which was for the building of the Hankow-Peking railway line: "It did not fail because of any lack of interest on the part of the American Minister, Charles Denby. Denby went so far as to call at the Foreign Office in Peking and demand that instructions be telegraphed to the Chinese negotiator at Shanghai to contract with the American company for the building of the line." (Citing *United States Foreign Relations,* 1897, pp. 57–8) C. F. Remer, *Foreign Investments in China,* 1933, p. 256.

[69] It should be mentioned that while the Wilson policy rejected American participation in the old consortium of 1913, it tended to encourage American participation in the new consortium, steps toward which began in 1918. In October, 1920, the China Consortium Agreement was signed. Remer accounts for this change of attitude principally by the new position attained by Japan in the Far East after the first few years of the World War, evidenced in the political field by the 21 Demands and in the financial field by the Nishihara

declared at Paris, May 23, 1923, the international bankers, instead of desiring rivalry and hatred, preferred coöperation in financing on terms more reasonable to China and more secure for investors than the individual projects so passionately pushed by the ministers and agents of the respective powers represented at Peking.[70]

What conclusions can be drawn from these minute glimpses of national interest in action? The search for truth requires extreme caution, but some conclusions are possible. Within the periphery of vision we see certain persons, private and official, operating in Washington, in Nicaragua, in China. Within the same circle we see certain things, objective and measurable—plantations, factories, mines, forests, stores, goods, and claims, all susceptible of expression with more or less exactness in mathematical terms. Intangible, but open to realistic inferences, are hopes, purposes, and desires—for gain, profits, extension of operations, fame, and promotion. Equally intangible, yet highly dynamic, are shadowy imaginings of achievements to be accomplished, achievements that can ultimately be brought into objective form. By imperceptible degrees realities shade off into potentialities of unknown quantity and quality.

With respect to the persons involved relations are intimate. In Nicaragua and China, American citizens and officials, civil and military, are closely associated. They form local colonies. They have business and social affiliations. They communicate constantly with one another. They have many common ideas about the scenes in which they find themselves and the opportunities of economic development there. In some matters the initiative for government action comes from private citizens; in others it comes from the official side. By such processes private and public views are fused, altered, con-

loans. Subsidiary causes for the change of policy were the new position of the United States in world finance, the course of events in Paris during the discussions which preceded the Versailles Treaty, and the events which led up to the Washington Conference of 1921–1922. *Foreign Investments in China,* pp. 329ff. and 334–335. Remer might have added that beginning with 1917, certainly after 1920, the control of American foreign policy passed from the Democratic party to the Republicans (the party of the restoration) with its traditional conceptions of national interest in commercial expansion.

[70] Text in *The China Year Book* (1924), pp. 809–811.

solidated. The result is not an exact pattern of either original. Even the two patterns are not clear-cut in origin; and both are subject to change and development. Yet out of plan and inchoate designs comes a certain concentration of program, will, resolve, action.

This concentrated program is primarily economic in object.[71] It covers the protection of property and property rights already obtained, the acquisition of concessions, opportunities, and privileges from which profits may be derived, the collection of damages for losses, real and prospective, already suffered, and the establishment of legal and other conditions conducive to advantageous operations.

In some relations each particular interest stands on its own bottom and is only indirectly or remotely connected with surrounding interests. Occasionally interests are conflicting: American citizens sell munitions to revolutionists in Nicaragua whom the Government of the United States is informally aiding and also to the administration which it is desirous of ousting. In other relations many interests make common cause, especially when the home Government's support and coöperation are sought. For practical purposes the Government serves both: it helps individual citizens and concerns to realize their desires and provides diplomatic pressure and naval force to create conditions that are regarded as generally favorable to private enterprise.

Since the business is primarily economic in nature, it should be possible to express the result in the form of a balance sheet showing gains in wealth accruing to the American nation set over against the cost of government operations charged to the American taxpayer. Is there, in the papers and documents thus subjected to minute examination, evidence that any of the participants viewed their operations in the light of such a final statement or adjustment or made an effort to strike a balance

[71] With respect to American activities in China, Remer intimates that "investments" were evidently not contemplated within the term "economic." Only trade and political policy were emphasized, not investment. "I have yet," he says, "to find a strong statement by a responsible American political leader advocating the encouragement of American investment in China on the ground that it is desirable in itself for economic reasons." *Foreign Investments in China,* p. 317.

of this kind? **None at all.** Whatever may have been their formulas of patriotism, they were proceeding with reference to the instant need of particular things. Speaking in philosophical and, therefore, fundamental terms, they were nominalists, not realists.

CHAPTER VII

FOREIGN IMPLICATIONS OF DOMESTIC AFFAIRS

DOMESTIC affairs and foreign relations are intimately associated with each other. Often both are but different aspects of the same thing. Separating them into distinct compartments, if pursued to the logical conclusion, results in misleading conceptions concerning the processes of national life and their actual ramifications throughout the texture of world societies. And yet there has been a persistent tendency in many quarters to treat domestic and foreign affairs as if they were either wholly independent of each other or only remotely related. This tendency is conspicuous among many modern writers.

The custom, no doubt, is open to partial explanations. It makes for convenience of academic treatment. It conforms to the tendency of specialization which often yields usable findings in details; but which, by the practice of narrowing the vision, raises the danger of limiting the understanding of the whole. It is due also, in part, to the legalistic views of the state employed in diplomacy—the idea of states as independent entities with fixed boundaries, represented by governments at home and diplomats abroad. To some extent it may also be ascribed to the use, in international law, of the abstract doctrine of sovereignty originally developed with reference to internal struggles for power and then projected into the field of international relations, where it does not have even the substance that it possesses in domestic affairs.

Again, the practice of treating each subject as if it were independent is in a large measure due to the content of the subjects themselves. The connection between the two is often obscure. Domestic affairs seem to be more pertinent, real, and pressing in the routine life of the nation. Foreign relations —witness the very connotation of the word *foreign*—seem to concern things outside the nation, things which appear remote from the daily routine and which do not necessarily demand immediate consideration. If, however, attention is drawn to the realistic forces which condition international intercourse, if the vision is broad enough to observe the constant repercussions the one phase has upon the other, the unity of domestic and foreign issues, policies, and events, is seen as an inescapable fact.[1] All foreign policies are internally, as well as externally, conditioned.

There are, to be sure, some domestic developments and actions which have no relation to foreign affairs, or at least, very remote relations. For example, the construction of a highway between two inland towns with no military purpose in view or the erection of a city hall in Springfield, Illinois, is not likely to have any direct foreign implications. But few important aspects of domestic development fail to have some bearing upon foreign relations. The geographical position of the national territory, its store and use of natural resources, the character of its population, the nature of its economic structure, even the manner in which it enacts and executes its domestic legislation, are but a few examples of the seemingly domestic concerns which fundamentally affect its relations with other nations.

There is, for instance, the matter of the growth of population; Japan's policy toward China has a relation both real and ideological to the pressure of its population upon the means of subsistence. Again, the diplomatic course of the United States at the turn of the nineteenth century can be traced largely with reference to the increasing saturation of the domestic market and the growing pressure for selling opportunities abroad. The existence and systematic cultivation of the warlike spirit, though confined entirely within the geographical borders of a particular country, have repercussions abroad; news of it is carried by telegraph, cable, wireless, and press to

---

[1] An excellent illustration of this principle is to be found in E. Kehr, *Schlachtflottenbau und Parteipolitik,* where the roots of German foreign policy are traced to domestic developments mirrored in party conflicts and combinations. An instance of this in the United States was the conflict between the eastern and western sugar refiners, an important factor reflected in American policy toward Hawaii just previous to annexation.

the corners of the earth, affecting the diplomatic attitudes and policies of other nations.[2]

The movements of domestic forces which set in train lines of actions and events in various parts of the world do in fact create obligations, contribute to the formation of attitudes, produce diplomatic and naval interventions, and raise issues of policy, whether accompanied by treaties and conventions or not. While the lawyers, for mental convenience, may separate the nations into sovereign, territorial, and administrative entities, the underlying realities of domestic actions and international intercourse correspond to no such verbal distinctions. Washington advised his countrymen to avoid the European system of alliances and to cultivate commercial connections with all countries; but the very commercial relations which he favored and advocated led to powerful obligations abroad and to actual entanglements more binding than the prescriptions of formal treaties.

A treaty is merely one way of creating international responsibilities and obligations. The United States stood wholly outside the paper alliances which fixed the lines for the World War; and yet was drawn into the holocaust under conceptions of interest and moral obligation. "The World War," said Curtis Wilbur, speaking as Secretary of the Navy, "furnished a clear instance of violated commercial right and our defense thereof. We fought not because Germany invaded or threatened to invade America, but because she struck at our commerce on the North Sea, and denied to our ships and to our citizens on the high seas the protection of our flag."[3] If this oversimplifies the case, it at least expresses substantial truth; no commerce, no violation of rights, no entanglements of diplomacy and war. On the other hand, obligations solemnly undertaken by formal treaties are not proof against the operation of other forces or domestic decisions. Treaties may be broken and have often been denounced under such pressures.

[2] The acts of the Hitler government in Germany, for example, have had powerful repercussions in other countries. See also the reactions abroad to a speech delivered by Admiral Plunkett before the National Republican Club at New York on the subject of commerce and war. New York *Times,* January 24, 1928. (See text pp. 349–350 and note 89 on p. 350.)

[3] New York *Times,* May 8, 1925.

Italy, though solemnly bound to the Central Powers, severed the written ties and joined the Entente largely in exchange for more substantial promises.

Measures of law adopted in a country, though mainly in response to a movement of domestic forces and viewed as domestic in essence, may bear heavily on international relations. Even the form of government cannot escape this imputation. As Doctor Oliver Wendell Holmes said, more than half a century ago, the Government of the United States was long a standing menace to governments founded on different, that is, monarchical, principles.[4] Assertions suspiciously like this are today being made respecting the form of government in Soviet Russia and its relation to the so-called "capitalist" governments.

Although this is not the place to attempt a microscopic analysis of all the bearings of domestic policy upon diplomatic relations, the subject deserves illustrations by pertinent examples. Tariff legislation and accompanying measures, while treated as matters solely of "domestic concern," cut into international trade, and often add stimulus to the rivalries of commerce and government.[5] Armaments, even if innocently conceived as instrumentalities of mere territorial defense, are in themselves expressions of foreign policies and produce repercussions in the policies of other governments, whatever verbal assertions of pacific intention may accompany them. The development of a merchant marine comes under the same head. Finally, immigration legislation, however justified by domestic ideals and necessities, awakens reverberations in distant foreign offices and deflects the currents of world thinking and action. Not without warrant did Yusuke Tsurumi inform his audience at the Williamstown Institute of Politics that the American exclusion act would have grave consequences in over-

[4] When an American benefactor established a chair in American Constitutional History in the University of Tokyo several years ago, conservative Japanese professors objected on the ground that such teachings would be a menace to the Japanese imperial system.

[5] So flagrant have been the upsets due to national tariff legislation within recent years that the connection between the tariff and international affairs is now commonly recognized, and the former belief that the tariff is solely a matter of domestic concern has lost much of its efficacy and many of its adherents.

throwing the liberal group in Japan and driving that country back upon a purely Asiatic policy.[6] Time justified his prophecy.

Illustrations of the close intimacy of domestic affairs and foreign relations could be expanded indefinitely and along a broad front of diverse subjects. In some instances the connection is commonly recognized. In others, it is not readily admitted. The conditions of modern life are increasingly lifting matters forcibly out of a sphere naïvely declared to be "purely domestic" and casting them into the wider arena of international affairs. Thus it may be said that tariff legislation, armament provisions, merchant marine laws, and immigration measures, to single these out for consideration here, are intimate phases of foreign policy; and in truth, they must be considered as aspects of national interest projected on a world stage.

TARIFF RESTRICTION AS A NATIONAL INTEREST

From the establishment of the Constitution to the latest presidential administration the restriction of imports through tariff legislation has been treated by distinguished statesmen as a phase of national interest. "The safety and interests of the people require," said Washington in his first annual address, "that they should promote such manufactures as tend to render them independent of others for essential, particularly military, supplies." Hamilton expressed similar views: "It is the interest of nations to diversify the industrious pursuits of the individuals who compose them. . . . It is the interest of the community . . . to encourage the growth of manufactures. . . . If Europe will not take from us the products of our soil upon terms consistent with our interests, the natural remedy is to contract, as far as possible, our wants of her."[7] Even Madison, as the Jeffersonian party shifted its ground, declared in 1811: "The national interest . . . requires that . . . we should not be left in a state of unnecessary dependence on external supplies."[8]

---

[6] *Reawakening of the Orient and Other Addresses,* Publication of the Institute of Politics, pp. 107–110.

[7] Report on Manufactures, *Works* (Lodge ed.) Vol. III, pp. 321, 352, 325.

[8] Message to Congress, November 1, 1811.

During the long evolution of tariff policies, sponsors of the system continued to emphasize the foundation principle of national interest. After declaring that he would effectually protect American industries, Henry Clay added: "I would afford them protection not so much for the sake of the manufacturers themselves as for the general interest." [9] In quoting this passage from Clay's speech, William McKinley insisted on the unity of all interests defended by protection. "There is no conflict of interest," he said, "and should be none between the several classes of producers and consumers in the United States. Their interests are one. . . . That which benefits one, benefits all." [10] Though somewhat lukewarm on the subject, Theodore Roosevelt declared that when changes were made in the tariff there must be something like "a general agreement among the citizens of the several states" that alterations were "needed and desired in the interest of the people as a whole." [11] President Taft laid stress upon the provisions of the Payne-Aldrich bill which he deemed to be "of the utmost importance in the interest of this country." [12] Illustrations could be multiplied indefinitely to support the statement that tariff advocates have consistently based their reasoning on some conception of national interest or have employed the term in defense of their position.

The more thoughtful among the early sponsors of protection for American industries were not content with the general covering phrase, "national interest." They broke it down into its constituent elements and visualized it in the form of the kind of social order deemed desirable for the United States as a nation. First of all they laid stress upon the importance of "independence and security," upon emancipating the country as far as possible from reliance upon the vicissitudes of foreign trade for its primary needs—"the means of subsistence, habitation, clothing, and defense," to employ Hamilton's phrasing.[13] In the early days of the Republic statesmen of both political parties maintained that commercial policy should rest upon

---

[9] Henry Clay, quoted in McKinley, *The Tariff*, p. 2.
[10] Ogilvie, *Life and Speeches* (1896), p. 7.
[11] Roosevelt, Annual Message, 1905.
[12] Address at Winona (Sept., 1909).
[13] Hamilton, *Works* (Lodge ed.), Vol. III, pp. 356–357.

this fundamental maxim of social philosophy. Washington more than once dwelt upon the advantage of freeing the country from dependence upon other countries "for essential, particularly, military, supplies." Madison elaborated the thesis: "The national interest requires that, with respect to such articles, at least, as belong to our defense and primary wants, we should not be left in a state of unnecessary dependence on external supplies." [14] Again and again Madison returned to the argument that the country must produce its materials of defense and supply its primary wants, as a matter of sheer prudence, to escape the hazards of interruptions in foreign commerce. For these elementary necessities, he urged, "a provident policy would favor an internal and independent source as a reasonable exception to the general rule of consulting cheapness alone." [15]

Even Jefferson himself, although he once ardently wished to keep workshops and working people in Europe and to avoid the rise of great urban centers as "sores on the body politic," later came to support the argument of "independence and security." Taught by the bitter experiences of the Napoleonic wars, which disrupted American commerce and spread ruin among his favorites, the agriculturists, he made a frank avowal of a change in opinion. In a letter to Benjamin Austin, written on January 9, 1816, he declared: "We must now place the manufacturer by the side of the agriculturist. Experience has taught me that manufactures are now as necessary to our independence as to our comfort; and if those who quote me as of a different opinion will keep pace with me in purchasing nothing foreign when an equivalent of domestic fabric can be obtained, without regard to difference in price, it will not be our fault if we do not soon have a supply at home equal to our demands, and wrest that weapon of distress from the hand which has wielded it." [16] By this time his party had swung into line and was preparing to escape dependence on the vicissitudes

---

[14] Quoted in Start, *Early American Statesmen on the Tariff*, p. 18; message to Congress, November 1, 1811.   [15] *Ibid.*, pp. 7–20.

[16] *Ibid.*, p. 16. Andrew Jackson, leader of the agrarian uprising took a similar view. After describing the richness and diversity of American natural resources, he insisted that protection should be afforded to all industries which supply "those leading and important articles so essential to War." *Ibid.*, p. 23.

of European commerce by fostering domestic industries—"in the agricultural interest"—as its leaders were fond of saying.

Alexander Hamilton went far beyond the bare limits of "independence and security" in interpreting the national interest of commercial policy. He underlined the superiority of a reliable and steady domestic market as compared with the foreign market; it would prove an outlet for agricultural produce and contribute to a flourishing state of agriculture.[17] He dwelt upon the advantages of a diversified system of industry which would "cherish and stimulate the activity of the human mind by multiplying the objects of enterprise."[18] Such a diversified system, he thought, would encourage the natural aptitude of the American people for mechanical work; foster the genius of invention and contrivance so marked among the intellectual characteristics of American civilization.[19] Diversified industry, he continued, would provide employment for persons who would otherwise be idle, especially women and children.[20] By providing new opportunities in the United States, it would also stimulate immigration from abroad, adding to the human resources of the country.[21] In other words, Hamilton had clearly in mind a type of social and economic order to be created and fostered by commercial policy. He did not assume a fixed order of "natural" industry for the United States and base public actions upon the economy of "cheapness," but viewed the American people as endowed with ingenious capacities to be unfolded and with diversified material resources to be developed. For him society was not a stereotype, but an organism capable of modification and growth under stimulants properly applied to private enterprise.

With the principle of national interest objectified in a type of society in development, Hamilton applied the principle of selective protection and encouragement, as distinguished from indiscriminate support for all applicants. In choosing the objects of public favor, he explained, "five circumstances seem entitled to particular attention: the capacity of the country

[17] *Works* (Lodge ed.), Vol. III, pp. 318, 320.
[18] *Ibid.*, p. 317.
[19] *Ibid.*, p. 317.
[20] *Ibid.*, p. 314.
[21] *Ibid.*, pp. 315–316.

to furnish the raw materials; the degree in which the nature of the manufacture admits of a substitute for manual labor in machinery; the facility of execution; the extensiveness of the uses to which the article can be applied; its subserviency to other interests, particularly the great one of national defense." [22] Thus Hamilton lays down criteria for judging the expediency of extending government assistance in the form of tariffs, bounties, premiums, prohibitions, improvement of transport, and encouragement of invention. His point of departure is an idealized conception of society deemed desirable, not subservience to particular interests; he provides the criteria of judgment with respect to the objects chosen and the instrumentalities to be applied; in short, he rests his case upon a philosophy of society and of historical development. In this view national interest is something to be objectively realized by policy.

In the course of time the clear conception of the system of protection and encouragement as serving the national interest —realistically viewed in terms of independence, security, continuity of market and employment, diversity of enterprise, and stimulus to the unfolding of popular talents—became confused with other issues and sharply traversed by criticism. The original contentions were continued but their vividness was dimmed by other considerations, and the course of thinking on the subject was deflected by the movement of economic forces. When particular industries flourished under measures deemed temporary, they became vested interests to be protected in their own right.[23] As urban laborers multiplied in number, with the rise of protected industries, another appeal to particular interest was made: the vested interest of labor in high wages made possible by discriminations against Europe.[24] Agriculture was not overlooked, to be sure: a home market for farm produce was to be maintained; but the principal concern of those who defended the protective system,

[22] Works, op. cit., p. 383.

[23] Taussig, State Papers and Speeches on the Tariff, p. 34. Speech of Clay in 1832.

[24] J. R. Commons, Annals of the American Academy of Political and Social Science, Vol. XXXII, No. 2 (September, 1908), p. 315; Taussig, Tariff History of the United States (5th ed.), pp. 63–65.

as manifested in their speeches and party platforms, was the profits of industry and the wages of labor. With amazing exactness the ideology of national interest in the program of discriminations conformed to the economic transformation which marked the course of American history.

As the memories of the twenty-three years of European war, opening in 1793 and closing in 1815, faded away, and the long peace afforded an unimpeded outlet for American agricultural produce on the seven seas, the old arguments of the older Jefferson and Madison respecting American security and independence were dropped by their followers. Their agrarian party, under the leadership of cotton planters, ceased to regard protection as a phase of national interest and assailed it as a scheme of vested and private interests. In 1840 the Democratic party presented this formulation of the case in a concise plank: "Justice and sound policy forbid the federal government to foster one branch of industry to the detriment of another, or to cherish the interests of one portion to the injury of another portion of our common country." With some fluctuations, due to particular occasions, this declaration of faith runs through the pronouncements of the Democratic party until 1916: Protective tariffs reflect special interests, not the national interest. In 1912 the contention took the following form: "The high Republican tariff is the principal cause of the unequal distribution of wealth; it is a system of taxation which makes the rich richer and the poor poorer; under its operations the American farmer and laboring man are the chief sufferers. . . . The farmer sells largely in free markets and buys almost entirely in protected markets." Perfect consistency was not maintained during these years but the main current was clear: Interest in the protective tariff and its affiliated policies is a special, not a national, interest.

Under this formulation the national interest became substantially identified with the agricultural interests, and had the facts of American economic evolution conformed to the hypothesis the country might have remained primarily agricultural, an exporter of food stuffs and raw materials to be exchanged for manufactured commodities with the more advanced nations of Europe. But the trend of development ran against the static-rural assumption. And as manufacturing expanded, as the proportion of exports of manufactures in the total export trade rose higher and higher until it overtopped agricultural produce, and as the urban wing of the Democratic party grew in size, the pattern of the Democratic conception of interest in trade control changed. While the party continued to condemn particular tariff acts as "class legislation," it shifted its general position. In its platform of 1928 it announced that its policy would include: "The maintenance of legitimate business and a high standard of wages for American labor. . . . Actual difference between the cost of production at home and abroad, with adequate safeguard for the wage of the American laborer, must be the measure of the tariff rate." Although in 1932 the party declared in favor of "a competitive tariff for revenue," its candidate, Franklin D. Roosevelt, explained that it meant protection for "American business and American labor," [25] thus marking a long departure from the party advocacy in 1856 of "progressive free trade throughout the world."

It is evident from this record that the principle of free and unrestricted trade as a conception of national interest has practically disappeared from political calculations and the doctrine of controlled trade has become almost universally accepted outside academic circles. As a result of long development the United States became a large-scale exporter of both agricultural produce and raw materials on the one side and finished manufactured commodities on the other, the special interests of each seeking to enlarge its foreign market by the management of imports into the United States. The theory and practice of unrestrained commercial intercourse have disappeared from government circles.

But even this situation raised a serious problem. How far was it possible to enlarge indefinitely the outlet for both manufactured commodities and agricultural produce? The high degree of self-sufficiency, the rapid approach to a stage of productive maturity with its attendant abundance of goods, the beginnings of the shift from a debtor to a creditor status, intensified the problem and turned it into something of a dilemma

[25] Acceptance Speech, New York *Times,* July 3, 1932.

in which adjustments and sacrifices of some sort appeared to be inevitable. The difficulty was further aggravated by the conflict between the broad interests of the two classes—industry and agriculture—within the country itself. The industrial groups seemed to bend their efforts toward cheap raw materials, low cost of living for wage earners, and the maximum consumption of manufactured products, which, interpreted in terms of the tariff, meant high duties on refined products and little or no duties on raw materials. The agricultural groups and those immediately dependent upon farm prosperity sought high protection against raw products competing with those of American agriculture, cheaper manufactured articles, and the maximum consumption of home-produced farm products; and these were interpreted in tariff terms as high duties on raw and refined products competing with home agricultural produce and little or no duties on articles, especially manufactured products, consumed by the farmers. In such circumstances, the position which the country should take toward foreign nations on the matter of the tariff became a serious and difficult problem.

This dilemma has long been recognized by both parties to the tariff controversy. Early in the last decade of the nineteenth century, after American manufacturers had developed the continent, fairly saturated the domestic market, and begun to cast abroad aggressively for new outlets for their enterprise, the idea of managing foreign trade through reciprocity legislation, treaties, and agreements began to flower in Republican thinking for various reasons and from various motives. Leaders of the party came to the conclusion, as McKinley phrased it in his famous Buffalo address, that "we cannot forever sell everything and buy little or nothing," and that arrangements must be made with foreign countries whereby they will favor certain American exports and send in exchange "such of their products as we can use without harm to our industries." The general philosophy and practice, under which this project for expanding the market for American products was to be realized, were covered by the loose term, of pleasing connotations, "reciprocity."

For a time efforts were made to promote this form of national interest by tariff provisions, treaties, and agreements. Although some earlier steps had been taken in this direction, emphasis on the design came with the great expansion of American industries near the close of the nineteenth century. By the revenue act of 1890 the President was given power to impose duties on certain commodities whenever, in his opinion, the countries exporting such goods to the United States imposed duties on American goods, which he deemed "unjust or unreasonable." This was directed especially against Latin-American countries and was characterized as a weapon which "might be used [by the American Government] to club weaker nations into compliance with its demands."[26]

Under this provision a number of reciprocal agreements were negotiated. Four years later, by the Wilson Act of 1894, these arrangements were cancelled, ostensibly on the ground that reciprocity was a weapon of commercial aggression and produced ill-will in foreign countries. Upon their return to power, the Republicans restored the system, with modifications, by the Dingley Act, and authorized the President, with the consent of the Senate, to negotiate treaties reducing duties in return for favors and to make minor executive agreements as well. But no treaties were concluded under the authorization, and only a few agreements. The next tariff law, the Payne-Aldrich Act of 1909, swept the slate clean and provided for a scheme of maximum and minimum rates to be applied by a tariff board with reference to the policies of other countries. This experiment was short lived, for the Underwood Act of 1913 abolished the maximum and minimum schedules and empowered the President to enter into reciprocal arrangements with other countries, by formal treaties ratified by the Senate. Returning to their old interpretation of the most-favored-nation clause, the Republicans in 1922 struck a blow at the earlier form of reciprocity; and the high hopes of trade expansion once entertained under this head were practically abandoned.[27]

[26] W. C. Ford, *Reciprocity under the Tariff Act of 1890*, International Statistics Institute, Chicago, 1893, p. 6.

[27] For parallel comparisons on countervailing duties, "flexible" provisions, and powers of the tariff commissions, and for the Anti-Dumping Act of 1921, see *Comparison of the Tariff Acts of 1913, 1922, and 1930*, prepared for the

As the treaties and agreements negotiated under various reciprocity provisions indicated, the range of commodities for which adjustments could be made was too narrow to admit of a marked expansion of American exports by this process. The experiment had been disappointing to its sponsors. So a new tack was taken—in favorable circumstances. The Department of Commerce was largely transformed into an aggressive selling agency with representatives in all parts of the world. Owing to the events of the World War, the United States had immense accumulations of capital, and the market for American goods was swiftly expanded by lending money to prospective purchasers. For the moment the impasse from which reciprocity was designed to save the country was avoided. High tariff schedules were retained and the outflow of manufactured goods swelled to enormous proportions. According to appearances, the fortunate state of affairs for which McKinley longed had been established: an expansion of exports was possible without taking in exchange any goods that might bring "harm to our industries and labor." Unfortunately for the believers in the new order, the decline in foreign trade which followed the crash of 1929 revived the old problem in a still more difficult form, the problem of expanding exports, plus lending, while closely restricting imports.

Meanwhile the Democrats, who had looked coldly upon reciprocity projects or regarded them as weapons for coercing weaker countries, felt compelled to attack the problem by similar methods. In their platform of 1932 they endorsed "reciprocal tariff agreements with other nations; and an international economic conference designed to restore international trade and facilitate exchange." In commenting on this platform, the Democratic candidate, Franklin D. Roosevelt, declared that "by our acts of the past we have invited and received the retaliation of other nations"; and then he proposed "an invitation to them to forget the past, to sit at the table with us, as friends, and to plan with us for the restoration of world trade." Thus, while "American business and labor" are to be protected, foreign trade is to be restored, to some level

use of the House Committee on Ways and Means. Government Printing Office, Washington, D. C., 1931.

not stated, by the process of negotiation with other countries. Despite the efforts of the Republicans to escape the dilemma of expanding output by reciprocity adjustments, the Democrats hoped to accomplish the desired result by "reciprocal tariff agreements" and negotiations at "an international economic conference." [28]

To the apparent unanimity of opinion on national interest in protection, in principle, expressed by the political parties, only one powerful dissent was opposed—bankers largely engaged in floating foreign loans. As early as 1921 Otto Kahn suggested that the creed of commercial protection was outgrown. "We are facing a fundamentally novel problem," he said in an address to the Traffic Club of Pittsburgh, "in the fact that within the past six years, we have for the first time in our history become a creditor nation, and, at the same time, that

---

[28] That the Democrats had reached a state of serious confusion upon the solution of the tariff and associated problems became obvious from the very start of the World Economic Conference. Topics *suggested* by the American delegation for the consideration of the economic commission on the matter of tariffs included "A. Reduction of trade barriers by multilateral agreements. . . . C. Encouragement of reduction of trade barriers by bilateral agreements. . . . Such reciprocal agreements should be based on the most-favored-nation principle in its unconditional and unrestricted form. . . ." New York *Times,* June 18, 1933, item, "Text of United States Tariff Proposal." (Immediately following the publication of this item a sharp controversy, involving the home Government and the American delegation at the Conference and centering about the question whether an American position on tariff matters had been definitely taken, arose over the issue whether the American memorandum was a "suggestion" for the agenda or a definite "proposal.") Again in his opening address to the Conference Secretary of State Hull, criticizing existing tendencies, had declared: "In the making of tariffs thought was given only to the safeguarding of the home market. . . . The home market was to be kept separate from the world market, and prices bearing no relation to those of other countries would be fixed arbitrarily within each nation." Almost at the moment this criticism was being levelled at "thought . . . given only to the safeguarding of the home market," the Industrial Recovery Bill of the home administration, with its broad provisions for keeping the home market separate from the world market, was being prepared for passage by the Congress. The same trend appeared in the confusion arising subsequently over the question of international stabilization of monetary exchange wherein the efforts in one direction of the American delegation were met with President Roosevelt's statement maintaining that "The sound internal economic system of a nation is a greater factor in its well being than the price of its currency in changing terms of the currencies of other nations." (For the full text of the President's declaration, which is itself somewhat vague and confusing, see New York *Times,* July 4, 1933.)

our industrial activities demand, to a greatly enhanced extent, the supplementary utilization of foreign markets. We simply cannot maintain our trade with the world unless we enable adequate imports to take place. . . . We can only hope that our party leaders and legislators will realize that old formulas no longer fit what has become a wholly new issue." [29]   Five years later a group of international bankers, including important leaders from the United States, signed a plea for the removal of restrictions on European trade, in connection with which the declaration was made: "If we check their dealings, their power to pay their debts diminishes, and their power to purchase our goods is reduced. Restricted imports involve restricted exports, and no nation can afford to lose its export trade." [30]   But the voice of finance had little or no effect, so far as it concerned the American bankers' particular interest in international trade, on the policies of nations respecting home protection.

From this survey of the facts in the history of protective and restrictive measures certain conclusions emerge. The tariff has been consistently defended by its sponsors as an instrument and a phase of national interest. The idea of "progressive free trade throughout the world," proclaimed by the Democrats in 1856, has been completely abandoned by them as a controlling principle. Although they now condemn particular aspects of protection, they no longer denounce it officially as a creation of special interests and they promise to safeguard, by customs duties and other provisions, industry, labor, and agriculture—which, in fact, represent all phases of national interest broadly considered in economic terms.

In other words, the two great parties, which between them comprise the overwhelming majority of the people, have shown a decided tendency to return to the original principle—the Hamiltonian philosophy of nearly one hundred and fifty years ago—that the control of imports in the national interest is a responsibility imposed by the nature of things on the Government of the United States. They appear to be faced with

[29] *Pressing Problems and Some Suggestions,* pp. 23–24.
[30] *Annals of the American Academy of Political and Social Science,* No. 230, January, 1929, p. 47.

the necessity of restating that philosophy in terms of modern conditions and of establishing the criteria by which to determine what particular forms of restriction actually serve the national interest—the philosophy and the criteria depending upon a searching inquiry into just what is the national interest to be sought, measured, and served.

Steps in this direction appear to have been taken. Both parties have been drawing together on the matter of criteria. As early as 1892, the Republicans declared that the duties levied on commodities coming within the range of control should be "equal to the difference between wages abroad and at home." Twelve years later they asserted that "the measure of protection should always be at least equal to the difference in the cost of production at home and abroad." In their platform for the next campaign they reiterated this "true principle of protection"—"the difference between the cost of production at home and abroad"—and added as a kind of after thought, apparently, "together with a reasonable profit to American industries."

In 1928 the Democrats definitely accepted the fundamental criterion by declaring that "actual difference between the cost of production at home and abroad, with adequate safeguard for the wage of the American laborer, must be the measure of the tariff rate." Although they favored in 1932 "a competitive tariff for revenue," they omitted the significant word "only" and their candidate committed them to the protection of "American business and labor," implying at least a criterion of discrimination. Furthermore, both parties propose to "take the tariff out of politics" by having an impartial board apply automatically a mathematical standard of measurement to particular schedules. According to these findings, therefore, control of trade in the national interest is to be a fixed principle, and is interpreted to mean that the difference between the cost of production at home and abroad is the criterion for determining the nature of that control. The problem raised by this course is to be solved by fact-findings and the use of economic and engineering rationality.

Such is the point to which the conception of national interest in commercial control has been brought in the process of historical development; but practice, lagging far behind theory, has not caught up with principle. When the tariff bill of 1930 was being framed, few schedules seem to have been fixed by reference to the mathematical formula—the difference between the cost of production at home and abroad—and many were based on pertinent suggestions by particular parties interested in them. Senator Bingham, of the Senate Finance Committee, was assisted by Mr. Eyanson, a gentleman selected by the President of the Connecticut Manufacturers' Association, "loaned" to Senator Bingham, and by him commissioned as one of his own clerks on the Senate payroll. Declaring that he was himself uninformed about tariff matters, the Senator found "an extremely good teacher" in Mr. Eyanson; and the President of the Manufacturers' Association was delighted that he had been able to handle the tariff measure "here in the office." [31] During the same controversy, Mr. Grundy, of Pennsylvania, explained how he raised money for the Republican campaign fund from contributors interested in tariff rates, and declared that individuals and concerns directly interested in the tariff should write the rates, protesting against the disproportionate representation accorded to agricultural states in the Senate. [32]

Other testimony presented at Senate hearings about the same time disclosed the pressure of powerful private interests on the making of rates and the tactics employed by them to advance their own special interests. In connection, for example, with the principle of protection according to the "cost of production" at home and abroad, it was shown that one group of fish processors owned substantial interests both in the United States and Canadian industries. In such a situation it was possible for their representatives, when testifying before the Tariff Commission of either country, to set up costs of production in each case as the particular interests of the fish companies might dictate, since the same group was in control of the determinants and accounts of production costs at home and

[31] *Hearings Before the Sub-Committee of the Committee on the Judiciary,* (71st Cong., 1st Sess., 1929), pp. 202–203. (Investigation pursuant to Sen. Res. 20 relating to lobbying.)

[32] *Ibid.,* pp. 432, 464–474; 500–503, 574, 575, 579.

abroad.[33] Moreover, the efficiency and purity of the impartial agency, which was to take the tariff out of politics and arrive at conclusions by scientific methods, were not a little endangered by the tactics of particular private interests. Thus, also in the case of fish, it was shown that between the time the House of Representatives passed upon a bill making no change in the fish duties and the Senate Finance Committee reported out a bill in which it altered the rates to meet the requests of the private interests, one of the fish groups active before the Senate Finance Committee induced an employee of the Tariff Commission in charge of matters dealing with the fish industry to leave the Commission and enter its own employ.[34] It was testified elsewhere in the hearings by one witness, and as directly denied by another, that the said employee, while in the service of the Tariff Commission, had made the statement "that it would be comparatively easy to fix up a group of figures on either side of the fence; that in the confusion they could be believed."[35]

In the matter of the rate on sugar, likewise, it might be difficult indeed for any impartial "fact-finding" body to protect its findings against such an interference with scientific principles as was shown to have been fostered by private sugar interests, both in the United States and in Cuba, associated with and representing the Cuban industry.[36] Nor could the "cost of production" analysis gain much headway in the face of the strict control exercised through decrees secured from the Cuban government by the associated producers united in a selling agency to eliminate competition.[37]

[33] *Ibid.*, pp. 323–337; 341–342. For the motive for the American control of Canadian plants and its relation to international competition, see pp. 346–347; 480–481.

[34] *Ibid.*, pp. 345–346; 403–431.

[35] *Ibid.*, p. 282.

[36] The testimony on the activities of sugar and associated interests is quite voluminous and is continued at intervals throughout a large part of the Senate *Hearings*. The more pertinent passages may be found on the following pages: 375–400; 1263ff.; 1505–1526; 1549, 1568–1581; particularly such pages as 1216, 1506, 1507, 1510, 1511, 1560, 1561.

[37] *Ibid.*, pp. 1573–1574. Indeed the Cuban sugar interests were anxious to keep true production costs in strict confidence at a time when they were seeking a change in rates which ostensibly was to be based upon such costs. When one of their own agents, engaged to disseminate publicity in their behalf, gave

The record of the hearings from which this information is taken, to which reference has been made, is replete with other examples along the same line, but the illustrations given are typical enough to illustrate the points indicated without going to the extreme of belaboring the record. Certainly it is clear that the practice of tariff-making falls far short of the fixed "scientific" principles designed for its guidance. When the Democrats returned to power shortly afterward, the modifications in rates which they adopted had immediate reference to the demands of particular constituencies.

Hence the same dichotomy appears here as in other parts of the conception of national interest. Irrespective of the extent to which it may represent the true national interest, the conception itself assumes a transcendent consideration controlling details with reference to supreme bench marks; and yet in practice policy as reality is the product of the pressure of special interests. Even as the political parties appear to be moving toward transcendent criteria in declared policy, practice appears to move flagrantly in the opposite direction. Only on the theory that the equilibrium or movement created by the confluence of pressures automatically reflects the national interest can practice be accepted as in conformity with the idea. But the analogy drawn from the realm of physics is scarcely applicable to the conduct of human affairs. Throughout the processes of negotiation and conflict which produce equilibrium or movement there are appearances of choice; the statesman is not an inert weight moved by an impact of a given force; he resists, compromises, chooses, and deflects, always with respect to some standards and predilections composing his pattern of the social order deemed desirable or of the particular interests to be fostered and cherished.

However made, tariff schedules strike into the economies of other countries and usually evoke commercial readjustments, if not open retaliations. It may be, as the Secretary of the

out information bearing too closely upon production costs, a letter was despatched from the Cuban interests to their representative in the United States asserting: "It is very dangerous to stress the fact that Cuba can make sugar cheap. I think it very important that some one visé all of Mrs. Jones' publicity, or I am afraid she may do something that might hurt the cause." (P. 1744.)

Treasury, Ogden Mills, declared in 1932, "that the rates in our tariff laws are a purely domestic question to be determined by the Congress of the United States without consultation with foreign governments"; but, whether those governments are consulted orally or not, their responses to American tariff legislation, both actual and potential, form a part of the data which the wisdom and discretion of statecraft must take into account.[38] Whatever the legists may say, the making of tariff rates and the control of commerce generally are not in substance and effect unilateral operations. Here the realization of what appears to some as a purely domestic policy conceived in the national interest becomes inevitably a projection of lines of force into the complex of international relations.

DEFENSE THE SUPREME NATIONAL INTEREST

Towering above all other interests is that of national defense. By general consent this is the supreme consideration of every government. At all events no other appeal commands such wide-spread popular support, receives such undivided allegiance. Those who resist it are loaded with the heaviest social opprobrium and those who betray it are stamped with the highest of crimes, treason. By almost unanimous consent it is held that the right of self-defense is rooted in the nature of things.[39] The Darwinian conception of the struggle for existence lends a biological sanction to the exercise of the right; and the municipal law, which brands murder as a capital crime, makes an exception of killing in self-defense. "The first law of states, as of men," says Admiral Mahan, "is self-preserva-

[38] Although not necessarily in retaliation for the American tariff, trade barriers in more than half of the sixty-five commercially important countries increased by various means during the year 1932. This is in addition to restrictions upon trade by means of exchange controls. *Foreign Tariffs and Commercial Policies During 1932*. Trade Information Bulletin No. 812, United States Dept. of Commerce, Washington, D. C., 1933.

[39] In developing the "fundamental rights" of states into a system, Fauchille derives them all from "the primary right of existence," from which flows first, ". . . defense." Cited in Clyde Eagleton, *International Government*. For a discussion of self-preservation as a fundamental right of states, see Oppenheim, *International Law*, Vol. I, p. 234 and Chapter II: Fenwick, *International Law*, Chapter X.

tion." [40] Few there are who will deny it, who will rather insist that the first law of states, as of men, is sacrifice for the benefit of others, even unto death.

In recognition of this fact the Constitution confers upon Congress the power to provide for the common defense, to raise and support armies, to provide and maintain a navy, to make rules for the government and regulation of the land and naval forces, to declare war, and to call the militia into the service of the United States. The authority thus granted is almost plenary, is plenary for practical purposes. "Security against foreign danger," wrote Madison in the *Federalist,* "is one of the primary objects of civil society. It is an avowed and essential object of the American Union. The power requisite for attaining it must be effectually confided to federal councils. . . . With what color of propriety could the force necessary for defense be limited by those who cannot limit the force of offense? If a federal Constitution could chain the ambition, or set bounds to the exertions of all other nations, then, indeed, might it prudently chain the discretion of its own government and set bounds to the exertions for its own safety." [41] Congress must, no doubt, observe certain formalities in laying taxes and making appropriations for military purposes, but in the last resort as a practical proposition it may make unlimited use of persons and property in war.

Although the conception of defense against aggression bulks large in the writings of the Fathers, the powers conferred upon Congress were by no means limited to this purpose. It is true that, according to the letter, the militia is to be called forth "to execute the laws of the Union, suppress insurrections, and repel invasions," and that during the War of 1812 vigorous objections were made to the employment of the militia beyond the borders of the United States; but Congress has the power to declare a war of aggression, if it so pleases, and the right to unite the militia with the Army of the United States has been established by law and practice. Under the Constitution, defense is not limited to the territory and waters of the United States nor to the protection of American lives and property on

[40] *The Problem of Asia and Its Effect upon International Policies,* p. 97.
[41] The *Federalist,* No. XL.

the high seas. It extends to the realization of any rights, clear or inchoate, which Congress in its wisdom may see fit to effectuate by arms. Only by such an interpretation could authority be found for the acquisition of territory from Mexico or Spain, to say nothing of "thrashing the Barbary pirates" and employing gun boats on the Yangtse River.

In the course of American history, however, there has developed no little confusion on the subject of national defense. The reasons for this state of affairs are not difficult to discover. For many years before and after the Civil War the people of the United States were particularly absorbed in the development of the continental resources; and the expanding domestic market furnished generous outlets for developing industries and accumulating capital. In this period the country was inclined to turn in upon its own economic activities and little or no emphasis was laid upon the navy, a merchant marine, or the prosecution of foreign trade. "We look to no foreign conquests, nor do we propose to enter into competition with any other nation for supremacy on the ocean," wrote President Tyler in 1841; "but it is due not only to the honor but to the security of the people of the United States that no nation should be permitted to invade our waters at pleasure." [42]

Long afterward, during the World War, when Germany was assailed as an "aggressor on land and sea" and the American nation was enlisted in the struggle against the Central Powers, denunciations of aggressive warfare became common in high official circles, and millions were led to believe that there was something sinister about all wars of "aggression." Article 10 of the Covenant of the League of Nations provided for security against a war of external aggression. This restricted view of national defense was attempted in the Kellogg Pact; [43] and

[42] *American Naval Policy as Outlined in Messages of the Presidents*, (Washington, 1924), p. 8.

[43] It is questionable how far the attempt has been successful. James T. Shotwell, *War as an Instrument of National Policy*, pp. 216, 218. But see pp. 157, 168, 173. For the effect of Secretary of State Kellogg's "explanations" of the treaty, see also Clyde Eagleton, "The Attempt to Define Aggression," International Conciliation Document No. 264 (November, 1930), especially p. 607. For another view on this point see John B. Whitton, "What Follows the Pact of Paris?" International Conciliation Document No. 276 (January, 1932), particularly p. 40 thereof.

President Hoover on more than one occasion spoke of defense
as covering merely the American nation. In partial answer to
the attack of William C. Gardiner, at the time head of the
Navy League, President Hoover, on Navy Day, October 27,
1931, expressed his view of the national defense as follows:
"The first necessity of our government is the maintenance of
a navy so efficient and strong that, in conjunction with our
army, no enemy may ever invade our country. . . . Ours is
a force of defense, not offense. . . ." In his acceptance speech
of August 11, 1932, he said: "I insist upon an army and navy
of a strength that will guarantee that no foreign soldier will
land on American soil. The strength is relative to other nations.
I favor every arms reduction which preserves that relationship."

On the other hand, the weight of governmental opinion has
been against this limited view of the national interest in the
objectives of warfare. The authors of the *Federalist,* as we
have seen, took the opposite tack. President Monroe looked
upon the Navy as obliged to extend "its aid to every interest
on which the security and welfare of our Union depend"—
"even when remote from our coast." [44] Jackson, in urging an
increase of the Navy, declared this to be "true policy," for
"your Navy will not only protect your rich and flourishing
commerce in distant seas, but will enable you to reach and an-
noy the enemy, and will give defense its greatest efficiency by
meeting danger at a distance from home." [45] Lamenting the
neglect of the Navy by Congress, President Grant underlined
his recommendations for an increase by giving specific reasons:
"With an energetic, progressive business people like ours, penetrating and forming business relations with every part of the
known world, a Navy strong enough to command the respect
of our flag abroad is necessary for the full protection of all
their rights." [46] Among the things covered by defense, President Arthur included "the protection of our commercial interests." [47] By this time the export of manufactured products

---

[44] *Writings* (Hamilton ed.), Vol. VII, p. 6.
[45] *American Naval Policy,* p. 7.
[46] *Ibid.,* pp. 9–10.
[47] *Ibid.,* p. 10.

amounted to only 11 per cent of the total export.[48] Congress was still reluctant to vote the enlarged appropriations requested by the Navy Department.[49]

As the proportion of manufactured goods rose in the export business, the demand for "defense of world-wide commercial interests" became more insistent. McKinley called for a navy and a merchant marine which meant "more work and wages to our countrymen as well as a safeguard to American interests in every part of the world." [50] His successor, President Roosevelt, continued the emphasis: "The American people must either build and maintain an adequate navy or else make up their minds definitely to accept a secondary position in international affairs, not merely in political but in commercial matters." [51] Carrying forward the tradition, President Taft advocated a strong navy "as the best conservator of peace with other nations, and the best means of securing respect for the assertion of our rights, the defense of our interests, and the exercise of our influence in international matters." [52] After the interregnum under President Wilson, President Harding renewed the assurance by declaring that the Navy is "the right arm of the Department of State, seeing to the enforcement of its righteous pronouncements. It guards the security of American citizens wherever they are the world over." [53]

It remained, however, for President Coolidge and his Secretary of the Navy, Curtis D. Wilbur, to formulate the philoso-

[48] For the year 1880. Bogart, *Economic History of the American People,* Table on p. 682. Dividing the total export into two broad divisions—Agricultural and Non-agricultural Products—the United States Commerce *Yearbook* (1931) gives the proportions for each respectively for the period 1896–1900, 66.2 and 33.8 per cent of the total export (p. 93).

[49] President Arthur took office in 1881. Yearly average expenditures of the Navy Department, on the basis of warrants issued, were: for the period 1871–1875, $23,328,000; 1876–1880, $15,990,000; 1881–1885, $15,863,000; an average of approximately $16,000,000 was fairly evenly maintained from 1876 to 1888. In the following year the figure rose to $21,379,000 and thereafter increased steadily. (The figures relate solely to the expenditures of the Navy Department for its naval functions and exclude civil expenditures of the Navy which until 1920 were included under another separate heading of Civil and Miscellaneous.) *United States Statistical Abstract,* 1931, p. 176.

[50] *American Naval Policy,* p. 13.

[51] *Ibid.,* p. 18.

[52] *Ibid.,* p. 29.

[53] *Ibid.,* p. 31.

phy of defense in its all-embracing scope. Their predecessors had spoken of the national interest to be defended in general terms, having in mind upon occasion, no doubt, specific contents, but they had not given a bill of particulars. President Coolidge, by contrast, speaking in the naval tradition, went more directly to the point. In an address before the United Press Association in 1927, he opened by explaining how the economic development of the United States had turned it into a nation extensively engaged in exporting capital and goods to foreign countries, and then came to the issue of defense. "Our Government," he said, "has certain rights over and certain duties toward our own citizens and their property, wherever they may be located. The person and property of a citizen are part of the general domain of the nation, even when abroad. . . . The fundamental laws of justice are universal in their application. These rights go with the citizen. Wherever he goes, the duties of our Government follow him." This, President Coolidge recognized, brought "inevitable criticisms," but he continued, "if, even where our national interests and the protection of the rights of our citizens are involved, we attempt to assist in composing difficulties and supporting international law, we must expect to be charged with imperialistic motives." Nevertheless, he denied that this policy meant "military aggrandizement" or any departure from established doctrine.[54]

Going into greater detail, Secretary Wilbur, in an address to the Connecticut Chamber of Commerce, enumerated the items of property abroad that composed the economic portion of national interest. He listed "twenty million tons of merchant shipping . . . worth $3,000,000,000 . . . loans and property abroad, exclusive of government loans, of over $10,000,000,000 . . . the volume of exports and imports for a single year—about $10,000,000,000 . . . the $8,000,000,000 due us from foreign governments." Adding these together "we have a total of $31,000,000,000, being about equal to the total wealth of the nation in 1878." Here is the material substance of national interest. "These vast interests must be considered when we talk of defending the flag. That flag must be defended unhesitatingly and with all our power whenever attacked. It makes

[54] New York *Times*, April 26, 1927, and January 11, 1927.

no difference whether it floats from an army post in Montana or from an American ship in the harbor of Calcutta or Sitka. . . . To defend America we must be prepared to defend its interests and our flag in every corner of the globe. . . . World-wide interests require world-wide defense. An American child crying on the banks of the Yangtse a thousand miles from the coast can summon the ships of the American navy up that river to defend it from unjust assault. Any nation facing the sea can be called to account by our navy. . . . A wise and sane development of the army and navy, a reasonable advance along lines of progress in all means of national defense, will remove serious thought of aggression by others." [55] Somewhat later Secretary Wilbur added sea lanes to the national domain: "Our trade routes as well as our international trade are essential parts of our national life. We are committed to the protection of this traffic upon the high seas." [56]

Running parallel with the evolution of the theory that defense means the protection by force of every American citizen and every American dollar in every part of the world on land and sea, as the official civilian conception, was a similar development in naval circles. The idea has firm roots in the *Federalist*, written in defense of the Constitution; it was expounded as a system by naval officers in the middle period of American history; and it was given outward expression by the Wilkes expedition to Samoa in 1839, Perry's opening of Japan in 1854, and Meade's acquisition of a naval base at Pago Pago in 1872. Beginning in 1890, with the appearance of *The Influence of Sea Power upon History*, the idea was worked out with great elaboration and documentation in the voluminous writings of Captain Alfred Thayer Mahan. While it cannot be said that his work was marked by strict philosophical consistency, he did particularly emphasize the conception of interest as the motive force of international relations, the object of defense, and the grounds of war.

"Self-interest," he said flatly, "is not only a legitimate, but a fundamental cause for national policy; one which needs no cloak of hypocrisy. . . . It is vain to expect governments to

[55] New York *Times*, May 8, 1925.
[56] Speech in Thomaston, Maine, July 25, 1927.

act continuously on any other ground than national interest. They have no right to do so, being agents not principals." [57] This formulation he applied to commerce and naval warfare: "The history of the Sea Power is largely, though by no means solely, a narrative of contests between nations, of mutual rivalries, of violence frequently culminating in war. The profound influence of sea commerce upon the wealth and strength of countries was clearly seen long before the true principles which governed its growth and prosperity were detected. To secure one's own people a disproportionate share of such benefits, every effort was made to exclude others, either by the peaceful legislative methods of monopoly or prohibitory regulations, or, when these failed, by direct violence. The clash of interests, the angry feeling roused by conflicting attempts thus to appropriate the larger share, if not the whole, of the advantages of commerce, and of distant unsettled commercial regions, led to wars." [58] Commercial aggression is a powerful source of wars. "The armaments of Europe," Mahan wrote in 1912, "are now not so much for protection against conquest as to secure to themselves the utmost possible share of the unexploited or imperfectly exploited regions of the world—the outlying markets, or storehouses of raw materials, which under national control shall minister to national emolument." [59]

The interests thus to be defended by sea power are not static or attached to any territorial area of fixed boundaries; they are subject to inevitable development from inner necessity. "The first law of states, as of men, is self-preservation—a term which cannot be narrowed to the bare tenure of a stationary round of existence. Growth is a property of a healthy life. . . . It does involve the right to insure by just means whatsoever contributes to national progress, and correlatively to combat injurious action taken by an outside agency, if the latter overpass its own lawful sphere. When a difference between two states can be brought to the test of ascertained and defined rights, this carries with it a strong presumption in favor of submission of arbitration; but when a matter touches only

[57] *The Problem of Asia,* pp. 97, 187.
[58] *Influence of Sea Power upon History, 1660–1783,* p. 1.
[59] *Armaments and Arbitration,* p. 113.

advantage, not qualified by law or prescription, and the question, therefore, is one of expediency, it is justly and profitably considered in the light of self-preservation." [60]   Indeed even the law is not always a bar to the pursuit of interests: "The legal right of one country, or of two countries, may so far contravene the natural—that is, the moral—right, the essential interests, the imperative policy of a third, that resistance would be necessary, and therefore justifiable. Diplomacy then enters, and armament is simply an incident of diplomacy." [61]   Although in other places Mahan laid stress upon moral obligation and, indeed, flatly denied the potency of interests in policy (below, pp. 268 ff.), he nevertheless made interests the central objects of defense. [62]

From this standpoint Mahan assailed as erroneous the fundamental proposition: "That the United States needs a navy 'for defense only.' ... That a navy 'for defense only' means for the immediate defense of our seaports and coast-lines; an allowance also being made for scattered cruisers to prey upon an enemy's commerce." [63]   As an escape from this restriction he chose a re-definition of defense. "The way out of this confusion of thought, the logical method of reconciling the political principle of non-aggression with a naval power capable of taking the offensive, if necessary, is to recognize, and to say, that defense means not merely defense of our territory, but defense of our just national interests, whatever they be and wherever they are. ... No military student can consider efficient a force so limited, in quantity or quality, that it must await attack before it can act." [64]   For this reason Mahan insisted that the United States should have a navy strong enough to defend its interests in all parts of the world; able to "go out and assail the enemy and hurt him in his vital interests." [65] Hence it follows that "a 'navy for defense only' is a wholly misleading phrase, unless defense is construed to include all national interests, and not only the national territory; and fur-

---

[60] *The Problem of Asia*, pp. 29–30.
[61] *Armaments and Arbitration*, p. 81.
[62] *Current Fallacies upon Naval Subjects*, p. 281.
[63] *Ibid.*, p. 281.
[64] *Ibid.*, p. 281.
[65] *Ibid.*, p. 286.

ther, unless it be understood that the best defense of one's own interests is power to injure those of the enemy." [66]

Having developed the formula that "national defense" is the defense of national interests, wherever they may be and whatever their form, Mahan proceeds to enumerate them. They include defense of national territory, the extension of American maritime commerce, the acquisition of territorial positions which contribute to command of the seas, "when it can be done righteously," [67] the maintenance of the Monroe Doctrine even though the United States does participate in European controversies,[68] hegemony in the Caribbean,[69] and active promotion of the China trade.[70] Perhaps the American nation does not fully comprehend these realities and this policy, but events are inexorable. "That the mass of United States citizens do not realize understandingly that the nation has vital political interests beyond the sea is probably true; still more likely is it that they are not tracing any connection between them and the reconstruction of the navy. Yet interests exist, and the navy is growing." [71]

In due time the philosophy unofficially formulated by Captain Mahan was officially accepted by the Navy Department and substantially incorporated in a declaration of naval policy (below, p. 320). Fearing that members of the Department had been "hampered by a lack of definitely enunciated policies which could be followed by all concerned" and desirous of aiding Congress "in framing legislation for the Navy," the Department took upon itself the responsibility of defining its duties.[72] In this official declaration the Department set forth the purposes of the Navy: "to support national policies and national interests, . . . to support its [the United States'] policies and its commerce and to guard its continental and overseas possessions, . . . to develop and organize the Navy for operations in any part of either ocean, . . . to make

---

[66] *Ibid.*, p. 300.
[67] *Interest of America in the Sea Power*, pp. 124, 129.
[68] *Ibid.*, p. 154.
[69] *Ibid.*, pp. 265–266.
[70] *Problem of Asia*, p. 17, pp. 109–110, 122–123, 166–167.
[71] *Interest of America in the Sea Power*, pp. 51–52.
[72] *Annual Report of the Secretary of the Navy* (1932), p. 33.

strength of the Navy for exercising ocean-wide control of the sea, with particular reference to the protection of American interests and overseas and coastwise commerce, . . . to support in every possible way American interests, especially in the expansion and development of American foreign commerce and American merchant marine." [73] Thus a whole program of foreign economic policy, accompanied by conceptions respecting the nature and objects of defense, was prepared by the General Board of the Navy, approved by the Secretary, and promulgated as the official doctrine of the United States Navy, apparently without reference to the fact that policy, under the Constitution, is a matter for the determination of the civil branches of the Government.[74]

Moreover, the Navy Department, through its official publications, lays emphasis on its function in promoting as well as defending national interests in all parts of the world. "Another great rôle of the Navy," it reports, "not generally appreciated is its part in initiating trade through diplomacy." [75] In support of this statement it cites the Jones treaties with a Hawaiian

[73] New York *Times,* November 13, 1928.

[74] The composition, functions, duties, and work of the General Board were set forth in considerable detail by Rear Admiral Mark L. Bristol in his testimony before the Senate Foreign Relations Committee in its hearings on the Treaty on Limitation of Naval Armaments (May, 1930), 71st Cong., 2d Sess., pp. 101ff. Parts of the Text of the Memorandum of the General Board touching policy as well as technical matters were placed in the official record of this hearing, printed as a public document, and made available through the Government Printing Office, Washington, D. C. According to the information given at this hearing, the policy of the General Board, embracing the matters in the text above, was set forth in full detail in a memorandum or report on May 16, 1922, and revised and approved on October 6, 1928, and as so revised was in force at the time of the hearings. The intimate connection in practice between the navy, through its officers, and the Department of State, is brought out clearly by Admiral Bristol who stated that he served in the Near East for eight years as high commissioner representing the State Department, and also was in command of the naval forces in those waters, with headquarters at Constantinople. *Ibid.,* p. 115. As regards the relation of the navy to commerce, Admiral Bristol produced a trade map showing trade and commercial interests in dollars in various areas, stating at the same time that when naval policies and affairs are discussed, both by the Admirals and the General Board, this map is before them. *Ibid.,* pp. 231–233. His testimony is supported by the other naval officers who appeared before this committee, particularly Rear Admirals Frank H. Schofield (*Ibid.,* p. 236), L. M. Nulton, and Hilary P. Jones.

[75] *What the Navy Has Done* (Annual Report of the Department, 1930), p. 5.

chief in 1826, the Wilkes expedition to Samoa in 1839, and Perry's action in opening Japanese ports in 1854. Turning from historical illustrations it cites recent activities, particularly in the Near East. "The competition for trade in this part of the world," it continues, "is very keen, the various European countries using every means at their disposal to obtain preferential rates, etc. The Navy not only assists our commercial firms to obtain business, but when business opportunities present themselves, American firms are notified and given full information on the subject." [76] In this way Mahan's theory that interests are dynamic, not static, is accepted by the Navy Department and the additional assumption is made that it is the duty of the Navy to participate with the civilian branches of the Government in making them dynamic.

Although not afloat on the seas and not easily transferable to any part of the world, the Army of the United States is officially regarded as having responsibilities for protecting national interests in places far scattered from the continental domain. To use the language of the War Department, "the Army must provide an adequate organized, balanced, and effective mobile force which shall be ready and available for emergencies within the continental limits of the United States or elsewhere; which must patrol the 1500 miles of Mexican border; and which constitutes a nucleus for a complete and immediate mobilization for the national defense in event of an emergency declared by Congress. It must provide adequate defense for our coasts and oversea possessions. To this end, garrisons are stationed in Alaska, Hawaii, the Philippines, Panama, Porto Rico, and China, both as a safeguard for Americans who have settled there and as an added protection for the continental United States and for its commercial and political interest in the Far East." [77] Thus the military as well as the naval branch of the Government has arrived officially at the broad conception of defense as *the protection and promotion of world-wide American interests.*

Evidently the conception of defense as national interest, like

---

[76] *What the Navy Has Done,* p. 5. On the activities of the Navy in the Near East, see Admiral Bristol's reference to his service in that area. Note 74, p. 341.

[77] *The Work of the War Department* (1924), p. 18.

all other ideas, is intimately associated with particular interests. By general agreement in military and naval circles, defense now covers not only the entity known as the nation in its geographical setting but also American citizens, property, and opportunities for profitable commerce throughout the world. These particular interests demand and receive both diplomatic and military protection in varying degrees according to circumstances.[78] They exert pressure on the Government and its departments, shaping more or less its policies and actions. That much is declared officially and written firmly in the record of history. And naturally the statesmen most vigorous in support of these particular interests have the support of the latter in domestic politics—moral and economic—indicated by political affiliations and the lists of campaign contributors.

In addition to the particular interests operating abroad, there are powerful interests at home directly concerned with the extension and enlargement of the material instruments of defense, such as ships, armor plate, fuel, guns, tanks, airplanes, and explosives. Indeed, owing to the technological character of modern warfare, nearly every industry is involved in the

[78] As explained by Henry Kittredge Norton, speaking on "Backward Countries as a Field for Investment:" " . . . where American money goes into a backward country, American managers and superintendents go with it to supervise its application in the same manner in which American administrators are sent to supervise government loans. These American citizens usually take with them their wives and children. . . . In the event of an upheaval in which American interests are threatened, there is thrust upon these expatriots the duty of protecting and preserving the properties committed to their charge. Their lives are at once endangered. And the United States is called upon to protect them. American citizenship would be worth little outside our own borders, Americans could take little part in the reclaiming of backward areas, if the government did not respond by sending them the protection necessary." Lectures on the Harris Foundation. University of Chicago Press, 1928, pp. 221–222. That this observation is borne out in practice and that the United States does respond to the call upon it, even upon rumor of trouble, is well illustrated in a series of dispatches concerning "consistent rumors of imminent uprisings . . . recruited entirely from the unemployed 'communists' and the riffraff of northern Honduras," a district where an American fruit company carried on substantial operations. "Minister Lay requested that the U.S.S. *Memphis* at Ceiba make a visit to Tela where a high nervous tension existed. These visits were said to have had a very beneficial effect." . . . "The U.S.S. *Memphis* reported all quiet at Ceiba and stated that cargoes were being loaded as usual. . . ." Department of State Press Releases. Weekly Issue No. 82 (April 25, 1932), No. 184.

business of furnishing supplies. The wider the area of defense to be covered on land and sea, the more intense the rivalry of nations over commercial opportunities, the greater the imminence of war, the larger the demand for the machines and commodities of defense. And, as in other divisions of politics, private interests which supply these goods at a profit to themselves, from time to time, bring pressure to bear on the Government.[79] They favor increases in armaments and oppose efforts to effect reductions by international agreements. They engage lobbyists to work on members of Congress, carry on propaganda through the press, send out speakers to arouse patriotic societies, and contribute to campaign funds. Moreover army and navy bureaucracies, like all other bureaucracies, become interests in themselves,[80] and as a matter of course call for more officers and men, larger salaries and wages.[81] In fact, so involved is the question of defense in private considerations that it is difficult to discover just where the public interest in security ends and particular interests in gains and emoluments begin. Here as everywhere else, those who exercise large powers in the determination of the public interest are constantly subject to the influences of private considerations.

THE MERCHANT MARINE

As the conception of national defense was worked out to include the protection and promotion of American economic

[79] For illustrations see Beard, *The Navy: Defense or Portent?*, pp. 111–184. General recognition of this fact led Congress in 1930 to order an inquiry into methods and measures for "taking the profit out of war."

[80] Writing in the June, 1933, number of *Scribner's Magazine* ("Congress— The Nation's Scapegoat"), Mr. F. H. La Guardia, formerly a member of Congress from New York, observes on this point: "Now we come to the most peculiar and let me say the most effective form of lobbying in Washington. That lobby is not conducted by any private interest but by two of the executive departments of the government itself, that of the army and navy." He then continues with a description and illustration of the workings of these lobbies.

[81] In the same article Mr. La Guardia explains how these lobbies "play practical politics too" . . . when "in the consideration of the 1932 army appropriation bill . . . efforts were made to reduce the cost of the army by eliminating a number of superannuated and supernumerary officers." He further illustrates a connection between political party leadership and the interests of the army with respect to the legislation on the appropriation bill. *Ibid.*

interests in all parts of the world, the development of the idea of a merchant marine as a beneficial interest and as an arm of defense ran parallel with it.[82] And, on the whole, there was a fairly clear-cut division of the major parties on this issue previous to the disruption of sea-borne traffic by the World War. As early as 1884 the Republican platform called upon Congress "to remove the burdens under which American shipping has been depressed." In this declaration no specific measures were suggested but in the next campaign there was a direct demand for appropriations to encourage "the shipping interests of the Atlantic, Gulf, and Pacific states." From that time forward the Republicans continued to insist upon government aid for merchant shipping. Successive platforms commended the policy. Presidents endorsed it. Efforts were made in Congress to carry the project into realization. "To the spread of our commerce in peace and the defense of our flag in war," insisted President Roosevelt, "a great and prosperous merchant marine is indispensable." But the opposition of the Democrats and the agrarian wing of the Republicans long delayed the voting of the subsidies and other measures designed to effect the end in view.

[82] The early statistical background of the status of the American merchant marine is as follows: The proportion of American carriage in foreign trade rose rapidly from 1789 to 1795 to 92 per cent of the imports and 88 per cent of the exports. Thereafter, except for a slight dip between 1811–1815, a fairly even level was maintained as follows: for the period 1796 to 1800, an average of 91.6 of imports and 87.8 of exports; 1826–1830, 93.46 of imports and 86.78 of exports. Beginning with 1830 a consistent decrease commenced and continued to the last decade of the century as follows: 1831–1835, 90.6 of imports and 76.7 of exports; 1841–1845, 85.6 of imports and 75.48 of exports; 1851–1855, 74.06 of imports and 69.3 of exports; 1861–1865, 40.52 of imports and 44.54 of exports; 1871–1875, 28.8 of imports and 27.3 of exports; 1881–1885, 20.7 of imports and 13.52 of exports. The proportion of loss, or falling off, in the American carriage in foreign trade for the 75 years after 1815 was approximately 82.52 of imports and 89.92 of exports. William W. Bates, *American Marine,* Houghton, Mifflin & Co., New York, 1893. The proportion of total American foreign trade carried in American vessels fell from 66.5 per cent in 1860 to 9.3 per cent in 1900, which was the lowest point reached. Bogart, *op. cit.,* p. 696. See also, the text and tonnage chart (IX) in United States Commerce *Yearbook,* Vol. I, 1931, pp. 597 and 598, as well as the comparative statistics of world tonnage in Vol. II, 1931. Conditions since 1910 have operated to increase American participation in the carriage of its foreign trade. Just prior to the depression American vessels carried close to 40 per cent of the total American foreign trade.

With a high degree of consistency the Democrats, as a party, stood out against public assistance to private shipping. In 1900 their platform denounced "such bare-faced frauds upon the taxpayers as the Shipping Subsidy bill, which, under the false pretense of fostering American shipbuilding, would put un-earned millions into the pockets of favorite contributors to the Republican campaign fund." Again, in 1908, they con-demned the ship subsidy bill recently passed by the Senate as "an iniquitous appropriation of public funds for private purposes"; they favored "the upbuilding of a merchant ma-rine" but "without new or additional burdens upon the people and without bounties from the public treasury." Four years later the formula was repeated. The platform declared in favor of fostering "by constitutional regulation of commerce . . . the growth of a merchant marine . . . but without im-posing additional burdens upon the people and without bounties or subsidies from the public treasury." Upon this platform Woodrow Wilson was elected President. Two years later the World War broke in upon oceanic commerce. Farmers as well as manufacturers were confronted with the problem of securing enough bottoms in which to carry commodities, now at a high price, to foreign markets. A new note was then heard in agrarian circles.

In these circumstances a shipping bill was prepared under President Wilson's direction and he went before Congress in December, 1914, to press for the immediate enactment of legis-lation. Having long denounced open and direct subsidies to private shipping interests, the Democrats chose, as an alterna-tive, to "put the Government into the shipping business." At once a bitter fight was precipitated between the two parties, but the need was urgent. To win support the President took the issue to the country. Speaking in Indianapolis, on Janu-ary 8, 1915, he made the agrarian appeal. "Do you know, gentlemen," he said, "the ocean freight rates have gone up in some instances to ten times their ordinary figures, and that the farmers of the United States, those who raise grain and those who raise cotton . . . cannot get any profit out of the prices they are willing to pay for these things on the other side of the sea because the whole profit is eaten up by the extortionate charges for ocean carriage?" [83] Later in that year the same point was made in the same city by W. G. McAdoo, Secretary of the Treasury: "Our farmers, because they produce the bulk of our exports, ought to be protected against extortionate ocean freight rates, and ought to have the assurance of sufficient steamship service and reasonable rates to secure fair treatment and enable them to compete in the open markets with their rivals in the other great farm-producing regions of the world." [84]

In due course the shipping bill was passed and the Government of the United States went into the business of buying, leasing, building, and operating merchant ships. [85] After the stress of the war was over, the Government, now under Republican auspices, adopted a policy of selling its ships at a low price to private concerns and retaining for itself only the "pioneer" lines which did not pay their way. Under Harding and Coolidge efforts were made to wring a direct subsidy from Congress for private companies, but in vain. Yet in the end the goal was reached by other routes. Money was lent by the Government at low rates to shipbuilding concerns; operating companies were granted lucrative mail contracts and the services of naval officers. [86] Thus the strength of the Gov-

[83] E. C. Brooks, *Woodrow Wilson as President*, p. 422.

[84] *Ibid.*, p. 427.

[85] By act of Congress, approved September 7, 1916, the United States Shipping Board was created and empowered to organize one or more corporations to carry out the broad purposes of the act. In April, 1917, it organized the United States Shipping Board Emergency Fleet Corporation, the name of which was changed subsequently to United States Shipping Board Merchant Fleet Corporation. Under the maximum allowance for all shipping activities of the board, the enormous total of 4,500 vessels of 24,500,000 dead-weight tons came under its jurisdiction and control. Approximately $3,000,000,000 was spent on the war shipbuilding program. Prepared statement of T. V. O'Connor, Chairman, United States Shipping Board, *Hearings of the House Committee on Merchant Marine, Radio, and Fisheries,* 72d Cong., 1st Sess.; *General Inquiry Into the American Merchant Marine,* etc. (January-April, 1932); Government Printing Office, Washington, D. C., pp. 24ff.

[86] The Merchant Marine Act of 1920 combined in its law and administration the two purposes of liquidating the war-time activities and encouraging an American privately owned and operated merchant fleet. The Jones-White Act of 1928 materially expanded the activities designed to carry out the broad purposes expressed in the Act of 1920; and brought to the aid of American shipping services substantial subsidies for the carriage of ocean mails; and through its loan arrangements made possible the private construction of many new

ernment and its enormous financial resources were thrown on the side of extending American shipping operations to the four corners of the globe as a form of national interest affiliated with the promotion of trade and naval defense.

An examination of the debates in Congress which have accompanied marine and naval legislation reveals the fact that the weight of opinion favors the extension of shipping as an instrumentality for expanding commerce as well as for gathering into American purses the profits which now accrue to foreign carriers. The whole case, which is spread over hundreds of pages of print, is tersely and vigorously summed up by Senator Hiram Johnson, of California: "Ours, sir, is a producing Nation. The cycle of development through which we have just passed has been principally internal, but our huge resources have given us a productive capacity almost beyond belief and far in excess of our power to consume. The surplus must be marketed abroad if our general prosperity and our standards of living are to be maintained. . . . The desideratum can be accomplished in one fashion; that is, with a due measure of sea power. By sea power I mean a sufficient merchant marine and an adequate navy. Neither can exist separately; they are mutually dependent; they are the two elements which, when combined, are the sea power which every producing nation must have in order to be prosperous and stable. We must have first a merchant marine to carry our goods abroad and we must next have a navy to conserve, preserve, and protect that merchant marine. . . . To depend absolutely upon our trade competitors for the carriage of our goods would be like a merchant intrusting to his commercial rival and competitor the distribution of his wares. . . . We need a merchant marine because our unrivalled resources have, with an unparalleled

vessels for service on a broad front. For a statistical summary of the construction of vessels and the loans under these Acts, see *Cong. Record* (day to day session print), 73d Cong., 1st Sess. (April 12, 1933), pp. 1600ff. It should be noted, however, that the policy and the means of carrying it out as embodied in these two acts has been subject to persistent attack in many quarters, particularly among Democratic members of the Congress. See Hearings of the House Committee on the American Merchant Marine, etc. *Ibid.* See also, *Cong. Record* (day to day session print), 72d Cong., 2d Sess., pp. 1303, 2794, 2861, 2934, 3183, 3455, 3500, 4219, 5257, 5410, 5470.

genius and capacity for production, gone far beyond our ability to consume. We need it because exporting our surplus products is essential to maintain our standards of living and prosperity. We need it because we must of necessity import large quantities of essential products from overseas. We need it because the United States is at the center of the maritime world, with a position unequalled for the carrying trade to the great continents of Europe, Asia, and Africa. We need a merchant marine, lastly, because American commerce requires it and American national defense demands it." [87]

In a practical sense, then, the Navy and the merchant marine are, as Senator Royal Copeland, of New York, expressed it, "Siamese twins. One cannot live without the other. Without merchant ships acting as supply ships to feed the Navy, the Navy cannot exist, and unless we have the cruisers to give protection to our travel routes our merchants ships cannot continue to operate in the high seas." [88] Or to put the issue in the language of Senator Oddie, of Nevada, "the importance of a merchant marine as a factor in winning trade for national defense has been so great that foreign countries have made, and will continue to make, greater concessions to ship owners than would be justified if the shipping individuals alone were to be considered. For these reasons the United States must now meet the keenest and most strongly intrenched foreign competition that has ever existed and on a scale far greater than before. . . . The prestige, prosperity, and security of the nation depend upon an adequate and permanent merchant marine, and to maintain such a merchant marine will demand adequate naval protection."

If Admiral Plunkett is to be accepted as authority, this policy also requires adequate preparation for the supreme exigency. In a speech before the Republican Club in New York, on January 21, 1926, he said with quarter-deck directness: "If I read history correctly, and what we are doing today, we are nearer war today than we have ever been in our history, . . . the business men of this country have awakened

---

[87] *Congressional Record,* July 17, 1930, Special Senate Session, 71st Cong., Vol. LXXIII, p. 224.

[88] *Ibid.,* July 14, 1930, pp. 139–140.

to the fact that where they would sell they must deliver (they can no longer depend on their competitors to deliver their goods in the markets of the world) and that we must build a merchant marine and go back to the sea where we were in 1850. . . . Just so long as you make that your policy and you follow it through you are going to have war. I don't care whether it is with Great Britain or some other nation, you are going to have war just as surely as you are sitting in the room with me if you dare to contest the control of the sea with your goods. . . . It is economic in its origin, and as long as we proceed along the lines which we are traveling today war is absolutely inevitable." [89] The logic of the facts, the Admiral thought, required adequate naval preparation to meet the test when it came.

In conclusion, the conception of government support for a merchant marine as serving the national interests may be summarized in the following formulas. A merchant marine is an indispensable factor in the wealth and progress of a nation. Part of that wealth consists of the profits of the carrying trade which should go to American citizens instead of being left in the hands of foreign shipping interests. The merchant marine is also an instrument of trade promotion which has become an essential activity in the progress of the United States on account of the ever-increasing volume of production which must continuously find widening outlets abroad for goods. The merchant marine, also, as a part of the maritime potential, is an important element in national defense, the supreme interest of nations. It is a nursery of seamen and provides the navy with auxiliaries in time of war. On the other hand, the navy is an affiliate of the merchant marine. It must protect the foreign trade and commercial opportunities which the merchant marine helps to create. The larger the commerce

[89] New York *Times,* January 26, 1928, item "Plunkett Pictured Armed Trade Ships." Admiral Plunkett's speech was originally published in the January 22, 1928, issue of the *Times,* and in other papers on that date. Owing to a controversy over the exact wording of the speech—a controversy made all the more important by the international repercussions of the speech (see New York *Times,* January 24, 1928)—a full stenographic report was later released and published as first above stated. The extracts in the text come from this official report.

and the marine, the larger the navy; and the larger the navy, the more merchant auxiliaries required for its maintenance and operation. The reciprocal expansion of both is, therefore, an outcome of economic transactions of American nationals abroad and the desire of the Government to promote commerce. To employ the dictum of Admiral Benson, pronounced before the thirteenth annual convention of the National Rivers and Harbors Congress: "Anything that helps commerce helps the navy; anything that helps the navy helps commerce; and whatever helps both helps the country. (Applause.)" [90]

These formulas go further and include the conviction that private ownership and control are the best means of building up and maintaining a strong merchant marine. But in view of the discriminations constantly being made in favor of foreign carriers; in view of the pressures of foreign governments upon their own carriers on behalf of their nationals; and taking into account the intense competitive conditions in the carrying trade, the subsidizing of merchant marines by other nations, the difficulty of bringing American costs down to competitive costs owing to the higher American living standards reflected in the construction and operation of American vessels—for all these reasons, a strong American merchant marine under private ownership is impossible without substantial government aid in the form of subsidies, mail contracts, loan arrangements, and shipping regulations. These formulas are largely interdependent and together they build up the unity under which the conception of government support for a merchant marine has been realized. It is a conception which the Republican party has advocated and which the Democratic party has opposed, although extraordinary conditions, at times, have forced the latter to seek another solution than the one implied by mere opposition.

In the development of the merchant marine, as with the more direct instrumentalities of defense, private as well as public interests appear. While defense is strengthened by every increase in the number of merchant vessels under the financial stimulus of government aid, certain private enter-

[90] W. S. Benson, *The Relation of Inland Waterways to Naval Efficiency*, Washington, D. C., p. 4.

prises profit from the transaction—ship yards, operating companies, and purveyors of materials and supplies of many kinds. This, too, is well known and is written large in the documentary history of the conflict over ship subsidies. Here also appear propagandists, lobbyists, and political manipulators, supplied with money by particular concerns, and engaged in attempting to force the Government into enlarging the amounts granted from the Treasury.[91] On account of such political pressures, it has become difficult, if not impossible, for the statesman to determine the issues of the merchant marine with reference to national interest as a transcendent conception having a fixed bench mark of its own.

CONTROL OF IMMIGRATION IN THE INTEREST OF NATIONALITY

Although the conception of national interest was early advanced as the pivot of American diplomacy, emphasis was usually placed on the noun "interest" rather than on the adjective "national." It is true that the Fathers of the Republic laid stress on the significance of a common race, tongue, system of laws, and principles of government in their pleas for the establishment of a federal government. Recognizing the importance of personal attachment and sympathetic understanding in assuring the stability and efficient functioning of government, they placed certain restrictions on the participation of aliens in official operations. They provided that a Representative in Congress must have been seven years a citizen of the United States before assuming authority, and a Senator, nine years a citizen. The supreme office, that of the presidency, they closed to all persons except natural born citizens. As R. L. Garis states, after an examination of the history of legislation bearing on naturalization, "the statesmen of the Revolution did not entertain any idea that aliens had an *absolute right* to participate in the prerogatives of government."[92]

Nor did the Fathers look upon America as the asylum of the oppressed of all nations. Washington wrote to a corre-

[91] For illustration see Beard, *The Navy: Defense or Portent?*, pp. 60–67.
[92] *Immigration Restriction*, p. 27.

spondent in England: "I have no intention to invite immigrants, even if there are no restrictive acts against it. I am opposed to it altogether." Reënforcing this conviction he declared in a letter to Patrick Henry: "I want an *American* character, that the powers of Europe may be convinced we act for *ourselves* and not for others. This, in my judgment, is the only way to be respected abroad and happy at home." John Adams was equally emphatic. Jefferson looked with misgivings on "the importation of foreigners," and took note of "inconveniences" that might arise from the practice. Besides entertaining objections to the immigration of mechanics with their "manners and morals," he held that success in government depended on homogeneity in population. "It is for the happiness of those united in society," he said, "to harmonize as much as possible in matters which of necessity they must transact together. Civil government being the sole object of forming societies, its administration must be conducted by common consent." Immigrants from countries ruled by absolute monarchs, he thought, would bring disturbing ideas and practices into the United States. "These principles, with their language, they will transmit to their children. In proportion to their numbers, they will share legislation with us. They will infuse into it their spirit, warp or bias its direction, and render it a heterogeneous, incoherent, distracted mass." [93]

In spite of these views and precautions, however, the doors of the country, for nearly one hundred years, were open to all comers of every race and clime. Although the importation of slaves was forbidden by federal law in 1808, the smuggling of Negroes into the slave states continued and the breeding of slaves for sale became one of the profitable industries of the South. These processes went on until there were large sections of the country in which Negroes outnumbered the whites and nearly everywhere the blood of the two races was commingled in a new amalgam, neither Negro nor white. Here powerful economic forces ran counter to the realization of homogeneity. At the same time economic motives, in the United States, Europe, and Asia stimulated other streams of

[93] For these and other opinions, see Garis, *op. cit.*, pp. 22ff.

immigration. The rise of industries and the opening of western lands made an enormous demand for workers to run the factories and till the soil. So mill owners and land speculators found a huge influx of labor highly advantageous to their particular interests, and mill owners, land speculators, and speculative farmers were powerful in the legislative councils of the nation.

For many years there was a marked antagonism between these two groups in American society, sharpened by the insistence of land-hungry citizens upon the division of the federal domain into free homesteads. Obviously, if the public land was to be given away to settlers, an exodus from the industrial regions would diminish the labor supply and cause a demand for higher wages on the part of those who remained. At last a compromise was reached. The Republican party took the fateful step. In 1860 it endorsed the principle of free homesteads on western lands and then gave manufacturers their portion in a promise of higher tariffs on imports. Four years later it supplemented the latter concession by a declaration in favor of stimulating immigration: "Foreign immigration, which in the past has added so much to the wealth, development of resources, and increase of power to this nation— the asylum of the oppressed of all nations—should be fostered and encouraged by a liberal and just policy." And in the same year Congress incorporated this pledge in a law providing for the importation of laborers under contract—a kind of limited indentured servitude. Although this law was repealed shortly, the practice of importation long continued, facilitating the inflow of immigrants—white, black, and yellow—from the four quarters of the globe.

At the close of the colonial period, about the year 1773, the white population was approximately 82 per cent English, while the remaining 18 per cent included Scotch, Irish, Dutch, French, and Germans. Successive waves of immigration radically altered not only these proportions but submerged the whole in a new stream, composed of groups with distinctly different racial characteristics. Two great waves of immigration contributed to make over the racial stock in America. Until about the year 1880 the peoples coming to America

were from the north and west of Europe. They consisted
principally of Germans and Irish with negligible numbers of
Norwegians, Danes, and Swedes. Despite the differences between them, they harmonized with one another and with their
new environment sufficiently well to make the process of assimilation relatively easy. The percentages of foreign-born
white stock in the United States in 1890 were: German 33.2,
Irish 23.3, British 13.2, Scandinavian 7.5, and the remainder
covering a wide variety, 22.8. But this population content
had no time to become fixed in characteristics or amalgamated
before the full impact of the second wave of immigration,
starting in a trickle in the 80's, was upon it.

Before the close of the century, with the growing maturity
of the nation as an industrial country demanding an abundant
supply of cheap labor, the stream of immigration changed.
Whereas formerly it had come chiefly from the north and west
of Europe, it now shifted to the south and east. Anglo-Saxon,
Teutonic, and Scandinavian immigration shrank, while Slavic,
Italian, Jewish, and Russian immigrants crowded the steamship offices clamoring for a chance to come to the land of
paradise described for them in glowing terms by the agents
of shipping companies seeking business. Coming as they did
from the densely populated countries of eastern and southern
Europe, they brought with them a low standard of living, and
an ignorance of American customs, systems of law, and administration, which militated against assimilation in the new environment. Many of them were of peasant origin and had been
laboring under the burden of a harsh class system, oppressive
taxes, and greatly restricted civil and religious liberties. Their
adjustment to the new country was a long and difficult operation. The early homogeneity was definitely broken and entirely new racial contents, flowing into the old stream, radically altered its earlier appearance and characteristics. By
1930, even though restriction of immigration had already
commenced some years earlier, the percentages of foreign
born were as follows: Germans 17.7, Italian 11.7, British 9.4,
Irish 9.8, Austro-Hungarian 8.8, Polish 8.6, Scandinavian 8.3,
Russian 8.1, and all others 17.6. Facing the new century the
United States was a polyracial nation, with large sections,

urban and rural, occupied by races of radically different origins.

The dilution of the old stock with this flood of strange races and peoples, aside from the multitude of problems of adjustment, brought with it a renewed feeling of uneasiness early in the new century.[94] Yet the opposition to the "liberal" policy of the Republicans came not so much from the leaders of the old stock, as from the leaders of organized labor composed extensively of newcomers.[95] Henry Ward Beecher, a son of New England, held membership in a corporation engaged in importing laborers under contract to work in American industries; somewhat later, Samuel Gompers, an English Jew stood at the forefront in a struggle to restrict immigration— to assure to "American" laborers protection against alien competition, a protection similar to that accorded to American manufacturers. The blow fell first upon the Chinese and at length Congress was forced to enact legislation, at first contrary to treaty, providing for their total exclusion. Finally under heavy pressure from the American Federation of Labor, Congress, in 1917, established the literacy test which, though on its face applied generally, in operation discriminated against Slavic, Jewish, and Mediterranean races and made a drastic cut in the immigration from countries of their origin. Seven years later came the first law based frankly and definitely upon the concept of nationality—the National Origins Act—which adopted the quota system based on the social composition of the population of the United States in 1920 and put up positive bars against the Japanese. But this left the door still open

[94] One phase of that uneasiness appeared in an acute form when the war opened in Europe in 1914. There was much apprehension in the United States over the reaction that would follow among the diverse, unassimilated, racial groups. The uneasiness was considerably increased as the war continued and as it became increasingly apparent that the United States would be drawn into it. That the danger was more apparent than real was subsequently assured when the United States actually entered the war in 1917, and Briton and Frank, Italian and Russian, Slav and Jew, and even German and Irish despite the exceptional conditions bearing upon their positions, stood shoulder to shoulder in the Expeditionary Forces which through the war maintained an unusual and distinctive American quality and solidarity.

[95] The "Native American" movement which flourished before the Civil War died away as an effective political force, and legislation excluding criminals, paupers, diseased persons, etc. had no bearing on the issue of nationality.

to immigrants from American overseas possessions and certain countries of the Western Hemisphere; so agitation was immediately begun to cut off immigration from the Philippines, apply the quota system generally, and complete the restriction of immigration on the principle of nationality.

Thus it happened that, after the Government of the United States was supposed to have become a "world power," as certain writers of the new direction were fond of phrasing it, and engaged in a redoubled effort to prosecute national interests in all parts of the world, it confronted other countries with discriminating legislation against the migration of their nationals. At the same time, by restricting immigration on the rule of national origins, it sought to consolidate its heterogeneous population, to protect it against more alien infiltrations, and to develop a nationality marked by a certain racial unity. Interests were to be prosecuted with vigor abroad and nationality nourished at home. Here was a new course intimately related to national interest, indeed, inseparable from it; and it had almost universal approval, for both the major political parties were substantially united in advocating the continuance and strengthening of immigration restriction in racial terms.

However vigorously it may be asserted that tariffs, armaments, merchant marine, and immigration restriction are matters "of purely domestic concern," the fact remains that they are outward thrusts of power which produce repercussions in various parts of the world, as surely as do trade promotion, investment protection, and demonstrations of force in the national interest. This is not to say that the nation has no "right" to control its imports, armaments, merchant marine, and immigration in its own interest, but that the exercise of such control and the manner thereof have a distinct bearing on the interpretation and enforcement of national interest in the field of foreign affairs. To insist upon treating them as absolutely separate is to increase, not diminish, the hazards of foreign affairs, and to place obstacles in the way of a consistent and efficient foreign policy.

CHAPTER VIII

MORAL OBLIGATION IN NATIONAL INTEREST

THE emphasis thus far upon the economic and political content of national interest should not be permitted to obscure the moral aspects which have come to be closely associated with the idea. It is true that the national interest has been conceived primarily in materialistic and a-moral terms, as springing from utilitarian purposes and concerned with power and practical ends. This is in keeping with the ordinary conception of politics. As Croce says, when we speak of "political sense" we think of a sense for adaptation, for opportunity, for the actual, and for positive goals,[1] and not of the control of conduct by some abstract scheme of moral idealism, some utopian dream of human perfection, near or remote. By general consent the statesman must avoid the appearances of quixotism, must refrain from imperilling the practical affairs of his own country by adventures in the moral improvement of others. Yet the separation of economics, politics, and morals has never been absolute in theory or practice. It is a question of emphasis and usage. Nevertheless, the nineteenth century was wearing on to a close before directors of foreign policy in the United States spoke of themselves as bound by moral obligation to embark upon projects for uplifting, civilizing, or Christianizing other peoples beyond the confines of the country.

EARLY ABSTENTION FROM MORAL ENTERPRISES ABROAD

For nearly a hundred years the Government of the United States consistently and insistently maintained that it would

---

[1] Politika in Nuce, *Die Dioskuren* (1924), p. 14. The problem of the relation of justificatory moral ideas to political and military actions has never been explored. The only realistic approach, for the Western world at least, is through the earliest historical sources, such as the *Anglo-Saxon Chronicle* where adjectives having moral implications come late in the record. The earliest entries bear upon deeds substantive, and moral ideas come later in the story of war and politics.

not employ the engines of diplomacy and force for the purpose of doing good to other peoples by interfering with their domestic and international quarrels, by imposing on them American systems of economy, politics, and morals, and by withholding recognition from *de facto* governments whose theories and principles were not pleasing to the administration in Washington. The idea was foreign to the conceptions of the Fathers who founded the Republic. With justifiable pride they felt that their experiment in self-government set a noble example to countries ruled by despots, and on occasion they showed sympathy for other peoples that cast off absolutism or broke alien yokes by declaring their independence. But they shrank from taking up arms for the purpose of aiding in "wars of liberation" and refused to jeopardize the safety of the country by moral adventures in diplomacy.

If the *Federalist* may be taken as representing their general view of things, they thought that wars sprang from the cupidity of monarchs and nations; that nations fought when they believed there was a chance of getting anything by the operation; and that entanglements in the jealousies and disputes of Europe were likely to sacrifice American blood and treasure for the advantage of others—a thing that could not be defended on any realistic ground of national interest. And Washington's Farewell Address was a warning against expectations of favors without price from other countries, a caution against allowing sympathies to override practical considerations, and a standing admonition against attempting to improve the manners and institutions of other peoples by resorting to diplomacy and arms.

In keeping with the original idea, the Government of the United States followed the practice of recognizing *de facto* governments, thrown up by revolutions and wars, without attempting to pass too close a judgment upon their wisdom, their virtues, or their domestic policies. Always holding an even balance, it did business with the bloody and despotic Tsars of Russia, the haughty Emperor of China, and the revolutionary republics of France and Spain, guided by the policy of nonintervention and bent on safeguarding national interest, practically viewed. It did sometimes show more speed in recognizing a new republic born of popular uprising than a despotism established on the ruins of a constitution, but in both cases it observed the proprieties of international ceremony. There was, also, an implied thread of idealism running through the Monroe Doctrine which sought to insure by unilateral action the benefits of democratic principles to other countries, particularly those in the Western Hemisphere; but the attitude was negative rather than positive, and was more in the substantial interest of self-preservation for the United States than out of compassion for other peoples still under the oppression of autocratic rule. If any political or moral teaching was to be done, the Government of the United States relied on the weight of example rather than on diplomatic fulminations and displays of force. Likewise, in case of quarrels among nations, when its aid was suggested, the Government stood aloof on principle, assuming that it had no authority to take risks in efforts to pacify the warlike or improve the manners of the backward or incorrigible.

The principle may be illustrated by historical references. For example, early in the year 1863,[2] revolutionists in Poland made a desperate and heroic effort to cast off the tyranny of the Tsar, and the effort appealed to liberal sentiments everywhere, besides giving diplomats an opportunity to fish in troubled waters. Moreover, Europe was disturbed generally by movements in the direction of political democracy and national unifications. In these circumstances, for reasons not here germane, the French government, under Napoleon III, appealed to the Government of the United States for aid in exercising "a moral influence on the Emperor of Russia."[3] On May 11, 1863, Secretary Seward wrote to his minister in France as follows: "We learn that the proceeding which has . . . been adopted at Paris, with a view to the exercise of a moral influence with the Emperor of Russia, has received the approbation and concurrence of the court of Vienna and the cabinet at London, and that the Emperor of the French . . . would be gratified with a coöperation in that important pro-

[2] February 23, 1863. *Diplomatic Correspondence* (1862-3), Part 2, Department of State, p. 713.

[3] Henderson, *American Diplomatic Questions*, p. 207.

ceeding by the government of the United States."[4] Secretary
Seward then goes on to recognize the moral element in the situation. "This government is profoundly and agreeably impressed with the consideration which the Emperor has manifested toward the United States by inviting their concurrence
in a proceeding having for its object the double interests of
public order and humanity. . . ."

After the customary preliminaries, Mr. Seward stated positively: "Notwithstanding, however, the favor with which we
thus regard the suggestion of the Emperor of the French, this
government finds an insurmountable difficulty in the way of any
active coöperation with the governments of France, Austria,
and Great Britain. . . ." Then he explained: "Founding our
institutions upon the basis of the rights of man, the builders
of our republic came all at once to be regarded as political
reformers" and "revolutionists in every country hailed them in
that character," looking to the United States for "effective
sympathy, if not for active support. . . ." Stamped with this
character, it was only with extreme reluctance that the American nation yielded to "the wiser counsels" of Washington that
"the American people must be content to recommend the course
of human progress by the wisdom with which they should exercise the powers of self-government, forbearing at all times,
and in every way, from foreign alliances, intervention, and
interference."

Mr. Seward was aware that Washington took a broad view
of world affairs. "It is true," the dispatch continued, "that
Washington thought a time might come when, our institutions
being firmly consolidated and working with complete success,
we might safely and perhaps beneficially take part in the con-
sultations held by foreign states for the common advantage
of the nations." But Mr. Seward was anxious to dispel all
thought that such a time had now arrived. Thus he went on
to observe: "Since that period, occasions have frequently happened which presented seductions to a departure from what,
superficially viewed, seemed a course of isolation and indifference."

[4] For the proposal of the French Government, see *Diplomatic Correspondence*, p. 829.

He enumerated them in detail. "One was an invitation to a congress of newly emancipated Spanish American States; another an urgent appeal to aid Hungary in a revolution aiming at the restoration of her ancient and illustrious independence; another, the project of a joint guarantee of Cuba to Spain in concurrence with France and Great Britain; and more recently, an invitation to a coöperative demonstration with Spain, France, and Great Britain in Mexico; and later still, suggestions by some of the Spanish American States for a common council of the republican States situated upon the American continent."

But all these "seductions" were "suggestions successively disallowed by the government. . . . Our policy of non-intervention, straight, absolute, and peculiar as it may seem to other nations, has become a traditional one, which could not be abandoned without the most urgent occasion, amounting to a manifest necessity. . . ."

He closed his dispatch with a note of finality which even the niceties of a diplomatic apology could not obscure: "The President will not allow himself to think for a single moment that the Emperor of the French will see anything but respect and friendship for himself and the people of France, with good wishes for the preservation of peace and order, and the progress of humanity in Europe, in the adherence of the United States on this occasion to the policy which they have thus far pursued with safety, and not without advantage, as they think, to the interests of mankind. . . ."[5]

It was not, however, a case of clear-cut balancing of the national interest of one people against the calls of a broader humanity. Rarely does a situation of such clarity arise. It was a weighing of interests in keeping with the manner in which they did arise; and the note of irony which crept into the dispatch reaffirmed the essentially practical view taken by the American Secretary of State in connection with questions of moral obligation and the national interest. It must also be considered in the light of the fact that the United States was particularly disturbed by the French attitude toward the Civil War and Mexico; while no such exasperation disturbed

[5] For the full despatch, see *Diplomatic Correspondence,* pp. 737–739.

Russian-American relations.[6] Moreover, a critical period of
the Civil War in the United States had just set in; and, while
there was neither the possibility nor any thought of positive
American action regarding the Polish situation, the friendship
of Russia was needed by the American government strictly in
its own behalf.

Mr. Seward's dispatch closed the American relation to the
Polish uprising, except for the amusing reaction of the French
government upon the American refusal to be drawn into the
matter. As reported by Mr. Dayton on May 29, 1863, "He
[the French Minister] said he was not at all disappointed in
the result of their application to us, and more especially was
he not so in view of the precedents cited by you, illustrating
the history and showing the past practice of our government in
respect to the question of intervention. He said, indeed, that
the application to us had been made rather as a matter of
'homage' and respect than otherwise . . . and here our conference ended." [7]

Subsequently the Polish uprising was put down without any
government rising sufficiently above the exigencies of national
interests to sacrifice itself on "the altar of humanity." On this
point Mr. Dayton reported to Mr. Seward: "France will not
move . . . without England and England will not embark in
war for Poland. . . . It has been said that France is the
only nation that goes to war *for an idea*. However this may
have been in the past, her present rulers are as little disposed
to overlook *material* interests as the people of other countries. . . ." [8]

---

[6] Indeed, Russian-American friendship was on a firm material footing at
the time. In the dispatches between Mr. Seward and Mr. C. M. Clay, American
Minister at St. Petersburg, in which the progress of the Polish insurrection was
noted, the progress of a grant to an American company to explore Russian
territory with a view to establishing an overland telegraph line was also discussed. See *Diplomatic Correspondence;* Sec. Russia. And Mr. Seward had
sent to Mr. Clay a copy of his views concerning the proposed intervention of
the European Powers on moral grounds, with the observation that, "There
can be no impropriety in your informally making known the contents of the
paper to Prince Gortchacow. . . ." *Ibid.*, pp. 867, 871. Thus the invitation
from France was used for practical purposes.

[7] *Ibid.*, p. 741.

[8] *Diplomatic Correspondence*, (1862-3), Part 2, pp. 753-754.

Even more clear-cut and illuminating, with respect to the policy of non-intervention on moral grounds, were the instructions given by Secretary Frelinghuysen to the American diplomatic representative in Chile, on January 9, 1882, when a quarrel between that country and Peru threatened to eventuate in war, and the interest of the United States was suggested. "The President," said the Secretary, "wishes in no manner to dictate or make any authoritative utterance to either Peru or Chile as to the merits of the controversy existing between those republics. . . . Were the United States to assume an attitude of dictation towards the South American republics, even for the purpose of preventing war, the greatest of evils, or even to preserve the autonomy of nations, it must be prepared by army and navy to enforce its mandate, and to this end tax our people for the exclusive benefit of foreign nations." [9] In this simple statement is found the conception of national interest on which the statesmen of the Republic once put aside opportunities to do good everywhere on the assumption that it had no moral obligations to aid quarreling nations and backward peoples.

THE INTRODUCTION OF MORAL OBLIGATION AS A RULE FOR THE CONDUCT OF EXTERNAL AFFAIRS [10]

This principle of abstention from interference in the affairs of other peoples with a view to improving their manners and morals was first broken, it is said by Henderson, in the case of Samoa—in the first permanent acquisition of an over-seas dependency. It was claimed that the naval base at Pago Pago, won single-handed by an American navy officer, offered decided advantages to the United States and that there was a prospect of some trade in the Islands; but there was good ground for regarding the naval base as a liability rather than as an asset and the trade was certainly trivial as compared with the cost involved. In any event, there was no deliberate cal-

[9] Henderson, *American Diplomatic Questions*, p. 207.

[10] The politics of moral addresses to urban and rural masses that have no immediate interests in a particular affair but may be "interested" by propaganda presents a problem that has not been realistically explored.

culation of national interests. With the aid of a naval officer, a few traders, and some missionaries, the Government of the United States stumbled into the Samoan quarrel between half-savage chieftains on the one side and British and German capitalists and authorities on the other and nearly came to blows with Germany in an alleged effort to protect the natives.

As Mr. Gresham, Secretary of State, reported to President Cleveland in 1894: "It is in our relations to Samoa that we have made the first departure from our traditional and well-established policy of avoiding entangling alliances with foreign powers in relation to objects remote from this hemisphere. . . . If the departure was justified, there must be some evidence of detriment suffered before its adoption, or of advantage since gained, to demonstrate the fact. . . . Every nation, and especially every strong nation, must sometimes be conscious of an impulse to rush into difficulties that do not concern it, except in a highly imaginary way. To restrain the indulgence of such a propensity is not only the part of wisdom, but a duty we owe to the world as an example of the strength, the moderation, and the beneficence of popular government." [11]

President Cleveland, in his annual message of December 2, 1895, also declared, concerning the American attitude respecting Samoa, "that our situation in this matter was inconsistent with the mission and traditions of our Government, in violation of the principles we profess, and in all its phases mischievous and vexatious." [12] And speaking in the same message of Cuba, he observed: "Whatever may be the traditional sympathy of our countrymen as individuals with a people who seem to be struggling for larger autonomy and greater freedom, deepened, as such sympathy naturally must be, in behalf of our neighbors, yet the plain duty of their Government is to observe in good faith the recognized obligations of international friendship"; and this must prevail over "any shock our human sensibilities may have received from the cruelties which appear to especially characterize this sanguinary and fiercely conducted war." [13]

[11] Henderson, *op. cit.*, p. 208.
[12] *Messages of the Presidents*, p. 6067.
[13] *Ibid.*, p. 6068.

These were echoes of the policy of the Fathers and of its reaffirmation in the Seward dispatch on the Polish insurrection. But the voice was somewhat uncertain and feeble; [14] the die had been already cast; and the new course was taken by the directors of the Government at Washington.

As an operation on a larger scale, in a larger theater, and with wider consequences, the war with Spain and the conquest of new territories afforded a more extended opportunity for the assumption of "moral obligation" than the affair in Samoa. So far as formal and official proclamations and statements are concerned the war on Spain and the settlement which ensued were mainly excursions in the domain of morals, and during the entire performance declarations respecting moral obligation appeared side by side with professions of national interest which emphasized investments, commerce, and national defense. "In the name of humanity, in the name of civilization, in behalf of endangered American interests which gives us the right and the duty to speak and to act," said President McKinley in his special message of April 11, 1898, "the war in Cuba must stop." [15] The resolution reported to the House of Representatives authorizing the President to employ armed forces against Spain announced that the action was "to the end and purpose of securing permanent peace and order there [in Cuba], and establishing by the free action of the people thereof a stable and independent government of their own." The Senate resolution, which was finally adopted, added a preamble declaring that the "abhorrent conditions" in the Island "have shocked the moral sense of the people of the United States; have been a disgrace to Christian civilization." The body of the resolution limited the purpose of the war to the establishment of Cuban independence, and announced that the United States disclaimed any intention to "exercise sovereignty, jurisdiction, or control over said island, except for the pacification thereof." Officially the war was a war of libera-

[14] Fourth Annual Message. In relation to Turkey. With regard to Cuba, President Cleveland later went far beyond this position and spoke of a situation "in which our obligations to the sovereignty of Cuba will be superseded by higher obligations, which we can hardly hesitate to recognize and discharge." *Ibid.*, pp. 6147–6148, and 6150–6154, respectively.

[15] *Messages of the Presidents*, p. 6292.

tion, although of course the consequences were accompanied by collaterals that had a more direct bearing on national interest, historically conceived.

After the Spanish War was over and order was being established in Cuba under United States military authority, President McKinley specifically renounced national interest in favor of moral obligation. In his instructions to Major-General Brooke, whom he designated Military Governor of Cuba, the President informed the Governor that "the government to be maintained under this authority by you on behalf of the United States is not in the interest or for the benefit of this country, but in the interest and for the benefit of the people of Cuba and those possessed of rights and property in that Island. It is important, therefore, that you keep in mind this fact so that all your conduct may be guided and inspired by that consideration." While suggesting to the Governor that "our commercial relations" should be "close and reciprocal," the President emphasized the importance of helping to realize "the best aspirations of the Cuban people." [16]

Kindred sentiments connected with moral obligation were expressed with reference to the acquisition and government of the Philippine Islands. Senator O. H. Platt, one of the leaders in the acquisitive movement, illustrated them in the following form in a letter written on August 15, 1898, while the issue was yet being debated: "During the past week I have been well over the state of Connecticut and I am satisfied that nine-tenths of the people of the state have an intense feeling that we should insist upon the cession of all the Philippine Islands. Those who believe in Providence see, or think they see, that God has placed upon this government the solemn duty of providing, for the people of these islands, a government based upon the principles of liberty, no matter how many difficulties the problem may present. They feel that it is our duty to attempt its solution. Among Christian thoughtful people the sentiment is akin to that which has maintained the missionary work of the last century in foreign lands. . . . If, in the negotiations for peace, Spain is permitted to retain any portion of the Philippines it will be regarded as a failure on the part of the

[16] C. S. Olcott, *Life of William McKinley*, Vol. II, pp. 196ff.

nation to discharge the greatest moral obligation which could be conceived." [17]

Between the conception of the moral motive for the acquisition and government of the Philippines, as formulated by Senator Platt, and the presentation of the case by President McKinley there is a striking uniformity. At a conference with a committee representing the General Missionary Committee of the Methodist Church, on November 21, 1899, the President explained the process by which he arrived at the determination to hold the Islands for the United States. He said that he did not want the Philippines, that he had ordered Dewey to destroy the Spanish fleet at Manila to prevent it from ravaging the Pacific coast, and that when "they came to us, as a gift from the gods," he did not know what to do with them. He sought counsel from Republicans and Democrats, "but got little help." Then, he said, "I went down on my knees and prayed Almighty God for light and guidance more than one night." And late one night the answer came. We could not give the Islands back to Spain; "that would be cowardly and dishonorable." Nor was it possible to "turn them over to France or Germany—our commercial rivals in the Orient—that would be bad business and discreditable." We could not give them independence; "they were unfit for self-government." Hence "there was nothing left for us to do but to take them all, and to educate the Filipinos, and uplift and civilize and Christianize them, and by God's grace do the very best we could for them as our fellowmen for whom Christ also died." If this statement is to be taken as representing the whole case, then the determining motive in President McKinley's mind in asserting sovereignty over the Philippines was a sense of moral obligation, tinged with a theological sanction.

A kindred spirit was expressed in the instructions to the Philippine Commission sent out to undertake the organization of government in the Islands—the "magna charta of the Philippines," signed by the President on April 7, 1900. The Commission was instructed, of course, to establish order, uphold law, and safeguard the rights of property and person, but it was distinctly informed that the government to be established

[17] Coolidge, *Life of Platt*, p. 287.

is "not for our satisfaction or for the expression of our theoretical views, but for the happiness, peace, and prosperity of the people of the Philippine Islands, and the measures adopted should be made to conform to their customs, their habits, and even their prejudices to the fullest extent consistent with the accomplishment of the indispensable requisites of just and effective government." Since Secretary Root, in general charge as head of the War Department, interpreted the moral obligation to mean, as applied to the Philippines, "those principles which are declared in our constitutions, which embodied the formative idea of the Declaration of Independence, that all men are endowed with inalienable rights, among which are life and liberty and the pursuit of happiness," and since President McKinley thought it meant educating, uplifting, civilizing, and Christianizing the Filipinos, it was clear that the instructions to the Commission involved a certain compromise in the moral campaign—a compromise adapted to Filipino susceptibilities and institutions inherited from former times. Yet in spite of some contradictions in terms, the keynote of moral obligation was firm and strong in the official literature of annexation and administration.

Conforming to the rule of moral obligation assumed by President McKinley to civilize, Christianize, and uplift the Filipinos, Dr. Jacob Gould Schurman, a member of the first Philippine commission, declared American policy in the following terms: "The destiny of the Philippine Islands is not to be a state or a territory in the United States of America but a daughter republic of ours—a new birth of liberty on the other side of the Pacific, which shall animate and energize those lovely islands of the tropical seas, and, rearing its head aloft, stand as a monument of progress and a beacon of hope to all the oppressed and benighted millions of the Asiatic continent." Beyond question, in this passage, Dr. Schurman voiced the sentiments of millions of American people who had no commercial or military interests in the Philippines and yet warmly supported the policy of annexation, conquest, subjugation, and pacification.

After scrutinizing carefully the papers left by President McKinley, his biographer, Charles S. Olcott, came to the conclusion that this note of moral obligation to other peoples marked a new turn in the evolution of American policy: "William McKinley was the first of our Presidents to respond to the call of broad philanthropy toward other less fortunate people. Lincoln heard a similar call and responded with the emancipation of four million slaves. But that was within our own boundaries. McKinley saw that the time had come when the United States, no longer a weakling nation threatened with dissolution, but strong and able, should take to itself the apostolic injunction, 'now we that are strong ought to bear the infirmities of the weak and not to please ourselves.' He realized that those inalienable rights of life, liberty, and the pursuit of happiness which our forefathers so ardently desired for themselves were not intended by the Creator as the exclusive privilege of our own countrymen, but were a part of the endowment of the people of Cuba, of Porto Rico, and of the Philippines as well. It was no part of the duty of the United States to watch the corners of the globe for violations of these rights, but when the current of events placed the destinies of these people within our hands, it became our duty to extend to them the same blessings of freedom which we ourselves enjoyed." [18]

Students of causation in human affairs, of course, may properly take note of the qualification placed on moral obligation by McKinley's biographer. Mr. Olcott does not say that the obligation lays on the United States the duty of watching the corners of the globe for violations of human rights, but merely imposes on the nation the responsibility for enforcing such rights when "the current of events" places the destiny of other peoples in our hands. This undoubtedly gives to policy a passive character that does not correspond exactly to the realities of historic movements. Acts of will and force on the part of the Government of the United States certainly helped to make the current of events which led to the acquisition of new territorial dominions. Governments are not inert and will-less bodies. They are composed of active and vigilant personalities, civilian, military, and naval. The range of their vision and will power is large; its boundaries are vague and impalpa-

[18] Olcott, *Life of William McKinley*, Vol. II, pp. 190–191.

ble, and strictly speaking there is no reason why moral responsibility, where the power to make extensive application is possible, should be limited to occasions produced by "the current of events." Be that as it may, however, the thesis must be accepted that near the close of the nineteenth century a new note was heard in American diplomacy, the note of moral obligation, self-imposed and subject to interpretation by duly constituted authorities.[19] It did not take the place of national interest, practically construed, but rather, supplementing national interest, it entered into all discussions pertaining to the determination of foreign policy.

THE DEVELOPMENT OF MORAL OBLIGATION

The idea of moral obligation, to which President McKinley appealed so frequently in conducting foreign relations, was broadened to include the moral improvement of the American people at home through the assumption of responsibilities abroad. President Theodore Roosevelt carried into the White House for the first time the conception that war was certainly a good thing for "the moral fibre" of the nation, if "righteous," and probably in any fortunate case. The Fathers of the Republic and their immediate successors, as a rule, looked upon war as a necessary evil to be avoided if possible, to be met heroically, if thrust upon them, or, as the authors of the *Federalist* put the matter, to be employed only when there was a chance to realize a substantial interest. If some of them believed it a virtue in itself without respect to national interest in a pragmatic sense, they left no reasoned arguments to that effect. Nor did Roosevelt, for that matter; but he

[19] Upon landing in Porto Rico in 1898, Major-General Nelson A. Miles issued a proclamation, saying, "The people of the United States in the cause of liberty, justice and humanity . . . come bearing the banner of freedom, inspired by a noble purpose . . . (to) bring you the fostering arm of a nation of free people, whose greatest power is in justice and humanity to all those living within its fold, . . . to bring you protection, not only to yourselves, but to your property, to promote your prosperity, and to bestow upon you the immunities and blessings of the liberal institutions of our government, . . . to give to all within the control of its military and naval forces the advantages and blessings of enlightened civilization." Cited in Bailey W. and Justine W. Diffie, *Porto Rico: A Broken Pledge*, p. 3.

expressed both privately and publicly opinions on the subject that admitted of no misunderstanding.

While the controversy was raging with Great Britain over Venezuela in 1895, he declared to Henry Cabot Lodge: "I most earnestly hope that our people won't weaken in any way on the Venezuela matter. The antics of the bankers, brokers, and anglomaniacs generally [in opposition to belligerent tactics] are humiliating to a degree. . . . As for the editors of the *Evening Post* and *World* [also opposed to belligerent tactics] it would give me great pleasure to have them put in prison the minute hostilities began. . . . Personally I rather hope the fight will come soon. The clamor of the peace faction has convinced me that this country needs a war." [20]

There is other evidence to support the proposition that Roosevelt approved war as a good in itself for the regeneration of the American people in peril of growing "soft." In private conversations with the German ambassador, Sternberg, reported in December, 1898, Roosevelt often referred to the weakening of fibre that was becoming more and more marked among sons of the upperclasses, especially in the East; and he declared that a war was desirable to strengthen national character, that he had worked for years to bring one about, and that for more than ten years one of his greatest wishes had been to take part in a war himself. [21] This conception of Rooseveltian philosophy is also sustained by the contemporaneous testimony of a member of the House committee on naval affairs, who stated that Roosevelt came to Washington "looking for war. He did not care whom we fought as long as there was a scrap." [22]

In public addresses Roosevelt often declared that where considerations of honor, justice, and righteousness were involved everything else must give way, even though the result is war. "The good man," he said in his famous address at the University of Paris, "should be strong and brave, that is to say, capable of fighting, of serving his country as a soldier, should

[20] *Selections from the Correspondence of Theodore Roosevelt and Henry Cabot Lodge,* Vol. I, p. 204.

[21] German Foreign Office Mss.; Sternberg an AA., 11:15, 1898.

[22] Pringle, *Roosevelt,* p. 171.

the occasion arise. . . . War is a horrible thing; and an unjust war is a crime against humanity. But it is a crime of this sort because it is unjust, not because it is war. The choice should always be in favor of right, whether the alternative is peace or war. The question should not be simply: 'Is there going to be peace or war?' The question should be: 'Shall the cause of right prevail? Are the great laws of justice once more to be observed?' And the reply of a strong and virile people will be: 'Yes, whatever the risk may be.' . . . No self-respecting individual and no self-respecting nation, should submit to injustice." [23] Thus the way was prepared in the public mind for the acceptance of the black and white war-guilt and war-innocence doctrine.

Although it would be difficult to make a logical pattern of Roosevelt's moral, political, and economic philosophies, it is certain that, according to his formulas at least, he claimed to base policy on honor, justice, and righteousness. The fact that men of high character could interpret these terms differently in the same case apparently did not disturb him; he felt sure that his interpretations backed by his prestige were correct, unanswerable, and invincible. On such grounds he insisted that questions of "honor," as well as of "vital interests," should be excluded from matters subject to international arbitration, and vehemently assailed the "foolish and mischievous all-inclusive arbitration treaties recently negotiated by Mr. Bryan under the direction of President Wilson." [24] Those who regarded peace as the supreme moral obligation he condemned in vigorous adjectives. What he called "the whole flapdoodle pacifist and mollycoddle outfit " [25] was considered by him a moral disgrace and a physical danger to the country. For their pacific policy with regard to Mexico in 1914, Roosevelt severely condemned both Wilson and Bryan, as "the very worst men we have ever had in their positions. . . . I really believe that I would rather have Murphy, Penrose, or Barnes as the standard-bearer of the nation in the face of international wrong-

[23] Fullerton, *Problems of Power*, p. 31.
[24] D. F. Fleming, *The United States and the League of Nations*, p. 6.
[25] *Selections from the Correspondence of Roosevelt and Lodge*, Vol. II, p. 464.

doing." [26] There is every reason for believing that he only tolerated peace propaganda for electioneering purposes.[27]

As a corollary to his philosophy of honor, justice, and righteousness, Roosevelt condemned with equal vigor those who believed that the actions of nations in foreign affairs are based upon considerations of practical interest. "It is a mistake," he said in his annual message of 1906, "and it betrays a spirit of foolish cynicism, to maintain that all international governmental action is, and must ever be, based upon mere selfishness, and that to advance ethical reasons for such action is always a sign of hypocrisy. This is no more necessarily true of the action of governments than of the action of individuals. It is a sure sign of a base nature always to ascribe base motives for the actions of others. Unquestionably, no nation can afford to disregard proper considerations of self-interest, any more than a private individual can so do. . . . A really great nation must often act, and as a matter of fact often does act, toward other nations in a spirit not in the least of mere self-interest, but paying heed chiefly to ethical reasons; and as the centuries go by this disinterestedness in international action, this tendency of the individuals comprising a nation to require that nation to act with justice toward its neighbors, steadily grows and strengthens. It is neither wise nor right for a nation to disregard its own needs, and it is foolish—and may be wicked—to think that other nations will disregard theirs. But it is wicked for a nation to regard only its own interest, and foolish to believe that such is the sole motive that actuates any other nation. It should be our steady aim to raise the ethical standard of national action, just as we strive to raise the ethical standard of individual action."

Not content with generalities, Roosevelt frequently illustrated his conceptions of honor, justice, and righteousness. In explaining and justifying specific actions he continually referred to ethical considerations. In conquering rebellious Filipinos and establishing American sovereignty over them, in extending American trade and investment opportunities in the Philippines, in exercising protectorate powers over Cuba,

---

[26] *Ibid.*, p. 450.
[27] *Die Grosse Politik*, Vol. XXIII-i, p. 57.

in "taking" the Panama Canal strip, in bringing Santo Domingo under American financial hegemony, and in resorting to kindred measures of a practical character, Roosevelt never failed to emphasize the moral aspects of the proceedings. Peace had been extended to disorderly regions, justice had been secured, liberty advanced, education introduced or improved, habits of industry encouraged, capacity for self-government enlarged, "fakirs and religious fanatics" put down, and the living standards of the peoples affected uplifted—at the same time that roads and canals were being built, industries founded, trade increased, investments enlarged, and material advantages gained by American citizens and other persons involved in the transactions. Meanwhile the nation was winning "added dignity," for it was "proving that we are capable honorably and efficiently to bear the international burdens which a mighty people should bear." [28] Although numerous contemporaries, both within his party and outside, ridiculed his "long moral dissertations," there was no doubt among those who knew him about the sincerity of his moral convictions and the depth of the emotions behind them.

The messages and state papers of Mr. Roosevelt's successor in the presidency, William Howard Taft, were shorter and more practical in tone, and carried fewer references to moral obligations with respect to domestic as well as foreign affairs. With his accession to power the era of "dollar diplomacy" was frankly inaugurated under Secretary Knox. Yet neither confessed that he was controlled entirely by a conception of national interest. The former, for example, in explaining his policy in connection with disturbances in Nicaragua in his first message to Congress, announced that his Government was "intending to take such future steps as may be found most consistent with its dignity, its duty to American interests, and its moral obligation to Central America and to civilization." A few weeks later in a public address Secretary Knox also saw transcendent requirements in international affairs. The number of international conferences, he said, supplied "evidence that the common interest of nations is being recognized as superior to their special interests and that unity of action in interna-

[28] *Messages of the Presidents,* pp. 7051f.

tional matters may yet control the unrestrained, unregulated, or isolated action of independent states." Practical events were bringing this about. "The development of commerce and industry and the necessary exchange of commodities have caused nations to see that their interests are similar and inter-dependent, and that a like policy is often necessary as well for the expansion as for the protection of their interests. . . . Indeed, the tendency is very marked to substitute interdependence for independence, and each nation is likely to see itself forced to yield something of its initiative, not to any one nation, but to the community of nations in payment for its share in 'the advance in the richness of existence.' " [29]

In his message of December 3, 1912, President Taft set forth with no little ingenuity the conception of intertwined material interest and moral obligation so characteristic of the polity which he represented in public life. "The position of the United States," he said, "in the moral, intellectual, and mate-rial relations of the family of nations should be a matter of vital interest to every patriotic citizen. The national prosperity and power impose upon us duties which we cannot shirk if we are true to our ideals." He then emphasized "the tremendous growth of the export trade," its relations to the industrial and commercial prosperity of the nation, the increasing importance of foreign commerce for the economic welfare of the country, the inadequacy of "narrow views befitting an infant nation," and the opportunity "for promoting the interests of the whole people." Treasures are to be laid up on earth, but good is to be done at the same time. "Because modern diplomacy is com-mercial," President Taft continued, "there has been a dispo-sition in some quarters to attribute to it none but materialistic aims. How strikingly erroneous is such an impression may be seen from a study of the results by which the diplomacy of the United States can be judged." By way of illustration he then cited efforts to secure arbitration treaties with Great Britain, mediation in Latin American quarrels, and coöperation with international bankers to secure "essential reforms" in China. "In Central America the aim has been to help such countries as Nicaragua and Honduras to help themselves." The new

[29] Quoted in Fleming, *The United States and the League of Nations*, p. 10.

commercial diplomacy, he insisted, "appeals alike to idealistic humanitarian sentiments, to the dictates of sound policy and strategy, and to legitimate commercial aims."

With even greater emphasis, akin in fervor to that of President Roosevelt, President Wilson brought moral obligation to bear upon public policies, but in different forms and with different applications. He came to the White House possessed by the conviction that "our Government has been for the past few years under the control of heads of great allied corporations with special interests," and that "the masters of the Government of the United States are the combined capitalists and manufacturers of the United States."[30] In the circumstances, he deemed it his duty to "restore the Government to the plain people" and administer it in the popular interest. In the first year of his administration he declared, with particular reference to Latin America: "Human rights, national integrity, and opportunity as against material interests—that . . . is the issue which we now have to face. I want to take this occasion to say that the United States will never again seek one additional foot of territory by conquest. She will devote herself to showing that she knows how to make an honorable and fruitful use of the territory she has, and she must regard it as one of the duties of friendship to see that from no quarter are material interests made superior to human liberty and national opportunity."[31]

Throughout his two administrations, President Wilson's declarations of foreign policy were based on assumptions of moral values as distinguished from national interest conceived in commercial terms. He raised national purpose high above material gain. He assumed that democracy, as practised in the United States, was a decided good and that other nations should be assisted in attaining it. "Only free peoples can hold their purposes and their honor steady to a common end and prefer the interests of mankind to any interest of their own."[32] The right of the peoples of the respective nations to choose their

[30] *The New Freedom*, pp. 25, 57.

[31] Thomas, *One Hundred Years of the Monroe Doctrine*, p. 240.

[32] War Message of April 2, 1917. *Selected Literary and Political Papers and Addresses of Woodrow Wilson*, Vol. II, pp. 234–237.

own government and determine their own fate he laid down as a fundamental postulate of international polity. He would realize this by lifting the Monroe Doctrine out of its provincial sphere and by extending its self-denying principles to the entire world. He insisted "that no nation should seek to extend its polity over any other nation or people, but that every people should be left free to determine its own polity . . . unhindered, unthreatened, unafraid, the little along with the great and the powerful." [33] He carried to the finality of an axiom the principle that all nations, small as well as large, should be secure in their territorial and administrative integrity against aggression. The particular process of imperialism known as the conquest and exploitation of backward peoples for the benefit of the metropolis President Wilson utterly repudiated and proposed instead that the idea of trusteeship should be substituted for sovereignty—trusteeship conceived in the interest of the ruled instead of the ruler.[34] Other elements of his avowed policy, such as freedom of the seas and the removal of barriers in the way of commerce, were logical extensions of his theory of security and self-determination for nations, and designed to eliminate frictions of interest that are dangerous to the peace of free and democratic nations.

Whatever may be said about the merits of these proposals, they were primarily value determinations of high moral purpose and were founded on the desirability of maintaining the geographical and administrative integrity of each nation. They offered a moral conception of a limited national interest, as distinguished from the primary pursuit of national interest with the use of war, conquest, and economic pressure as instrumentalities of realization. They also betrayed a faith in the power of moral influence. "The example of America," President Wilson declared, "must be the example, not merely of peace because it will not fight, but of peace because peace is the healing and elevating influence of the world and strife is not.

[33] Message to the Senate, January 22, 1917, *Selected Papers,* Vol. II, pp. 218–227.

[34] In his message to the Filipino people, delivered by Governor General Harrison in 1913, he said: "We regard ourselves as trustees acting not for the advantage of the United States but for the benefit of the people of the Philippine Islands." Quoted in *Cong Record,* 72d Cong., 1st Sess., p. 13949.

There is such a thing as a man being too proud to fight. There is such a thing as a nation being so right that it does not need to convince others by force that it is right." [35]

Before the United States entered the war, President Wilson spoke of the kind of peace that must be sought, lest in the heat of the battle the clear mandates of a transcendent morality should be dragged down into the slough of greed. It was to be a "peace without victory," a "peace that will win the approval of mankind," not "a peace that will serve the several interests and immediate aims of the nations engaged." [36]

When President Wilson carried the country into war, he sounded a note of high moral purpose. "Our object . . . is to vindicate the principles of peace and justice in the life of the world as against selfish and autocratic power and to set up amongst the really free and self-governed peoples of the world such a concert of purpose and action as will henceforth insure the observance of those principles. . . . We have no selfish ends to serve. We desire no conquest, no dominion. We seek no indemnities for ourselves. . . . We are but one of the champions of the rights of mankind." And in the broad peroration at the end of his war message he exclaimed: "It is a fearful thing to lead this great people into war . . . but the right is more precious than peace," and to right "we can dedicate our lives and our fortunes, everything that we are and everything that we have" with full pride in the knowledge that "America is privileged to spend her blood and her might for the principles that gave her birth and happiness and the peace which she has treasured." Instead of negotiating secretly for a share of the spoils of war, as had the Allies to whose rescue he came, he openly put aside all such pretensions, much to their satisfaction, no doubt. Without going into other motives or inquiring closely into the economic considerations that carried

[35] Quoted in David F. Houston, *Eight Years with Wilson's Cabinet*, Vol. II, p. 227. That Wilson was striving, by that much-discussed passage, to raise the United States to the position of a strong "reserve moral force" is attested by the ideas brought out in his speeches before the Associated Press of New York (April 20, 1915), in his special message on Mexico (August 27, 1913), and at Chicago (January 31, 1916), and on the Panama Canal Tolls (*Cong. Record,* 63d Cong., 2d Sess., Vol. 51, p. 4313).

[36] Message of January 22, 1917.

weight in American counsels, it may be said with confidence that the fundamental aims of the Government as expressed in the words of President Wilson were non-material rather than material.[37]

This statement of the case rests squarely on the authority of President Wilson's official biographer, R. S. Baker, who had access to all his papers, both public and private. The President "abominated" the dollar diplomacy of Secretary Knox; [38] he rested his policies on *"a priori* or moral principles"; [39] and based his program "upon a determination to restore moral principles as a guide." [40] Moreover he distinctly repudiated the doctrine of interest as the source of policy. In his address at Mobile in 1913 he disclosed his opinion of this conception and set forth its opposite: "Interest does not tie nations together: it sometimes separates them. But sympathy and understanding do unite them. . . . It is a spiritual union which we seek. . . . It is a very perilous thing to determine the foreign policy of a nation in terms of material interest. It is not only unfair to those with whom you are dealing, but it is degrading as regards your own actions . . . human rights, national integrity, and opportunity as against material interests . . . is the issue which we have to face." Then he applied this philosophy by attacking directly the concessions given to foreign investors by Latin American states, as bargains made hard on the ground of risk and then fortified by the use of the diplomatic and military engines of the American Government.[41] Henceforward, as far as he was concerned, American diplomacy was to be controlled by broad principles of human rights.

While objecting vigorously to the moral internationalism of his predecessor, President Harding continued the tradition of moral obligation. In dealing with the Philippines, as a member of the Senate, he had expressed convictions on the subject,

[37] Consider the connotation of the following words and phrases all taken from his single message to the Senate on January 22, 1917: Equality, candor, trust, intimacy, comity, coöperation, unite, community, silent mass of mankind, convictions of mankind, and *common* benefit, participation, organization, strength, interest, and protection. *Selected Papers.*

[38] Baker, *Woodrow Wilson: Life and Letters,* Vol. IV, p. 239.

[39] *Ibid.,* p. 76.

[40] *Ibid.,* p. 59

[41] *Ibid.,* pp. 283ff.

which, according to his biographer, he entertained until his death in the presidency. "We are the first nation on the face of the earth," he said, "that ever unsheathed the sword on behalf of suffering humanity. . . . [President McKinley] disavowed any intention of the acquirement of territory, and literally went to war for humanity's sake. Then out of the fortunes of that war, we acquired the Philippine Islands. . . . Our work in the Philippine Islands in education, in sanitation, in elevation, and civilization, has been the most magnificent contribution of a nation's unselfishness ever recorded in the history of the world. . . . A nation leading in civilization and in that uplifting work which contributes to the weal of humanity can no more limit its influences to its territorial and coast-bound sphere than can the man who stands high in his community. . . . It seems to me . . . that we ought to go on with the same thought that impelled Him who brought a plan of salvation to the earth. Rather than confine it to the Holy Land alone, He gathered his disciples about him and said, 'go ye and preach the gospel to all nations of the earth.' . . . Clad in our convictions of conscientiousness and righteousness, let us go on, Mr. President and Senators, in our efforts to fulfill the destinies of what I believe to be the best republic on earth." [42]

The creed of President Harding's party is summed up in the address by Senator Simeon D. Fess delivered before its national convention in 1928: "Our history under Republican administrations shows a new standard of cosmopolitan philanthropy never before aspired to by any nation of history. In Cuba we intervened partly on behalf of our peace of mind and partly from humanitarian motives. . . . In Santo Domingo, after forty years of perennial insurrections, we answered the call of duty, reorganized the financial structure, and supervised its operations. . . . The result is a well-ordered administration of local self-government and wonderful progress of a people which formerly lived in constant turmoil. In Haiti we are pursuing the same course in the interest of the welfare of these people, and in pursuance of a treaty. . . . No chapter in the history of nation-building has ever been written that will show

[42] W. F. Johnson, *The Life of Warren G. Harding,* pp. 172–178.

more unselfish service and greater humanitarian regard than that relating to what we have done for people like the Filipinos and the peoples of the West Indian Islands. . . . We have unfailing faith that a policy of unselfish service as displayed in our dealing with all struggling nations in their efforts toward law and order, including China, must meet with the approval of all friends of good government." [43]

FORCE AS AN INSTRUMENT OF MORAL OBLIGATION

In the course of time the idea of moral obligation which accompanied the extension of American economic power was emphasized by official writers on military and naval affairs. Indeed, Alfred Thayer Mahan worked it out into a system of sociology. He had declared that it was "vain to expect governments to act continuously on any other ground than national interest," had argued that the history of the sea power was largely, though not solely, the story of rivalry for material advantage, and had characterized self-interest as a legitimate and fundamental cause of policy (above, p. 223), but he also laid stress on the weight of morals in policy. His early writings on the sea power left the door ajar for moral considerations and as the idea of self-interest and national interest drew fire from critics, Mahan gave increasing attention to ethics.

Although he said in 1900 that self-preservation is the first law of states and that matters of advantage could not be submitted to any court of justice for arbitration, he later made consciousness of "rightfulness" the turning point of decision. "The resort to arms by a nation, when right cannot otherwise be enforced," he wrote in 1907, "corresponds, or should correspond, precisely to the acts of the individual man. . . . A state, when it goes to war, should do so not to test the rightfulness of its claims, but because, being convinced in its conscience of that rightfulness, no other means of overpowering evil remains. Nations, like man, have a conscience. . . . It is not the accuracy of the decision, but the faithfulness to conviction, that constitutes the moral worth of the action, national or individual. The general consciousness of this truth is wit-

[43] *Republican Campaign Text-book* (1928), pp. 63–65.

nessed by the common phrase which excludes from suggested schemes of arbitration all questions which involve 'national honor or vital interests.' " [44] From this point of view, resort to arms is not merely to realize interests; it is to satisfy the righteous dictates of the nation's conscience; if the decision is inaccurate, still faithfulness to conviction gives moral worth to the nation's action.[45]

In the same volume Mahan makes war apparently inherent in the nature of things; but still a human instrument for the control of evil. "War," he declares, "is the regulator and adjuster of those movements of peoples which in their tendencies and outcome constitute history. These are natural forces, which from their origin and power are self-existent and independent in relation to man. . . . His provision against them is war. . . . By this he can measurably control, guide, delay, or otherwise beneficially modify results which threaten to be disastrous in their extent, tendency, or suddenness. So regarded war is remedial or preventive." [46] To say that war is wicked "amounts to saying that it is wicked for society to organize and utilize force for the control of evil. It will scarcely be denied that evil in various forms now exists; not evil of thought or word merely, but evil of act; of overt violence, legal as well as extra-legal; evil, aggressive, persistent, insolent, and ultimately subversive, if unchecked, of all social order and personal happiness." [47] Here Mahan's test of war is not faithfulness to conscience but the suppression of objective evil. By way of illustrating this principle, he referred to "the righteous objects" of the Spanish War and the Boer War, which had been "unattainable by milder methods." [48] Besides satisfying the conscience, war is a means of attaining moral ends, not otherwise attainable.

After Norman Angell had taken hold of the theory of national interests, self-interest, and self-preservation, which

[44] *Some Neglected Aspects of War,* pp. 29–32.

[45] Just what is meant by "accuracy of the decision" is not clear. Does it mean a rightful interpretation of right or a right guess respecting the outcome of the war?

[46] *Some Neglected Aspects of War,* p. 92.

[47] *Ibid.,* pp. vi–ix.

[48] *The Problems of Asia,* pp. 141–142.

bulked so large in Mahan's writings on the sea power, and sought to show in *The Great Illusion* that modern war really damages the interests of victors as well as vanquished, the Admiral turned upon him with unwonted vigor. In making this assault on Angell's position, Mahan almost, if not quite, reversed himself. As if oblivious to the nature of his former arguments, he stated positively: "A mature consideration of the wars of the past sixty years, and of the occasions also in which war has seemed imminent and has been averted, will show that the motives to war have not often been 'aggression for the sake of increasing power, and consequently prosperity and financial well-being.' The impulses to war . . . have risen above mere self-interest to feelings and convictions which the argument of *The Great Illusion* does not so much as touch. . . . To regard the world as governed by self-interest only is to live in a non-existent world, a world possessed by an idea much less worthy than those which mankind, to do it bare justice, persistently entertains. . . . The inciting causes of war in our day are moral; a statement which includes of course immoral, though opposite in meaning, as are 'good' and 'bad,' belonging to the same category of motives. . . . Even where material self-interest is at the bottom of the trouble, as possibly in the present [1911] state of feeling between Germany and Great Britain, it is less the loss endured than the sense of injustice done, or apprehended, that keeps alive the flame." [49]

Finally Mahan went all the way over to conception of war as an advance agent of morality. "To right what is amiss, to convert, to improve, to develop, is of the very essence of the Christian ideal. Without man's responsive effort, God himself is not powerless but deprived of the instrument through which he wills to work. Hence the recognition that, if force is necessary, force must be used for the benefit of the community, of the commonwealth of the world." [50] The obligation rests squarely upon the nation and cannot rightfully be avoided. "I think, and have always thought, that the possession of force, of power, to effect ends is a responsibility—a talent, to use the Christian expression—which cannot by the individual

[49] *Armaments and Arbitration,* pp. 126, 153, 154.
[50] *Armaments and Arbitration,* p. 117.

man or state be devolved upon another." [51] In the spread of civilization the British Empire and the American Empire have obligations to increase "the world sum of happiness." If there is peril of hypocrisy in this doctrine it can be escaped: "If a plea of the world's welfare seems suspiciously like a cloak for national self-interest, let the latter be accepted frankly as the adequate motive which it assuredly is. Let us not shrink from pitting a broad self-interest against the narrow self-interest to which some opponents of imperialism would restrict us." [52] In other words, the wider the theater in which self-interest operates, the more defensible it is in Admiral Mahan's eyes. Advancing self-interest on a large scale and doing moral good are parts of the same thing.

In support of the moral aspects of his thesis, Admiral Mahan cited passages from the Bible, as for example: "[The ruler] beareth not the sword in vain: for he is the minister of God, a revenger to execute wrath upon him that doeth evil" (Romans, 13:4). This is in accord with the conception of war as right against wrong. Mahan then takes up the case of Saint Peter's tilt with the guard, and employs it as an illustration of his reasoning. " 'Now he that hath no sword, let him sell his cloak and buy one; for the things concerning me have an end' (Luke, 22:36, 37). The spiritual things concerning him ended not then, nor since; but, unless the sword was bought for ornament, not for use, the use of it in the approaching stage of his dispensation is recognized—nay, authorized. . . . St. Peter, by misunderstanding our Lord's purpose and necessary death, and prematurely—because the end was not yet—used the sword wrongfully and was rebuked (John, 18:10, 11, Matthew, 26:52–54); but the general command was not rescinded." [53] Whatever critical scholarship might say about this particular form of biblical exegesis, Mahan employed it extensively in developing the moral aspects of warfare. Thus he combined nature, morality, Christian doctrine, human motives, and failings, in perfecting his conception of war as an instrument of obligation and responsibility.

[51] *Ibid.*, p. 30.
[52] *Interest of America in Sea Power,* p. 50.
[53] *Some Neglected Aspects of War,* pp. 107–110.

Supported by the authority of Admiral Mahan, other writers on naval affairs have emphasized the point of moral obligation. Speaking of the navy "as a motor in geographical commercial progress," the publicist, G. W. Littlehales, declared in 1899 that the spirit of honorable adventure and the persistent striving against the obstacles of nature "have placed the naval service of the United States among the forceful agencies of the nineteenth century in extending the confines of knowledge to a wider horizon and in opening avenues through which the industries of the people have poured millions of treasure into the nation's lap, and coördinated it with the missions of the Christian Church in bringing the people of distant lands within the generous folds of western civilization." [54] Writing in 1932 on the work of naval officers and men in maintaining "an ever vigilant guard against the savages and atrocities of the ever revolting Chinese and the pillaging of Chinese pirates," Ensign E. Marshall, handing back to his teachers their own teachings, insisted that "the navy is constantly striving to aid China in her progress toward a better civilization, and has always endeavored to protect China from exploitation by greedy foreign powers, even as it protects Central and South American states from similar colonization. . . . To withdraw American interest would seriously handicap the countries involved, since they owe much of their economic, social, and political developments to the work of Americans." [55]

Similar references to moral obligation are found in official publications emanating from the United States Army. "In other lands—the Philippines, Hawaii, Cuba, Porto Rico, and Panama—the Army has given impetus to the forces of civilization," states the War Department in a review of its own work. "It has built public utilities, stamped out disease, educated the children, promoted the spiritual welfare. After setting up these institutions it has protected them from aggression." [56] In laying this case before the nation, the Secretary of War presented

[54] *Bulletin of the American Geographical Society*, No. 2 (1899), p. 123.

[55] *United States Naval Institute Proceedings*, February, 1932; A Prize Essay at the Naval Academy.

[56] *The Work of the War Department* (1924), p. 28.

the argument in another form: "The Philippines, Hawaii, Cuba, Porto Rico, and Panama—all have histories of achievements— history in which the progressive forces of civilization have struggled against reaction and decadence. That civilized forces are triumphant is due primarily to the intelligent administration and constructive talents of the American Army. Building up public utilities, eradicating terrible diseases, educating the children, attending even to the spiritual needs, creating the institutions of self-government, and protecting these institutions from aggression—in all these has the Army left its seal upon our possessions and protectorates and proven itself once more the Pioneer of American Pioneers." [57]

THE UTILITIES OF MORAL OBLIGATION

To summarize the above survey, the American system of political morality, as applied to imperial affairs, consists of maintaining order, bringing backward and primitive peoples under a régime of industry, building roads, introducing sanitation and medicine, establishing popular and secular education, and gradually granting self-government with a view to the spread of democratic institutions on the American model. Funds for the realization of this moral program are derived partly from local sources and partly from the Treasury of the United States. Such operations of course are not entirely without economic aspects. They help to furnish a supply of labor for American industries. Roads, water works, sewers, hospitals, schools, and institutional building in general offer lucrative contracts and the financing of various projects brings bankers into the scene. The raising of the standard of life all around increases buying power and the demand for commodities associated with civilization in Western countries. While it cannot be said that doctors, nurses, teachers, and government officers expect substantial gains from their participation in moral enterprises, entrepreneurs and investors count on more than the rates of return that are customary at home. In other words, American morality is earthly. Its

[57] *Address of John W. Weeks* (before the Boston Chamber of Commerce, November 14, 1922), p. 8.

visible and outward signs of things desired are material conditions adapted to a comfortable and convenient life and a
population well-fed, well-clothed, and literate.

Although accompanied by great enthusiasm, conviction, and
sense of rectitude, it cannot be called a sacrificial morality
without self-regardant aspects, except so far as soldiers and
marines give their lives in helping to carry it into effect. Nor
do efforts to spread it under government auspices extend beyond places where it can be realized in conjunction with economic advantages to American citizens and with a reasonable
degree of safety and expedition.

If American action in Samoa may be deemed a departure
from the original rule against interference in the affairs of
others on moral grounds, the new policy thus inaugurated has
not been without limits. It cannot be said that the Government of the United States has sought to do good in every possible place without respect to perils and sacrifices. When, for
example, after the distribution of the spoils of war at Paris
in 1919, it was proposed, not without a certain degree of irony,
that the United States accept a mandate over Armenia and assume moral and material responsibility for a race struggling
for existence against powerful neighbors, the offer was rejected by Congress. The opportunity to do good was enormous,
but the risks and possible disadvantages outweighed the moral
obligation. Hence it would seem that the moral obligation of
American policy is not absolute, but conditional, is more of
an aspect or support of national interest, than an independent
force of its own.

Moral obligation as employed in American foreign policy is
not, therefore, a transcendent point of reference far above
national interest practically conceived. It is admittedly secular
and utilitarian. It does not command the people of the United
States to sell their goods and set out on a crusade to rescue the
tomb of the Savior or seek any object that is wholly intangible
and incorporeal, utterly beyond outward signs and balance-
sheet estimates. It stands part way between the requirements of sacrificial ethics and the frank exploitation of the
province for the benefit of the metropolis. But whether viewed
as a covering ideology or as an independent political philoso-

phy it constitutes a psychological force in determining the course of external relations.

MORAL OBLIGATION A FORMULA FOR DOMESTIC CONSUMPTION

It requires only a slight knowledge of diplomatic papers to disclose the fact that the use of the term, moral obligation, by the Government of the United States, or any other government for that matter, is effective for domestic purposes mainly. Foreign offices are all well acquainted with the formula and privately regard it as dubious, if not hypocritical. Evidences of this truth are obtrusive in the thousands of pages of diplomatic documents published since the end of the World War, such as *Die Grosse Politik* and *British Documents on the Origins of the World War*. British, French, and German delegates at the first Hague Conference, for example, declined privately to take American pretensions respecting disarmament and arbitration at face value, and American delegates privately had no illusions about the aims and purposes of their collaborators. German diplomats looked upon American operations in the Philippines "in behalf of benighted peoples" as sheer subterfuge.

Writing privately of the public professions made by the American delegates at the Hague Conference, Colonel Charles A Court, British military attaché, reported to his government: "The American Delegates have, it is true, stated that they stand apart from Europe, and that their naval policy has not relation to, and can have no importance for, the Powers of Europe. Mr. [Andrew D.] White indeed made an eloquent speech in defence of the policy of protection for private property at sea, and laid stress on the sentimental side of American character; but it is difficult to get credit for good intentions, and the French Admiral remarked to me at the close of the speech that the Americans had destroyed the Spanish navy and commerce, and now wanted no one to destroy theirs." [58]

The skepticism of the British military attaché was further

[58] *British Documents on the Origins of the World War*, Vol. I, p. 231.

deepened by a private conversation with Captain Alfred Thayer Mahan, another American delegate at the Hague Conference. In the same memorandum the attaché reported to his government: "Captain Mahan has not only stated that his Government will on no account even discuss the question of any limitation of naval armaments; but he has also informed me that he considers that the vital interests of America now lie East and West, and no longer North and South; that the great question of the immediate future is China, and that the United States will be compelled, by facts, if not by settled policy, to take a leading part in the struggle for Chinese markets, and that this will entail a very considerable increase in her naval forces in the Pacific, which again must influence the naval arrangements of at least five Powers."[59] Hence the British government, having been privately informed that the United States had extended the scope of its vital interests to include the Far East, would increase its naval forces there, and would take part in the struggle for Chinese markets, was compelled to regard American professions respecting moral obligation as accompanied by very practical considerations.

THE MORAL ANTITHESIS TO MORAL OBLIGATION

Though immensely popular and spread over wide areas of official papers, the thesis of moral obligation has not passed unchallenged. It was early attacked on its own merits and on the ground that it was likely to lead to quixotic actions dangerous to national interest, realistically conceived. Senator George Gray, a member of the commission which negotiated the treaty of peace with Spain, at first opposed the annexation of any part of the Philippines for the very reasons chosen by President McKinley to justify his policy, namely, on the ground of moral obligation. "Conceding all the benefits claimed for annexation," Senator Gray said in a telegram from Paris to Secretary Hay, "we thereby abandon the infinitely greater benefit to accrue from acting the part of a great, powerful, Christian nation; we exchange the moral grandeur and strength to be gained by keeping our word to nations of the world and by exhibiting

[59] *Ibid.*, p. 231.

a magnanimity and moderation in the hour of victory that becomes the advanced civilization we claim, for doubtful material advantages and shameful stepping down from high moral principle boastfully assumed. We should set example in these respects, not follow the selfish and vulgar greed for territory which Europe has inherited from mediaeval times. . . . Above all let us not make a mockery of the injunction contained in those instructions [of the President to the Peace Commission], . . . that we took up arms only in obedience to the dictates of humanity and in the fulfillment of high public and moral obligation, and that we had no design of aggrandizement and no ambition of conquest." [60]

In sharp contrast to President McKinley and Secretary Root, who held that moral obligation required annexation and the application of the principles of our constitutions and the Declaration of Independence to the peoples of the Philippine Islands, Senator Hoar took the opposite view and set himself firmly against the policy of his party and the administration: "The war which followed it [the treaty with Spain] crushed the republic which the Philippine people had set up for themselves, deprived them of their independence, and established there, by American power, a Government in which the people have no part, against their will. No man, I think, will seriously question that that action was contrary to the Declaration of Independence, the fundamental principles declared in many state constitutions, the principles avowed by the founders of the Republic and by our statesmen of all parties down to a time long after the death of Lincoln." [61]

Carl Schurz was particularly active in the group of citizens who attacked the thesis that moral obligation required overseas expansion. This group applied to the thesis the European name of Imperialism. The principal agency through which they maintained close contact with one another, and presented a united front to the public, was the American Anti-Imperialist League, with headquarters, significantly enough, in Chicago. In the early days of the war, Mr. Schurz wrote to President McKinley: "If we turn this war, which was heralded to the

[60] G. F. Hoar, *Autobiography of Seventy Years,* Vol. II, p. 314.
[61] *Ibid.,* Vol. II, p. 304.

world as a war of humanity, in any sense into a war of conquest, we shall forever forfeit the confidence of mankind, and we shall be met with general distrust in our international relations." [62]

As the war moved on toward American success, and as the note of annexation began to sound louder and clearer above the tumult, Mr. Schurz increased his efforts to raise the moral issue to a high point. Speaking of the Congressional resolution adopted on April 19, 1898, he said that it was designed "to justify our war with Spain before the public opinion of mankind . . . that only a sense of duty put arms in our hands; that we were impelled by a high purpose of noble disinterestedness; that this was to be a war of liberation and humanity, not of conquest or self-aggrandizement. . . . It is quite evident that if this proclamation had been open to the construction that, while we would not annex Cuba, we would annex whatever else might come conveniently our way, it would have met with general derision and contempt." Does not annexation of any of the Spanish colonies, he asked, "turn this solemnly advertised war of liberation and humanity into a war of self-aggrandizement?" [63] Decrying the "policy of Imperialism" which would transform a war of liberation and humanity into a war of conquest, "a land-grabbing foray," Mr. Schurz declared that "American Democracy will have lost its honor. It will stand before the world as a self-convicted hypocrite. . . ." [64]

But in the tumult of the hour, amid the success of American arms, amid cries of "destiny," "divine Providence" and "obligation to benighted peoples," the opinions of those who sought to oppose the rush toward overseas empire could not be heard; or having risen above the confusion and din of the times were weighed, after a fashion, and found wanting. For on December 21, 1898, in a letter of instructions for the American command in the Philippines, President McKinley declared that

[62] Letter of June 1, 1898. *Speeches, Correspondence and Public Papers of Carl Schurz* (ed. by Frederic Bancroft), Vol. V, p. 472.

[63] Address, "Our Future Foreign Policy," before the National Conference of the Civic Federation. Saratoga, N. Y., Aug. 19, 1898. *Op. cit.*, p. 479.

[64] "Thoughts on American Imperialism." First published in *The Century Magazine* (September, 1898). *Op. cit.*, p. 510.

as a result of the success of American arms, and of the treaty of peace with Spain (not at the time ratified by the American Senate) "the future control, disposition and government of the Philippine Islands are ceded to the United States" whose military government is now "to be extended with all possible dispatch to the whole of the ceded territory." All persons in the Philippines who "coöperate with the government of the United States to give effect to those beneficent purposes, will receive the reward of its support and protection. All others will be brought within the lawful rule we have assumed, with firmness if need be, but without severity so far as may be possible." [65] Shortly after these instructions were made known to the Filipinos through the proclamation issued by General E. S. Otis hostilities broke out between the Filipinos and the American forces, the former seeking independence, the latter executing President McKinley's order of "benevolent assimilation."

The reaction in the United States to these events brought forth a vehement address from Mr. Schurz. Speaking at Chicago, in October, 1899, he gave his version of the whole affair in broad outlines: "We go to war with Spain in behalf of an oppressed colony of hers. We solemnly proclaim this to be a war—not of conquest—God forbid!—but of liberation and humanity. We invade the Spanish colony of the Philippines, destroy the Spanish fleet, and invite the coöperation of the Filipino insurgents against Spain. We accept their effective aid as allies, all the while permitting them to believe, that, in case of victory, they will be free and independent. . . . When we have captured Manila and have no further use for our Filipino allies, our President directs that, behind their backs, a treaty be made with Spain transferring their country to us; and even before this treaty is ratified, he tells them that, in place of the Spaniards, they must accept us as their masters, and that if they do not, they will be compelled by force of arms. They refuse and we shoot them down. . . . I ask you

---

[65] Quoted in "McKinley's Declaration of War" (against the Filipinos who had expected liberty under a government of their own choosing). Professor Albert H. Tolman, *Liberty Tracts*, No. 5, American Anti-Imperialist League, Chicago, January, 1900.

now what epithet can you find justly to characterize such a course? . . . President McKinley himself has furnished the best when, in a virtuous moment, he said that annexation by force should not be thought of, for according to the American code of morals, it would be 'criminal aggression.' . . . I pity the American who can behold this spectacle without the profoundest shame, contrition and resentment." [66]

"In the vocabulary of our imperialists," Mr. Schurz declared, " 'order' means . . . submission to their will. . . . This 'order' is the kind that has been demanded by the despot since the world had a history." "I am pleading," he cried, "for the cause of American honor and self-respect, American interests, American democracy . . . against an administration of our public affairs which has wantonly plunged this country into an iniquitous war; which has disgraced the Republic . . . which makes sport of the great principles and high ideals that have been and should ever remain the guiding star of our course." [67]

Picking up the catchwords of "destiny" and "Providence," he subjected them to analysis, and concluded: "Thus the record shows most conclusively that the conquest of the Philippines was not thrust upon the administration by a mysterious and overruling power, but that it was deliberately planned with a cool calculation of profit . . . and when President McKinley tries to make the American people accept his interpretation that the Philippines were simply 'intrusted to our hands by the providence of God,' and that 'it is a trust we have not sought,' he has, to say the least, taken liberties with Providence which he may answer for." [68] "Indeed, disguising the character of imperialism is cultivated as a fine art by its devotees," he said in his Cooper Union address, and "President McKinley . . . furnished an example . . . bold enough to make us gasp." [69]

When the next presidential election came around, Mr. Schurz carried the note of moral obligation into the campaign. In the previous election he had supported McKinley, the man of "sound money"; now he turned against him on "the policy of

[66] "The Policy of Imperialism," *Speeches,* Vol. VI, pp. 91–92.
[67] *Ibid.,* p. 119.
[68] Address "For the Republic of Washington and Lincoln," Philadelphia, February 22, 1900, *Ibid.,* p. 158.
[69] Sept. 28, 1900, *Ibid.,* pp. 219–220.

imperialism" and contrasted McKinley's public utterances with his acts: "He devotes 10,000 words to the task of persuading us that it is only a war of duty and humanity, . . . 'not for aggrandizement, nor for pride of might, nor for trade or commerce, nor for exploitation, but for humanity and civilization'; . . . [but] when Spain was ready for peace, the Secretary of the Navy telegraphed to Admiral Dewey as follows: '. . . The President desires to receive from you any important information you may have of the Philippines; the desirability of the several islands; the character of their population, coal and other mineral deposits; their harbor and commercial advantages; and in a naval and commercial sense, which would be the most advantageous.' There was nothing about 'humanity and civilization' in this. . . ." How "low an opinion of the intelligence of his countrymen" must the President have to tell them that we are not trying to subjugate the Filipinos for our "aggrandizement," for "trade or commerce," or for "exploitation," while "every nook and corner of the land is fairly ringing with the appeals of the President's spokesmen to the coarsest greed of wealth and the most vainglorious pride of might, describing in absurdly gorgeous colors the riches somebody might get on those islands, and the magnificent position as a great world-power their possession will give us!" [70]

Writing to Charles Francis Adams, Jr., on October 25, 1900, Mr. Schurz declared: "I have laboriously and carefully studied what has happened in all its details . . . and that study has profoundly convinced me that the story of our 'criminal aggression' upon the Philippines is a story of deceit, false pretense, brutal treachery to friends, unconstitutional assumption of power, downright betrayal of the fundamental principles of our democracy, wanton sacrifice of our soldiers . . . cruel slaughter of tens of thousands of innocent people, . . . without a parallel in the history of republics. . . . This is my honest conviction. . . ." [71]

Other critics of the new code—moral obligation—added their voices and contributed their influence and money in the effort

[70] Cooper Union Address. September 28, 1900. *Speeches,* Vol. VI, pp. 221–222.

[71] *Speeches,* Vol. VI, p. 263.

to stem the tide. In a letter to Mr. Schurz, William James, the philosopher, wrote: ". . . Your Philadelphia address stirs my heart to overflowing. . . . I think the Administration talk, Dewey's talk, about never having committed ourselves in any way to Aguinaldo . . . is the most incredible, unbelievable, piece of sneak-thief turpitude that any nation ever practiced. . . ." [72] Asserting that "The people of the United States today are face to face with a question of right and wrong," Moorfield Storey, of the Boston Bar, in a speech at Philadelphia on February 23, 1900, reviewed the history of the case and asked: "Is it right? Test it by any principle, political, moral or religious, that we have ever learned at home, in church or at school, test it by all that the great leaders of this country have taught us, is it right? This is a question which every citizen must answer. Evade it, disguise it, deny it as he will, he cannot escape it. . . ." [73] Quoting the words of Charles Sumner, who on a former occasion in American history had declared that there is something above commercial and material prosperity, Mr. Storey continued: " 'It is the honor and good name of the Republic, now darkened by an act of wrong. If this territory so much coveted by the President were infinitely more valuable than it is, I hope the Senate would not be tempted to obtain it by trampling on the weak and humble.' " [74]

Even Andrew Carnegie entered the lists against "imperialism," and in a very substantial way. "Print your speech," he wrote to Mr. Schurz on December 27, 1898, ". . . and distribute it and I will be your banker. . . . You have brains and I have dollars. . . . Do not lose faith in the Republic or Triumphant Democracy. It is sound to the core." [75]

Responding to such criticism of the new course and adhering to tradition, the Democratic party in its official platforms chose to reject the moral-obligation thesis of the Republicans and to emphasize the foreign aspect of their policy as economic greed. In 1900 it declared that the Administration's treatment of the Porto Ricans "dooms to poverty and distress a people

---

[72] From France, March 16, 1900, *Ibid.*, p. 190.
[73] *Liberty Tracts;* "Is It Right," No. 8.
[74] *Ibid.*
[75] *Speeches,* Vol. V, p. 531.

whose helplessness appeals with peculiar force to our justice and magnanimity." It denounced the Philippine policy as sacrificing the lives of the Republic's sons, as placing the country once applauded as the champion of freedom in the false and un-American position of crushing with military force "the efforts of our former allies to achieve liberty and self-government." It asserted that a "greedy commercialism" had "dictated Philippine policy" and condemned the war against the insurrectionists as "the war of 'criminal aggression.' " In succeeding campaigns the Democratic party repeated this criticism in various forms, and in 1912 reaffirmed "the position thrice announced by the Democracy in national convention assembled against a policy of imperialism in the Philippines and elsewhere." If moral obligation, imposed by fate as alleged or by choice, was the pivot on which territorial expansion in connection with commerce really turned, the theory was thus directly denied by a belligerent opposition.

The thesis of moral obligation was also challenged in the name of anthropology and religion, as well as national tradition. On the side of anthropology it was said that the whole conception was based on an unscientific and impractical view of human nature—on an untenable assumption, namely, that all races are capable of assimilating civilization in its American form and would be better off if they should take on its outward aspects. Obviously this contention opened up views of world history which could not be disposed of finally by a political debate.

In the name of religion, representatives of the Catholic Church insisted that spiritual damage was being wrought by American morality, particularly in the Philippines. Speaking, in 1932, at a farewell ceremony for fifteen Jesuit missionaries about to depart for the Philippines, the Reverend Charles G. Herzog, professor of theology at Woodstock College, while conceding that the United States had brought "many lasting benefits" to the people of the Islands, "may have bettered their material life and given them opportunities of becoming better schooled in the sciences and the arts, it has, on the other hand, carried to these Islands the same indifference to religion which is rampant in this country." Once the people were Catholics, but under American rule "their Catholicism is being endangered by the materialistic teachings of the American school, from which religion is excluded." These evils must be combated, the speaker insisted, by sending out more Catholic missionaries.[76]

Ever since the war with Spain, in fact, debates dealing with Philippine independence and collateral issues have turned on moral obligation and interest, both parties to the discussions emphasizing the one or the other, according to circumstances. When, at length, the "oppressed and benighted millions," to whom Dr. Schurman referred (above, p. 255), really began to stir after the agitations of the World War, when the passion for "self-determination" began to spread ominously through the entire Orient, and when American advocates of independence for the Philippines began to speak of the moral obligation to grant freedom to the Islands, critics on the other side laid stress on practical interests and on the moral obligation of the United States to aid in preserving the old *status quo* in the Far East. Speaking before a Senate Committee, in 1930, Nicholas Roosevelt, whom President Hoover, an opponent of Philippine independence, had tried in vain to make governor of the Islands, insisted that independence would destroy the balance of power in the East and endanger order in the possessions of the imperial nations. "It is to the particular interest of Great Britain, the United States, and Holland," he said, "to see that there is no change in the political equilibrium of the Far East, because they want two things. They want peace from the point of view of international affairs, and they want internal tranquility in their possessions and in those territories which they govern out there." Mr. Roosevelt went on to discuss the unrest in the Dutch East Indies, the Malay States, India, and Korea, and expressed the opinion that "even talking of granting independence to the Philippines" might contribute to the serious outbreaks against imperial governments and threaten the peace of the Orient. In other words, by a strange turn of fortune, the United States owed an obligation to other ruling powers in that region and, after

[76] New York *Times,* June 6, 1932.

having undertaken the evangelization of the East through the spread of the Declaration of Independence, must now renounce the program lest its success prove disastrous elsewhere. The moral obligation remains, but its objectives are no longer the same.[77]

Especially, during the controversy that raged while the bill granting provisional independence to the Philippines was under consideration, did participants on both sides toss *moral obligation* and *interest* forward and back. When agrarian and labor representatives cited practical interest as a reason for granting independence, representatives of industry and commerce taunted them with sacrificing moral obligation to sordid considerations. When the latter brought forward moral obligation as a ground of opposition to independence, agrarian and labor representatives charged them with using the phrase to cover their profit-making activities in the Islands (below p. 406). Yet, in the course of their arguments, the two parties were assiduous in collecting and presenting facts and figures designed to show that the retention or independence of the Philippines, as the case might be, would bring material benefits or do material damage to the United States. And by no process of research or logical analysis is it possible to discover whether the sense of moral obligation or estimates of substantial advantages weighed heavier in the minds of those who freely employed the terms.[78]

---

[77] *Senate Hearings*, "Independence of the Philippines" (1930), pp. 347ff.

[78] For example, see speech of Senator Hawes; *Cong. Record*, 72nd Cong., 1st Sess., p. 13230. See also a kind of summary in the speech of Senator Vandenberg, June 13, 1932, *Ibid.*, pp. 13254ff; and accompanying discussions by other Senators during the same month. See also the reasons given by President Hoover for vetoing the Bill passed during the 2d Session of the 72nd Cong. Subsequently the Philippine Independence Act became a law over the President's veto. For President Hoover's veto message and the House vote overriding it, see *Cong. Rec.*, 72d Cong. 2d Sess., No. 30 (Jan. 13, 1933), pp. 1818–1828. For the Senate discussion and vote on the same see, *ibid.*, Nos. 31, 32 and 33, particularly pp. 1995–2013 of the last. Under elaborate clauses providing for a convention to draft a constitution which must receive the approval of the President of the United States, as well as a majority vote of the Philippine people, and which must then be made the basis of a ten-year probationary period during which certain acts must have the approval of the President of the United States; and under long, detailed provisions bearing upon American sovereignty, naval bases and trade relations with the Islands, and for the

What conclusion "of strict scientific determination" is possible? None. After reviewing, more or less casually, evidence in the case as it appeared at the turn of the nineteenth century, the historian, James Ford Rhodes, came to the conclusion "that the attempt of many anti-imperialists to hint that love of gain was the prime cause of our taking the Philippines is not borne out by the record." [79] While this finding does not settle the dispute or prove that moral obligation was the "prime cause," there can be no doubt that a sense of moral responsibility was an active factor in bringing about the annexation of new territorial possessions and the efforts to improve the material and spiritual condition of the inhabitants—the sense which Senator Platt found so prevalent among the people of Connecticut. It was a potent force throughout the country, among millions of American citizens who knew little or nothing about the Philippine Islands, who had no practical interests at stake in their retention or emancipation, who had little information about the possibilities of profit from the development of their natural resources or from the use of them as a base for the enlargement of the China trade. Indeed, Senator Hoar himself, opposed though he was to the Philippine adventure, conceded that President McKinley was moved to renounce his former hostility to "forcible annexation," by the "apparently earnest desire of the American people, as he understood it, as it was conveyed to him on his Western trip." [80] The roots of that sense, this swelling passion to do good, to impose inherited principles of government and civilization on other peoples, lie deep in the process of history. Its form is nebulous; under skillful leaders it may make crusades and holy wars; but its existence is scarcely to be questioned, and the McKinley administration, in departing from the austere aloofness of earlier days, gave to moral obligation a fixed place in the ideology and reasoning of American diplomacy.

neutralization of the Islands, and so on—Philippine independence, in so far as it is not restricted by the provisions of the act, may be attained after an interval not less than approximately fourteen years, with possibilities in the bill of stretching the period over several additional years. For the salient points of the bill, which became law on Jan. 17, 1933, see N. Y. *Times*, Jan. 18, 1933; or for the bill itself, see H. R. 7233.

[79] *The McKinley and Roosevelt Administrations*, p. 185.

[80] *Autobiography of Seventy Years*, Vol. II, p. 309.

MORAL OBLIGATION: A SUMMARY

To take the words and ideas associated with moral obligation out of the context of which they are a part, or away from the events and conditions which they describe, is ordinarily an exercise of dubious validity. And if the purpose in doing so were to subject them to a critical analysis and appraisal, the undertaking would be specious indeed. But in a work primarily expositional, no harm is likely to be done if the words and ideas previously presented in their proper connotations are removed therefrom and recapitulated in more succinct form. By thus casting into sharper relief the basic or key elements of moral obligation, free from the surrounding detail, such a summary may serve to clarify the concept as a whole and place it in the larger perspective of national interest objectively revealed.

Moral obligation used in practice as a motive force influencing the actions of men and governments covers a wide range. The content, the scope, the purpose, the consistency, and the utility of moral obligation are revealed in the words and phrases and the ideas used to make it articulate in the course of history. These words, phrases, and ideas provide the raw materials of fact from which an understanding of the concept of moral obligation may be gained, if at all, and upon which a reasoned pattern of moral obligation and its relation to national interest may be tentatively formed, and squarely presented.

From the examples above given—the presentation is not, of course, exhaustive—the mandate of moral obligation appears to be operative in three spheres which, on occasion, seem to overlap: (1) the nation itself, as something of an independent entity; (2) the nation in respect of other single nations and certain limited groups of nations; and (3) the nation as one unit in a larger whole made up of many diverse units forming what is commonly called the "community of nations." In practice, there is no positive exactitude about any of these spheres. Consequently they are here used merely for the convenience of exposition since in the literature and practice of moral obligation these spheres have appeared, in a rough way, to constitute the physical theaters in which action was intended to take place and in which action did take place.

In the first sphere—bearing upon the nation itself—moral obligation assumes several forms. It enjoins upon the nation the desirability, the necessity, and the duty of strengthening the "moral fibre" of its citizens, and of the nation as something of a unified personality, even if an abstract one. With this is associated the desirability of increasing the "self-respect" and the "dignity" of the nation, placing upon the nation the necessity of raising its "ethical standard" to approximate the "code of morals of the individual" so that it may earn the "approval" and the "confidence" of all "mankind." There is a certain "moral grandeur" in keeping our word. Moral obligation in this sphere urges the nation to respond to the call of "philanthropy," even as, in the domain of private life, the rich man responds to the needs of the community. The nation, when strong, must aid the weak; when richly endowed in culture and "the blessings of freedom," must share them with other nations. Like the individual, the nation has a "conscience" which it must satisfy to keep its own "peace of mind," and this requires the nation to perform innumerable acts of infinite variety. The nation must eternally strive for "justice," for "righteousness," and to "overpower evil." The nation must forever cultivate those instincts of "humanity" and "civilization" which impel it to "resist oppression," to "vindicate the principles of peace and justice . . . against selfishness and autocratic power," to foster "good understanding," "friendship" and "happiness," and to extend to all the "sympathy" by which humanity may assuage the hardships and misfortunes visited upon it from whatever cause. Having undertaken an operation in the moral sphere, the nation must have the courage to see it through even though such action may demand great sacrifices and may endanger its own material interests. When in a position of responsibility toward the lives and possessions of others, the nation must adopt the rectitude, the self-effacement, and the solicitude of the personal "trustee."

There are other qualities which the "deep sense of moral obligation" demands from the nation purely for its own sake. But those mentioned—strengthening its moral fibre, adding to its dignity and self-respect, preserving its honor, cultivating philanthropy and magnanimity, satisfying the dictates of its conscience, sharpening its sensibility to justice, righteousness, humanity, and civilization, enlarging its capacity for sympathy, and placing these things above its own material interests—may be said to be the principal mandates which moral obligation prescribes as necessary to establish the *character* of the nation as a nation and to develop it in its own sphere of life, even as the same qualities and virtues define the character of the individual and sustain him in the development of his whole personality. The nation should do these things for itself alone, for its own well-being, apart from the duty it may owe either to other nations or to the "community of nations" in which it moves and has its being.

The second of these spheres in which moral obligation may be observed to be practically operative—the nation's relationship with other single national entities and with certain groups of nations—also reveals distinct characteristics. The nation is under a duty to "observe good faith" toward other countries, a duty which embraces a range of acts impossible to detail. Abstention from "interference with the affairs of other nations" is another broad admonition commonly encountered in practice. The nation must respect the security, the territorial and administrative integrity of other nations; but there are occasions, it seems, when moral obligation requires mediation and even forcible intervention in the affairs of other countries.

There are also to be found in this sphere certain real or implied interests, material and cultural, associated with groups and sub-groups of nations. The identifications are always rather vague to be sure, but they are usually clear enough for moral obligation to operate. There is, for example, a group of nations associated with the idea of "Western Civilization." Mere association with such a group, unauthenticated in any objective way, seems to place upon the nation the moral obligation to maintain the solidarity of the group, spread its "benefits," defend it, and refrain from any act which, either directly or indirectly, might weaken its position or destroy its influence. On this ground it has been urged, for example, that the United States should not free the Philippine Islands because to do so would upset the "equilibrium," the peace and stability now maintained by certain Western Powers under the peculiar circumstances existing in the Far Eastern area of the world. To upset such an "equilibrium" would not be "keeping faith" with the group of Western nations concerned, and may even amount to a violation of an implied covenant not to interfere in their affairs, all of which is covered by the dictates of moral obligation. Finally, all those qualities, virtues, and acts, described as establishing the character of the nation as a nation, must also be manifest in the relations of the nation with its "fellow-nations." [81]

It is in the third sphere—the relation of the nation to the "society of nations" of which it is declared to be a member— that the dictates of moral obligation are said to be the strongest and the broadest. Here, not only must the nation carry all its "personal" attributes and the qualities which should make of it a "good neighbor," but also many other duties and virtues of a wider nature. For here, it must answer to the dictates of "international friendship," of "humanity," of "civilization" in the broadest sense. It must "Christianize," "educate," "uplift," fight any number of things—oppression, disease, ignorance, "raise living standards," and "overpower evil." It must extend the "blessings of freedom," secure the "inalienable rights of man," (sometimes viewed as crystallized in the Declaration of Independence), and help others to obtain the "benefits" of democratic government.[82] It must help other countries to realize the "best aspirations of their people." It must not permit infant nations to "wreck themselves" upon dangerous economic rocks or run aground upon treacherous political shoals.

In this sphere the moral obligation envisages some sort of a régime of "peace, law, and order," which lays upon the nation the duty to strive to bring about everywhere "stable" government, "independent" government, "just and effective" government, and government based upon "the principles of liberty."

---

[81] President Franklin D. Roosevelt, in his inaugural address, dedicated the nation to the policy of being "the good neighbor."

[82] A duty performed, for example, for Nicaragua under the supervision of the United States Marines after a system of American suffrage and elections had been installed in that country.

Flowing from this is the necessity that the nation do its share in achieving everywhere such conditions as "protection," "security," "pacification," and "prosperity." These concepts pass into a still larger one. There are certain "common interests" too which must be realized. They spring from "progress"—scientific, economic, political, and social. They arise out of the interdependence of nations. They even flow from the abstractions of universal nature; from the operation of some "higher" laws; and from the commands of some "divine" being. Thus to reiterate a view advanced by Mahan, nations may be under the moral obligation to go to war as a sort of "compensatory action" against subversive "natural forces," performing, what would be termed in the field of medicine, the work of immunizing and prophylactic agents. According to Mahan also, and to many others as well, there are circumstances under which a nation may be an instrumentality to carry out "God's will," even to the extreme of war. It is the moral obligation of the nation to aid in regimenting these "common interests," crystallizing them in the shape of national and international institutions, formal and informal, and enlarging the area of their operation.

These, then, are the spheres in which moral obligation may be seen to be operative. The words, the phrases and the several concepts above presented are not theoretical, but are the verbal forms through which moral obligation finds expression in practice. All of them may be observed in use in connection with the relations with Samoa, Cuba, Porto Rico, the Philippines, China, the Central American countries, and so on. All of them may be found in the diplomatic conversations and correspondence and in the official documents in the government archives. The broad fields of economic, political, and social literature abound with them. They indicate the substance of moral obligation.

At times, moral obligation appears as an independent force. At others, far the most frequent, it seems to supplement national interest, or give meaning to it. When, for example, a policy or an act has been deemed desirable "in the national interests," the appropriate mandates of moral obligation have been drawn upon freely to substantiate, support, or provide justification for, the deed. There do not seem to exist any independent, objective criteria for determining the relationship between moral obligation and the national interest, either as currently conceived or as may be conceived under any known system of knowledge and thought. That is to say, objective criteria appear to be lacking, both for the interpretation and testing of moral obligation, and for determining "the true" national interest. Nevertheless, allegedly to realize the precepts of moral obligation in action, all the engines of war, conquest, economic pressure, religious dogma, social control, and political power have been employed.

CHAPTER IX

INTERPRETATION, ADVANCEMENT, AND ENFORCEMENT OF NATIONAL INTEREST

FROM the above record it is clear that the promotion of national interest is widely represented as the prime concern of American statecraft. And by a process of reasoning, none the less clear because inferential, the conclusion must be drawn that the advancement of national interest is also officially regarded as the primary concern, the result, if not the conscious aim, of all legitimate private enterprises in American life—economic or otherwise—as well. That true national interest may or may not be served either by statecraft or by private enterprises is another matter which, for purposes of the present inquiry, may be considered irrelevant. This much is certain, namely, whenever the question arises in its simple, direct form: What is the supreme, ultimate motive underlying a given process, policy, or act in public or private life?—the answer is given just as simply, that the primary motive is the national interest, or to use variants, "national welfare," "public interest," or "the general welfare."

Materials have already been presented to illustrate the proposition that promotion of national interest has been widely held to be the supreme objective of public and private life, and also to indicate what the substance of national interest is conceived to be. It is now appropriate to inquire by what processes and agencies that interest is to be disclosed and applied in particular cases and as a general rule. In short, how and by whom is the national interest interpreted, and in what ways is the national interest advanced and enforced?

Interpretation, advancement, and enforcement of national interest are in reality parts of the same process. It is true that enforcement usually calls to mind "police" action, the application of force in a concrete situation for the accomplishment of some desired end. But such a procedure is merely one aspect of enforcement, broadly viewed. In point of time it is usually the last resort, the ultimate sanction, by which objectives are sought to be attained. In content enforcement is almost always the application of some positive, physical form of coercion. One of its principal elements is the manner of its appearance, which represents an act of will—the assertion of a positive intent to use some agency of compulsion, or the doing of a positive act designed to compel acquiescence, in a situation where there is opposition to the intent, or resistance, open or covert, to the act. This is the common connotation— the popular conception—of enforcement. Applied to national interests it covers the entire range from the thinly veiled threat in diplomatic intercourse to the full engagement of the nation in war. It is not, however, the only, or even the principal, means by which national interests are advanced or enforced. By far the greater proportion of what are conceived to be national interests is achieved in the daily, routine conduct of men and governments, in the field of "enforcement" outside the sphere of the coercive action above described, which, in point of time, is usually preceded by preliminaries of enforcement.

This broader phase of enforcement is none the less enforcement because it is at the same time the routine action of men and governments; because it lacks the obvious concomitants of coercion. Like the narrower conception of enforcement, it concerns objectives; it deals with conflicts of interest; and by sanctions far more subtle and delicate in their operation, it compels and achieves desired results. It is inseparably bound up with interpretation and together they help to substantiate and express the daily routine of private enterprise and government action.

There are three categories of "entities," "subjects," or "persons," existing in modern world intercourse, which are involved in interpretation and enforcement. They are: private individuals, private corporations, and public corporations—states. For many purposes the number of these categories may be reduced to two by combining the private individuals and private corporations into a single group—private subjects.[1] These "entities" of private subjects and states have their being and move in a series of physical environments: private subjects in the locality, the village, the country, the province, the nation and, in modern times, the world;[2] and states within the region (such as Europe, the Near East, Central America, etc.), the continent, and the world.

From the dawn of history a process has been in the course of development by which men and the groups they formed, impelled by instinct, necessity, or desire, have interacted upon each other and upon the particular physical environment as a result of the inevitable and ever-widening contacts of man with man, man with the group, and group with group. Out of these contacts, conditioned as they were by the "natural" needs and desires of men, by the limitations of the environment, and by an infinite number and variety of "forces," conflicts of interests were bound to arise. Inherent in the clash of interests was the necessity of adjusting them if the consequence of the conflict was not to be a complete annihilation of both the interest sought and the individual seeking it. Likewise with the crude attempts at human association and coöperation came the recognition of a body of interests common to the group, and later to the several groups. Gradually the conditions of individual adjustment and the recognition of common interests became crystallized into an institution of human association, called custom. In the further course of development many things sanctioned by custom took on the more concrete character of convention, from which in the passage of time

---

[1] "At the present day, practically all states recognize the civil capacity of foreign corporations as they do that of natural persons." Edwin M. Borchard, *Diplomatic Protection of Citizens Abroad*, p. 42.

[2] For illustrations as to the individual, see Count E. C. Corti, *The Reign of the House of Rothschild*. As to partnerships, the world-wide operation of J. P. Morgan & Co. is an excellent example. As to corporations, the number and variety of examples are almost unlimited. Such concerns as the General Motors Corporation, the Ford Motor Company, the General Electric Company, the International Telephone and Telegraph Company and the International Harvester Company are well-known illustrations. A partial analysis of corporations whose direct, material operations go beyond the national boundaries discloses, for example, two hundred American concerns having some eight hundred subsidiaries throughout Europe. See Frank H. Southard, *American Industry in Europe,* particularly Chapter II, and pp. 111, 189, and 200ff.

certain "rights," carrying with them correlative duties, arose.[3]

Without intending to be arbitrary or to become involved in any theoretical discussion of "rights," inalienable or otherwise, an enumeration of these rights may be ventured. In the case of individuals and later of private corporate bodies, these "rights" may be said to fall into two broad categories: "public rights" and "private rights," although neither the particular "rights" nor any of the classifications into which they may be grouped have achieved universal recognition and interpretation.

Among the so-called "public rights" are included individual liberty, freedom of worship, freedom of speech and of the press, the right of association and assembly, liberty of commerce, trade, and industry, and the right to resort to the courts of foreign countries. "Private rights" include the ownership of real estate, the right of succession to property, the power and freedom to acquire, own, and dispose of personal property, the right to industrial and literary property, and so on.[4]

With greater indefiniteness and inconclusiveness, but with some similarity to the treatment of "rights" of private subjects, the "rights" of states are declared to be the right of existence which implies self-preservation, the right of liberty of action or of independence, the right of holding and acquiring property which involves exclusive control over the territory within the boundaries of the state, and the right to do whatever is necessary for the attainment of these rights and for the continued development of the state.[5]

[3] It is hoped that the text dealing with the discussion of "rights" will make clear that the broader conception of rights is intended rather than the narrower aspect which conceives of rights in legal terminology and institutions alone. For a discussion of the legal rights in the light of these broader institutions, see Sir Henry S. Maine, *Ancient Law* (ed. Sir Frederick Pollock). For an illustration of the influence of interests upon the development of a prevailing institution—neutrality—see Oppenheim, *International Law*, Vol. II, pp. 463–464, 468.

[4] For a discussion of these "rights" as they enter into international intercourse, see Edwin M. Borchard, *Diplomatic Protection of Citizens Abroad*, pp. 40–43; 73–86. Also p. 15, where Fiore's enumeration of "rights" is cited. In the Declaration of Independence these rights are reduced to their simplest and broadest expression in the phrase "Life, liberty, and the pursuit of happiness."

[5] Moore, *Digest of International Law*, Vol. I, p. 60, sec. 23. The American Institute of International Law, at its first session held in Washington, January 6,

These "rights," broadened by an infinite number of "secondary," or "derived" rights, eventually found expression in various fields of human thought and action. They were continued in custom, confirmed in convention, woven inextricably into the doctrines and institutions associated with economics, politics, and social intercourse, and many of them found concrete expression and authority in municipal and international law. They make up the substance of the daily routine of men and governments. They enter into the current conception of "national interests." Through their interpretation and their application to economics and politics, for example, they become the link between the American national interest and gunboats on the Yangtse River, between commercial expansion and the marines in Haiti and Nicaragua. Their interpretation and enforcement in the daily routine may be considered generally in the two broad fields in which national interest is operative: business enterprise, particularly that branch more directly involved in foreign commerce, and the "area" occupied by the Government of the United States.

Another approach is also necessary to round out the discussion. Items of national interest are frequently lifted out of the daily routine by the conditions of existence and human association, and appear in the character of specific issues. This is the point at which enforcement proper (in the nature of "po-

1916, adopted six articles which it declared to be the "Rights and Duties of Nations." Abridged, they are "I. Every nation has the right to exist, and to protect and to conserve its existence. . . . II. Every nation has the right to independence . . . to the pursuit of happiness and is free to develop itself without interference or control from other states. . . . III. Every nation is in law and before law the equal of every other nation belonging to the society of nations. . . . IV. Every nation has the right to territory, . . . to exercise exclusive jurisdiction over its territory, and all persons . . . found therein. V. Every nation entitled to a right by the law of nations is entitled to have that right respected and protected by all other nations. . . . VI. International law is at one and the same time both national and international: national in the sense that it is the law of the land, . . . international in the sense that it is the law of the society of nations . . . [that it is applicable in both spheres when questions involving its principles arise]." Running through these rights is the qualification that they may not be exercised so as to "interfere with or violate the rights of other states," and that "rights and duties are correlative." *American Journal of International Law (1916)*, Vol. X, p. 124. See also Amos S. Hershey, *The Essentials of International Public Law and Organization*, Chapter X, pp. 230–252, Rev. Ed., Macmillan, N. Y., 1927.

lice" action) begins. For convenience, it has been made the subject of a second review under the title: Diplomacy and the Enforcement of National Interest (below).

By these two approaches to the subject it is not intended to imply any definite separation between the processes by which national interest is interpreted and enforced. As indicated the process is a whole one. The daily routine forms its major content, and by degrees it shades off, through the specific issues thrown up by the routine, into diplomatic representation and negotiation and finally into the use of all the agencies and procedures of enforcement proper—resort to the compulsion of armed violence.

INTERPRETATION BY BUSINESS ENTERPRISE

According to one common hypothesis, business enterprise discovers what is good for itself, and whatever is good for business enterprise is *ipso facto* good for the country. In the first instance, therefore, business interprets the national interest and the Government acts as a protective and executive agency upon occasion. Thus the underlying operations, intellectual and physical, are in private hands and the Government in promoting national interest needs merely to follow the leadership and course of business enterprise. In this view the task of interpretation is relatively simple: the natural reason of business men acting under the guidance of the acquisitive instinct supplies most, if not all, of the necessary information.

In interpreting national interest, business enterprise so conceived does not employ a common organization, endowed with a collective mind and will. It has no such sovereign agency. At bottom it is a congeries of particular interests carrying on widely diverse operations. Within its embrace are included manufacturers whose prosperity may be mainly dependent on high protective tariffs, importing merchants whose profits hang upon a large volume of imports though these may conflict in the market with domestic products, international bankers engaged in remunerative activities by lending money abroad, local bankers who finance domestic industries principally, transportation companies interested only in securing car loadings whether of foreign or domestic goods, farmers raising produce for domestic consumption, farmers raising wheat and cotton for the world market, and so on through the complicated arrangements of American economic society. Although the several departments of economic life—industry, commerce, agriculture, and labor, for example—are each organized after a manner and occasionally bring collective pressures upon the the Government, they are not sovereignties endowed with plenary power to define national interest in particular cases and as a general rule. They have no organ to express a single will.

According to the operating hypothesis here under review, the interpretation of national interest flows rather simply out of economic activities themselves—financial and commercial—and the function of the Government is to protect and promote them by various means. A loan to a foreign government or industrial enterprise is about to be arranged by private bankers; if necessary the Government is to provide appropriate diplomatic assistance. An outlet for commodities is sought; the Government should aid in discovering markets and should protect them against discriminations and disorders. The carriage of goods on the high seas is deemed useful to business in general and advantageous to ship-owners and builders; it is the duty of the Government to arrange the conditions in which profitable operations may be pursued. To be sure, under the dicta of classical economy, there is to be as little as possible or no political interference at all, but those criteria have been modified by American practice. Acquisitive enterprises in the United States are to supply the data and the substance for the policy of national interest and the Government of the United States is to derive its responsibilities in the premises from these sources.

By what intellectual processes does business enterprise discover that its multitudinous activities—diverse in nature and often conflicting in purpose—really redound to the national interest? Although engaged in pecuniary transactions it does not present its picture of national interest in the form of a balance sheet showing gains or losses in national wealth resulting from its individual transactions. With all its searching and compiling of statistics, economic science has not demonstrated mathematically, as it could if it were a science, just how the ardent pursuit of particular interests by individuals actually promotes the general welfare. On the contrary it merely makes the assumption and clothes it in mystery. Adam Smith, the founder of political economy, puzzled by the problem, evaded it by referring to "an invisible hand" that overrides evils of egoism and turns them to the good of the Commonwealth.[6] "There was," as George Peel says, "a touch of mysti-

[6] The belief that the activities of private enterprise automatically inure to the national interest draws its justification or support from the "law" of natural evolution. The reasoning, starting from fundamentals, is something like the following:

A. Man moves within (or confronts) a natural, physical environment capable of yielding up certain things which man calls the necessities of life, and wealth.

B. The primary desires of man are economic—each individual will strive for subsistence and security for himself and his family, and for as many comforts, luxuries, and possessions as his desires dictate and he can get—within the stated environment.

C. If each man is permitted to seek his own interests (which only he can know best since only he can know the food, the clothing, the shelter, the possessions, which he wants and will satisfy his wants) the aggregate wealth of all individuals in the same environment will be increased, even though each single individual follows his own interests without any thought for the community as a whole. The "mysterious way" in which the whole community is enriched without any planned or conscious effort in that direction is rather simple and not so mysterious as it seems—at least in broad theory.

D. In following his own desires and interests, each individual will have to meet other individuals who are striving in a similar manner within the same environment. The limitations upon man himself, and the limitations of the environment in which he moves—physical and human—are such at any given time as to turn this contact of man with man and of man with his environment into a complex process of competition. Under the influence of this competition, each individual will be induced or forced to put forth his best and utmost efforts. The result will be a more intensive assault by all men upon the environment in which they find themselves to extract from it the maximum yield of subsistence and security, of comforts and luxuries, of possessions. The process naturally will lead to better methods of production, more product, better quality. It will lead to the most advantageous employment of capital. It will result in a better division of labor, since each individual, following his own interests and knowing himself, will discover the things he is best able to do. The process will also throw up, naturally, many beneficial arrangements—such as coöperation—by which skills and facilities are coördinated and the results shared and exchanged.

E. Thus with every individual motivated solely by his own desires and interests, and left wholly free to pursue them as he will, the result will be a community of individuals all seeking the maximum amount of subsistence, se-

cism here. The fixity of the old abandoned mediæval economy had been justified also, in its day, on supernatural grounds. It had been defended by St. Thomas Aquinas and his school as a part of the Divine Order. This mysticism, expelled at the Renaissance, was thus returning to rule us, and to be re-incorporated, throughout the nineteenth century, into the most prosaic and materialistic of schools! Perhaps the explanation is that this mysticism of Adam Smith and of his followers was of a modernized type. It was mysticism arm in arm with the main chance." [7] However that may be, the general assumption of American business enterprise is that the pecuniary gains of individual and corporate concerns are synonymous with general welfare and that its innumerable requirements automatically constitute the fundamental interpretation of national interest.

This hypothesis of interpretation has been, of course, oversimplified, for the sake of sharpness in presentation. Private interests have not always taken the lead in developing foreign commerce, nor have they made the complete pattern of interpretation for political action in the national interest. From the foundation of the Republic, no doubt, they have sought government aid in opening new opportunities; but the Government, on its part, has not blindly followed a course plotted by the private pecuniary quest. In fact the Government has often foreshadowed and searched out paths for private enterprise to follow. It has framed economic policies of its own, sought to enlist the support of bankers, industrialists, and merchants, and

curity, comforts, luxuries, and other possessions, within a given environment in the best way possible. The competition in wants raises a competition in efforts in which all individuals are seeking the "best," the "most efficient," the "maximum," both in what the environment can yield and in the capacity, ingenuity, and skills with which each individual is by nature endowed. It follows from this process, *ipso facto*, that the individuals, and the community as a whole, are constantly and increasingly piling up wealth. If the community is a nation, then it is the nation which is thus enriched along with the individual; and when, in turn, the environment is enlarged to include the whole world, the philosophy of this process whereby the enrichment of the individual becomes the enrichment of the environment, is equally applicable and efficacious. In short, the enrichment of the whole automatically follows—so the theory teaches —from the enrichment of constituent members and parts. The grand design of it all is a "mystery," the act of "an invisible hand."

[7] *The Economic War*, p. 28.

aided in the creation of the vast network of interests which it has covered with the collective term, national interest. With much justification, it has been said that there was more diplomacy than dollars in dollar diplomacy. The Government is, therefore, an interpreter of national interest on its own account as well as the promoter and executor of interpretations provided by private parties.

INTERPRETATION BY AGENCIES OF THE GOVERNMENT

Although the Government of the United States is sometimes supposed to be a single agency for the purpose of expressing and realizing the national interest and controlling foreign policies to that end, it is not in law, theory, or practice, a unitary body save, perhaps, in time of war when the executive becomes supreme. The Federal Government is divided into three branches, each of which possesses high powers with respect to the interpretation and enforcement of national interest. The Congress is composed of two houses, which exercise separate functions bearing on foreign affairs. It is also divided into parties and factions reflecting more or less precisely the private economic processes which are supposed to constitute the national interest. It may pass laws and resolutions embodying particular expressions of the conception. The Senate exercises a powerful supervision and control over treaties with foreign countries. The executive branch, though headed by a single officer, is divided into numerous departments, agencies, and establishments—a large number of which can exert influence on the determination of concrete cases in foreign relations. Although the Supreme Court is supposed to hold all agencies of the Government within the orbit of the Constitution, it has often declined to perform the full function on the ground that large questions of foreign relations are "political" and thus outside the scope of its intervention. There appears to be the same separate striving of individuals and agencies in the political or public sphere that there is in the sphere of private enterprise, with the same belief and assumption that the aggregate of all separate efforts inures to the benefit of the whole, the national interest. Moreover the processes and mechanics of diplomacy are in many respects the same as the processes of business among individuals.[8]

A somewhat minute examination of this immense, disjointed federal organization is, therefore, necessary to an understanding of the ways and means by which national interest is interpreted and determined. Let us first take the office of President. His powers in this respect are so striking and so well known that a mere enumeration will suffice for our purposes. He alone can initiate treaties with foreign countries. He acts as official spokesman for the nation in the formulation of foreign policies and the conduct of negotiations. He nominates ambassadors, consuls, and other public ministers. The right to receive and dismiss agents from foreign countries is vested in him, and he may thus recognize, refuse to recognize, and break off relations with, foreign governments. Through messages to Congress and other official pronouncements he may formulate significant policies for the guidance of foreign relations; Monroe's famous message is merely one illuminating example. As head of the Navy, he may order a fleet or single ship to any waters of the world and may in fact authorize the use of limited force, without calling upon Congress for a declaration of war. Scores of examples are available. The Army is likewise subject to his command and may be moved to any frontier as a gesture to support his policy-determinations. The illustration of the Mexican War will suffice. He may, in point of fact, create a diplomatic situation which will make a declaration of war by Congress its only choice. By common consent President Wilson could have kept the country out of the World War, perhaps as easily as he took it into the War. Practically considered, the determination was his own. Besides all this, the President may enter into executive agreements with other powers and reach understandings with them, open or secret. President Roosevelt's personal arrangement with Japan as to the Far East may serve as an illustration.[9]

Such are the President's formal and actual powers in out-

[8] DeWitt C. Poole, *The Conduct of Foreign Relations under Modern Democratic Conditions.*

[9] Tyler Dennett, *Roosevelt and the Russo-Japanese* War, p. 112. A wide variety of illustrations is presented in Samuel B. Crandall, *Treaties: Their Making and Enforcement* (2d Ed.), pp. 108ff.

line. What any particular President may do in fact depends upon his training, personality, and sympathies, upon the pressure brought to bear upon him by private interests, economic and moral, organized and unorganized.[10] His interpretation of national interest in particular cases will not be derived from abstractions alone; it will be the result of complex forces, among which corporate and individual private interests must always be reckoned. He is as much subject to the pressures of lobbies in his sphere as Congress is within its domain—through the leaders of his party and through personal connections. He brings a heritage of theories, sentiments, ideas, and attachments with him into his office. Though a single person, he often finds himself, as Emerson said of every man, at war with himself in his own bosom, balancing conceptions, pressures, and appeals over against one another. Seldom can his decisions be determined by statistical demonstrations or the clear weight of facts duly found by experts. Not always can he tell in advance whether any single action will be supported by Congress, his party, or the majority of the voters. Yet, under the assumption that "politics stops at the water's edge," it is widely supposed that the President's determination of national interest in foreign affairs must receive unconditional support on grounds of loyalty. More than one President has taken this position.

For example, on December 31, 1926, President Coolidge, at a conference of newspaper correspondents, informed the press that it should, by its attitude, make plain to the world "that it supports the Government when it is doing what it can in protecting American interests at home and abroad." With reference to the pending crisis in Nicaragua, he gave the press

[10] According to a recent study it was neither the plan nor the early practice to have the President act as a single, independent agent in foreign affairs. "The longer one reflects upon the discussions of this matter in the 'Federalist,' " wrote Henry W. Wriston, "the more certain it seems that the authors envisaged President and Senate working together in the formulation of policies, in the appointment of diplomatic officers, in the drafting and approval of instructions, in the discussion of negotiations during their progress, and in placing the stamp of approval upon the work when completed. No other interpretation makes their statements intelligible." (P. 77.) And Washington's relations with the Senate confirmed this conception. *Executive Agents in American Foreign Relations*, pp. 77 and 103.

representatives to understand that the administration would "continue its present program which is aimed solely at protection of American interests," and he recalled "that the executive was charged with doing what it could to protect American lives and property and to take such action as was best suited to that end." The phrase "American interests" as used in connection with Nicaragua, the President explained, meant a policy "founded entirely upon action to safeguard American lives and their property." [11] In the course of his interview, the President made it clear that he resented attacks on his foreign policies by certain Senators and sections of the press, and regarded them as verging on disloyalty to the country.

The plain facts and the implications of this official pronouncement are significant. Although President Coolidge, near the close of his statement, referred to "peace," "good will," and "international justice" as ideas to be cherished, he indicated clearly that, in his opinion, American foreign policy is founded on "national interest," that national interest means safeguarding American lives and property, and "promoting American commerce." Mr. Coolidge also looked upon the definition and enforcement of national interest in the foreign sphere as an executive function, particularly where American lives and property were implicated, and felt that Congress, the press, and private citizens should "back the Government," namely, the President, "in its foreign policies," giving other countries no cause for suspecting that American opinion was divided on any foreign issue at stake.[12] Although the doctrine was not novel, this statement of the presidential thesis, for comprehensiveness and simplicity, is scarcely excelled by any other passage from American diplomacy.

The contention, however, is countered by innumerable precedents. For example, when, in 1918, the Congressional elections went against President Wilson, a distinguished Republican leader, Ex-president Roosevelt, denied the right of the former to determine the foreign policies of the country. In commenting on the election, Roosevelt exclaimed that "in no other free country in the world today would Mr. Wilson be in office."

[11] New York *Times,* Jan. 1, 1927.
[12] See p. 304, note 10.

Then he wrote emphatically: "Our allies and our enemies and Mr. Wilson himself should all understand that Mr. Wilson has no authority whatever to speak for the American people at this time. His leadership has just been emphatically repudiated by them. . . . Let them [the Allies] impose their common will on the nations responsible for the hideous disaster that has almost wrecked mankind." [13] Similar illustrations of open opposition to presidential determinations of policy, from political leaders, members of Congress, and the press, can be cited from the passages of history dealing with every diplomatic crisis. Hence, efforts to throw the protection of lese majesty around executive pronouncements on national interest have only a shadowy claim to validity in law and none whatever in practice. The President is merely one of the interpreting agencies in the Federal Government and his efficiency in realizing his decisions depends upon shrewd calculations respecting particular situations and the possibility of winning popular support for his resolutions.

Next to the President, the Secretary of State is supposed to be the interpreter and special guardian of national interest in foreign affairs. He is the member of the cabinet through whom the President generally carries out the functions relating to foreign affairs vested in him.[14] Although in a peculiar sense the President's personal appointee, the Secretary may exercise a high degree of independence. He cannot, of course, run counter to the former's policies with respect to important matters; if driven by conviction into an antithesis, he must resign, as did Secretary Bryan in 1915, and as was expected of Secretary Lansing in 1919; but in all circumstances he enjoys a powerful influence in his own right and it sometimes happens that he is the real director of policy, especially if the President is weak or unconcerned. Charles E. Hughes undoubtedly was supreme during the Harding administration.

[13] Shippee, *Recent American History*, p. 473.

[14] Radio Address of Secretary of State, Henry L. Stimson. May 9, 1931. Publication No. 195 of the Department of State. Washington, D. C. For a brief historical review of the operations and functions of the Secretary of State and of the Department of State, see *The Department of State of the United States*. Publication No. 232 of the Department of State, Washington, D. C. 1931.

Despite the extent of the powers vested in him and the complications of the business placed in his hands, the Secretary of State is not ordinarily a "diplomat" by training. Usually he comes into office directly from business or professional life or from some branch of politics remotely concerned with foreign affairs. At all events, unlike foreign secretaries in Europe, he does not reach his post after long political service in and out of power—service in which he is designated by a process of natural selection for the place in question. As a rule his experience in foreign affairs is likely to be slight, his knowledge fragmentary in character. If in the course of his preoccupation with other matters he has found time, before his installation, to develop a consistent thesis of national interest, he has had no opportunity to test his theories by the touchstone of trial and error.

Owing to the cast and working of American politics, and to the intimate connection between politics and economics, the Secretary of State is almost certain to be powerfully impressed by the importance of commercial interests. Often he has been a lawyer associated with industry and trade and comes from a seaboard state. His affiliations are generally commercial rather than agrarian, and, apart from the personal difficulties of American citizens, the business which comes before him is primarily connected with trade rather than agriculture. It was with fullness of feeling that the Assistant Secretary of State, W. R. Castle, speaking to a convention of exporters, said in 1928: "Mr. Hoover [Secretary of Commerce] is your advance agent and Mr. Kellogg [Secretary of State] is your attorney." [15] Ever since industry overtopped agriculture in the United States this has been increasingly true. In the modern age the Secretary of State is an attorney, acting under the impulses of commercial forces and compelled to interpret national interest with reference to the requirements of commercial economy. [16]

Although the Secretary of State may be commercial in this affiliation and an attorney for business, his procedures are partial, not comprehensive. His Department acts continuously

[15] Quoted in Kirkland, *History of American Economic Life,* p. 711.
[16] Kirkland, *ibid.*

on the initiative of others: on appeals, claims, and demands filed by interested parties, on proposals from foreign countries, on incidents in world affairs. The Secretary may stand idly by while millions of dollars of American capital are poured into a foreign country which he suspects to be insolvent,[17] and yet feel moved to solicit the extension of bank credit to that same country, simply because the matter has been brought to his attention through formal diplomatic channels. Often, therefore, in matters of undoubted national interest, realistically conceived, he is deprived of initiative by the traditions and rules of his office. With good and sufficient warrant John Hay lamented that much of his time was taken up with pressing the more or less dubious claims of American citizens upon other countries and beating off claims against the United States.[18]

Yet the Secretary, in truth, is more than an attorney speaking for interested clients. Whatever his qualities and bent, he is, in a certain measure at least, a statesman, charged with a sense of high responsibility, and must act also as a judge controlled to some extent by great principles evolved in the long history of the country: the Monroe Doctrine, the open door, and the profession of love for peace. He has a wide variety of functions, relating both to domestic and foreign affairs, to perform.[19] His Department has traditions and precedents. He must fit his decisions, like the good judge, into the pronouncements of his predecessors, whatever may be the practical demand for a change in policy.

The statements of Secretary Stimson during the collision with Japan over Manchuria provide a case in point. Under various notes and treaties Manchuria was recognized as a part of China, saving the interest of Japan in her zone of influence, and the door was supposed to be open for equal trade. In accordance with its historic commitments, the State Depart-

---

[17] Below, p. 396.

[18] "The real duties of the Secretary of State seem to be three: to fight claims upon us by other States; to press more or less fraudulent claims of our own citizens upon other countries; to find offices for friends of Senators when there are none." Hay to Adams in *The Education of Henry Adams*, p. 374.

[19] For a summary listing of these functions, see *The Department of State of the United States*, pp. 1–2.

ment was bound to protest against the action of Japan in occupying Manchuria in 1931 and in setting up a puppet government there. With some justification it could be said that such
protests were in the national interest as conceived by merchants
with goods to sell immediately in Manchuria. But on the other
side it was argued with great cogency and with statistical display that, if Japan could stabilize Manchuria and develop its
resources, American bankers would be called upon to help
finance the operation and that an improvement in the economic
position of Japan would mean a large increase in the sale of
American merchandise within the Empire. For example, the
American cotton export business would probably be injured
by a closure of the Manchurian market, but American bankers
and automobile manufactures would profit from an enlargement of Japanese economic operations in Manchuria. So, it
might have been possible to contend with some degree of logic
that, according to a balance-sheet conception of national interest, the inherited formulas of the State Department with
respect to the Manchurian sphere did not correspond with national interest in point of fact. Yet tradition prescribed a
resort to them.

Since the Secretary of State is partly controlled by historic
doctrines and partly by the pressure of special claimants, wide
variations appear in the interpretation and practice of national
interest. In the case of Nicaragua and Haiti, for example, the
Department of State took the initiative in enlisting the interest
of American bankers in making loans and rehabilitating local
finances, and, by one expedient or another, gave them, in effect, the official protection of the United States Government.
Indeed it is doubtful whether they would have embarked upon
uncertain financial ventures in these two countries if the Department had not insured them against adverse eventualities.
On the other hand, during the post-war period when billions
of American capital were pouring into all parts of the world,
the State Department attempted no positive control and made
no guarantees. It did, as we have seen, require the submission
of loan proposals to it for scrutiny, reviewed them with reference to certain "political" considerations, and usually gave its
approval by interposing no "objections." Where particulars

and generals are not referred to a common bench mark or
where the rule or guide is so general, ambiguous, or made up
of a wide variety of flexible criteria, uniformity of interpretation and action is scarcely to be expected or achieved.

As a matter of fact, whenever large issues are at stake, the
Secretary must move with circumspection in making commitments in the name of any policy of national interest. If a
treaty is necessary, an appropriation of money, or a demonstration of armed force, the coöperation of one or both houses
of Congress is required by the Constitution. And Congress is
a large and miscellaneous body representing conflicting interests. However careful the Secretary may be in conciliating
Senators and Representatives, he has no way of making certain
in advance that any stroke of policy will be supported in
Congress. Treaties are often defeated. Prolonged congressional
debates may vitiate the atmosphere of negotiation. The best
of compromises may be assailed as contrary to national interest. Standing between the President, who may repudiate
him, and Congress, which may baffle him, the Secretary of State
is scarcely in a position to pursue a steady course of his own
with respect to national interest. Unable to take the initiative
in some important economic matters and often forced to act
on trivialities in others, he occupies a position of great uncertainty.

To some extent this condition of affairs is to be explained
by the organization of the Department and the operations of
its divisions.[20] Its structure is regional, not functional. It has
separate divisions dealing with Oriental, European, Near-
Eastern, and Latin-American affairs, each proceeding with
reference to certain local conditions and historical traditions.
No common agency for dealing with policies of trade, concessions, and loans brings them all to a focus. Though furnishing the channels through which expert knowledge of foreign
political and economic conditions flow into the United States,
the Department is not provided with machinery for utilizing
the results. On the contrary it must turn over to the Department of Commerce the essential materials contained in the

---

[20] For a detailed description of the State Department, see *The Department
of State of the United States.*

consular reports which pour into its office daily and, since the establishment of that Department, it has confronted a powerful rival in the field of economic affairs—the chief domain of modern diplomacy.[21]

In recent years, it is true, the office of economic adviser has been instituted in the State Department, but however great may be the merits of the incumbent the establishment which he directs has neither the staff nor the power required for the discharge of such an important duty. Nor could the adviser function effectively without the coöperation of colleagues in other Departments—Commerce and Treasury, for instance. Indeed, recognizing the need for drawing together and working out a common policy, subordinates in these Departments do hold occasional conferences on particular matters.[22] But all is haphazard, dependent on the intelligence and enthusiasm of individuals; there is no effective coördination conceived as a necessity of grand policy.

In recognition of the difficulties confronting the State Department in dealing with the enormous mass of economic business, special efforts have been made since the opening of the twentieth century to provide it with more adequate equipment. The reorganization of the Department, the establishment of regional divisions to deal with specific geographical areas, and the introduction of permanent tenure in the foreign service [23] grew largely out of the determination of the President and

[21] On resigning in 1928 a consul-general said flatly: "As diplomatic functions today are mainly economic, this places the Department of Commerce in control of the substance of diplomacy, and leaves the Department of State with social representation only." Kirkland, *op. cit.,* p. 711.

[22] So far as foreign representation is concerned, an Executive Order of April 4, 1924, among other things, provided: "Whenever representatives of the Department of State and other Departments of the Government of the United States are stationed in the same city in a foreign country they will meet in conference at least fortnightly under such arrangements as may be made by the chief diplomatic officer or, at posts where there is no diplomatic officer, by the ranking consular or other officer. . . . It shall be the purpose of such conferences to secure a free interchange of all information bearing upon the promotion and protection of American interests." The Order also contains other provisions tending to coördinate American representation in foreign countries. *The Department of State of the United States,* pp. 24–25.

[23] For the details of these changes see *The Department of State of the United States,* p. 21. See also "Congress, the Foreign Service, and the Department of State," *Pol. Sci. Rev.,* Vol. XXIV (1930).

Congress to make the Department a more efficient instrument for the promotion of national economic interests abroad. In his message of December, 1910, President Taft explained the motive force behind the new departures: "All these tariff negotiations [respecting the elimination of foreign discriminations], so vital to our commerce and industry, and the duty of jealously guarding the equitable and just treatment of our products, capital, and industry abroad devolve upon the Department of State. The Argentine battle-ship contracts, like the subsequent important one for Argentine railway equipment, and those for Cuban government vessels, were secured for our manufacturers largely through the good offices of the Department of State. The efforts of that Department to secure for citizens of the United States equal opportunities in the markets of the world and to expand American commerce have been most successful. The volume of business obtained in new fields of competition and upon new lines is also very great and Congress is urged to continue to support the Department of State in its endeavors to further trade expansion."

On January 1, 1933, there were fifty-nine American diplomatic missions in foreign countries, consisting of fifteen embassies and forty-four legations. There were also some three hundred and forty-two consular offices abroad, and the total of employees abroad exceeded 4,000.[24] In the Department at Washington there were thirty-five divisions, offices, and bureaus, with approximately 800 employees.[25] The Department had the handling of affairs dealing with fifty-five diplomatic missions and 1,174 consular offices established by foreign countries in the United States and its territorial possessions. Appropriations for the Department of State for the fiscal year ending June 30, 1934, total approximately $12,500,000.[26] Attempt-

[24] For a list of the diplomatic missions, the consular offices, and the number and classification of American employees abroad, as of January 1, 1933, see *Foreign Service List*. Department of State. Publication No. 420. Washington, D. C.

[25] *The Department of State of the United States*, p. 9.

[26] Specific appropriations total $12,196,519, but this figure is increased by "unexpended balances" in several funds, the amounts of which are not given in the appropriation bill. For the details of the large number of items comprising this total sum, see (Public No. 387—72d Congress) H.R. 14,363, "An Act, making appropriations for the Department of State, etc." The average

ing to express the value of its consular service to American foreign trade, the State Department estimated that "the total value to date of the new business effected and savings realized to American export interests by American consular officers situated in two hundred and ninety-eight posts in all parts of the globe during the fiscal year ended June 30, 1932, was $15,-022,421.03." [27] A table of similar concrete results achieved in previous years shows business secured or safeguarded as follows: 1928, $16,092,734; 1929, $10,597,638; 1930, $83,784,-800; and 1931, $19,361,237. [28] Over against this business secured, the State Department sets the salaries of "those officers of the Foreign Service . . . serving under consular commissions" which, for the five-year period, 1928–1932 inclusive, averaged $2,414,050 per year. [29]

annual appropriation for the Department of State (operating and non-operating expenses) for the 5-year period, 1919–1923 inclusive, was $12,507,794.20; for the period 1924–1928 inclusive, $16,034,052.13. The appropriation for the year 1929 was $14,618,863.42. For the appropriations from 1919 to 1929 with a breakdown into the large categories, and for an itemized distribution of the 1929 appropriation, see William T. Stone, "The Administration of the Department of State." Foreign Policy Association Information Service. New York. Vol. IV, Special Supplement No. 3 (February, 1929) particularly Tables I, II, III, Appendices pp. 41–44.

[27] The principal items included in this total are: Merchandise sold through trade opportunities submitted, $2,052,588.96; Merchandise sold through contacts provided in commercial letters, $2,151,557.49; New business provided by consular officers to the traveling representatives of American firms, $1,301,620.40; Savings realized to American interests through consular activity in the protection of American trade, $4,191,757.28; Important assistance rendered by consular officers in obtaining contracts for construction and development enterprises abroad where the value of the contracts was $4,673,662.52. Department of State, Press releases (December 24, 1932). Weekly Issue No. 169, Publication No. 411.

[28] It must be realized that in any estimate or computation of this character the values stated can neither be precise nor accurately allocated. At most they are broad generalizations expressed in concrete figures, and are merely intended to give an idea, express an approximation, of the utility of the consular service to American business interests.

[29] Department of State Press Releases. Even under the admitted approximations of business secured over against cost involved, this figure is not a complete expression. To give the salaries of the consular officers only is a minimization of the true cost involved; and consequently a distortion of the idea sought to be conveyed by the computation. Proper accounting methods would require the computation of the whole cost of the consular establishment and service, in so far as that could be ascertained, to be set off against the business secured, with adjustments for services performed by consular officers for the general

Notwithstanding all that has been done to furnish the Department with a stronger structure and more efficient instruments, it is still lacking in the centralization and equipment necessary for dealing organically and effectively with economic matters involved in diplomacy. It has no officer corresponding to the British Under-Secretary for Foreign Affairs who gives continuity and consistency to policy through all the changes and vicissitudes of politics, in spite of all parliamentary efforts to secure control and re-orientations. Moreover, the Department has been positively weakened with respect to economic matters by the development of the Department of Commerce, with its army of commercial agents [30] in all parts of the world, duplicating in part the work of the consular officers. Thus, while diplomacy pertains more and more to economics, the Department charged with diplomatic functions has not been provided with adequate organization and staff to assure coherence and competence in economic policy—in the continuous and consistent interpretation of national interest.

Still the State Department is one of the many influential organs of the Federal Government engaged in the interpretation of national interest and its application. The Department has theories, traditions, and formulas, both political and economic. Whenever occasion requires or suggests, it makes pronouncements of policy, broad or narrow, comprehensive or fragmentary. It acts upon its own initiative at times, taking leadership and enlisting private economic enterprises in the realization of its projects. At other times it acts upon impulses from the outside—the demands of individuals and corporations, suggestions from consular and diplomatic agents abroad,

purposes of the United States not commercial in character. Some of the items likely to enter into such a proper computation (using the year 1929 as an example) would be in addition to the salaries of the consular officers for that year: clerk hire, $1,645,000; contingent expenses, $1,035,000; expenses of Foreign Service inspectors, $25,000; and part of such items as transportation, emergency fund, post allowances, foreign service retirement fund, rent and maintenance of buildings and the like; as well as such parts of the home establishment increased in cost by the necessity of supplementing the consular establishments and services. Such a "balance sheet" would be much more complicated, of course, than the simple approximation shown in the text above.

[30] The number was materially reduced by the Roosevelt administration in 1933.

and requests from the representatives of foreign governments.[31] In numerous cases it proceeds with reference to powerful and active interests within the United States and unless it be assumed that these particular interests, often conflicting in aim, constitute in the aggregate the national interest, freedom from contradictions in policy is scarcely to be expected from the Department.

No less zealously than the State Department, the Navy Department has assumed the responsibility of interpreting national interest, in gross and detail. The Director of Naval Intelligence was fully justified in writing in 1931 that, "contrary to uninformed opinion, American naval officers are not narrow-visioned technicists. . . . Some of the brightest pages of American diplomatic history have been written by the exploits and sagacity of our early sailor diplomats."[32] It is true that according to widely accepted theory, the civilian branches of the Government are supreme and prescribe policies for enforcement in peace and war. It is true also that under this theory, the military and naval arms of the Government are mere instruments, taking orders from the duly constituted civilian authorities. But practice has by no means conformed to the hypothesis.[33] Although the Army, owing largely to

---

[31] It is said that when public interests are inherent in or incidental to private activities abroad, the Department of State becomes active in support of the private interests, ostensibly for the achievement of the public interest believed to be involved. An excellent example of this may be seen in the efforts of the Department of State under Mr. Bayard in 1885, Mr. Blaine in 1889 and again in 1892, and Mr. Gresham in 1893, to secure a grant of landing rights at Rio from the Brazilian Government when the Argentine Government granted to the Central and South American Telegraph Company permission to extend its line from Buenos Aires to Brazil. J. B. Moore, *Digest of International Law*, Washington, D. C., 1906, Vol. VI, p. 326, hereinafter cited as Moore, *Digest*.

[32] *The United States Navy in Peace Time*, p. iv.

[33] Discussing the respective provinces of the political and naval representatives of the United States Government in a dispatch to Mr. Asboth, American minister to the Argentine Republic, dated May 18, 1867, Secretary of State Seward stated: "There is no subordination of the ministers to the commander of a squadron, and no subordination of the commander of the squadron to a minister." Where coöperation between them is "practicable and useful, that coöperation is distinctly commanded by the President." Otherwise, "the agent of each class is necessarily left to proceed according to his own discretion within the range of the general instructions received from the Department under which he is employed." Moore, *Digest*, Vol. IV, pp. 616–617.

problems of frontier defense, has never been an active force in the determination of foreign policies, as in many countries of Europe, the Navy has occupied and assumed a different position. Unlike the Army, it has had the wide world for its range and in considering issues of strategy confronts the possibility of operations in the seven seas against the enormous naval forces of other countries, taken singly or in combination.

From the early years of the Republic until the Civil War, naval officers were active in the formulation of policy and in applying it as occasion and opportunity offered. Accepting at face value the doctrine of the Fathers, expressed in the *Federalist,* that the Navy was an instrument for the promotion and protection of trade and extending the power of the nation in the determination of affairs, naval officers took their responsibilities seriously. And in an age when there were no cables or other means of rapid communication, they often felt compelled to act on their own authority in the national interest, as circumstances dictated. In 1803 Preble and Rogers, by a show of force, compelled the emperor of Morocco to sign a treaty safeguarding American commercial rights; and several years later Commodore Decatur, after bringing the Dey of Algiers to terms, joined William Shaler in signing a treaty with that ruler, which abolished the tribute formerly exacted from the United States. While acting under official authorization couched in general terms, these officers exercised a high degree of discretion in defining and enforcing American rights.

In the Pacific theater, it is not too much to say, naval officers have been mainly responsible for determining national policy. Leaders among them early came to the conclusion that the Pacific Ocean was to be the next great scene of international rivalry for markets, that the Orient offered enormous possibilities for lucrative commercial operations, that naval bases and the acquisition of territory in the Far East were necessary to economic aggrandizement, and that only by demonstration of armed force, especially against England, could American trading rights be fostered and secured. As we have seen, Commodore Matthew C. Perry formulated a complete system of *Machtpolitik* for the United States in the Orient.[34] "It is self-

[34] *Ante,* p. 97.

evident," he wrote near the middle of the nineteenth century, "that the course of coming events will erelong make it necessary for the United States to extend its jurisdiction beyond the limits of the western continent, and I assume the responsibility of urging the expediency of establishing a foothold in this quarter of the globe, as a measure of positive necessity to the sustainment of our maritime rights in the east." [35]

Recommendations which they made to their Government in Washington, naval officers sometimes sought to carry out on their own motion. As early as 1826, Captain Catesby Jones, on his own initiative, entered into negotiations with the government of Hawaii and drew up a treaty incorporating provisions safeguarding American interests; but his designs were defeated by the failure of the United States Senate to ratify the document. Thirteen years later Commodore Wilkes, while cruising in the distant Pacific, visited the Samoan Islands and entered into an agreement with native chiefs with a view to protecting American whalers and traders operating in that region. Still more bold, Commodore Perry, without waiting for instructions from home, seized some of the Bonin Islands, bought land for a naval depot in the Lew Chews, and would have gone further if he had obtained support from his superiors in the civil administration at Washington. It is not without warrant that the Director of Naval Intelligence claims that "the 'open door' policy was first proclaimed by a resolute naval officer," for Commodore Kearny, taking advantage of the situation created by the Opium War, insisted on obtaining from the Chinese government for Americans equal trading rights with the British.[36]

During the Civil War and the years immediately following, when the attention of the country was largely concentrated on domestic affairs and the development of the West, naval officers continued their thinking about national interest on the sea and put no brake on their activities designed to realize their conceptions. They furnished support for Seward's policy of expansion in the Caribbean, particularly the acquisition of a naval base in Santo Domingo. They kept sharp eyes on the

[35] F. R. Dulles, *America in the Pacific*, p. 73.
[36] *The United States Navy in Peace Time* (1931), pp. iv and 163.

potentialities of the Pacific as divined by Commodore Perry, and from time to time they combined action with design. It was a naval officer, Commander Meade, who took matters in his own hands in 1872 and obtained from the "great chief of Pago Pago, in Samoa," a concession which granted to the United States "the exclusive privilege of establishing a naval station in that harbor." History may well ascribe to that determination of national policy by a naval officer, on his own initiative, the origins of the program which established American empire in that distant seat and brought the country almost to the verge of war with Germany over the division of spoils. Naval authorities took the lead, and, against vigorous opposition in Congress, involved the country in their transactions, gradually educating the nation, directly and through interested parties, to an acceptance of their interpretations of policy.

Near the close of the nineteenth century, as we have seen, a naval officer, Captain Alfred Thayer Mahan, formulated a positive theory of national interest under the general head of "sea power," which he incorporated in numerous works on the influence of the navies upon history. His general thesis was that maritime concerns are superior to military, political, and economic movements in the making of history and the shaping of national destinies. Mahan accepted at face value, without examination, the doctrine that "the natural course of trade," whatever that may be, is advantageous to a nation, that the promotion and protection of this trade is the prime business of the Navy, and that the rise and fall of civilizations hang upon the possession of predominant sea power.

Referring specifically to the United States, Mahan said: "Henceforth the greatest producer and economic unit which the world has known, situated at the world's greatest maritime center, must inevitably link up domestic production, foreign sources of raw materials, overseas markets, merchant marine, and Navy. In coast defense, protection against invasion, safeguarding overseas possessions, reënforcing our diplomacy, and supporting our general political policies, the Navy as always will continue to play an important rôle. But in the largest perspective, the Navy must more and more come to be recognized as an economic agency—as a basic factor in the country's business upon which the livelihood and prosperity of our citizenry depend." [37]

Although Mahan's works were hailed in the imperialist circles of Great Britain, Germany, Japan, and the United States as definitive, as marking an epoch in historical interpretation, they were in fact characterized by evident lapses in logic. At one point he treated naval power as if it were an independent force operating under its own momentum and at another as a mere agency of economic interests. Obviously it could not be both. Then while pointing out the economic superiority of the United States, Mahan accepted British naval supremacy as a beneficent force—"not to make war, but to preserve peace, not to be predatory, but to shield the free development of commerce, not to unsettle the world, but to stabilize it through the promotion of law and order." [38] Yet from his own pages he could have discovered that the British navy was at peace only after it had destroyed all its serious rivals—Holland, Spain, and France—on the sea; and he lived to witness the greatest war in history precipitated largely by an effort of Germany to acquire for the protection of her commerce the very kind of sea power which he had recommended to all countries. If the purpose of the British navy was to preserve peace and promote the free development of commerce, why did any other commercial country need a navy at all? Equally curious was Mahan's assumption that the United States, the world's greatest commercial emporium, should be content with inferiority in naval construction. By what array of facts could such a low position be justified? Nor did he explore the possibility that two or more inferior navies might by combination overcome the largest single navy in the world. There were many other serious lapses in Mahan's logic, but they did not reach his consciousness as such. However that may be, the naval writings of Captain Mahan had a profound influence on civil policy, particularly after the accession of President Theodore Roosevelt, and must be reckoned among the great American formulations of national interest.

In due course the slips in Mahan's logic were discovered in

---

[37] Quoted in *United States Navy in Peace Time,* p. 4.
[38] *Ibid.*

the naval circles of the United States. During the World War, if not earlier, American naval officers discovered that national interest required unquestioned naval supremacy, helped to convert President Wilson to this view, and aided in inducing Congress to authorize a building program designed to attain that end. Although the United States had joined Great Britain in destroying the German navy, naval officers began to doubt the Mahan hypothesis that the British navy was in fact an instrument of peace engaged in protecting the free development of commerce and promoting law and order. At all events, they now vigorously urged the establishment of superiority over the British navy and were in a fair way to secure it when the rivalry thus engendered, the expenses, and perils ostensibly involved, brought about the Washington and London conferences which compromised on the strange and elusive principle of "parity." Then naval officers accepted the inevitable with such grace as they could command, justified no doubt in wondering why, if the Navy was to defend commerce and enforce rights, superiority should be surrendered for equality. Indeed, some of the boldest among them continued to insist that national interest had been jeopardized by failure to attain the kind of dominance which had made Great Britain a supreme arbiter in all parts of the world from the downfall of Napoleon to the rise of the United States.

After the great outburst of enthusiasm for naval construction that occurred during the World War, however, there came a lull in congressional interest, and it became impossible to secure even appropriations sufficient to build up to the limitations set by treaty. It looked as if the country, as distinguished from the Navy Department and its allies, might be content with inferiority after all. Thereupon the General Board of the Navy adopted the practice of issuing, with the approval of the Secretary, a periodical statement known as the "United States Naval Policy." Although it would appear, from the formalities of the Constitution, that the Navy could have no policy except that of enforcing the decisions of the civil branches of the Government, naval technicians rejected this view of their responsibilities. They declared the general purposes of the Navy. The statement of policy presented to the country in

1922 by the Navy Department set forth its aims as follows: "The Navy of the United States should be maintained in sufficient strength to support its policies and its commerce, and to guard its continental and overseas possessions. . . . To create, maintain, and operate a Navy second to none. . . ." Elaborating upon these aims, the General Board declared its intention "to make every effort, both ashore and afloat, at home and abroad, to assist the development of American interests, and especially the American merchant marine." Excursions in empire are certainly implied in the direction: "To have always in mind that a system of outlying naval and commercial bases suitably distributed, developed, and defended is one of the most important elements of national strength." [39]

An examination of the items in the official statement of "United States Naval Policy" shows that most of them bear on conceptions of national interest rather than upon the mere technology of warfare—the peculiar province of the Navy under the Constitution. The proposal to maintain a Navy second to none is not a matter of naval arithmetic, but involves issues to be determined by the civil branches of the Government with reference to the political and economic policies to be pursued in foreign relations. Support for it and objections to it are not to be derived from any branch of knowledge or information in which naval officers as such are experts. Whether the Navy is to be used for "exercising ocean-wide economic pressure" [40]—another avowed aim of the Navy Department— whatever that sweeping phrase may mean, is likewise an issue of large national policy, not one that can be decided on purely technological grounds. But for present purposes, these comments are an excursus. The point to be emphasized is that naval officers, the General Board of the Navy, and the Secretary of the Navy, though presumably subordinate to the President and Congress, have exerted and continue to exert a powerful independent influence on opinions and decisions pertaining to the interpretation of national interest.

[39] The above extracts from the statements of the aims of the Navy, as formulated by the General Board in 1922, are cited in the *Annual Report of the Navy Department,* 1922, Washington, D. C., 1923, pp. 2–3. See also, Walter Millis, *Atlantic Monthly,* June, 1932, p. 765.

[40] *Ibid.*

Official statements expounding national policy published by the Navy Department are frequently supplemented by declarations of admirals acting as individuals. For example, a naval policy designed for the full and effective protection of the interests of the United States was presented to the Committee on Naval Affairs of the Senate by Admiral Hilary P. Jones in 1930 in the following form, as "basic and unassailable," to use his words:

> 1. No limitation of its [the United States'] sovereign powers.
> 2. A Navy adequate for the protection of its continental territory and overseas possessions.
> 3. A Navy adequate for the maintainence of its vital interests and the protection of its citizens in all parts of the world.
> 4. A Navy adequate to insure open lines of communication for its world-wide commerce, and full protection thereof.[41]

Although Admiral Jones added that "a Navy second to none in actual strength" was necessary to assure the full realization of the above principles, he did not indicate how all the obligations outlined above could be discharged by a Navy merely equal to the largest competitor in combatant power. For more than a hundred years British naval experts had advocated similar principles: no limitation on sovereign power and a naval force sufficient to protect British interests and citizens in all parts of the world, and to keep the commercial lanes open at all times, in peace and war. But British naval experts did not think that mere parity with the nearest competitor was adequate for such purposes. On the contrary, they tenaciously held to the doctrine that nothing short of absolute superiority was sufficient for the execution of the policy thus avowed. On this assumption Great Britain struck down Spain, Holland, and France and reduced them to a footing of inferiority. On this ground also Great Britain was alarmed by the attempts of Germany to build a formidable navy, insisted on a two-for-one program in naval ship construction, and finally joined France and Russia in driving the German navy from the seas. On substantially identical principles, American naval experts,

---

[41] *Hearings before the Committee on Naval Affairs, United States Senate . . . on the London Naval Treaty of 1930,* p. 109, hereinafter cited as *Hearings, London Naval Treaty.*

at the close of the World War when the American navy was in a fair way to exceed the British navy in fighting strength, demanded absolute superiority as essential for the adequate defense of American interests, and condemned the ratio and parity rules adopted at the Washington conference as a surrender of the supremacy necessary to the protection of American territorial and commercial rights.[42]

Certainly it is widely held in American naval circles today that mere equality in fighting ships does not assure the adequate defense of American interests as defined by Admiral Jones. This was clearly brought out in the hearings before the Senate Committee on Naval Affairs on the London treaty of 1930. Senator Walsh of Massachusetts asked Admiral Pratt whether the country that had "the larger and stronger and faster merchant marine" would not have the advantage over another country which merely possessed parity in combat strength, and the Admiral answered in the affirmative.[43] Senator Walsh continued: "My questions are now for the purpose of trying to impress the committee and the country that mere parity of naval combat vessels does not mean that we are secure, or that we are in equality in time of conflict with other countries which have, plus the same number of naval vessels we have, a very large and powerful merchant marine." To this Admiral Pratt replied: "You will get every naval man to agree with you, sir, that we should like to have a large merchant marine." Not yet content the Senator went on: "Now then do you agree with me that the important thing for us to do in America, if we are really concerned about defending our property and our people against hostile attack, is to build up some way, somehow, a strong, powerful merchant marine, equal to that of any other country?" Again Admiral Pratt agreed: "I say 'amen' to that."[44] Thus American naval policy apparently supplements economic policy and calls for additions to the merchant marine which in turn, besides increasing ships available for combat, extends the commercial interests requiring naval protection and multiplies the sea lanes to be defended.

[42] *Hearings, London Naval Treaty,* p. 61.
[43] *Ibid.,* p. 62.
[44] *Ibid.,* p. 63.

American naval policy relative to the protection of national interest also involves strong naval bases as well as an auxiliary merchant marine. Probably all naval experts will agree on this point.[45] Admiral Pratt gave a concrete illustration when he said a few years ago: "The 3–5 ratio gave Japan ample strength for defense, and article 19, which preserved the status quo of Pacific bases (preventing a development in Philippine strength), drew our teeth, both in a defensive and an offensive sense and really gave Japan a preponderance in the eastern Pacific. We have no right to put the United States in a position of inferiority in the matter of foreign relationships, and, as is well known historically, a country's strength in international relations bears a direct ratio to its naval strength. The generations that come after us, if they be good Americans, will not thank us for having done it. . . . Before 100 years have passed we may be helping to fight China's battles for her."[46] A similar view respecting the importance of a Far Eastern naval base, well protected, in case of a war with Japan, was advanced by Admiral Bristol during the hearings before the Committee on Foreign Relations of the Senate on the London naval treaty of 1930.[47]

These naval policies are more than abstractions presented to the country in official pronouncements. In truth, the Navy is continuously engaged in concrete demonstrations. The Yangtse naval force was constantly employed in protecting "United States interests, lives, and property" on that strategic river along which at least half of the commerce between China and the United States flowed. "Considering the perpetual banditry, piracy, and revolutionary conditions obtaining in this area," says the Secretary of the Navy, "without the protection of our Navy this commerce would be practically non-existent." Yet it

---

[45] The intimate relation between the merchant marine, the navy, and national defense, brought out clearly by Mahan in his works on sea power, particularly *Naval Strategy* (1911) and *Mahan on Naval Warfare* (Ed. Allan Westcott, 1918, Little, Brown & Co., Boston) and other naval strategists, may be illustrated by the equation:

$$\underset{\text{(Navy)}}{N} \quad + \quad \underset{\text{(Merchant Marine)}}{M. M.} \quad + \quad \underset{\text{(Naval Bases)}}{N. B.} \quad = \text{Sea Power}$$

[46] *Hearings, London Naval Treaty*, p. 93.
[47] *Ibid.*, pp. 114ff.

is repeatedly said that the protection afforded is not adequate.[48] "During the past ten years there have been continually recurring protestations from the American Chamber of Commerce and similar business organizations about the inadequacy of this patrol and a persistent demand for its enlargement." [49]

In the Near East also the American Navy exercises its protective functions, making policy by concrete actions. Its operations in this sphere may be best described in the language of the Director of Naval Intelligence: "The termination of the [World] War left the Near East in a very unhealthy and unsettled state. . . . American interest in oil, tobacco, flour, and other commodities of everyday necessity, both to and from this country, were jeopardized and the constitution of our business interests seriously threatened. Our warehouses in Turkey and Greece, for example, contained hundreds of thousands of dollars worth of American-owned tobacco, the loss of which would have meant the loss of so much American capital. The situation was acute . . . we could and did send the Navy. We sent a number of destroyers, small, light-draft and almost self-supporting vessels to anchor off the principal centers of our business interests and to see that fair play and justice were accorded to all. These vessels were based on Constantinople, and from there cruised almost continuously in the Black Sea, the Ægean, and the Mediterranean Sea, always mindful of the fact that their specific mission was the protection of American life and property." [50]

Inevitably in the formulation of its policies respecting national interest, the Navy Department relies fundamentally on the economic doctrines current among the commercial classes

[48] The force of gunboats patrolling the Yangtse river "cost the Navy something like $3,000,000 a year to operate." *The United States Navy as an Industrial Asset*, p. 4.

[49] *The United States Navy in Peace Time* (1931), p. 3.

[50] *The United States Navy in Peace Time*, p. 3. In an earlier publication of the Office of Naval Intelligence *(The United States Navy as an Industrial Asset)* it was stated: "One destroyer is kept continuously at Samsun, Turkey . . . and the American tobacco companies represented there depend practically entirely on the moral effect of having an American man-of-war in port to have their tobacco released for shipment" (p. 5). The cost of the service so rendered is some $4,000,000 annually (pp. 4–5). See also note on Rear Admiral Bristol, *ante* p. 341, note 74.

engaged in overseas trade.[51] Of necessity it is closely associated
with the shipbuilding industry and the commercial activities
of the seaboard towns. Its personnel is partly recruited from
the mercantile marine, and while in service is affiliated with
commercial rather than agrarian circles. The substratum of
Navy opinion, therefore, is current commercial economics, however sound or unsound that may be; at all events it is not
isolated, operating in a vacuum on its own philosophy, despite
the intimations of Captain Mahan. "We know," wrote the
Director of Naval Intelligence in 1931, "that our Navy, like
those of foreign powers, had its inception in the need for trade
protection. And our Navy is coming more and more to be
recognized as a potential force in American commercial security. Moreover, in less settled portions of the world it is accepted as a potent, and at times extremely active, trade
stabilizer." [52]

Unlike the other branches of the Federal Government engaged in the determination of policy with respect to national
interest, the Navy Department is itself an immense economic
interest. It employs more men than the State Department and
the Commerce Department combined.[53] It has a natural interest in promotions and increases in salaries. It maintains
yards, bases or stations at leading centers of business along
the Atlantic and Pacific coasts: Portsmouth, Boston, New
London, Newport, Brooklyn, Philadelphia, Washington, Nor-
folk, Hampton Roads, Charleston, Pensacola, New Orleans,

[51] For example, in the publication *The United States Navy as an Industrial
Asset*, p. 2, after stating that our production greatly exceeds the home market
and must seek foreign outlets "if economic stability is to exist," the author,
speaking officially for the Navy, declared that "in this phase of the Nation's
economic life the Navy has always played a conspicuous part."

[52] *The United States Navy in Peace Time*, p. 1.

[53] The number of employees in the Federal Executive Service of the three
departments (on January 1, 1932) was as follows: Department of State: 4,944;
Department of Commerce: 20,709; Navy Department: 47,304 (exclusive of
commissioned officers and enlisted men). The total appropriations of the three
departments for the year 1932 (covering full personnel and all functions) were:
State, $18,951,175; Commerce, $54,960,530; and Navy, $377,973,000. *Statistical
Abstract of the United States*, 1932, pp. 155, 168, 171. See also the respective
Hearings, Subcommittee of the House Committee on Appropriations, 72d
Cong., 2d Sess., Washington, D. C., 1933 as follows: State Department, p. 29;
Commerce Department, p. 22; Navy Department, pp. 668, 671 and other ap-
propriate pages.

San Diego, San Francisco, and Bremerton (Washington). At each of these points it makes large expenditures for labor and supplies, thus attaching to itself powerful local interests which are usually felt in Congress when naval appropriations are on the carpet. A large part of the naval construction is done in the yards of private companies, thus engaging the solicitude of shipbuilders, steel, machinery, and electrical manufacturers, and other purveyors of goods—purveyors whose economic interests are on the side of increases, not reductions, in naval outlays, and are often in evidence when the curtailment of armaments is under consideration.[54]

Well aware that support for the Navy is likely to be found in circles directly or indirectly interested in its construction and operating activities, the Department issues literature showing its service in the protection of overseas commerce and its practical utility to purveying enterprises. After presenting abundant pertinent data, the Director of Naval Intelligence states: "The preceding facts have been set forth to illustrate, in a few respects out of many, the close relation existing between the activities of the Bureau of Yards and Docks of the Navy Department and the Nation's industries and engineering developments. It should be recognized that almost the entirety of the expenditure of funds under the Bureau are for the employment of American labor and the purchase of materials of American manufacture. . . . The closest contact of the Navy with the business world . . . is through the purchasing activities of the Bureau of Supplies and Accounts. . . . The money value of the purchases by the Bureau of Supplies and Accounts is well over $100,000,000 annually, and this includes almost every imaginable commodity. The Bureau is always anxious to interest responsible manufacturers and dealers in Navy business and is constantly adding to its list of business men in every section of the country who are desirous of engaging in the business of selling to the Navy."[55] Similar representations are made before committees of Congress concerned with naval appropriations.[56] All this proceeds on the

---

[54] C. A. Beard, *The Navy: Defense or Portent?* pp. 112ff.

[55] *The United States Navy in Peace Time*, pp. 80, 83.

[56] For illustrations see *Hearings*, House Committee on Appropriations.

assumption apparently that modern business is a unity, that it does not embrace conflicting interests, that what is good for one part is good for all, that the revenue side of expenditures is negligible, and that the interests of taxpayers are identical with those of naval purveyors.

Yet it would not be in strict accordance with the facts in the case to say that the Navy is a mere interest in the pecuniary or commercial sense of the term, even though in practice it is intimately associated with such interests. Unlike the State Department and the Department of Commerce, the Navy represents fighting traditions and standards of "honor" older than commerce and purely civil institutions. It inherited a code of prestige, right, and propriety which sublimated the ancient motive of fighting, namely, desire for territory and loot. And that code has often been presented by naval writers as opposed to the "low" or "money-making" motives of the capitalist class, and made the basis of an appeal to "idealistic" or anti-pecuniary considerations.

An appeal ingenuously combining both motives was set forth early in the great naval upswing near the close of the nineteenth century by Alfred Thayer Mahan in an article in *The Forum*. "The attention of United States citizens," he says, "has restricted itself almost exclusively to the interior affairs of their country and has attached to the making and having of money an importance paramount to that of all other factors in life. Undoubtedly many other human interests claim and receive a certain share of attention, but money, as the representative of power and the means to gratification, may without exaggeration be said to have no competitor so close as to be accurately called a rival. In the Navy, money will not be found; and as, if it stands for anything, it stands for the representation of external interests, it fails to touch keenly the chords that represent danger or advantage near at hand. As a matter of fact, the external interests which are generally recognized as calling for the existence and maintenance of a navy concern but a very small proportion of our citizens—those who reside or have business interests in foreign lands where political conditions are unsettled and justice at times hard to obtain. Whether a wide-embracing view of national interests will in the future be justified, and, if justified, will be reached by so large a number of our own people as to constitute anything like a national sentiment, is a question upon which it is impossible to speak with authority. My own opinion is that within the probable lifetime of some now entering the service such a sentiment will have become general, owing to the course that external events are likely to take; not by the initiative of our own country, but by the action of other states. If that should come to pass, the Navy will undoubtedly gain that growth of sympathy and recognition which, by the dignity it confers, is of itself no slight advantage to be considered in the choice of a profession. In no event will there be money in it; but there may always be honor and quietness of mind and working occupation which are better guarantees of happiness." [57]

Although endowed with less power to take the initiative in foreign affairs than the State and Navy Departments, the Department of Commerce also represents policy in respect of national interest, and acts as an important agency in the formulation of policy. One of the relatively newer establishments of the Government, its inception and development mark a departure from the theory that the immediate solicitation of foreign trade is a private function to be entrusted to interested parties. Its progress is in keeping with a general tendency of Western countries to place powerful engines of state behind the extension of trade, the sale of goods, the acquisition of concessions, the placement of foreign loans, and the enforcement of claims.

In the discharge of its statutory duties the Department of Commerce performs three primary functions in the field of foreign commerce. Through its own agents, and the consular officers of the State Department, it collects an enormous mass of concrete, realistic materials on the economic conditions of foreign countries, their laws and trade policies, their public and private finances, their products for export, and their potential and actual demands for American goods. The results of findings based on these materials are sifted, collated, and distributed widely among American merchants and manu-

[57] *The Forum*, November, 1895.

facturers and are used as the basis of personal advice and correspondence. In the second place, the Department maintains a large staff of commercial agents abroad, engaged in searching out trade opportunities for American citizens, forming contacts with key persons in foreign commerce, and otherwise promoting the sale of American goods in foreign markets. In the third place, it seeks to arouse the interest of American business men in foreign trade and investments, shows them how to find new markets abroad, and coöperates with them individually and collectively as trade associations in extending their foreign operations.[58]

In part the Department of Commerce is a fact-finding agency, but it formulates policies both positive and negative. Its fundamental business in the foreign field is to increase the sale of American commodities abroad and to promote the activities of American business men in other countries by all legitimate means, without inquiring closely into the immediate or long-run consequences of these activities. Apparently with an even hand it aids American manufacturers in establishing branch factories in foreign countries and American manufacturers who make commodities which compete with these branch factories. It furnishes facilities for the encouragement of foreign lending, whether the loans go into wasteful public expenditures, into the development of local resources advantageous to the United States, or into industries that are actual rivals of American industries in the world market. Through publications, public statements, and addresses by its prominent officials, the Department gave its support to the trade and investment policies which culminated in the *débâcle*

[58] A wide variety of periodical publications is utilized to disseminate this information. Aside from the regular annual statistical and associated reports, the principal periodical publications include: *Survey of Current Business* (monthly, with weekly supplement); *Monthly Summary of Foreign Commerce; Commerce Reports* (weekly; it is this publication which contains, on the back page, information on specific commodity wants and commercial opportunities for American business concerns in foreign countries). Periodical studies of markets, commodities, trade conditions, etc., at home and abroad, are issued under the *Trade Information,* and the *Domestic Commerce,* Series of publications. For a more complete list of the publications of the Department of Commerce, see "Monthly Catalogue, United States Public Documents," Superintendent of Documents, Washington, D. C., Monthly section, "Commerce Department."

of 1929.[59] It accepted and made its own, without critical analysis, the dominant commercial philosophy of the post-war period. Like the United States Chamber of Commerce it assumed that business was a unity, consistent in all its parts, and that what was good for business was good for the country —that is, "in the national interest." Only occasionally, when the results of its fact-findings carried conclusions on their face, as in the case of Bolivian finances, did it exercise its negative powers by publishing a report, without open recommendations, which indicated perils ahead.

Broadly speaking, its reports are founded on the assumptions of current and popular business philosophy. On its own motion it has made no broad inquiry into the total effect of export practices on American economy, viewed in the light of permanent national interest. Only in response to a resolution of the Senate did it make a critical report on *American Factories Abroad* in 1931 and examine the economic repercussions of that tendency on American trade at home, in the local markets, and in neutral markets; and even that document was lacking in conclusiveness.[60] Not until 1932 did it begin a close analysis of the influences of foreign trade on the economic conditions in the United States. Of course, it may be said on behalf of the Department that thoroughgoing inquiries into fundamental problems of international trade and exchange raise enormous difficulties, involve the possible antagonism of conflicting interests, and raise distressing controversies. By operating on the current philosophy dominant in the circles of the export trade, the Department is on safer ground, immediately at least; and it can rightly plead likewise that there is nothing in the law governing its operations which require it to act positively as the chief determining agency in the field of foreign economic policy. Like other Departments it is constantly impressed by the instant need of many things, sometimes reciprocally antagonistic.

The Department of Commerce does not confine its opera-

---

[59] *Frontiers of Trade,* by Dr. Julius Klein, Assistant Secretary of Commerce under Robert P. Lamont, is an excellent single example of the way in which officials have encouraged the current trade and investment policies.

[60] See below, p. 393.

tions to investigation and promotion. It sometimes takes leadership in the presentation of broad policies to the public. An excellent illustration of its methods and potentialities in this relation is afforded by its action in 1926 on the prices of certain imports under the control of foreign governments—especially rubber, coffee, camphor, nitrates, and potash. On his own motion Secretary Hoover made an open attack on the policies of the governments concerned and called upon the Interstate and Foreign Commerce Committee of the House of Representatives to inquire into the causes of the high prices of these commodities. He estimated that the American people were "gouged" to the amount of more than a billion dollars a year by artificial efforts to maintain price levels.

Under his supervision the Bureau of Foreign and Domestic Commerce issued a bulletin declaring that American users of rubber imports paid about $300,000,000 a year "in excess of the fair price." Bringing his argument before the world to a sharp point, Secretary Hoover assailed Great Britain directly, accusing her of controlling most of the raw material and deliberately adopting a plan to raise the price of rubber bought in the United States. Besides making an assault on the economic policies of foreign powers, Mr. Hoover suggested an economic policy for the United States, namely, the development of the rubber industry in the Philippines.

Before he had gone very far in the promotion of his projects, however, efforts at price-pegging abroad proved ineffective and in due course the prices of the commodities in question fell to ruinous levels, seriously affecting American interests in another direction. When, for example, Brazil could not hold coffee up to a level that yielded a fair return to the growers, her finances crashed and Brazilian bonds went into default, to the great distress of American investors. Whether this excursion of the Department of Commerce into the field of foreign affairs worked good or evil in the long run need not concern us here; the point is the potential powers of the Department in the interpretation and advancement of national interest.

By tradition and law, the Secretary of the Treasury is made an instrument for the determination of national interest in certain relations. He may from time to time present projects of taxation which affect the duties imposed upon imports and thus bring his policies forcibly to the attention of the country. Under the tariff acts, he is given wide powers over the conduct of foreign trade. Whenever he finds that an industry cannot be established in the United States or that one already established is being injured on account of the importation of foreign goods to be sold at less than fair value, he may publish the fact, and may impose a special "dumping" duty in addition to the existing rate, if there is one. Since he is in charge of customs appraisals, valuations, and collections, the Secretary is in a strategic position to keep watch on foreign merchants and manufacturers likely to engage in "irregular" transactions to get rid of their surpluses. In administering the revenue and tariff laws, he may employ treasury attachés, customs representatives, and other agents to search the factories, accounts, and procedures of foreign enterprises engaged in manufacturing goods for the American market. Under his power to exclude goods made by forced labor abroad, he may bar commodities from any country if he has reason to believe the law has been violated. Indeed a wide latitude is permitted here, as the country discovered when American competitors sought to bar certain imports originating in Soviet Russia. The Secretary of the Treasury has at times been given the power to negotiate specific agreements with foreign governments for loans, for the establishment of credits, or for the funding of debts owing to the national Government.[61]

On the assumption that the organization of American business for efficient competition abroad is a proper subject for governmental action, Congress has authorized the Federal Trade Commission to supervise American combinations for export business and has exempted them from the limitations of the anti-trust laws in that respect. "One of the primary purposes of the law," says the Commission, "was to enable American exporters to operate on an equal footing with foreign

---

[61] Such, for example, were the agreements signed by the Secretary of the Treasury who served as Chairman of the World War Foreign Debt Commission under Acts of Congress approved February 9, 1922, February 28, 1923, and January 21, 1925.

combines. This has been accomplished through coöperative agreements stabilizing export prices, reducing selling costs, standardizing grades, contract terms and sale conditions, improving the quality of the products exported, and assuring buyers of prompt and efficient services in the filling of orders. The Webb law association is also in a position to present a solid front to the buying combines which might otherwise play one exporter off against another and beat down the prices to an unprofitable basis." Export associations must file with the Federal Trade Commission certain statements respecting their organization and methods. Unless the Commission finds that it is restraining domestic trade or the export trade of a rival, an association has practically a free hand abroad. Thus the Commission enters into the determination of export methods and carries certain responsibilities in foreign affairs. In addition it has a general authority to investigate foreign trade relations in and with foreign countries where there are combinations and practices of manufacturers, merchants, and traders which may affect the foreign commerce of the United States. In other words, an independent Commission of the Federal Government, subject to no departmental supervision, acts as an agency for interpreting and determining national interest in particular cases.

Although emphasis is laid in public opinion at least upon the flow of capital and manufactured commodities in international commerce, agriculture is by no means neglected. The Department of Agriculture has jurisdiction affecting commodity prices more or less directly. Like the Department of Commerce it is represented abroad by special agents engaged in promoting the sale of agricultural produce.[62] It exercises control over domestic production, commodity markets, and warehousing, with more than incidental bearing on export and import. With a view to protecting American products against pests and diseases, it may exclude certain competing commodities from other countries, thus combining sanitary measures with the bestowal of economic benefits upon certain

---

[62] Under the act approved June 5, 1930, establishing the Foreign Agricultural Service, the Department of Agriculture may send agricultural attachés and other officers to represent it abroad. *United States Statutes at Large,* Vol. 46, p. 497.

producers, and influencing American foreign relations in no small degree. Thus this powerful federal agency has direct responsibilities for interpreting national interest as expressed in terms of agricultural activities, prices, and profits.

The Department of Labor is charged with the general administration of the laws bearing upon the admission of aliens into the United States; but the Department of State, through its consular officers, helps to administer the Immigration Act of 1924 and other laws and regulations touching upon immigration. As a result of overlapping jurisdictions the consuls are "assisted" by immigration inspectors and technical advisers from the Department of Labor.[63]

While current theory sometimes makes the President the official spokesman of the United States in interpreting national interest in the field of international relations, the theory possesses only a partial validity in fact. It is true that Congress does not carry on official correspondence with foreign governments, does not write them notes dealing with particular cases and applying the creed of national interest, but that function, important as it may be, is only one of the activities bearing on foreign affairs. Under the Constitution, Congress, the separate houses, and the Senate especially, exercise fundamental powers in determining and applying national interest.

Congress alone can provide the money required for military and naval preparations—and such preparations are national policy—can declare war, enact tariff legislation, make laws regulating foreign commerce, control immigration, levy tonnage duties, subsidize the merchant marine, determine the status of overseas possessions, and resort to other measures pertaining to the definition and enforcement of national interest beyond the borders of the United States. In the discharge of these functions each house makes use of a number of committees which carry on investigations, develop news for the creation and expression of opinion, and prepare reports on policies and measures. On the floor of each house members may make speeches without restraint on the policies of other

[63] *United States Statutes at Large,* Vol. 39, pt. 1, pp. 874, 892; Vol. 43, pt. 1, pp. 153, 157, 160–162, 166.

countries, on the relations of the United States with them—speeches which are cabled abroad as representing "American opinion." No small part of the great world pattern of ideology respecting the foreign policy of the United States is made up of views expressed in debate by Senators and Representatives.

It is not necessary to expand this theme, but two striking events may be cited as illustrating immense potentialities. The first is the action of Congress in wresting the regulation of Japanese immigration from the State Department, where it had once been determined by a secret executive arrangement known as "the Gentlemen's Agreement," and in making it the subject of angry debate in which certain members gave great offense to the susceptibilities of the Japanese people. It was said at the time that this action, accompanied by irresponsible oratory, would have "grave consequences" in the Far East; and there is good reason for believing that American action and methods, especially the methods, in barring immigration, were partly, if not largely, responsible for straining American-Japanese relations and driving Japan back upon a purely Asiatic policy which found expression in her Manchurian expansion in 1931 and 1932. While the merits of this controversy are not germane to the present argument, the power of Congress in such affairs and its possible methods are decidedly pertinent. A division of authority which makes impossible the formulation of policy consistent in all its parts and directed to unitary ends has a distinct bearing on the problem of creating and realizing efficiently any system of national interest in the large or in detail.

A second illustration of the power of Congress in interpreting national interest is the investigation of Mexican affairs conducted by a subcommittee of the Senate Committee on Foreign Relations, under the presidency of Senator Albert B. Fall in pursuance of a formal Senate resolution.[64] At the time American relations with Mexico were strained and President Wilson was pursuing lines of policy which were subject to hostile criticism in both houses of Congress. Convinced that the President was bent on going his own way, the Senate intervened, and the subcommittee held hearings in which ex-

[64] Above, pp. 138ff.

tensive testimony was collected indicating an immense loss of American life and property in Mexico. A "murder map" purporting to show places in which American citizens had been killed in Mexico was presented, creating a huge sensation in the daily press, which surged up in a cry for a war of revenge.

At the conclusion of its hearings, the subcommittee reported the measures which, it decided, should be taken "to prevent a recurrence of such outrages." These proposals included a delay in recognizing the new president of Mexico, a demand for modification of the Mexican constitution, under which the rights of American teachers and missionaries in Mexico had been curtailed and restrictions imposed on the rights of property held by American citizens, and finally, if warnings were without avail, action by the military and naval forces of the United States against Mexico to maintain communications in that country, to restore peace and order, to return to American citizens "their properties," to afford opportunity "for the opening of mines, fields, and factories," and to assist the Mexican people in establishing a "government of serious, competent, honest, and honorable men who will meet the civilized world upon friendly ground and bind themselves to deal with other people as they themselves would be dealt with." Although the report was not carried into effect by congressional action, it had a profound influence on public opinion and on the course of diplomatic relations. It showed what even a subcommittee of the Senate could do in the way of defining national interest and creating popular support for it.[65]

Of the power of the Senate over international relations through control over diplomatic appointments and the ratification of treaties, it is scarcely necessary to speak. A library on this subject is available. Nor is it necessary to go into the vexatious question whether the Senate is a mere ratifying body or may participate in the formulation of treaties at various stages of the process. Experience seems to indicate clearly that no President or Secretary of State is wise in venturing to undertake an important negotiation with a foreign government without consulting at least some members of the

[65] *Investigation of Mexican Affairs*, 66th Cong., 2d Sess., Sen. Doc. No. 285, Washington, 1920. See also text and notes beginning p. 138 above.

Senate, unless perhaps he is reasonably sure of support in that body. Again and again, in spite of precautions, treaties have been rejected or amended in vital particulars. It is not too much to say that whenever a treaty definition is involved, the determination of national interest is vested in the Senate. Strictly speaking it is vested in a small minority of the Senate—one third plus one—the vote required to defeat the ratification of a treaty formally negotiated by the President. Moreover, the working of the constitutional provision as regards Senatorial control over treaty negotiation is further narrowed by the power of individual Senators, and of the Senate Foreign Relations Committee, to delay proceedings, often for considerable periods of time.[66]

Whatever errors of detail and inference there may be in the above outline of the federal agencies engaged in interpreting national interest and of their methods, certain conclusions are inescapable. These agencies are several in number and each moves more or less freely within its own orbit, confined in some relations by the requirements of legal specification. In certain cases they coöperate; in others, they are often found in antagonism. None of them is an isolated body operating in a vacuum under its own momentum. All are controlled by personalities with deep roots in the varied and complicated life of American society. No common authority unites and dominates them, forcing consistency in their scattered findings and actions, bringing their interpretations into a harmonious pattern which presents a conception of national interest that can be objectively verified with reference to gains or losses in national wealth and well-being. In short, at the heart of things, where national interest is interpreted and applied, there is a division of powers, a diversity of views, and an endless conflict of opinion subject to no ultimate tribunal of reconciliation and adjudication.

[66] D. F. Fleming, *The Treaty Veto of the American Senate,* pp. 282–289. The action of the Constitutional convention in vesting control over treaties in the Senate and requiring a two-thirds vote for ratification was a reflection of state particularism and sectional jealousies which ran counter to the formation of a national government—an instrument of national interest. It would be illuminating to inquire what sections of the country have been represented in the minorities that have repeatedly withheld their sanction from treaties.

The interpretation, advancement, and enforcement of national interest are not confined to the use of institutions and agencies of a national character only. Any means capable of assisting the state are seized upon and utilized. Thus the entire field of international organization, so far as it has been expressed in institutional form, has been made the vehicle for the attainment of national interest. National interests are sought through such procedures as international conferences, conventions, and the process of treaty negotiation, primarily those which are *ad hoc* devices for the attainment of specific objects.[67] Notwithstanding the fact that the United States was not a member of the League of Nations, it has participated both in the procedures of the League organizations and in the activities conducted under the auspices of, or with the aid of, the League.[68]

Rarely, however, are national interests either formulated or interpreted through these international procedures, institutions, and agencies. Rather should it be said that after the national interest is crystallized within the country, the effort to advance and enforce it enters the field of international organization whenever expedient. Undoubtedly this accounts for the large degree of particular nationalistic bias found so frequently in international gatherings even in cases where the subject under consideration is a common problem for all the nations of the world. Moreover, the practice of using international organization as an instrument of particular national purposes has a tendency to project into the international sphere the confusions, contradictions, and conflicts of interest that mark domestic

[67] For an excellent survey of the development in this field, see Pitman B. Potter, *An Introduction to the Study of International Organization*, 3d Ed. Also *Ten Years of World Coöperation*, League of Nations Secretariat, Geneva, 1930; and Felix Morley, *The Society of Nations: Its Organization and Constitutional Development*.

[68] For American participation in proceedings and activities of the League of Nations, see Ursula P. Hubbard, "The Coöperation of the United States with the League of Nations, and with the International Labor Organization." International Conciliation Document No. 274, Carnegie Endowment for International Peace, N. Y., November, 1931. An example of the use of an international procedure for the attainment of what is conceived to be an item in the national interest is Senator Key Pittman's negotiation of a "silver pact" at the World Economic Conference in July, 1933. New York *Times*, July 23, 1933, item "Silver Pact Signed by Eight Nations."

life, with the result that relations in the international sphere are devoid of conscious unity and direction, and oftentimes positively dangerous for the participating states themselves.

NATIONAL INTEREST AND THE BUREAUCRACY

In a survey of agencies engaged in interpreting, declaring, and enforcing national interest, a distinction appears between "political" or temporary officials and permanent or bureaucratic officials. The fundamental importance of this distinction has received little attention in the United States, partly because it is constantly assumed that political officers really make the policies which bureaucrats enforce and partly because the bureaucracy is of comparatively recent growth in the United States. But on second thought the significance of the distinction becomes evident.

From the foundation of the Republic there has been a bureaucracy in the United States—a body of permanent officials. At first and for a long time, it was confined mainly to the Army and the Navy. Since the adoption of civil service reform in 1883 there has been a steady extension of the permanent service in the civil departments of the Federal Government, including those establishments, like the State Department, which are vitally concerned with external relations. In fact the routine performances and many important operations affecting national interest are now carried on mainly by consular and diplomatic officers enjoying permanent tenure. As the body of career servants increases and business becomes more complex, growing reliance upon "informed" and "experienced" officials is inevitable. Inexorably also, the bureaucracy attains a higher degree of irresponsibility based on the supposition that its knowledge is "expert," if not esoteric.

The meaning of this for the interpretation, declaration, and enforcement of national interest is apparent. Every bureaucracy draws somewhat apart from the main currents of national life, tends to become an interest in itself, and is inclined to regard its interest and interpretation of interest as equivalent to the interest of the state. A bureaucracy likewise tends to affiliate itself with the dominant interests in society and in case of domestic conflicts to align itself with the parties and groups that have long been uppermost. That this should be so seems almost inexorable.

In sustaining itself, expanding its importance, and magnifying its prestige, a bureaucracy naturally looks around for opportunities and makes opportunities where it can, not without reference to general interests, to be sure, but most likely with reference to the best available special interests that can be enlisted. In this way the bureaucracy solidifies the position attained by permanence of tenure and makes its independent will, in general and in detail, prevail more effectively against that of temporary and passing political officials in the interpretation, declaration, and enforcement of policy, whether in domestic or foreign affairs. The facts in the case, therefore, require a recognition of the distinction between permanent and temporary officials when a statement is made respecting the processes by which national interest is interpreted and applied.[69]

DIPLOMACY AND THE ENFORCEMENT OF NATIONAL INTEREST

By far the most important means used to advance and enforce national interest is the "system," or institution, of diplomacy. From the earliest contacts of man with man, and of group with group, diplomacy in some form has played a conspicuous part in advancing particular interests and in effecting the adjustments between conflicting interests and policies. In the daily routine it sometimes makes and interprets national interests, but under modern conditions of communication, it

[69] By the Securities Act of 1933, Congress authorized the creation of a hybrid agency to be concerned with the interpretation and enforcement of national interest, when the President finds it "in the public interest," namely, a Corporation of Foreign Security Holders. This Corporation, now established, consists of directors originally named by the Federal Trade Commission and is to be self-perpetuating. It is called into existence under Act of Congress and set up by the Government, and yet, by the terms of the statute, it cannot "claim" or "pretend" to act for the State Department or the Government of the United States. The Corporation, thus created, is a kind of governmental agency authorized to operate in the foreign field and yet without responsibility to, and beyond the control of, the Government of the United States. New York *Times,* Financial Section, September 26, 1933.

assumes the current conception of national interests and devotes its efforts toward advancing and enforcing them.

Diplomacy operates in three distinct relations: that existing, first, between the state and its citizens abroad; second, between the alien and the state of his residence; and third, between two states concerned with respect to their mutual rights and obligations.[70] The existence of these three relations is confirmed first of all by the actual fact; and second by the recognition accorded to the fact by custom, convention, legal theory, and law. Action of the state in behalf of its nationals abroad appears to be inherent in what are called the fundamental rights of states; [71] and in the personal relationship existing between the home state and the individuals of which it is formed, whereby "its laws travel with them wherever they go, both in places within and without the jurisdiction of other powers." [72] Since each state exists, not in rigid isolation, but under the necessity of entering into relations with other states in the international community, and since other states possess similar fundamental rights, there has been cast upon each state "restrictions upon its freedom of action and a modification of any theoretical claim it may have had to *absolute*

[70] Borchard, *Diplomatic Protection of Citizens Abroad,* p. vi. Professor Borchard refers to these three relations as "legal" relations. Whatever these spheres or relations may mean in contemplation of law as commonly understood, diplomacy in actual practice does not seem to confine itself wholly to the field of "legal" relations, but operates as well in fields and upon subjects which lie outside the scope of law. See Charles G. Fenwick, *International Law,* p. 37; Amos S. Hershey, *The Essentials of International Public Law and Organization,* writes of *"Diplomacy* in the wider sense, or *Foreign Policy,* . . . generally based upon considerations of expediency or national interest rather than upon those of courtesy, humanity, or justice" (p. 4ff). As a matter of fact the "protection" and enforcement of national interests involves a wide variety of methods, procedures, instrumentalities, and sanctions, in which law and legal conceptions are only but one contributing part.

[71] Thus it is said that "The action of the state in exercising the right of diplomatic protection, being based upon its independent claim against other states to have its nationals treated in accordance with the rules of international law, has been founded by various writers upon its right of self-preservation, the right of equality, and the right of intercourse." Borchard, *op. cit.,* p. 25; 353 and notes.

[72] Hall, *International Law,* 8th Ed., Oxford, 1924, p. 56. See also Oppenheim, *International Law,* 4th Ed., 1928, Vol. I, p. 521. For the application of this concept to corporations, see Borchard, *Diplomatic Protection of Citizens Abroad,* pp. 621–622.

authority over its subjects abroad or over all the inhabitants of its territory. . . . The citizen abroad is thus subject to a certain control of both the personal and the territorial sovereign, each requiring forbearances upon the part of the other." [73]

If the laws of the territorial sovereign "are arbitrarily unreasonable and out of harmony with the standard of civilized states, or if the administration of the laws transgresses the prescriptions of civilized practice, or if in any respect there is an abuse of the rights of territorial jurisdiction as provided by treaties or established custom, the personal sovereignty of the home state reasserts itself and emerges in the form of diplomatic protection." [74] The right of the citizen to this protection, however, is, as to the citizen, an imperfect right in the sense that while his home state may insist upon protecting him and his interests, he may not, in turn, obtain it as a matter of course. To extend protection, or to refuse it, lies within the sole discretion of his state. [75] Nor can he waive the right of his state to protect him if it sees fit to do so; and even when he has so waived it, as concessionaires have done in contracts renouncing the right to resort to diplomatic support, his own state has sometimes denied and repudiated his capacity in that respect; [76] and international "commissions generally have sought to find a ground on which they could relieve the claimant from the binding character of the obligations." [77]

[73] Borchard, p. 345.

[74] *Ibid.*, p. 346. In this respect there are two rules for measuring the protection afforded to citizens abroad: the general rule based upon "actual ability to protect" and the "failure to prevent" which appears to operate with respect to China, Turkey, Morocco and similar countries (*ibid.*, p. 215). And it appears that ". . . The application of the rights of diplomatic protection increases in vigor in direct ratio with the weakness of the local protection accorded by the state of residence" (p. 346).

[75] Borchard, *ibid.*, pp. 356, 801.

[76] *Ibid.*, p. 797 and notes, citing the position taken by Secretary of State Bayard in 1888 to the effect that "this government cannot admit that its citizens can, merely by making contracts with foreign powers, or by other methods not amounting to an act of expatriation or a deliberate abandonment of American citizenship, destroy their dependence upon it or its obligations to protect them in case of a denial of justice." It is stated that Germany and Great Britain take the same view (p. 809).

[77] *Ibid.*, p. 801. For a specific example, see Dickinson, *The Law of Nations*, p. 893.

As already indicated, diplomacy assumes the current conception of national interests without question. It also functions within the current doctrines and ideology of economics and politics. It rarely questions or alters them; it does not appraise them, or subject them to the test of any yardstick or criteria over and above the mass of conflicting interests which they express. It accepts these conflicts and contradictions, as it sees them on the surface, as the scheme of things ordained by some force transcending man, and confines its efforts merely to composing the differences and adjusting the conflicts. It does not occur to diplomacy to question the system or the fundamental conditions out of which the conflicts arise.[78] This is the substance of the routine action of diplomacy and constitutes its principal activities in the advancement and enforcement of national interests.

Included in the subject matter of diplomatic negotiation and administration is the great network of treaties, consular conventions, and other concrete agreements, which are, perhaps, the most customary instruments for defining the rights of citizens abroad and assuring protection for their interests.[79] Treaties are one step removed from the ill-defined character of the current conceptions of national interest and from the loose assumptions upon which these conceptions rest, in the sense that treaties have brought interests and ideas into a realm of concrete expression where there is at least partial affirmation and acceptance upon the part of the participants.[80]

[78] For example, Borchard states: "In the encouragement of American enterprises abroad, the government lends its support to such as are legitimate and nationally beneficial, the degree of support being measured by the national advantages to be expected." *Op. cit.,* p. 400. Query: What are the criteria for deciding whether such enterprises are "legitimate and nationally beneficial"? Where is there a fundamental statement of the "national advantages to be expected"?

[79] Borchard, *Diplomatic Protection of Citizens Abroad,* pp. 75, 438. For a classification of Treaties and other International Compacts, and the procedures in international relations with which they are associated, see Sir Ernest Satow, *A Guide to Diplomatic Practice,* 3d Ed. (H. Ritchie, Ed.), Chapters XXIII to XXVII (pp. 318–421). For a classification and illustrations of "executive agreements" in the nature of treaties, see Samuel B. Crandall, *Treaties: Their Making and Enforcement,* 2d Ed., pp. 112–140.

[80] To the extent that treaties contribute to the establishment and acceptance of positive rules in international law, the latitude for manœuvring in the wider field of diplomacy is cut down. Hershey, *op. cit.,* p. 5.

Many of the agents of the state in its international relations have been discussed in previous sections. Some repetition will be unavoidable in this approach to the interpretation, advancement, and enforcement of national interest through diplomacy. Hall divides these agents into two groups: (1) the person or persons to whom the management of foreign affairs is committed; and (2) agents subordinate to these, who are: public diplomatic agents, officers in command of the armed forces of the state, persons charged with diplomatic functions but without publicly acknowledged character, commissioners employed for special objects, such as the settlement of frontiers, supervision of the execution of a treaty, etc. With international agents of the state properly so called may be classed consuls, who are only international state agents in a qualified sense.[81] Chief among those persons in the first group are the President and the Secretary of State, but the previous discussion indicates that in addition to these executive officers a number of other agents (some of whom Hall has classified as "subordinate" agents) have operated independently in the formulation and interpretation of national interest. Having already considered the first group, we now turn to the second —agents either permanently or temporarily abroad conducting the routine relations between the United States and other governments of the world. Principal among these are the diplomatic representatives proper and the consular officials.

With the classifications of diplomatic agents into such categories as ambassadors, ministers of various rank and degree, envoys, and the like, we are not particularly concerned. It is the unitary character and functions of these representatives through which national interests are advanced and enforced. The ambassador, or other diplomatic agent, is the spokesman for his country in the state to which he is accredited or at the conference to which he is sent. As such, he is in a position where he may and does formulate and interpret the national interest of his country, though often as he alone seems to view

[81] Hall, *International Law*, 8th Ed., 1924, p. 351. For a further discussion and classification of Diplomatic Agents, see Satow, *op. cit.*, Chapters XI (pp. 109–117) and XV (pp. 149–160). Examples of several groups of executive agents and the range of their activities may be found in Henry M. Wriston, *Executive Agents in American Foreign Relations*, Chapters V and VI.

it. Many such instances have already been given in the previous pages. But more important than his action in that respect are his daily activities over a wide range. Through him, a constant interchange of views is carried on,[82] as well as more formal negotiations leading, perhaps, to the conclusion of a treaty. Assisted by an expert staff,[83] he gathers information as to policies, military strength, economic situation, public opinion, or any other matter which might be of service to his own government. He is the principal agent engaged in protecting the interests of his own state and the interests of his fellow-nationals in the country where he is at work.[84]

Even to a greater degree than the strictly diplomatic representative, the foreign consul advances and protects the material interests of the citizens of his own country as part of the daily routine. A mere summary statement of the work he performs indicates the range of his influence. In general, he is expected to promote the interests of American citizens within his jurisdiction, protect them in all acquired privileges and facilitate trade relations. "For his fellow citizens abroad, he must keep a record of permanent residents, certify to births, marriages, and deaths; attest wills; perform notarial functions; protect them against injustice in the local courts, or from unjust detention . . . take charge of estates of deceased Americans. He has onerous duties with regard to shipping. . . . He provides visas for alien immigrants; . . . he arranges for the extradition of criminals; he observes the

---

[82] The almost direct and powerful influence exerted by the ambassador upon national interest is abundantly revealed by the letters of Walter Hines Page, American Ambassador to Great Britain immediately prior to and during the early years of the World War. Burton J. Hendrick, *Life and Letters of Walter H. Page,* Vol. III. A similar, and perhaps even more powerful, influence, in the case of an agent who was something of an ambassador-at-large, characterizes the activities of Colonel E. M. House which are described in the pages of Charles Seymour, *The Intimate Papers of Colonel House,* particularly the latter part of Vol. I and all of Vol. II.

[83] Secretaries of Embassy or Legation; under-secretaries; counsellors; attachés representing many fields such as military, naval, financial, technical, etc; experts in trade, agriculture, commerce, on legal matters, and so on; and a numerous staff of assistants, clerks, stenographers and other help. Moore, *Digest,* Vol. IV, sec. 625–626.

[84] Clyde Eagleton, *International Government,* p. 210.

execution of commercial treaties. In behalf of citizens back at home he maintains all possible contacts and acquires all possible information concerning local markets or materials, . . . which information he dispatches home in regular reports. . . . The range of his duties and of his service is amazing; it is the foundation of international commerce." [85] It should be added that in performing these services, the consul acts within the pattern and scope of the prevailing economic doctrines, within a wide and varied range of political policies, and under the general assumption that all his acts are for the advancement and protection of the "national interest." No other criterion seems to guide his acts than the fact of American citizenship. Whether the fostering of some particular commercial interest of a fellow-citizen does or does not in truth redound to the national interest does not occur to the consul in his daily routine; and even if it should disturb his private thought and judgment upon occasion, the pattern of the official institution through which he functions would dispel any doubts or misgivings that may have entered his mind. [86]

It is impossible to detail the multitude of services performed by diplomatic agents in behalf of the citizens and the national interests of their respective countries. [87] Their daily routine itself constitutes an important part of enforcement and protection even when it does not bear upon contested interests or carry specific assertions of an intention to coerce. Thus protests have been made in advance of municipal legislation believed to be prejudicial to established American interests, against proposed tariff rates curtailing American trade, against proposed monopolies (as the grant by Haiti of a soap monopoly to certain French concerns in 1907–1908), which appeared to violate treaty rights or was inimical to American trade. [88] Remonstrances have been made against legislative decrees in

---

[85] Clyde Eagleton, *International Government,* pp. 203–204.

[86] For a further discussion of the Consular Service as an agency of protection, see Borchard, *op cit.,* Chapter VI, pp. 435–438.

[87] For an exposition of the instrumentalities and processes of diplomacy, see Poole, *The Conduct of Foreign Relations under Modern Democratic Conditions,* Chapter II.

[88] Borchard, *op. cit.,* p. 401.

foreign countries as, for example, those protesting the debasement of currency in Venezuela.[89]

The early practice of the Department of State was to retain full control over the activities of diplomatic representatives in behalf of private interests, although the difficulties of communication often rendered such control ineffective and left decisions of this character to the discretion of the diplomatic agent. John Quincy Adams took the position that "a public minister cannot act as agent for the collection of private claims without injury to the dignity and decorum of the public service," [90] Mr. Adams, in 1823, and Mr. Marcy, Secretary of State, in 1856, adhered to the policy that the United States is not bound to interfere to secure the fulfillment of contracts made between American citizens and foreign governments, on the ground that the contract is presumed to have taken into account the ability of the foreign power to perform its obligations and the risk of failure involved.[91] In 1873 Secretary Fish observed that "the aid of the diplomatic representatives of the Government is frequently requested for the prosecution of private investigations, but this Department does not feel justified in being the medium of conveying requests of that character. . . ." [92]

But even as early as 1876 the impact of commercial expansion and the services it implied were apparent in the realm of diplomacy; for while, in that year, Secretary Fish affirmed his previous attitude, he indicated that the American minister might be permitted "to exert his friendly good offices" in behalf of the American citizen and his interests.[93] The attempt of the State Department to control the acts of diplomatic agents was never given up completely although the very latitude increasingly given to such agents in official instructions made home control difficult to maintain in the case of routine activities.

---

[89] Moore, *Digest,* Vol. VI, pp. 753–754.

[90] *Ibid.,* Vol. IV, p. 565.

[91] Borchard, *op. cit.,* p. 287.

[92] Moore, *Digest,* Vol. IV, pp. 565–566.

[93] Borchard, *op. cit.,* p. 288. By "good offices," Mr. Fish explained that he meant a direction to a diplomatic agent "to investigate the subject, and if [he] shall find the facts as represented [he] will seek an interview with the minister of foreign affairs and request such explanations as it may be in his power to afford."

Secretary Bayard in 1887 instructed Mr. Denby, American minister to China, to this effect: "Responsible citizens whose enterprises have the practical guarantee of pecuniary ability and personal character and standing will, at all times, receive whatever of aid it may be possible and practicable for the Department to lend, but such action should originate in this Department, where the opportunity for estimating the nature of the proposed enterprise and the character and responsibility of the parties proposing to embark in it can be better formed. Our representatives abroad will be less embarrassed by following this rule and abstaining from the furtherance of individual plans and contracts connected with foreign governments, until they have been submitted to this Department and received its approval." [94]

It is possible that such a policy did not square with the attitude which Mr. Denby took toward the functions and opportunities of his official position, for it appears from a dispatch in December, 1896, that he again sought for an expression of the policy of the State Department on the question of advancing American commercial interests. A much wider latitude was given to him by Secretary Olney's reply, which stated that "while agreeing with you that you should not assume, directly or impliedly, in the name of this Government, any responsibility for or guarantee of any American commercial or industrial enterprise trying to establish itself in China, the Department thinks that you should use your personal and official influence and lend all proper countenance to secure to reputable representatives of such concerns the same facilities for submitting proposals, tendering bids, or obtaining commercial enterprise in the country."

The discretion vested in a minister could scarcely be more complete than was given in this connection. "It is not practicable to strictly define your duties . . . ," the dispatch continued, "nor is it desirable that any instructions which may have been given should be too literally followed; your own judgment and experience, the standing of the firms who seek your assistance, and of their agents, must all be given due weight and your action shaped accordingly. Broadly speak-

[94] Moore, *Digest,* Vol. IV, p. 567.

ing, you should employ all proper methods for the extension of American commercial interests in China, while refraining from advocating the projects of any one firm to the exclusion of others." [95]

From the turn of the century, the practice of giving aggressive support to the interests of American citizens abroad grew until it appeared to attain almost world-wide range and received the authority of a positive official creed in the conception of dollar diplomacy under Secretary Knox. After a brief setback during the Wilson régime, the pattern was restored again with the return to power of a Republican administration in 1921. Throughout the following decade the practice of giving diplomatic support to private interests continued on a scale scarcely equalled in any other preceding period, until it culminated in the broad assertions of President Coolidge and Curtis D. Wilbur, his Secretary of the Navy [96]—assertions of policy which were given general affirmation by President Hoover, and vigorous detailed support by various departments of the Government, particularly the Department of Commerce, during his régime. And during the early months of the Roosevelt administration there was not as much alteration in the practice as the 1932 campaign seemed to forecast.[97]

Neither the advancement of American interests nor the advocacy of claims of American citizens can be said, however, to be an absolute function of diplomacy. Here, as elsewhere, consistency will be sought in vain, no matter how diligent the search or how broad an allowance is made for reasonable exceptions to any general rule. In a letter addressed by Secretary of State Bayard to Mr. Whitney, Secretary of the Navy, in 1885, the assertion is made that, "Generally speaking, persons who quit the shelter of their own flag to take up a voluntary residence in a foreign land do so at their own risk. . . ." [98]

---

[95] Moore, *Digest,* Vol. IV, pp. 568–569, where other instances of similar instructions relating to China, the Netherlands and "Hayti" in 1897 and 1898 are detailed.

[96] Above, pp. 221ff.

[97] An excellent illustration, concerning the situation in Liberia, is detailed by Raymond Leslie Buell in *The New Republic* (August 16, 1933), Vol. LXXVI, No. 976. See also the editorial "The State Department and the Old Deal" in the same magazine the following week (August 23, 1933), Vol. LXXVI, No. 977.

[98] Cited in Moore, *Digest,* Vol. VI, p. 29.

But such an expression applied to a rather limited character of circumstances. It does not express the general rule. "The United States has never taken the position that one who acquires a residence in a foreign country does so at his peril and assumes the risk of ill-treatment or injury identically with citizens." [99] And such a rule is not limited in its application to the person and property of citizens resident abroad, but operates as well in behalf of nationals resident in the United States who have ventured only their property and interests, and not their lives, abroad. [100]

It is now relevant to the subject in hand to refer to various formalistic principles offered to justify the advancement and protection of American lives and property abroad. As already explained, the practice is based upon the general foundation of the fundamental rights of individuals and states. Most of these find practical expression in international law. [101] Diplomatic protection also finds its justification in the fact that citizens domiciled abroad (and even those not resident abroad but having property and interests there) have no political share in the government of the foreign country; and thus being denied the opportunity to express disapproval and the privilege of bringing about a change of administration which native citizens enjoy, they are ultimately forced to rely upon outside protection as the only sanction they have for asserted rights. [102]

Another justification for the protection of citizens and their property abroad seems to grow out of a value-relation between the state and its own nationals, aside from the abstract claims of nationality. Such a ground for offering protection of indi-

[99] Borchard, *op. cit.*, pp. 106–107.

[100] There is some evidence to indicate that this was not always the case with respect to property and interests abroad. The earlier practice of the Government discloses a reluctance to venture too far in support of American material interests abroad. At any rate, the policy was neither clear nor positive until after the beginning of the period of commercial expansion in the closing decades of the 19th century. It should also be observed that prior to 1900, except for interests involved in the flow of trade and commerce, American investments and other property interests abroad were quite small (scarcely exceeding $500,000,000 in 1900 as against approximately $15,000,000,000 in 1930).

[101] Borchard, *op. cit.*, p. 14.

[102] *Ibid.*, p. 94; 106–107.

viduals abroad is brought out in the following excerpt from the brief of the United States in the Santa Ysabel case before the United States-Mexican Special Claims Commission of 1923: [103] "In the primitive stages of society the value of the citizen to the nation was largely measured in terms of his present or prospective value for military service. This is no longer true. From the standpoint of modern civilization and indeed of national existence under the present complex economic and social conditions of the world, military service is one of the less important elements in the value of a citizen to the nation. His productive power, his ability to contribute to the intellectual and social progress of the community, and other elements which are obvious, are under present conditions matters of primary importance in the national life and development, and any act of a foreign nation which destroys or impairs the productive, intellectual or social value of a citizen constitutes a material injury to the nation to which he belongs, entirely aside from any question of offense to the national honor or injury to the person himself or to those dependent upon or attached to him. It follows that the nation which thus sustains injury or damage through injury or damage to one of its citizens is entitled to indemnification commensurate with the economic and social value of such citizen, aside from any element of loss to his family. . . ." [104]

Following a similar process of reasoning, the protection of property and interests abroad is justified in the same brief in the following manner: "The same principles are applicable to cases of loss of or damage to property of a citizen either natural or artificial. The loss or damage is to property under the control and jurisdiction of the nation, constituting a part of the national assets and resources, for which the nation is entitled to indemnification in justice to all its citizens, aside from any right of the individual property owner. The very

[103] Cited in Frederick S. Dunn, *The Protection of Nationals,* Notes to Chapter III, Appendix, pp. 212–213.

[104] Of this, Dunn observes: "But if this rather vague and nebulous material value of the citizen to the nation is the basis of our concern for his welfare while abroad, we should feel the same concern about him to an even greater degree when he is at home, since he is then in a far better position to contribute to the 'intellectual and social progress of the community.'"

existence of any modern nation depends upon (1) the life and productive capacity of its citizens; and (2) the property or resources subject to its jurisdiction and control. All property of its citizens, wherever located, is subject to taxation and to expropriation in event of need. It may be reached directly when within the territorial jurisdiction of the government, or indirectly through governmental control of the person of the citizen or national if the property be outside the territorial jurisdiction. But this aspect only looks to governmental use of property for the purpose of taxation or emergency. The private use of property by the owners thereof is the chief basis of industrial and social progress. It is obvious, therefore, that any act of a foreign government, by which the property of a citizen of another is injured or destroyed or in any wise depleted, constitutes an injury to the nation through the diminution of the national assets and the impairment of the essential elements of national life, entirely aside from the direct or private injury or damage. For this damage to all the citizens of the nation there should always be full compensation or indemnification."

Theoretically, a citizen and his property are accorded protection through diplomatic negotiation and upon the basis of international law.[105] His right to protection is not absolute. Whether protection of any kind, or none at all, will be accorded to him rests in the discretion of the Government.[106] Some of the considerations influencing the State Department in the exercise of its sole right to decide for itself the appropriate time for advancing the claims of its citizens are: fear of the disapproval of the Senate if the means required must be expressed in a treaty; the financial weakness of the defendant state; the political instability of the defendant state; and the circumstances of the relations between the two states. The

---

[105] Nationals and material goods and things are said to be but *objects,* while states only are *subjects* of the Law of Nations. Amos S. Hershey, *The Essentials of International Public Law and Organization,* p. 267. It follows from this that if a national wishes to invoke the principles and processes of international law, he must find some way to induce his own government to take up the advocacy of his interest or claim. He cannot, in this respect, act in his own behalf.

[106] Crandall, *op. cit.,* pp. 108–110.

effect of these considerations, it is asserted, renders the pressure, even of a purely legal claim, "subject to every political consideration which affects the sensitive machinery of diplomacy, with the result that many meritorious claims have rested for years, unredressed, in the archives of the Department of State and in the Foreign Offices of other governments." [107]

Nor are these the only considerations entering into the decision concerning protection. The nature of the offense or injury to be redressed, the character and reputation of the local government for the proper administration of justice, the political expediency of instituting harsh or mild measures, the conduct and character of the claimant with respect to his title to diplomatic protection, the nature of the claim, as tortious or contractual, and the need of the claimant, are also matters influencing the attitude and decision of the State Department. "For these reasons, it is impossible to state with any degree of precision the measures of protection which in a given case will be accorded to American interests abroad, for the action of the government necessarily depends upon all the facts and circumstances of the case, and the principles of international law applicable thereto." [108]

The routine action of diplomatic agents is broadly covered by the principal functions of representation, negotiation, and interposition. [109] "In countries which habitually maintain effective government, the protective function of the national government of a resident alien is usually limited to calling the attention of the local government to the performance of its international duty." [110] Such a procedure not only applies to

---

[107] Borchard, *op. cit.*, pp. 372–373.

[108] *Ibid.*, p. 399.

[109] For some definitions and distinguishing features touching upon these functions, see Dunn, *op. cit.*, p. 20; Borchard, *op. cit.*, pp. 440–441; Poole, *op. cit.*, Chapter II; Oppenheim, *op. cit.*, Vol. I, pp. 622, 624.

[110] Borchard, p. 27. "Diplomatic protection is a complementary or reserved right invoked only when the state of residence fails to conform with the international standard." *Ibid.*, p. 28. One of the features coming under this standard is the general assertion of a "denial of justice" which, in theory at least, must be substantiated and consequently made somewhat more concrete, by the requirement that cases based upon contracts must be submitted to the local courts "as is provided by the local law or in the contract." *Ibid.*, pp. 281, 330. Like all other rules resting in theory, these are not always followed in practice, as American cases in Mexico, Central America, and the Caribbean

the protection of private interests, but embraces the interests of the political state as well; for it has been shown that the state has "fundamental rights," general and special interests, even aspirations, which are peculiarly associated with it in its corporate character as a political and material entity. Since many of these are expressed through private persons and have to deal with the same material things as do private rights and interests, the distinction is not always clear.[111]

As a routine matter, the action of the diplomatic representative in this respect is looked upon as the exercise of "good offices." [112] Representations of this character are perhaps the mildest form in which enforcement appears, aside from the fact of the daily routine which by its very nature is also a form of enforcement, though nowhere so regarded in technical treatments of the subject.[113] The mere exertion of good offices is a part of the daily routine, but it is also one degree nearer enforcement proper since it appears in cases which, by reason of the circumstances and their crystallization in the form of specific issues, are lifted out of the routine and require par-

amply demonstrate. In this respect the "denial of justice" principle is broadened to cover examinations into the very content and operation of the "local" law itself, and diplomatic protection or even more stringent protection is afforded upon the belief and the assertion that conditions are such that resort to the local agencies would be futile. (The claimant government decides for itself whether a denial of justice has taken place. *Ibid.*, p. 331.) Under such latitude the assertion of a "denial of justice" may be a mere subterfuge inspired by interested motives, or dictated by hauteur (in the case of a "strong" toward a "weak" state) or even by caprice; although there have been many occasions when none of these things, but a meritorious showing of the true fact, account for the assertion of a denial of justice. Moore, *Digest*, Vol. VI, p. 259, Sec. 913. (Although discussing intervention, as distinguished from "diplomatic intervention," the passage on p. 4 of the same volume, commencing: "A second caution in respect of intervention is . . . , etc.," is very illuminating in this connection.)

[111] The mere fact that there is an "international law," and that only states are the subject of such law, indicates a body of rights and interests associated with the state as such, above the private considerations of its constituent citizens. Moore, *Digest*, Vol. I, Secs. 3–13 (pp. 15–66); Fenwick, *op. cit.*, Chapter VI.

[112] The term "good offices" is employed in two senses—the unofficial, personal and friendly efforts of a diplomatic agent, and the official, formal, and governmental support of a diplomatic claim. Borchard, *op. cit.*, p. 440. But as Borchard states, the line between unofficial good offices and official interposition is not always easy to draw.

[113] Dunn, *op. cit.*, p. 20.

ticular or special attention.[114] The range of good offices may extend from any form of friendly attempts to compose differences, adjust interests, obtain recognition of asserted rights, simple redress, and remedies of various sorts, to formal protests, remonstrances, and in some cases, actual demands.[115] By far the greater number of cases involving both the interests of private enterprise and the interests of states themselves are disposed of by diplomatic negotiation of this character.

The assertion of national interests, the conflict of rights and interests, the failure to compose cases involving the alleged "rights" of private enterprise or of a public character, may persist beyond the efforts of diplomatic negotiations and interposition to dispose of them. Here, another series of agencies of enforcement are utilized and may be applied to the asserted national interests of the state as well as to the more limited specific interests of private enterprise which the state frequently makes its own. Conciliation commissions, commissions of inquiry, various procedures of mediation, various public and private arbitration boards, and judicial settlement are the principal agencies included within this series.[116] Either alone or in combination they are utilized for the enforcement of national interests, economic, political or otherwise.

Diplomatic negotiation, interposition, and the group of procedures just described are distinguished from all other methods of enforcement not only in that they are pacific measures, but also in that they do not consist of or utilize external pressures of force or coercion.[117] Whatever force these methods exert

[114] "When an injury has been inflicted upon an alien in such a manner as to involve the international responsibility of the state, an international case has arisen to be settled by the means recognized as legal for the settlement of any other international difference." Borchard, p. 439.

[115] Borchard, pp. 402ff.

[116] Oppenheim, *op. cit.*, Vol. II, pp. 13–14. These agencies may be *ad hoc* or permanent bodies; of such international character as the League of Nations' Council or the Permanent Court of International Justice; of quasi-international character, as jurists chosen from the panel which constitutes the Hague Permanent Court of Arbitration; or merely of private persons arbitrarily chosen to perform functions of conciliation, mediation, and arbitration. For a survey of these procedures, of the institutions through which they are operative, and of the qualifications and limitations upon them, see Fenwick, *op. cit.*, Chapter XXIV.

[117] That this is a real distinction may be seen in the common classification of

arises either out of the potentials of the negotiators or the character of the procedures themselves. Associated with the procedures are reason, logic, habit, custom, the sanction of opinion, the inherent sanction of the institution,[118] and that peculiar form of coercion which is manifested in self-restraint, a form of coercion scarcely considered as such because it is voluntarily accepted, not imposed from without.

ENFORCEMENT OF NATIONAL INTEREST BY COERCION

The measures which are now to be enumerated fall squarely within the field of enforcement proper. They all carry with them some form of arbitrary, physical, externally applied, force. They are all within the competence (though not always within the capacity) of the state to perform for itself.[119] They constitute coercion in the full sense of the word, notwithstanding the fact that some among them are designated "pacific measures." [120] They fall into two groups: (1) those measures set in motion within the state taking the initiative in enforcement, and not impinging directly upon the state proceeded against; and (2) measures operating directly against the state which is the object of the enforcement procedure.

Acts of enforcement falling within the first group may be

international remedies which include in "pacific measures," to which a state may resort, such procedures as pacific blockade, occupation of territory of the offending state, reprisals, and the like—"methods short of war." Fenwick, Chapter XXV.

[118] For example, if two nations should agree in a treaty that certain differences which may arise between them shall be settled by a conciliation commission, and the treaty sets up the commission and the rules by which it shall be constituted, operated, and governed, the obligation so created carries with it the implication of the further obligation that the nations concerned will resort to it when the situations contemplated by the treaty subsequently arise.

[119] "In the absence of a central authority for the enforcement of the rules of the Law of Nations, the states have to take the law into their own hands." Oppenheim, Vol. I, p. 14. "As international law is destitute of any judicial or administrative machinery, it leaves states, which think themselves aggrieved, and which have exhausted all peaceable methods of satisfaction, to exact redress for themselves by force." Hall, *International Law*, p. 81. See also Eagleton, *International Government*, pp. 78–81.

[120] By the very nature of the discussion in the text, the classification of procedures of this kind into "pacific measures" (or "measures short of war") and war, is disregarded.

said to be negative acts, though by indirection they may have a positive effect. The element of indirection is of considerable importance. The number and variety of acts of enforcement of this character may be quite broad, including any act or procedure designed to accomplish a desired result with respect to another state or group of states. In the wider field of state action to attain or secure national interests, many forms of alliances and state compacts have been construed as acts falling within this character. Domestic policies which may be regarded as aimed at the interests, the security, or the position of other states also fall within this group. Among the more concrete, specific procedures are: acts of non-intercourse, embargoes, boycotts, certain forms of retorsion, retaliation and reprisal, the severance of diplomatic relations, and when applicable and expedient, non-recognition. Some of these are definite, such as non-intercourse and embargoes; [121] some have a dubious status, such as the boycott; [122] some are rarely ap-

[121] For discussions, distinctions and cases bearing upon these two procedures, see Moore, *Digest*, Vol. VII, Secs. 1098 and 1099 (pp. 143–151). The denouncement of existing treaty relations may be associated with these procedures.

[122] The boycott is a relatively new measure of self-help. It has no legal status. It does not have official standing as an instrument of national policy. Its operation is limited by the economic character of the procedure as well as by the technique by which it is made effective. Owing to the possibility of construing an official boycott as an "unfriendly" act, or as an act of war, nations have been reluctant to resort to it. On account of these considerations, boycott activities have been set in motion largely by private persons without government sanction. It should not be gathered from this that the boycott may never be used to advance and enforce national interests. Economic and political conditions are so shaping themselves that the boycott may become a potent weapon in the hands of the state. Indeed it has been so used on several occasions by the Chinese against Western Powers and Japan. Dorothy J. Orchard, "China's Use of the Boycott as a Political Weapon," *Annals, Amer. Acad. of Pol. and Soc. Sci.*, Vol. 152 (November, 1930), pp. 252–261. For a Japanese point of view on China's use of the boycott in 1930–1932, see "The Present Condition of China." Document A. (Prepared by Professor Kenzo Takayanagi of Tokio Imperial University, Japan, for the American Council of the Institute of Pacific Relations, New York, 1932.) In connection with the Sino-Japanese controversy (1931–1932) considerable sections of public opinion urged the United States Government to boycott Japan. For a report by a group of prominent persons comprising a "Committee on Economic Sanctions," financed in an investigation into the use of the boycott and other economic sanctions by the Twentieth Century Fund, New York, as well as for a discussion of the boycott as an official measure of enforcement generally, see *Boycotts and Peace* (Evans Clark, Ed.). During the period of reorganization

plied in modern times, such as forms of retorsion, retaliation and reprisals; [123] while the device of severing diplomatic relations is so special in respect of the circumstances under which it is utilized,[124] and non-recognition is so narrowed by the conditions under which resort may be had to it,[125] that neither

of Germany under Adolf Hitler, accompanied as it was by agitation against the Jews, another demand arose in some quarters for an official government boycott of Germany. For several instances where this demand found expression in congressional speeches, see *Cong. Record,* 73d Cong., 1st Session, the index of which should be consulted under appropriate topics. That the boycott has been employed elsewhere between political units seems to be implied in the news item, "Danzig Asks Poland to End the Boycott." New York *Times,* July 8, 1932. In this connection, it would be interesting to analyze such devices as tariff controls, anti-dumping regulations, quota and licensing systems, sanitary measures, "Buy American" and "Buy British" movements, to determine to what extent and with what effect they utilize elements of the boycott technique in the advancement and enforcement of national interests in the accepted economic routine.

[123] For a discussion of the details of these measures and their present status, see Fenwick, *op. cit.,* Chapter XXV.

[124] For example, it has been asserted, not without foundation in fact, that "Before 1914, on the continent of Europe every important diplomatic discussion was conducted with the clear recognition that failure to achieve an agreement would be at once followed by war." Sir James Headlam-Morley, *Studies in Diplomatic History,* p. 50. The severing of diplomatic relations usually signified a failure to agree and thus became associated in point of time and consequence with the outbreak of war.

[125] Recognition (and its correlative non-recognition) is a process through which political entities (states) gain admission to the "family of nations." In a narrower sense, it is the procedure by which an existing state or states enter into direct, official relations with states newly formed, even though all the state-members of the "family of nations" may not concur in the act and policy of recognition. Fenwick, Chapter VII; Hershey, Chapter VIII, pp. 199–212. A summary enumeration of the consequences, in fact and law, which are said to flow from the practice of either recognizing or not recognizing a political state, indicates the uses to which this political act may be put to advance and enforce national interests. Oppenheim, Vol. I, pp. 154–156; Hall, pp. 39–40. By separating the principles of recognition into two aspects, *de facto* and *de jure* recognition, states have advanced their interests in such a way that they may secure many of the material advantages recognition may afford, without at the same time incurring many of the political disadvantages inimical to their interests which they seek to avoid. The most important modern case involving the policy of recognition concerns the status which respective nations have accorded to Russia. The United States refused to recognize Russia until 1933. In following this policy, it is clear that the United States was employing the principles of recognition in the advancement and enforcement of what it considered to be its own national interests. See International Conciliation, Document, No. 247; "Policy of the United States and other nations with respect to the recognition of the Russian Soviet Government, 1917–1929," New York,

is encountered very frequently in the ordinary routine. But irrespective of the qualifications, limitations, and conditions under which these devices may or may not be employed, all of them are within the competence of nations to employ in the advancement and enforcement of national interests. Every one of them, at some time or other—quite frequently in some cases—has been so utilized. With some few exceptions, all of them are policies, procedures, and mechanisms easily set in motion by the unilateral action of the state, are within its range of effective control, operate primarily upon the institutions, the interests and the life of the state, and only indirectly upon the other states affected or sought to be influenced. Moreover, even though these measures are, in every sense of the word, coercive, they are in most cases non-violent in a physical sense, and for that reason are considered less harsh, less disruptive of the routine relations between states, and less likely to produce dangerous crises or eventuate in war than the second group of procedures to which the state might resort to attain its national interests.

The second of these groups is made up, for the most part, of measures embodying the use of physical force externally applied and operating directly upon the state to be influenced or coerced. A wide range, from a direct threat of force to war, is covered. Often a threat of force is couched in diplomatic language and in such form as to be effective in achieving a desired result.[126] The diplomatic relations concerning

February, 1929. See also p. 135. Likewise, the United States followed a similar practice with respect to the Huerta government of Mexico in 1916. The rapid change of governments, particularly in Latin America, during the last decade, has afforded numerous examples of the employment of the practice of recognition as a device for the attainment of national interests. For a brief summary on this point, see Raymond Leslie Buell, New York *Times,* January 11, 1931, item, "New Latin-American Revolts Test Our Recognition Policy." The reluctance of the majority of the nations to accord recognition to Manchukuo is an illustration of the employment of this device to achieve results in the wider, international sphere.

[126] An illustration which has become something of a classic is found in the Monroe Doctrine as follows: " . . . we should consider any attempt . . . to extend their system to any portion of this hemisphere as dangerous to our peace and safety" and " . . . as the manifestation of an unfriendly disposition toward the United States." From the text cited in J. Reuben Clark, *Memorandum on the Monroe Doctrine* (December 17, 1928), Department of State. Publication No. 37, Washington, D. C., 1930. The action of the Western Powers with

the Caribbean, Central and South America, the Near East and the Far East are replete with illustrations of the use of the threat of force contained in words, not in physical acts. Such a device has even entered considerations connected with the effort to renounce resort to war as an instrument of national policy.[127]

Next to the diplomatic threat of force is the actual display of physical force in the enforcement of national interests. "It would be unintelligent," writes Poole,[128] "to belittle the direct relationship between the show of military force and national prestige." And Borchard observes that "The moral influence exerted by the presence of a war vessel is great." [129] "The United States," he says, "resorted to a display of force in Japan in 1852, in Turkey on several occasions, and within recent years in Haiti, the Dominican Republic, and Mexico." While expressly denying any intention of intervening in the domestic disturbances in Cuba in August, 1933, when agitation over a long series of internal abuses culminated in the flight of its president, Gerardo Machado, President Roosevelt ordered several American naval vessels to points on the Cuban coast as a "precautionary step to protect, if necessary, the lives of American citizens, pending the restoration of normal conditions of law and order by the Cuban authorities." [130]

respect to Japanese objectives at the conclusion of the Sino-Japanese War in 1895, is another case in point.

[127] In the British reply to the American note of April 13, 1928, which solicited the views of a number of governments upon the form and substance of a treaty renouncing war, a position practically embodying a threat of force was expressed in the following language: " . . . I should remind your excellency that there are certain regions of the world the welfare and integrity of which constitute a special and vital interest for our peace and safety. His Majesty's Government have been at pains to make it clear in the past that interference with these regions cannot be suffered." Text in International Conciliation Doc. No. 243, "The Pact of Paris" (October, 1928), p. 488.

[128] *The Conduct of Foreign Relations under Modern Democratic Conditions,* p. 9.

[129] *Diplomatic Protection of Citizens Abroad,* p. 447.

[130] Reported in the New York *Times,* August 14, 1933. The destroyers *Taylor* and *Claxton,* which "had been standing by in the vicinity of Key West for some days, cruising with the naval reserves . . . within a short run of Havana" were ordered to that port by naval authorities at the order of President Roosevelt, where they remained during the height of the Cuban crisis.

To determine the effect of the presence of these vessels, several circumstances must be considered. Important among them are: the political relations between the United States and Cuba, especially the implications of the Platt Amendment; the economic relations between the two states, particularly with respect to the commodity, sugar; and the enormous capital investments owned and controlled in Cuba by United States citizens; the relation of the Machado dictatorship to these same political and economic relationships; [131] and the efforts of Mr. Sumner Welles, American Ambassador to Cuba acting with the express, public approval of President Roosevelt, to compose the Cuban difficulties.[132] A study of these relationships sustains the conclusion that the "moral influence exerted by the presence of a war vessel is great."

[131] For an indication of the remarkable tie-up between the Machado Government in Cuba and American sugar and other interests, see the testimony of Mr. Herbert C. Lakin at the *Hearings of the Sub-Committee of the United States Senate Committee on the Judiciary*, 71st Cong., 1st Sess., pursuant to Sen. Res. 20 relating to the investigation of lobbying. Mr. Lakin, who described himself as an American citizen, president of the Cuba Company, a New Jersey holding corporation controlling large sugar-producing subsidiaries and other corporations in Cuba, asserted that he represented "substantially one-half of the sugar that is consumed in the United States." Under Senatorial questioning, he disclosed the intimate contact between himself, the Cuba Company, the Machado Government, and the United States Sugar Association, the American Chamber of Commerce in Cuba which is affiliated with the United States Chamber of Commerce, New York investment houses, the National City Bank and the National City Company, the Hershey Corporation, General Crowder, Colonel Carroll, representing the Cuban Embassy at Washington, and many other Cuban and American interests. Mr. Lakin reported his efforts to influence American legislation and other relations between the United States and Cuba "directly to President Machado." It is impossible in a note, the only space allotted for an observation on this subject, to detail the facts and circumstances brought out in these hearings which relate them to the display of force inherent in the presence of naval vessels in Havana harbor during the Cuban crisis. The reader is directed to the following pages of the testimony before the Senate committee from which his own conclusions on this point may be drawn: pp. 375, 376, 378, 379, 382, 383, 386–392, 1216, 1266, 1267, 1270, 1505–1526, 1560, 1561, 1568–1571, 1573, 1574, 1749. See also on this point Carleton Beals, *The Crime of Cuba*, J. B. Lippincott Company, Philadelphia, 1933.

[132] Particularly as reported in the press during the first fifteen days of August, 1933. See the consecutive issues of the New York *Times* and the New York *Herald-Tribune* for accounts of the situation during this period. The consensus of the press reports indicated quite clearly that the opinion was generally held that President Machado would have to relinquish his office before the efforts of Mr. Welles could succeed in composing Cuba's internal difficulties, if at all.

The display of force has long been a potent weapon in the enforcement of national interests. Political and economic history since the middle of the last century abounds with examples. European nations, grouped loosely (and often haphazardly) in what has been described as "the Concert of Europe," have frequently employed display of force in the Near East, ostensibly to keep the peace of Europe, but often, quite incidentally, to advance and enforce particular national interests.[133] Instances of the employment of a display of force are notorious in the case of China,[134] Africa, and the Caribbean.[135] A general formula covers the majority of cases in which a display of force is operative. It is found in the phrase "for the protection of the lives and property of American citizens," a phrase the substance of which is clothed by numerous forms of expression in diplomatic documents and official assertions of policy. The phrase has become so common, and the "lives and property" of American citizens are so widely scattered over the globe, that it is safe to say that the use of the formula

[133] R. B. Mowat, *The Concert of Europe,* Macmillan, London, 1930. For an excellent treatment of financial aspects of the numerous political manœuvrings for a third of a century before the World War, see Herbert Feis, *Europe: The World's Banker, 1870–1914.* For an excellent example of the operations of a diplomatic threat of force and a display of force in the advancement and enforcement of national interests, see the account of the Agadir crisis in G. Lowes Dickinson, *The International Anarchy, 1904–1914,* pp. 34, 120, 184–213, 368, 379.

[134] Indeed the device of a display of force in China has attained the dignity of a permanent institution, naval forces of a number of powers rarely leaving anchorage in the rivers and off the coast of China. In a broader situation affecting national policies in this area, it was not without some relation to the "moral effect of the presence of a war vessel" that during a tense moment of the Sino-Japanese controversy, practically the whole of the American fleet was concentrated in Pacific waters. See current newspaper accounts of the relation between national interests, diplomacy, and the display of force during this particular period, February 2 to March 5, 1932.

[135] So common a matter has the display of force become in American relations with the countries of the Caribbean that official Government publications can assert a fixed policy in the following words: "In case of a threatened revolution the mere arrival of an American cruiser, flying our flag, is usually sufficient to quiet the disturbance." *What the Navy Has Done for Industry and Commerce,* p. 4. The annual publication, *American Foreign Relations,* is replete with instances testifying to the effect of the mere appearance of an American naval vessel at points of "disturbance." For a specific instance with respect to a display of force concerning Honduras in April, 1932, see note 78, on p. 229.

is likely to accompany almost every serious political or economic disturbance, anywhere in the world. It is one of the principal covering justifications for the use of force in the advancement and enforcement of national interests as currently conceived. It finds dignity and legal sanction in the doctrines of recognized international law.

Many acts of force against other nations may be performed upon American soil and in American territorial waters in the enforcement of national interests. Embraced within the legal conceptions of retorsion and reprisals are acts which apply force in one way or another directly to the nationals and the property of nationals, of other countries. In connection with this aspect of retorsion, such acts are said to consist "in treating the subjects of the state giving provocation in an identical or closely analogous manner with that in which the subjects of the state using retorsion are treated." [136] In something of a like manner, reprisals "are resorted to when a specific wrong has been committed; and they consist in the seizure and confiscation of property belonging to the offending state or its subjects by way of compensation in value for the wrong; or in seizure of property or acts of violence directed against individuals with the object of compelling the state to grant redress; or finally, in the suspension of the operation of treaties." [137]

The forms of reprisals most commonly employed in recent times "consist in an embargo of such ships belonging to the offending state as may be lying in the ports of the state making reprisal, or in the seizure of ships at sea, or of any property within the state, whether public or private. . . ." [138] In short, retorsion and reprisals are devices in the nature of retaliation. They "are *prima facie* acts of war," but, because the state against which they are directed "determines for itself whether the relation of war is set up by them or not," they may not eventuate in a full state of war.[139] This being the case, these acts of retaliation are open to the state as "pacific measures"

[136] Hall, *op. cit.*, p. 433.
[137] *Ibid.*, p. 433.
[138] *Ibid.*, pp. 434–435.
[139] *Ibid.*, p. 434.

since, as a means of avoiding the graver alternative of war, "it must be conceded that anything short of complete war is permissible for sufficient cause." [140] Retorsion and reprisals are not as commonly employed in modern times as they have been in the past, largely owing to changes in the structure of international relationships and in the substance of diplomacy.[141]

It is but a short step from the display of force to the maintenance of a "pacific blockade," to the shelling by a war vessel of some area on the coast of a foreign state, and to the actual landing of forces upon its territory. "Since the beginning of the nineteenth century," writes Hall, "what is called pacific blockade has been not infrequently used as a means of constraint short of war." [142] Like every other practice, he continues, pacific blockade may be abused. "But subject to the limitation that it shall be felt only by the blockaded country, it is a convenient practice; it is a mild one in its effects even upon that country; and it may sometimes be of use as a measure of international police, when hostile action would be inappropriate and no action less stringent would be effective." [143] No instances are recorded showing use of the pacific blockade as such by the United States in the enforcement of national interests; on the contrary, American diplomacy appears reluctant to acquiesce in the employment of such measures. But numerous cases in which French, British, German, and Russian vessels, singly and in various combinations, were engaged in maintaining pacific blockade, have been reported.[144]

[140] *Ibid.*, p. 436. As to whether or not retorsion is regarded by some writers as a means of settling political differences or only to redress legal wrongs, see Hall, sec. 120; Westlake, Vol. II, p. 6, and Hyde, Vol. II, sec. 588.

[141] For a more complete discussion of retorsion and reprisal, the distinctions between them, and the place they fill in the enforcement of national interests, see Oppenheim, Vol. II, pp. 81–86. Borchard, p. 72, indicates that reciprocity relationships between states have been condemned by numerous publicists as a survival of the system of reprisals.

[142] Hall, p. 337.

[143] Hall, p. 441. One of the most important considerations concerning the pacific blockade in modern times, however, is the fact that it is rarely "felt only by the blockaded country," but impinges upon what other states assert to be their "rights."

[144] Hershey (*op. cit.*, p. 539, note 10) asserts that the instances of pacific blockade are said to have been twenty in number, the first reputed to have occurred in 1814 with the Anglo-Swedish blockade of Norwegian ports. Moore considers pacific blockade as "merely a form of reprisal." While giving a num-

Also closely associated with the display of force is the actual bombardment of a coastal area or the military occupation of an inland center. Under a call to the people of San Juan del Norte (Greytown), Nicaragua, to form a constitution, a government was set up and came into power May 1, 1852. Among the first acts of the new government was an order, issued by the City Council on February 8, 1853, to the Accessory Transit Company, an organization composed of citizens of the United States who held a charter from Nicaragua, to remove certain buildings within five days and its entire establishment within thirty days from a portion of land on the north side of the harbor known as Punta Arenas, as the land was needed for public uses. The order was not complied with and on February 21 certain of the buildings were demolished by a party of armed men. Thereafter a sharp controversy between the agents of the Transit Company and citizens of the town developed and continued, it appeared, until May 16, 1854, when an incident occurred in which Mr. Borland, United States Minister to Central America, took part. It is alleged that attempts were made to arrest him.

The United States Government was informed of the state of affairs, and Mr. Marcy, then Secretary of State, notified Mr. Fabens, the United States commercial agent at Greytown, that a man-of-war would be ordered to visit the area. Captain Hollins was ordered to proceed in the U.S.S. *Cyane* with instructions to the following effect: It is very desirable that the people of Greytown "should be taught that the United States will not tolerate these outrages, and that they have the power and the determination to check them. It is, however, very much to be hoped that you can effect the purposes of your visit without a resort to violence and destruction of property and loss of life. The presence of your vessel will, no doubt, work much good. . . ."

Shortly after his arrival on July 12, 1854, Captain Hollins issued a proclamation that if the demands which had been made

ber of examples occurring throughout the nineteenth century, he indicates that there is considerable question as to the status of pacific blockade both in legal theory and in actual practice. Moore, *Digest*, Vol. VII, Sec. 1097, where there also appear examples of the American attitude against approving the use of the pacific blockade.

by Mr. Fabens in a letter of the previous day to the town authorities were not complied with, he would, at 9 o'clock A.M. of the following day, proceed to bombard the town. The demands embraced an immediate payment of $24,000 as an indemnity for injuries to the Accessory Transit Company and for outrages perpetrated on the persons of American citizens and an apology for the indignity to Mr. Borland, together with satisfactory assurances of future good behavior. After waiving aside a protest against the bombardment from the Commander of a British war schooner in the harbor, and after preliminary preparations, including the provision of a vessel to take away such persons as desired to go, Captain Hollins, on failing to receive the satisfaction he demanded from the authorities on shore, opened a bombardment of the town at 9 o'clock on the morning of the 13th. On three separate occasions during the day firing was continued for periods of from one-half to three-quarters of an hour, and at four o'clock, P.M., a force was sent ashore to complete the destruction of the town by fire.

"The execution," says Captain Hollins, "done by our shot and shell amounted to the almost total destruction of the buildings, but it was thought best to make the punishment of such a character as to inculcate a lesson never to be forgotten by those who have for so long a time set at defiance all warnings, and satisfy the whole world that the United States have the power and determination to enforce that reparation and respect due to them as a Government in whatever quarter the outrages may be committed."

In subsequently discussing the incident in his second annual message of December 4, 1854, President Pierce characterized the Greytown settlement as a "pretended community, a heterogeneous assemblage gathered from various countries" which had given other indications of "mischievous and dangerous propensities." He referred to the people involved as "plunderers," and to their habitation as open to treatment in no other way than as a "piratical resort of outlaws or a camp of savages," clearly assuming the position that the inhabitants of Greytown were not, as a body, entitled to be considered as a civilized and responsible community. In such a manner the President justified the enforcement of American national interests by a bombardment which he observed "has been the subject of complaint on the part of some foreign powers." [145]

In most instances a display of force or a naval bombardment is accompanied by some form of actual occupation of the area proceeded against; and this intervention (or to use the milder term, interposition) so called, is one of the principal devices used for the enforcement of national interests. As with other measures of direct force, it is most frequently exercised in practice upon the general ground of "protection for the lives and property of American citizens." [146] That it is a device for the enforcement of national interest can scarcely be doubted. "No State will ever intervene in the affairs of another if it has not some important interest in doing so," writes Oppenheim, "and it has always been easy for such State to find or pretend some legal justification for an intervention, be it self-preservation, balance of power, or humanity." [147] There appears to be but little limitation in "international comity" upon the use of armed forces in interposition and intervention in the affairs of other states. Borchard observes that the practice of states "is at least cumulative evidence in establishing that intervention or the use of arms to collect public loans is a question of power and politics rather than a rule of law." [148]

It is not only with respect to the collection of contractual

[145] For a full account of the incident taken principally from British and Foreign State Papers, see Moore, *Digest*, Vol. VII, Sec. 1168, from which the account in the text above has been drawn.

[146] For a comprehensive discussion of the use of armed forces for protection, see J. Reuben Clark, *Right to Protect Citizens in Foreign Countries by Landing Forces*, United States Department of State Memorandum, Washington, D. C.

[147] Vol. I, *op. cit.*, pp. 271–272. For a discussion of the various kinds of intervention and the conditions under which it has been exercised, see Hall, *op. cit.*, pp. 337–346. Under the titles of "Intervention" (Chapter XIX), "The Monroe Doctrine" (Chapter XX), and "Claims" (Chapter XXI), practically the whole of Vol. VI of Moore, *Digest*, treats of the principles and instances associated with intervention.

[148] *Diplomatic Protection of Citizens Abroad*, p. 314. "The preponderance of authority," he asserts, "favors the view that under certain circumstances intervention to secure the payment of public loans is legitimate. Authorities differ merely as to the nature of the circumstances." *Ibid.*, p. 312. And this appears to be the case despite the fact that it was agreed by the nations assembled at the Second Hague Peace Conference in 1907 not to have recourse, except under certain definite circumstances, to armed force for the recovery of contract debts claimed from the government of one country by the govern-

debts or loans that intervention is a matter of power and politics.[149] Broader grounds have been offered in justifying intervention in state practices. "The grounds upon which intervention has taken place, or upon which it is said with more or less authority that it is permitted, may be referred to the right of self-preservation, to a right of opposing wrongdoing, to the duty of fulfilling engagements, and to friendship for one of two parties in a state."[150] The ground of self-preservation alone includes instances involving "dangers to the institutions, to the good order, or to the external safety of the intervening state."[151] The ground of a "denial of justice" appears to be extensive enough to cover any case in which "lives and property" may have been affected adversely in the opinion of the claimant. Especially does this seem to be true in the light of the keen and practical observation of the jurist, John Bassett Moore: ". . . admitting the propriety and duty of intervention in certain extreme crises, it is always open to a state, influential, designing, and unscrupulous, to foster in another state, subject to moral control, the very condition of things which will, sooner or later, bring about a fit opportunity for its own overt interference."[152] Moreover, "in the present condition of international law, in which states, large and small, have no common superior to control or check them, each state has the legal right of deciding for itself whether the conditions warranting intervention exist."[153]

That intervention is usually employed by "strong" states against "weak" states is not surprising, since an intervention in the affairs of an equal would most likely result in war because intervention, like acts of force in retaliation, is *prima*

ment of another country as being due to its nationals. See J. B. Scott, *Hague Peace Conferences,* Vol. I, Chapter VIII, pp. 386–422 and Vol. II (Documents), pp. 357–361. "In applying the rule of refusing diplomatic interposition in contract claims, the United States has always been careful to limit its strict interpretation to cases entirely free from the qualifying factors of a denial of justice or other tortious element." Borchard, p. 291.

[149] "Careful analysis of the rules of the Law of Nations regarding intervention and the practice of intervention as hitherto used makes it apparent that intervention is *de facto* a matter of policy." Oppenheim, p. 271.

[150] Hall, pp. 338–339.

[151] *Ibid.,* p. 339.

[152] Moore, *Digest,* Vol. VI, p. 4.

[153] Borchard, p. 313.

facie a hostile act.[154] In the case of equals, the state against which such action is taken is not likely to suffer in silence the indignity and the consequences of intervention, but may be expected to resist force by force, with war as the inevitable result.

The fact that intervention occurs so frequently in cases where a "strong" state and a "weak" state are the parties has been explained, however, in another way. Writing on the use of the army and navy for protective functions, Borchard states: "If these measures of constraint are applied by a strong against weak states, it is largely because it is in the latter that the treatment of aliens frequently falls below the standard prescribed by international law and civilized customs, and because in these states local protective agencies, both administrative and judicial, are often deemed unsatisfactory as guarantees of adequate remedies for defects in the measures adopted for the security of life and property." [155] But in view of the fact that even in the so-called "strong" states "the treatment of aliens frequently falls below the standard prescribed by international law and civilized customs," it seems to be the expediency of policy which most frequently accounts for the phenomenon and not some standard based upon well established law or degrees of civilization.[156] Especially is this true in view of the fact that economic practices are indulged in with respect to "weak" states, which, as between "strong" states, would not be countenanced; and that it is such practices that are likely to be sustained by intervention with a view to safeguarding their fruits.[157]

[154] Hall, p. 337.

[155] Borchard, pp. 406, 456.

[156] An incident such as the deliberate assault upon an American citizen by a Nazi storm trooper (see New York *Times,* August 20, 1933, item, "Nazis to Apologize to Us for Beating") may be expiated between "strong" states by an apology and a show of punishment of offending persons in the local courts, but between a "strong" and a "weak" state similar incidents have often ended in forcible interventions, which not infrequently have sought tangible satisfactions going far beyond a mere apology. (Upon the size of claims against "weak" countries, see Hershey, *Amer. Jour. of Int. Law,* Vol. I (1907), p. 44; and in the same proceedings, Latané, p. 137.)

[157] "Recent history has shown that the steps are often short ones from private investments, say in railroad building, in weak countries by nationals of strong countries, to spheres of influence for those strong countries with extra-

The United States has not been a stranger to the protection of its citizens and their interests abroad by force. On more than one hundred occasions, the armed forces of the United States have been landed on foreign soil for the protection of the lives and property of American citizens. "From the Ægean islands to Manchuria and from Mexico to the Falklands, American seamen and marines have been sent ashore to prevent by force of arms the injury of their countrymen wherever these have been endangered, or to exact reparation for wrongs committed against them." The forces employed have ranged from "only a dozen men in a cutter, who chased a piratical schooner ashore, pursued her crew into the hills, and burned the schooner or brought her off as a prize" to the engagement of "American armies of more than three thousand men . . . in long campaigns with the people of foreign states. . . ." [158] Specifically recorded cases, revealing various forms of action from the mere display of force to sustained combat,[159] cover thirty instances between 1813–1865; twenty-two from 1865 to 1899; and twenty-three from the turn of the century to 1927.[160]

During these periods, co-extensive with its growth in commerce and political power, the United States passed through an evolution in the practice of using armed forces abroad from a situation where its naval officers "have . . . the honor to propose" to the Captain General and Governor of Cuba "that your excellency should so far coöperate with me as to sanction the landing, upon the coast of Cuba, of our boats and men"

territorial privileges; from spheres of influence to political control as regards foreign relations; and from political control in foreign affairs to political control in domestic affairs; thus bringing the aggrandizing nation into complete control of the weaker and once independent state." Edwin W. Kemmerer, "The Theory of Foreign Investments," *Annals, Amer. Acad. of Pol. and Soc. Sci.,* November, 1916, p. 2.

[158] Milton Offutt, *The Protection of Citizens Abroad by the Armed Forces of the United States,* p. 1.

[159] " . . . wars if it were not for the fact that the Congress of the United States never recognized them as such by a formal exercise of the unique power to declare war." *Ibid.* In this connection, it should be observed that distinctions are made between intervention for "political" purposes and for "non-political" purposes. Offutt, *ibid.,* pp. 2–4. Yet it is difficult in practice, even in American practice, to sustain such distinctions of theory and of law. Frederick S. Dunn, *The Protection of Nationals,* pp. 87ff, 189, 190.

[160] The specific instances occurring during each of these periods are presented in Offutt, *op. cit.,* Chapters II, III, and IV.

in an action "not intended . . . to infringe upon the territorial rights of your excellency," to the positive declaration that, "this Government does not undertake first to consult the Cuban Government if a crisis arises requiring a temporary landing somewhere to protect life and property on the broad principles of international practice." [161]

Even though by the Paris Pact of 1928 the signatory powers condemned "recourse to war for the solution of international controversies" and renounced war "as an instrument of national policy in their relations with one another," acts of war and activities which are war in all but name still remain in the discretion of the state for the advancement and enforcement of national interests.[162] While in theory it might seem from the text of the Paris Pact that the use of war as an instrument of national policy was voluntarily renounced, it also appears that the renunciation was made in the light of two "principles" of international law, the effect of which is to render the renunciation nugatory in practice. "There is nothing in the American draft of an anti-war treaty which restricts or impairs in any way the right of self-defense," declared Secretary Kellogg in an address delivered on April 28, 1928, before the American Society of International Law; [163] and "every nation is free at all times and regardless of treaty provisions to defend its territory from attack or invasion and it alone is

[161] The comparative attitudes are respectively: the representation of Captain James Biddle to the Captain General and Governor of Cuba, April 30, 1822, and instructions of Secretary of State Knox to the United States Minister at Havana, May 29, 1912, for transmission to President Gomez. Cited in Offutt, *op. cit.*, p. 150.

[162] "It is a fact that without a declaration of war a large area of what was indisputably Chinese territory has been forcibly seized and occupied by the armed forces of Japan, and has in consequence of this operation been separated from and declared independent of the rest of China." From the "Text of the Conclusions of the Lytton Commission on the Manchurian Dispute." New York *Times,* October 3, 1932. See also the further report of the League of Nations Committee of Nineteen which reiterated a statement of the Lytton report that the situation in Manchuria and other parts of the territory of a member of the League was "war in disguise." New York *Times,* February 18, 1933.

[163] The parts of this address bearing upon "self-defense" and other questions concerning the effect of the treaty were incorporated in the note of the Government of the United States and circulated to the several powers concerned in the negotiations. For the text, see International Conciliation, Document No. 243 (October, 1928), "The Pact of Paris," p. 496.

competent to decide whether circumstances require recourse to war in self-defense." [164]

Regardless of theory and of the post-war efforts either to limit or to abolish war and to substitute the pacific instruments of international organization for the arbitrary action of the state, it can scarcely be maintained that resort to war has been abolished—withdrawn from the means which a state may employ in the enforcement of its national interest. For all practical purposes, as well as for the design of the present discussion, this much will have to be conceded; namely, that it is still open to states, in the exercise of their own discretion, to resort to the use of war as the ultimate means at their disposal for the enforcement of their national interests as they conceive them. Whether states possess a "legal right" to go to war or not, remains, in view of post-war practices, an academic question; the fact is that states do resort to activities identical with war, in the "national interest." [165]

SUMMARY

National interest is a prime concern of American statecraft, and, although by indirection, of private enterprise as well. Innumerable public and private agencies are engaged in formulating the policies and conceptions which may be said to constitute and express the national interest; and in interpreting, advancing, and enforcing it, which are all in fact parts of a whole process. Implied in the act of interpretation are the conditions under which the resultant interpretation or conclusion may be sustained by all the means available; while every act of enforcement is itself the expression of a previous interpretation. This is generally true, unless interpretation

[164] It should be observed that Secretary Kellogg's conception of "self-defense" seems to limit acts done under it to defense of a nation's "territory from attack or invasion," a conception much narrower than practice has established under the general "right" of a state to resort to any means deemed necessary by it to insure its "self-preservation."

[165] Clyde Eagleton, "The Attempt to Define Aggression," International Conciliation Doc. No. 264 (November, 1930), pp. 583ff. See also the discussion in International Conciliation Doc. No. 276 (January, 1932), "What Follows the Pact of Paris?" p. 39. Fenwick, *op. cit.*, Chapter XXVI. See Moore, *Digest,* Vol. VII, Chapter XXIII, for the general discussion.

and enforcement are considered separately, in the narrow and popular conception that regards enforcement and police action as synonymous. Common observation of the motives which actuate men and governments compels an acceptance of the broader view of interpretation and enforcement: "police action" is not the whole of the process, but only a special phase of it.

The greater part of the interpretation and enforcement of national interest is a routine process; the operation is not always performed in specific instances, with relation to specific objects, and with clearly defined results in view. The entire development by which interests and "rights" have come into being is itself interpretation and enforcement. Finding expression in all the fields of human thought and action, embodied in custom, crystallized in convention, and forming the very substance of the evolving doctrines and institutions associated with economics, politics, and social intercourse, the interpretation and enforcement of national interests are inherent in the very functions of society. And nothing less than a consideration of the routine actions of men and governments will disclose the means by which national interest is thus enforced. Only after this is done, and the coercive effect of normally accepted routine action is noted and understood, is it possible to comprehend the rôle of enforcement proper, that is, police action.

As already indicated the broader field of private interpretation and enforcement is occupied by the actions of private business enterprises, where conceptions of national interests and of the means to realize them flow rather simply out of economic activities themselves and their traditions. In the process, although remaining a passive force, Government is expected to substantiate private conceptions of the national interest whenever called upon to aid.

But since Government itself is an essential part of routine, it has taken the initiative, and on its account has interpreted, advanced, and enforced what it evidently conceived the national interest to be. Principal among the agencies by which this has been accomplished are the President, the Secretary of State, both Houses of Congress, the Departments of the Government such as State, Army and Navy, Commerce, Treasury, Agriculture, Labor, and various special bodies and commissions which are parts of the political and economic structure of the country. To avoid giving undue length to the discussion, many lesser phases of the subject, such as the semi-public activities of the Federal Reserve system, the influences of the Supreme Court, and other official pressures have not been emphasized where they have been treated at all.

Shading off from the routine activities, by reason of the special conditions and instances thrown up in the course of events, interpretation and enforcement enter the narrower field where diplomacy or negotiation disposes of innumerable conflicts of interest that arise. But some cases involving national interest persist, escape the efforts of diplomacy at composition, and enter upon what may be termed a third stage of interpretation and enforcement—wherein measures are set in motion by the state, which do not impinge directly upon the state proceeded against. Here, by a somewhat negative, indirect process, positive acts in the interpretation and enforcement of national interests are performed. Principal among them are non-intercourse, embargoes, boycotts, forms of retorsion and reprisals, the severance of diplomatic relations, and, under certain conditions, non-recognition.

What may be considered a fourth stage is that in which the state applies measures, involving the use of physical force, operating directly upon the state sought to be influenced or coerced. Such measures cover a wide range, extending from an open threat of force through displays of force, retorsions, reprisals, pacific blockade, bombardment, interposition, and intervention. The fifth and final stage is war.

CHAPTER X

THE HISTORIC SYSTEM OF NATIONAL INTEREST CHALLENGED BY FACT AND POLICY

At the noon of "normalcy," when economists spoke of the high plateau of permanent prosperity, and statesmen, looking upon the fruits of the capitalist system, pronounced it perfect, when European men of affairs were visiting the United States to learn the arts of rationalization, labor management, and commercial promotion—at this noon, a storm burst upon the scene. The great economic machine, which had seemed to function faultlessly under inerrant forces, in an ideal realization of national interest considered in material terms, slowed down to a ruinous pace, spreading bankruptcy, defaults, unemployment, and distress in every direction.

Just when the traditional thesis seemed to be beyond cavil, when the outflow of goods and capital, accompanied by vigorous promotion on the part of the Government, appeared to prove that expanding outlets for "surpluses" were forever possible, came the explosion of 1929 which shattered the fair prospects of endless and profitable advance in all parts of the world. Exports fell off with bewildering rapidity. The stream of capital export almost dried up. With some exceptions foreign bonds in the hands of American investors fell to low levels, and paper to the value of millions went into default,[1] scattering consternation among thousands of American citizens who had been "educated" in foreign bond buying. Imports of raw materials, such as oil and copper, stimulated in a large measure by the activities of American capitalists in Latin America, poured into the United States to depress still further the low prices of domestic products, and Congress, frightened by the havoc, made haste to raise tariff barriers against the

[1] See Appendix.

376

flood of additional supplies. The flow of agricultural produce from Latin America and the Philippines, partly set in motion by American business enterprise, and of other commodities from a number of countries, operating with depreciated currencies, drove prices downward in the markets of the world, adding to the distress of American agriculture which had continued almost unabated since the first post-war panic, and pressed hard upon industry itself, despite the protection of a tariff wall.

Thus what may be called the official thesis of national interest was rudely shaken by inexorable facts. President Taft, President Coolidge, and Secretary Hoover had induced American business men to believe that their very prosperity and security depended on the continuous expansion of foreign trade. American investors had been taught that by lending money abroad they obtained a higher rate of interest for themselves and promoted American interest by enabling foreigners to buy American goods. After having received official approbation of their business methods, American industrialists found themselves precipitated into the most ruinous panic in the history of economic crises—the more widely extended their plants and their credits, the wider the area of reduced production. The larger the expectations of profit, the deeper the sense of defeat. And when official guidance was sought for a way out of the slough of despond, the only answer was an expression of hope that the old course could soon be renewed—the very course which had ended in a devastating *débâcle*. At best this was not promising.

The only answer which the opposition could make at the outset was a promise, none too certain in the light of the conduct of Congress, that "a competitive tariff for revenue" would be established. This remedy, though offered with evident assurance, carried doubts with it. Would a sharp reduction of customs duties actually start up the cycle of production and make possible a continuous expansion of American industrial and agricultural enterprise in the face of powerful nations engaged in the same quest for markets? If so, why had Great Britain, with low duties, been unable to recover fully from the economic depression which overtook her after the collapse of

1920? What reason was there for believing that a deluge of European manufactures would bring "permanent and expanding prosperity" to the United States where warehouses were already full to bursting with identical commodities which could not be sold at home or abroad? Wheat and cotton producers might be benefited for the moment by the exchange of their crops for cheaper manufacturers, but would the advantage last and would it be in the national interest broadly conceived? Finally, in the long run would a general reduction of tariffs throughout the world do more than reduce the competition of industrial nations for markets to a lower price level, without eliminating the internal contradictions of the system which facilitated periodical expansions and explosions? And what tinkering could be done with international monetary exchange, an edifice rarely "stable" in "normal" times, and now completely demoralized by the blows of a world-wide panic?

With the official thesis of national interest bluntly challenged by the facts of commercial paralysis, with the chance for naval supremacy surrendered by concessions to Great Britain and Japan, the several parts of the thesis were now brought under critical review. The procedure of criticism was by no means orderly, or related to any well-knit, accepted conception of national interest. It appeared to respond to exigencies that arose in many quarters, and these concerned practices long embraced within the range of the official thesis of national interest. The simple hypothesis of ever-expanding foreign loans was subjected to a Senatorial inquisition, its elements examined, and the promotional methods associated with it exposed to public gaze. The easy assumption that any immediately profitable enterprise undertaken by an American businessman abroad—whether the construction of a branch factory or the exploitation of natural resources—redounded *ipso facto* to national interest was questioned by the Senate; and the Department of Commerce was directed to make an inquiry into at least one phase of the subject. Finally, the issue of the Eastern Empire, once regarded as closed by the party of McKinley, Roosevelt, Taft, Harding, Coolidge, and Hoover, was raised anew by a powerful demand for the independence of the Philippines made by American agricultural interests;

and an investigation into the economics of the adventure was conducted by committees of the House and Senate. A presentation of data developed at two of these inquiries will be of assistance in disclosing the doubts that arose, the nature of the official and professional attitudes, and the direction in which thought was beginning to turn. One summary deals with the inquiry into the processes and advantages of capital export; the other, with the merits of empire in respect of Philippine policy.

AN INQUIRY INTO NATIONAL INTEREST IN CAPITAL EXPORT

Aroused from its previous indifference by defaults on foreign loans and by the efforts of private creditors to secure a cancellation of the war debts which would strengthen their position, the Senate of the United States authorized a searching inquest into the whole business of foreign lending. During the course of swift expansion in the flush period of the restoration, it had been generally and perhaps carelessly assumed that loans abroad contributed directly and indirectly to the promotion of national interest in general, as distinguished from the interests of banking houses which made profits from underwriting specific loan transactions.[2]

The flow of capital had been explained in general terms. Thus, it was regarded as something like a "natural process" whereby "all foreign investments are the result of the flow of capital from areas where it is comparatively plentiful to those where it is relatively scarce. . . ." The creditor country, it was asserted, gets a higher rate of interest upon its "surplus" funds, secures needed raw materials and foodstuffs, and assures for itself new markets for the excess capacity of its home industries. The debtor country gets the funds which it needs to develop its buying power and resources and so increases its national wealth. Finally, by intensifying the economic interdependence of all countries, the international movement of

[2] "The basic principles of foreign investments are essentially the same as those of home investments. The chief motive power that drives the machinery of both is financial profit." Edwin W. Kemmerer, "The Theory of Foreign Investments," *Annals, Amer. Acad. Pol. and Soc. Science,* Vol. LXVIII (November, 1916), p. 1.

capital is declared to be a powerful force working towards world peace.[3] By making foreign loans, the United States increases its exports.[4] Again, ". . . the food, the raw materials, and the goods of the world move on credit," just as domestic goods move, for example, from the farmer to the consumer upon credit supplied at each step in the process by the banker.[5]

Or capital may move under the special circumstances of a highly elastic demand for goods accompanied by surplus savings which can be invested much more profitably abroad than at home, so that the savings help move the goods; England had enjoyed such conditions in the early stages of its modern economy.[6] Capital may even move abroad owing to the disadvantages in utilizing it at home. Thus Cassel intimates that if capital is forced to stay "at home," the result will be uneconomic use of it (through speculation, etc.), saving will become consuming in uneconomic directions, capital will be recklessly used in public enterprises, and anyway "the whole question of foreign investments is a subject far too complicated for the judgments and decisions of the average politician," who should leave it entirely alone.[7] It is also maintained, after the fashion of German pre-war finance, that large balances held abroad constitute invaluable liquid resources upon which the nation may draw to great advantage in times of stress.[8] These and similar assertions formed the accepted basis upon which capital export was simply assumed to be "in the national interest." Neither in economic literature nor in the public statements of those who made the assumption was there any unequivocal demonstration indicating the exact processes by which the general interest was actually advanced by capital exports; nor

[3] F. Cyril James, "Benefits and Dangers of Foreign Investments," *Annals, American Acad. of Pol. and Soc. Science* (July, 1925), pp. 76-79.

[4] *Trends in the Foreign Trade of the United States.* National Industrial Conference Board, N. Y., 1929, p. 16.

[5] Sir George Paish, "How Tariffs Affect Prosperity," *Annals, American Acad. of Pol. and Soc. Science,* July, 1931, p. 85.

[6] J. M. Keynes, "Foreign Investments and National Advantage," *The Nation* (London), August 9, 1924, p. 586.

[7] Gustav Cassel, *The International Movement of Capital,* Lectures on the Harris Foundation, pp. 50-51.

[8] Thomas Conway, Jr., "Financing American War Orders," *Annals, American Acad. of Pol. and Soc. Science,* Vol. LXVIII (November, 1916), whole No. 157, p. 145.

was a balance sheet presented showing the exact increments in real wealth accruing to the United States from such operations.[9] But the assumption had passed freely like current coin until the Senate investigation took up the issue.[10]

Throughout the inquiry the bankers who gave testimony generally adhered to the historic thesis, that foreign loans are in the national interest. When Senator Reed asked Thomas Lamont, of J. P. Morgan and Company, whether "American commerce has benefited from these loans in any way," Mr. Lamont replied: "Why, Senator Reed, I should think that American commerce had in the long run benefited very greatly by these loans. Of course it is quite arguable that in certain instances the matter of foreign loans has been overdone, but to take the situation as a whole we all know that foreign nations in Europe found themselves after the war denuded as to working capital. That applied to the industries; it applied to a very great many different phases of their situation. And these loans have been designed, as is quite manifest as stated on their face, either for stabilization purposes or to furnish funds that might be used for temporary credit in an attempt to restore the normal course of commerce.[11] We all know that our foreign trade is dependent upon the normality with which those processes can be carried on. And I go so far as to say that not only have they contributed very materially to our prosperity during those years of our foreign trade, but that they have contributed very materially to the capacity of the borrowing governments to enable them to discharge their obligations when due, and punctually, to the United States Government." [12]

Otto Kahn, witness for Kuhn, Loeb, and Company, went beyond the mere contention that foreign loans contributed to

[9] For a general "balance" sheet, see Lawrence Dennis, *Is Capitalism Doomed?* pp. 221–223.

Most of the views on the international movement of capital as given in the text above, as well as additional explanations in the "orthodox" tradition, are set forth in the small volume by Hartley Withers, *International Finance*.

[10] *Hearings on the Sale of Foreign Bonds and Securities in the United States,* before the Senate Committee on Finance, pursuant to S. Res. 19, 72d Cong., 1st Sess., Washington, 1931–1932; hereinafter referred to as *Senate Hearings.*

[11] See Appendix below, p. 556, for use of loans.

[12] *Senate Hearings,* I, p. 45.

the prosperity of the United States. That prosperity, he thought, was the controlling consideration: "Whether a man is an international banker or engaged in any other business, as long as he resides and works in, and owes allegiance to, America, his object is and must be beyond all other things America's prosperity, not merely from the point of view of a patriotic and decent citizen, but from the point of view of his own pocket. The international *banker's* profit, even in the case of foreign bonds, is made in this country and not abroad. European prosperity is desirable. America's prosperity is vital and indispensable." [13]

Yet neither in his testimony nor in his *Memorandum* submitted on the controlling policy of his Company with respect to foreign loans did Mr. Kahn give any statements, data, or balance sheets indicating that in reality foreign loans were governed by the paramount consideration of American prosperity or interest first of all. Indeed, the opening sentence of the *Memorandum* stated precisely: "Our primary consideration in any foreign loan, as it would be in any domestic loan, is to endeavor to appraise from the facts obtainable the intrinsic merit of the bonds to be issued and consequently estimate the assurance of their principal and interest and sinking funds, if any, being punctually paid when due." [14] This is undoubtedly what is called "good business practice," and is based upon the safe assurance of profits, but it presents no desiderata showing that loans are primarily made with a view to contributing to American prosperity, or advancing the national interest, no matter how that may be currently interpreted.

Although the Senate committee did not probe beneath the surface of Mr. Lamont's generalizations or the contentions of Mr. Kahn, it was somewhat more penetrating when Charles E. Mitchell, of the National City Bank and Company of the same name, made a similar sweeping assumption. "Foreign investments," said Mr. Mitchell, "very largely control the volume of export business of the United States. They should have, therefore, a sound basis of desirability to the most critically patriotic of Americans; and the fact that the banking in-

---

[13] *Senate Hearings*, II, p. 397; italics mine.
[14] *Ibid.*, II, p. 355.

terests of this country have floated foreign loans in America is
something which should have the praise rather than the criticism of any body of men." This broad statement was brought
under scrutiny in the following colloquy:

> *Senator Couzens.* You say $6,000,000,000 has been invested in for-
> eign countries, and I was wondering what proportion of that amount
> was used to produce goods that had heretofore been made in America.
> *Mr. Mitchell.* That I cannot answer, sir. . . .
> *Senator Couzens.* Is it not a fact that American industries have gone
> to foreign countries, including Canada, Great Britain, Germany, and
> France, to manufacture, in order to avoid having to pay the current
> tariff there?
> *Mr. Mitchell.* That is quite true; yes.
> *Senator Couzens.* You do not know what percentage that is of the
> $6,000,000,000?
> *Mr. Mitchell.* No sir; that I cannot answer from these figures.

While the bankers clung tenaciously to their theory that
foreign loans promoted national interest in general, a challenge was issued from industrial quarters. During the same
hearings, Francis P. Garvan lodged with the Committee a
protest against the extension of financial assistance to alien
competitors. He spoke for the Chemical Foundation, which, he
alleged, was "instituted by the United States Government to
encourage chemical industry and research for the protection
of the people of the United States in their national defense,
in their public health, and in the improvement of their standard of living."

Mr. Garvan attacked the whole policy of lending money to
foreign governments and concerns and thus building up with
American resources great industries abroad to compete with
American industries in domestic and foreign markets. "The
only defense these bankers have been able to suggest for themselves," he said, "is that they were encouraging foreign trade.
Your Commerce Department will expose this fallacy in detail
to you, but the whole fallacy appears in the fact that Germany's export trade today, with her natural resources and
only sixty millions of peoples, has been built up under these
foreign loans until it equals our own export trade, with our
natural resources and our one hundred and twenty millions of

peoples—she, the borrower, and we, the lender!" Coming directly to the chemical industry, Mr. Garvan declared that "these international bankers . . . have been persistently borrowing the savings of the American people and, for the bribe of huge commissions, have been loaning these savings to the international chemical cartel, or its constituent companies or allies, the cartel whose success is necessarily based upon the destruction of our industry and our independence." These generalities he then illustrated by appending a list of American loans to foreign competing chemical concerns.[15]

In another relation, the bankers' thesis was attacked—on the ground that foreign loans restricted the capital available to American industry and agriculture and raised the rate of interest on their borrowings. During the hearings, Senator Harrison asked Clarence Dillon, of Dillon, Read, and Company, whether the export of capital did not contract credit at home and exert an influence in slowing up domestic enterprise. Mr. Dillon answered: "I do not know at the moment of any demand for money by borrowers for the development of industry, for the sale of their goods, that is not being met." Senator Harrison pressed the point and Mr. Dillon countered again by saying: "I should think that if the credit were demanded and needed in this country it would be used in this country. The only credit that is available for foreign loans is the surplus of credit in this country."[16] Mr. Dillon continued to insist that the capital exported is "surplus" capital.

But members of the Senate committee, with equal insistence, argued that it was the higher rate of interest on foreign loans, not a domestic surplus, that was responsible for the outward movement of capital. Senator Gore renewed the inquiry: "Did that rate of interest have anything to do with our money going abroad, regardless of whether there was a surplus of credits in this country or not?"

> *Mr. Dillon.* I should say not.
> *Senator Gore.* And if you were offered a 5 per cent loan in this country and a 7 per cent loan abroad, you accept the lower rate of interest unless there is a surplus to respond to the 7 per cent rate?

[15] *Senate Hearings,* II, pp. 528ff.
[16] *Ibid.,* pp. 450ff.

Mr. Dillon. If there is a demand for money in this country and you can get equally good security abroad at a higher rate, why, the demand in this country would probably have to meet that rate.

Senator Gore. So it is not always a question of surplus. It is somewhat a question of the rate.

Mr. Dillon. No, it is a question of surplus, because this country would use its own money.

Senator Gore. If you call anything credit that goes abroad, regardless of circumstances or as to surplus, then of course that ends it. That is a mere matter of definition.

Mr. Dillon. I think it is, quite. . . .

Senator Gore. You would keep it [capital] here and lend it at a lower rate of interest unless it entered some sort of definition of surplus.

Mr. Dillon. I do not think you could get it here at a lower rate. I do not know how you would control that.

Senator Gore. That is the point.

Senator Couzens. It would automatically raise the rate in this country.[17]

Unquestionably the discussion during the Senate hearings, though somewhat tortuous, struck near the center of the problem. Capital, as described in the bankers' testimony, is a kind of international fluid. It flows to and fro without reference to national boundaries, unless impeded by actions of State. Where the demand is greater, the interest rate is higher and capital flows in the direction of the higher rate. In this connection international bankers appear as merchants, mediators; they are not governed primarily by considerations of national interest, but by the movement of capital in response to demand and interest rates. Nor are they particularly concerned as bankers about the use of the money they transfer as long as the security and the underwriters' profits are satisfactory. Whether it is devoted to war or peace, to production that competes with domestic industries, to governmental extravagance, or to the development of non-competing enterprises, is not their concern as bankers, whatever may be their private opinions or their individual practices with respect to particular loans. In theory, and to a large extent in historic practice, the movement of capital is as impersonal as the flow of the tides.[18]

---

[17] *Senate Hearings,* II, pp. 454ff.

[18] "Capital . . . has no sentiment. It is determined in its choice of a home by no other considerations than those of gain and security. Accordingly,

While this conception of international finance as a natural force responding to the impact of other natural forces runs through the testimony of the bankers during the Senate hearings, it is repeatedly countered by their own evidence respecting particular operations. Fundamentally it rests upon the old hypothesis of the classical school; namely, that economics is primarily concerned with the production of wealth by private enterprise and the distribution of wealth among individuals without intervention by the State. As far as international finance is concerned this theory never did square with the facts in the case. In cold truth the international movement of capital on any noteworthy scale began with the financing of kings engaged in carrying on dynastic wars, and it extended rapidly as dynastic conflicts widened into the commercial and territorial wars of states. It was not early associated with private enterprise or the production of wealth, to any considerable extent, and from the beginning it was subject more or less to the will of monarchs and ruling groups in particular countries. By the data produced at the Senate hearings it was abundantly demonstrated that a large part of the money gathered from American investors and sent abroad by the bankers did not flow "naturally" into "natural" economy, but was deflected hither and yon by the political decisions of foreign governments. The revelations of the witnesses were confirmed by other materials supplied by the Federal Government about the same time.

manufactures are freely transplanted from England to Belgium, or America, or India, without regard to the interests of the English people, the merchant navy of a state entering upon a war is transferred without delay to a neutral flag, and it constantly happens that a belligerent power is supplied with arms or food or money from its enemy." To this the following note is appended: "Two remarkable instances of that may be quoted from the history of the great war with France when feeling on both sides was strained to the uttermost. Rothschild having to transmit £800,000 to the Duke of Wellington, sent it through France (*Life of Buxton*, p. 289). Bourrienne, being ordered to provide 16,000 military cloaks, 37,000 jackets, and 200,000 pairs of shoes for the French army before the campaign of Eylau, procured them from England through a Hamburg house (*Mémoires de Bourrienne*, tome vii, chap. xx). In the first case, Frenchmen smuggled eight tons of gold through France to supply the needs of an army fighting against their own countrymen. In the second instance, whole factories in England must have been employed upon what— in the case of the jackets and cloaks, at least—everyone knew to be military equipment for the use of the enemy." Charles H. Pearson, *National Life and Character*, p. 184.

According to the *New Estimate of American Investments Abroad,* issued by the Department of Commerce in 1931, at the end of 1930 the private long-term American investments abroad, as distinguished from intergovernmental debts, were placed at $15,000,000,000 approximately. Of this amount $7,840,810,000 came under the head of "direct" investments in industrial and commercial enterprises abroad, and $7,204,-218,000 under the head of "portfolio" investments which included the bonds of foreign governments, central and local. The total obligations of foreign governments (exclusive of the "war debts") [19] held in the United States at this time amounted roughly to $5,000,000,000.[20] Of the American portfolio investments in Europe at the end of 1930, totalling $3,460,629,000, $894,100,000 was in private corporations in Europe and the balance was in governmental securities.

Undoubtedly a large part of the money lent to European governments was devoted to undertakings that may be classified under productive national economy: indeed, $632,194,000 worth of the governmental securities was classified as "government-guaranteed corporate investments." But the borrowings of governments, it is notoriously known, are not entirely controlled, as those of private business enterprises, by the prospect of creating wealth and earning profits in the process. Reasons of state which are not economic enter into calculations in this sphere. Particular governments temporarily in power may borrow to relieve themselves of the perils of heavy taxation, to entrench themselves or their parties in authority, to provide money for political purposes, and to accomplish other objectives which may or may not be to any national or international interest. Germany, for example, borrowed heavily in the United States to meet the requirements of the Dawes and Young plans growing out of the war indemnities imposed by the Versailles

[19] For further statistics on the total obligations of foreign governments (other than war debts) held in the U.S., see the Appendix.

[20] The computed total of foreign government obligations, set forth in the Department of Commerce study cited above, is $4,895,970,000. Adjustments for Chinese and Mexican obligations, omitted from this total, and deductions on account of the international securities movement, would confirm, roughly, the round estimate of 5,000,000,000 dollars used in the text. In addition to this amount, the sum of $1,188,413,000 is classified as Government-guaranteed Corporate.

Treaty, which, whatever its merits or demerits, had little or nothing to do with the so-called "natural course of productive economy."

Hence it appears that the export of capital is determined in part at least by the political policies; indeed often by the desperation of ruling groups in power in particular countries, without reference to the normal demand or the normal rate of interest in the realm of productive economy—or any consideration other than, perhaps, their willingness to promise high rates of interest to assure a flow of funds for the purposes they are eager to consummate. Nor were the international bankers who gave testimony before the Senate Committee impersonal watchers of financial currents, responding like the needle to the pole star of demand for loans. They themselves were active agents, at all events in many cases, in stimulating and creating the demand which they supplied. While some of the international banking houses apparently solicited no loan business from foreign governments, others maintained agents or agencies abroad engaged in negotiations with the officers of governments for the purpose of securing opportunities to float political obligations. The latter thus encouraged governments, central and local, to go into debt, to divert capital from the world pool into political enterprises, more or less productive, or not productive at all. This was particularly true in countries where political conditions were precarious, risks were great, and the commissions and interest rates correspondingly high. In one case, a New York banking house paid a large sum to a group of promoters who arranged for lending money to Peru—a group that included Juan Leguía, son of the President of Peru of the time the deal was consummated, and transferred to this local politician the sum of $415,000 for his "services" in connection with the undertaking.[21]

Illuminating glimpses into the methods of the less conservative banking houses in "stirring up business" in foreign loans are provided by the Senate hearings;[22] and the actuating motive is lucidly expounded by Frederick J. Lisman, an investment banker of forty years' experience in investment financing.

[21] *Senate Hearings*, III, pp. 1267ff.
[22] *Ibid.*, III, pp. 1267–1928.

Senator Johnson. Were there others who were competing with you for the loan there [Peru]?

Mr. Lisman. We understood that there were several banking houses there.

Senator Johnson. All of them trying to get the loan from the Peruvian Government?

Mr. Lisman. As usual.

Senator Johnson. That is so, all over Latin America?

Mr. Lisman. It was so during the period from 1925 to 1928, all over, I would say.

Senator Johnson. Seeking in every way to obtain such loans as you could for flotation here?

Mr. Lisman. To satisfy the public demand for securities. . . .

Senator Johnson. That was the sole purpose?

Mr. Lisman. Well, bankers do not knowingly float bad loans. But the purpose is to do a good business at a profit.

Senator Johnson. That is the main reason?

Mr. Lisman. The first essence of business is legitimate profit.

Senator Johnson. Exactly; and the desire was to obtain loans or induce loans to be made and then float them here at a profit. That was pursued by all the houses, was it not?

Mr. Lisman. Yes. I do not believe that there are many houses that would take up a piece of business that they did not think was good. They were all very keen to get business and bid against each other, and they had agents all over the world. I heard a good many amusing stories on that subject.[23]

None of the evidence adduced at the hearings revealed the existence of any comprehensive policy formulated by bankers for the purpose of controlling loans in respect of productive economy or national interest. A microscopic examination of the 2179 pages of testimony and documents yields no clue to the problem.

On the contrary, it shows all the banking houses operating mainly as merchants, conservative or reckless, considering each loan on its merits with reference to security and profits, and assuming more or less vaguely, where they thought at all, that loans "contributed to the prosperity of the United States." Even the distinguished specialist in banking and finance, Professor E. W. Kemmerer, while he often urged the foreign governments for which he worked to use loans "for productive public works that would be self-supporting in the main," ap-

---

[23] *Senate Hearings,* III, p. 1775.

parently did not make any statistical calculations showing that loans so used would promote the national interest of the United States.

Nor was he able to present to the Senate Finance Committee any plan for controlling foreign loans in the future with reference to the national interest. He recognized, he said, that these loans "are affected with a tremendous public interest. When they get into our commercial banks, our savings banks, when they become investments of trustees for widows and orphans, and become parts of the endowments of our educational and public welfare institutions and are bought by our life-insurance companies, the value of these bonds becomes affected with a great public interest, not only in our international relations, but in our own national affairs as well." But when asked by Senator Johnson to suggest a policy of public control in that interest, Professor Kemmerer confessed: "I have no conclusion except the feeling that something should be done." What, how, by whom, and with reference to what conception of public interest, he did not venture to explain.[24]

In short, the evidence presented at the hearings here under review does not furnish statistical or any other data to support the assertion of witnesses to the effect that the export of capital in general benefited "in the long run" the commerce of the United States—worked in the national interest realistically conceived. Was it in the interest of national economy to supply foreign industries with capital which made it possible for them to employ cheap labor and to compete still more vigorously with American industries in every quarter of the globe as well as in the United States? In what way did the loans which directly or indirectly aided in rehabilitating German chemical industry and German shipping contribute to the prosperity of the American chemical industry, protected by tariffs, and American shipping, subsidized by mail contracts at the expense of the public? If, as Mr. Lamont asserted, American capital helped to stabilize the governments of Europe and aided in creating the "normality" favorable to commerce, by what criteria can it be determined that the artificial stimulation furnished by American capital did more than postpone and

[24] *Senate Hearings,* III, pp. 1694ff.

intensify the crisis which came in 1929? To such questions the testimony of the bankers before the Senate committee supplied no positive answer—nothing except guesses and opinions.

Looking at the other side of the shield, did the contribution of these loans "to the maintenance during those years of our foreign trade" really redound to the economic interest of the United States in the long run? Was it really in the national interest to have the enormous domestic inflation and plant extension "during those years of foreign trade"? The testimony of those who defended the lavish export of capital provided no invincible answers to these questions either. The whole business was economic and if so then a statistical demonstration was feasible; or it was a matter of surmises, hopes, expectations, and ideology on which science could get no hold whatever. The national interest, expert witnesses declared, is promoted by the export of capital, but none of them proved it in general or particular.

In the writings of economists and publicists only general and theoretical explanations of the relation of foreign trade to the national interest were advanced. One or two of these will suffice to illustrate the reasoning followed by experts. "The United States," wrote Professor Harry T. Collings, long accomplished in the economics and practices of foreign trade, "produces more iron, copper, petroleum, coal, and cotton . . . than any other nation, and more than it needs for home consumption. . . . We have an aptitude for the use of machinery, a genius for its invention, and an indefatigable energy for organization which sweeps away all barriers to accomplishment. . . . How can we utilize these advantages to the full when our domestic market does not, and of necessity cannot, absorb at reasonable prices the total products of our potential energy? Only by consistent cultivation of the foreign market." [25] As a matter of plain business, maintained Dr. H. Parker Willis, it is necessary to get our foreign trade back, because "our plants have developed a manufacturing capacity that is very far ahead of our domestic consumption." According to Dr. Willis

[25] "The Basis of International Trade," *Annals, American Acad. of Pol. and Soc. Science*, January, 1929, p. 9. Many of the classical arguments in behalf of the desirability of foreign trade are set forth on pp. 9–10 of this article.

we have arrived at a very curious dilemma. "We do not want any more foreign bonds here than are absolutely necessary; certainly there are enough of them here now. And yet, if we do not accept them, how can we go on with this trade, which we have developed to a point where it must have a foreign outlet?" [26]

Another dilemma—between the operations of foreign investment and those of foreign trade—was also brought to light. "We have loaned abroad $16,000,000,000 of private investments. . . . How can we receive interest and the payment of principal on these foreign investments? There is only one way—through the importation of foreign goods and services. We need protection for our manufacturers, but can we slap in the face our investors in the foreign field?" [27] To these were added the voices of such distinguished publicists as Arthur Salter,[28] Raymond B. Fosdick,[29] and others, who, like them, spoke in broad and general terms emphasizing the "international" point of view.

These opinions and the theories they raised were not universally accepted, however. Other experts took up the challenge, with increasing vigor after the business recession intensified the violent collapse commencing in the fall of 1929. The voices of Frederic C. Howe,[30] Robert W. Dunn,[31] Dean Wallace B. Donham,[32] and J. M. Keynes at a much earlier date,[33] were raised in questioning doctrines and practices which seemed to be carrying everything before them. Many of the disserta-

---

[26] "A Tariff Policy for The Future," *Annals, American Acad. of Pol. and Soc. Science*, July, 1931, pp. 95, 97.

[27] Harry T. Collings, "International Problems of the Tariff," *Annals, American Acad. of Pol. and Social Science*, July, 1929, p. 77. Compare this with the situation previously described by Mr. Collings above, where our excess of productivity demands "cultivation of the foreign market."

[28] In the book *Recovery: The Second Effort*. Just what is to be "recovered" does not appear. The state of things in 1913?

[29] "Studies in World Economy." No. 1, International Conciliation Document No. 267 (February, 1931), Carnegie Endowment, N. Y. See also, New York *Times*, November 30, 1930, item: "The Ailing World: Two Able Diagnoses."

[30] "Some Overlooked Dangers in Foreign Investment," *Annals, American Acad. of Pol. and Soc. Science*, July, 1928.

[31] "Foreign Investments and Imperialism." *Ibid.*

[32] In the book, *Business Adrift*.

[33] "Foreign Investments and National Advantage." *Op. cit.*

tions on foreign trade and investments utilized the same principles to reach directly contrary conclusions. Very often it was possible to observe the inconsistencies in one argument become the affirmative supports of an opposing argument and vice versa. Nowhere, except in perhaps the broadest terms,[34] did any positive criteria related to a consistent conception of national interest rise transcendent above the medley of confused counsels.

Similar uncertainty with respect to national interest appeared in the investigation of the branch factory movement, conducted by the Department of Commerce in compliance with a Senate resolution,[35] which resulted in a report published early in 1931.[36] Among other things, one of the principal inquiries proposed by Senator David I. Walsh, when he presented the resolution referred to, was that ". . . this investigation . . . [should] . . . disclose the extent to which American capital invested in manufacturing in Europe constitutes a new competitive menace, directly or indirectly, to the industries carried on in the United States. . . ." The Secretary of the Department, in his letter of transmittal, stated that the document "obviously does not furnish an answer to all the questions raised by the Senate resolution," and then confessed that in the matter of the fundamental issue it produced no conclusions. "In view of the constantly increasing exports of the commodities figuring largely in the branch-factory movement, it is impossible to ascertain the effect of the branch factories on our export trade. It is quite evident, however, that there is a certain amount of competition between the branch factories and the parent plants in the United States as regards neutral mar-

[34] Such as the following, for example: "We are told that we are getting rich because we have given other countries fourteen billions of wealth and have taken in exchange fourteen billions of promises to pay. . . . The thing that is unseen is that we are in reality poorer by fourteen billions of real wealth and richer, if we may be termed richer, by I.O.U.'s of governments, cities and individuals for that amount." Howe, "Some Overlooked Dangers in Foreign Investment." *Op. cit.*, p. 19. See also the "balance" sheet set up by Lawrence Dennis in the book *Is Capitalism Doomed?*

[35] Senate Res. 128 of September 30 (calendar day, October 5), 1929, 71st Cong., 1st Sess.

[36] Sen. Doc. 258, *American Branch Factories Abroad.* 71st Cong., 3d Sess., January 22 (calendar day, January 23), 1931.

kets. The full extent of this competition cannot be ascertained from trade statistics which make no distinction between various commodities on the basis of the financial control of the plant in which they originate. The movement is intimately connected with the general industrial development of the United States and its future progress is likely to be determined primarily by the availability of capital and the economic policies of foreign countries." [37] In other words, the Department of Commerce found itself unable to answer a leading question pertaining to national interest in a single form of export promotion: What is the effect of the branch-factory movement on the domestic economy of the United States or on the outlets for American goods?

OFFICIAL ACTION ON FOREIGN LOANS SUBJECTED
TO SCRUTINY

The same hearings which demonstrated that leading financiers engaged in floating foreign loans had no reasoned conception of national interest but were guided by the instant need of things revealed a similar confusion among the promoting agencies of the Federal Government. During the boom years, when American capital was flowing out by the billions to all parts of the world, that Government, though presumably safeguarding national interest through its various Departments, particularly of State and Commerce, displayed no assured and consistent policy with respect to the economic content of national interest. In general, the Departments of State and Commerce appeared to proceed on the theory that, as a rule, they possessed no authority to take the initiative in checking loans, but could act in such a matter only when a specific case was brought to their attention by private parties or by the representatives of foreign governments. Thus official action might be taken on matters of slight importance because they were raised elsewhere; while issues of immense significance might be allowed to follow their own course—often to ruin. Each case apparently stood on its own bottom.

In the Senate hearings the controlling processes were abun-

[37] *American Branch Factories Abroad*, p. iii.

dantly revealed. Referring specifically to Bolivian loans, now in default, Grosvenor M. Jones, chief of the finance and investment division of the Bureau of Foreign and Domestic Commerce, explained how the question of expediency was treated: "The matter of these loans was frequently the subject of conversation between the economic adviser of the State Department, who handled them in the first instance for the State Department, and with persons in the Department of Commerce and in the Treasury Department, who were deputed to pass on them in the first instance for those departments. . . . As each loan came up—well, in many cases, I won't say in every case, but in many cases—the merits of the loan would be the subject of more or less discussion between the economic adviser and myself; not that it made a great deal of difference, except along the particular points that have been enunciated as a part of our foreign loan policy, but, sort of entre nous, speaking as man to man, we would exchange views as to whether we thought a certain government was overborrowing, or whether these loans looked good to us. I suppose we were amateur international bankers." [38] By such informal methods, official decisions, if any, were reached.

Whenever federal officials, working within the narrow limits imposed upon them, came to the conclusion that particular exports of capital were really contrary to national interest, in the sense that they were unsound loans, there were difficulties in the way of making conclusions public. The diplomatic difficulties are obvious. Equally troublesome are possible repercussions in the financial world. Hence circumspection, if not timidity, prevails—as is usual with a bureaucracy. In the autumn of 1928, for example, the Bureau of Foreign and Domestic Commerce, on the basis of concrete information, decided that Bolivia was in a perilous financial condition, but it could only publish a bulletin setting forth the salient economic facts in the situation, leaving the reader to draw his own inferences, if he could. This document was issued with the consent of the State Department and, though prudently and carefully worded, "created quite a little stir in New York." About the same time adverse findings were also made with

[38] *Senate Hearings*, II, p. 724.

respect to Colombia and published.[39] These findings did not seem to have any effect on practice. After the discovery had been made, three American banks gave Colombia a short-term credit of $20,000,000.[40] No establishment of the Government assumed that it had a right to take any initiative in protecting American investors.[41]

In fact, the State Department, under its system, felt compelled to intervene for the purpose of bringing about the last payment of the $20,000,000 credit after it knew that Colombian finances were in a dangerous condition, because, it alleged, the Colombian Government expressed a desire for the extension of the promised credit to the American diplomatic representative in Bogotá and the latter had cabled an official opinion to the State Department. Only from an outside stimulus, it was contended, could the State Department be correctly set in motion to negotiate with American bankers—to urge them to complete their contract. When asked by Senator Johnson whether the Department had in fact endeavored to straighten out differences over a particular loan between bankers and the Colombian government and yet done nothing to protect the American investors in general who had put $100,000,000 into Colombian bonds, the assistant chief of the Division of Latin American Affairs, answered in the affirmative. The question of the bonds in the hands of American investors had not come before the Department officially for action, and it was powerless to take the initiative in execution of its own policy if it had one.[42]

In this connection, it must be noted, however, that the State Department adopted a procedure calculated to subject international finance to a benchmark set up with reference to one phase of the public interest. In March, 1922, the following statement was issued: "At a conference held last summer between the President, certain members of the cabinet, and a number of investment bankers, the interest of the Government in the public flotation of issues of foreign bonds in the

[39] *Ibid.*, II, p. 727–728.
[40] *Ibid.*, II, p. 728.
[41] *Ibid.*, II, pp. 729ff.
[42] *Ibid.*, III, p. 1799. What actually went on behind the scenes in the State Department can only be surmised. O'Connor, *Mellon's Millions*.

American market was informally discussed, and the desire of the Government to be duly and adequately informed regarding such transactions before their consummation, so that it might express itself regarding them if that should be requested, or seem desirable, was fully explained. Subsequently the President was informed by the bankers that they and their associates were in harmony with the Government's wishes and would act accordingly. . . . Responsible American bankers will be competent to determine what information they should furnish and when it should be supplied. . . . The Department of State cannot of course require American bankers to consult it. . . . The Department believes that in view of the possible national interests involved it should have the opportunity of saying to the underwriters concerned, should it appear advisable to do so, that there is or there is not objection to any particular issue." [43]

In this statement, and in the subsequent practice of the State Department in conformity with it, there is the attempt to apply a criterion—"the possible national interests involved" —to the flotation of foreign loans in the United States. Nowhere did the State Department, however, supplement the general principle by providing the substance of the criterion intended to be applied. The "content" of "national interest" was not described or explained; and with this important omission tolerated from the start, the State Department proceeded to put the rule into practice. In the face of the details of the Colombian loan given above, and of the more eloquent testimony of fact supplied by the general state of the foreign security market after 1929, it would be redundant to marshal additional details concerning the fate of this attempt.

Yet, experience and practice in the case of certain German loans make a sufficiently interesting contribution to knowledge of the course of events under the practice of the State Department to warrant further reference. In a study devoted exclusively to German loans,[44] Robert R. Kuczynski found

[43] State Department Press Release, March 3, 1922. This and subsequent press releases bearing upon the same subject may be found in Kuczynski, *Bankers' Profits from German Loans,* Appendix E, Docs. Iff. Brookings Institution, Washington, D. C., 1932.

[44] *Bankers' Profits from German Loans.*

that: "American bankers have repeatedly been warned by American officials as to the safety of German borrowings; but these warnings were directed almost exclusively against loans to German states and municipalities." [45] To the Dawes loan, the Department of State offered "no objection." In the matter of the loan to the State of Bremen, proposed by the Guaranty Company, of New York, the State Department, while refraining from expressing its views, intimated a mild warning.[46] Notwithstanding the warning, the loan was floated. As to the dollar loans to private German enterprise, the State Department used the "no objection" formula. In the case of loans to German public agencies, it qualified this negative assent by calling attention to the relation of the proposed loan to the Versailles Treaty and the Dawes Plan.[47] From October, 1926, until July, 1929, the Department of State wrote letters to the bankers, calling attention to the large amount of American credits to Germany.[48] After the publication of the report of the Young Committee, the Department used the same brief formula then adopted for other foreign loans, namely, "The Department is not interested in the proposed financing." [49]

The responses of the bankers, for whom these warnings were intended, took many different forms. In some instances, bankers explained away, at least to their own satisfaction, the conditions on which the warnings were based. Often they settled any doubts by the covering phrase, "loans for productive purposes." In other instances they appeared to turn the warnings to their own advantage (as something in the nature of protective coverings) by inserting the doubts about the status of the loan in the prospectus apprising the public of technical conditions out of which difficulty might possibly arise.[50] But the financing was not interrupted merely on account of the advisability here and there of justifying some particular issue.

[45] *Ibid.*, p. 7

[46] *Ibid.*, pp. 7–9.

[47] *Ibid.*, p. 9.

[48] *Ibid.*, pp. 10–11. Warnings of a like character were made on various occasions by S. Parker Gilbert, Agent General for Reparation payments. *Ibid.*, pp. 12–17.

[49] *Ibid.*, p. 11.

[50] *Ibid.*, pp. 18–31.

Thus when a grave crisis in international economy, spreading ruin among American investors, forced an inquiry into the operations carried on under the presumed sanction of national interest, the bankers involved and the government officials concerned stood revealed in stark reality. The former contended that their transactions benefited American economy—promoted the national interest, but produced no evidence to prove their allegations. The latter, who were supposed to be dominated by "practical conceptions of national interest," to employ the language of a former Secretary of State, confessed that they had no reasoned policy of national interest in respect of capital export; and that, even if such a policy had existed in government circles, the limitations of their offices and their methods would not permit them to apply it save in particular cases set in motion by outside representations. The one attempt to set up a benchmark met with failure. Instead of precision in knowledge, statistical demonstrations in fact, consistency in policy, there appeared confusion, surmises, and contradictions.

THE ADVANTAGE OF EMPIRE DRAWN IN QUESTION

The movement of economic forces, stimulated by government promotion under an official thesis of national interest, which culminated in the disruption of commercial expansion abroad, revived on a more substantial basis the opposition to the Eastern Empire which William McKinley and Theodore Roosevelt had established in the Philippines. In the days of William Jennings Bryan, the agrarian antagonism to imperialist operations had been founded on more or less abstract considerations; but the tariff policy which pumped American capital and manufactures into the Philippines drew agricultural produce from them and created a competition that was keenly felt in powerful sections of American agriculture. Overseas empire had once been regarded as contrary to Jeffersonian traditions; now it was introducing into the American market commodities which slashed into the already depressed economy of agriculture. So, despite the opposition of the State Department, the War Department, and the Republican administration in general, the question of the Philippine independence was revived, with a stubborn insistence that could not be suppressed; and during the discussion of the issue it was made perfectly evident that the decision had to turn fundamentally on a conflict of economic interests within the United States and that the policy of the restoration effected in 1921 was to be challenged in another important direction.

In the winter and spring of 1930 a series of congressional hearings was held on various bills and resolutions, pertaining to the Philippine question.[51] The witnesses who made statements and gave testimony fall into six groups: officials of the Federal Government, official spokesmen for the independence movement in the Philippines, representatives of American commercial interests operating in the Philippine trade, representatives of American agricultural interests protesting against the competition of Philippine commodities admitted to the United States free of tariff duty, representatives of American labor objecting to the competition of Philippine labor, and a few miscellaneous individuals, including journalists and other persons more or less informed with respect to the issues in hand. Their testimony was supplemented by letters, telegrams, documents, and other materials bearing on the subject in debate —a veritable mine for the study of conceptions of national interest, covering ideology, moral obligation, and collateral considerations serving as "motives" in the formulation of policy and the determination of action.

The major part of this testimony, by far, is occupied by the declarations and arguments of witnesses who frankly admitted that they spoke for particular economic interests which would be favorably or adversely affected by the granting of independence to the Philippines. Yet no one of them would admit that he was actuated solely or even principally by economic considerations. Most of the concrete data presented were economic in character, but the warp, and sometimes the woof, of the arguments consisted of moral obligations—moral obligation to grant freedom to the Islands and moral obligation to

---

[51] Hearings, *Independence of the Philippines*, 71st Cong., 2d Sess. (On: S. 204; S. 3108; S. J. Res. 113; S. Res. 199; S. 3379), January 15, 1930, to May 22, 1930; 7 Parts; hereinafter cited as *Senate Hearings, Philippines*.

retain them, at least indefinitely, as if there were something reprehensible in the clean economic motive. Occasionally a telegram incorporated in the record was brief and pointed. For example, the Leslie Evans and Company of New York wired the Chairman: "We wish to record our protest against any unusual act of the Government in the matter of Philippine independence which would imperil American sovereignty and American trade interests." [52] But brief messages usually referred also to moral relations; a telegram from E. K. Hays, a business man of Cleveland, Ohio, ran: "Against King bill granting Philippine independence both on economic and ethical grounds." [53]

But there was no question about the location of the center of gravity. The representative of the American Farm Bureau Federation, Chester H. Gray, appeared in pursuance of a resolution adopted by a recent annual meeting of his powerful organization: "We demand an effective tariff on all agricultural commodities as advocated by President Hoover's message to the regular session of the Seventy-first Congress. It is an idle gesture to place even high rates of duty on farm commodities and then allow such commodities or substitutes therefor to enter our markets, duty free, from our so-called colonies or dependencies. Therefore, we favor immediate independence for such dependencies, but in the event that such independence cannot be granted, we insist most strenuously that the products from these colonies or dependencies be subjected to the rates of duty which are applicable to similar products from foreign nations." [54]

In this declaration of purpose there is no ambiguity or circumlocution. Philippine commodities cut the prices of domestic products; therefore, the Islands should be granted independence or discriminating duties should be laid on their exports to the United States.

In the course of his argument, Mr. Gray conceded that, had Congress earnestly grappled with the matter of tariff discrimination against the Philippines, the movement for inde-

[52] *Senate Hearings, Philippines,* p. 63.
[53] *Ibid.,* p. 65.
[54] *Ibid.,* p. 68.

pendence among the members of his organization would have been less marked, but he added that now it had almost unanimous support from the rank and file. When Senator Bingham referred to "our moral obligation" to the Philippine people, Mr. Gray replied that he was not unmindful of it and then extended the scope of his case to include historical promises of independence to the Islands, economic considerations, and humanitarian grounds. "Do not understand," he said, "that the farmers of America approach this question wholly from the economic point of view. They are not forgetting the historic point of view or the humanitarian point of view." Under the head of history and morals, Mr. Gray summarized various official statements from McKinley to Coolidge indicating that ultimate independence would be granted to the Philippines and drew the inference that a moral obligation rested upon the United States to fulfill the promise.

On the economic side, the agent of the Farm Bureau Federation presented certain data pertaining to the practical aspects of the subject. He stated that approximately 80 per cent of the imports into the United States from the Philippines were of an agricultural nature, while approximately the same proportion of the exports from the United States to the Philippines were industrial in character.[55] Although he admitted that there was a growing market for American wheat products in the Islands, it was small in comparison with the importation of Philippine agricultural products into the United States—products such as sugar, coconut oil, and copra which, he insisted, compete directly with sugar and animal and vegetable oil products of the American farmers.[56] This statement Mr. Gray followed by evidence designed to show that there was a possibility of an "expansion of agricultural and lumbering operations" in the Philippines "to many times the present volume." Thus the logical deduction was that the free importation of insular agricultural products had already made a grave inroad upon the earnings of American farmers—their standard of life—and the competition was likely to increase in the future, multiplying adverse results.

[55] *Senate Hearings, Philippines*, p. 69.
[56] *Ibid.*, pp. 77, 95.

This statement of the case for American agriculture in general by the representative of the Farm Bureau Federation was supplemented by arguments in detail from the Secretary of the National Dairy Union and from the Secretary of the National Coöperative Milk Producers' Federation. Both laid stress on the competition of Philippine oils with the animal and vegetable oils produced by American farmers. The former declared that "there will be plenty of vegetable oil in the United States to make all the oleomargerine that will be made and sold if all the coconut oil were shut out from the United States. . . . We want to develop the fats and oils producing industry of the United States, because that means new industries to the farmers in every part of the United States." [57] The latter added more minute specifications. "Of vegetable food products and beverages, we exported to the Philippines (in 1928) $7,379,361 and we imported free of duty, $51,401,931. Of other vegetable products, except wood and paper, we exported to them $6,016,-347 and imported $44,765,232." [58] To summarize the argument, the following commodities produced by American agriculture were subjected to downward price pressure by the free admission of Philippine products into the United States: sugar, hemp, cottonseed oil, animal oils and fats (dairy and pork products), and to some extent, tobacco. Considering the wide distribution of the areas in which these commodities were produced, it would seem that nearly every agricultural region of the United States was adversely affected by the existing economic relations with the Philippines.

The agriculturist demand for Philippine independence was supported by the American Federation of Labor on moral and economic grounds. The representative of that organization before the Senate committee opened with moral considerations and pointed out that the Federation, since 1898, had consistently opposed "forcing our system of government upon an unwilling people." Later its members began to feel the pressure of competition from commodities produced in the Philippines and from Filipino laborers who migrated to the United States. Then the Federation gave attention to economic aspects of

[57] *Senate Hearings, Philippines*, p. 108.
[58] *Ibid.*, p. 454.

independence, alleging that "the desire for cheap labor has acted like a cancer in American private and public life, destroying American ideals and preventing the development of a nation based on racial unity." By way of illustration, the spokesman of labor stated that Philippine cigar makers earned about $2.00 a week, while American cigar makers received $60.00. He also submitted a schedule, taken from a publication issued by the Philippine-American Chamber of Commerce, showing that the minimum daily wage of Philippine laborers ranged from twenty cents a day for casual workers to $1.20 for mechanics. He referred to the fact that special efforts were made to induce Filipinos to migrate to the United States "to enjoy the great prosperity existing there." [59] Like organized agriculture, the American Federation of Labor was willing to accept measures of restriction on imports and immigration, but its fundamental emphasis was on complete independence for the Philippines.

On the other side, representatives of commercial and manufacturing interests argued against immediate independence for the Philippines or at least any adjustment that would have an adverse effect upon their business operations. The president of Spencer, Kellogg, and Sons sought to show that coconut oil did not compete with oils or fats produced by American agriculturists, and contended that the large investment of $11,-000,000 in the industry would be "practically a total loss if economic barriers are erected against the free importation of coconut oil (and copra) into the United States from the Philippines." [60] He added that such a hampering of free trade in this relation would be "a blow to the American merchant marine" engaged in the carrying trade with the Islands. Then he touched upon the delicate matter of national defense. "Our supply of coconut oil in times of national emergencies would be indispensable as a source of glycerin for the manufacture of explosives." His prime concern was in the economics of the issue. Senator Tydings put to him this query: "As an abstract proposition, if trade relations between the United States and the Philippines could remain as they are at present, you would

[59] *Senate Hearings, Philippines,* pp. 113ff.
[60] *Ibid.,* p. 145.

not care as much about the Philippine independence problem as you do about the possibility you have just mentioned," that is, the danger of a trade barrier. The answer was: "Yes; that is true." [61]

The case of the cotton piece-goods exporting business was presented by J. F. Comins, of New York City. Mr. Comins sketched the rapid growth of the American export of cotton goods to the Philippines and declared that Americans could compete in the Philippines with Japanese manufacturers only because they had a free entry, while the latter had to pay a duty. The Philippine trade, he said, is vital to American industry. "You all know, I suppose, that the cotton industry in this country has had a hard time ever since 1920. Very few of the mills in this country have paid any dividends or, if they have, not sufficient to make it an attractive business. There is an overproduction in this country, approximately 10 per cent over what they can sell at a profit. In order to take this 10 per cent out of the country you have to find a foreign market for it. The Philippines are the largest market that this country has. It has grown in my own time from several million dollars, as I said before, to $13,000,000." [62] Mr. Comins proceeded to argue that a removal of the tariff discrimination in favor of the United States would result in serious injury to, if not the destruction of, the American cotton goods export, because Japanese and Chinese mills (many of the latter equipped with the latest American machinery) could undersell American manufactures. "Since the Philippines," he continued, "are a protégé of this country, we ought to give them some consideration. As a matter of fact, the way I understand it is that the balance of trade is in favor of the Philippine Islands." [63]

Besides the spokesmen of particular industries and commercial establishments interested in Philippine trade, a representative of the consolidated American-Philippine interests was heard, Charles D. Orth, president of the Philippine-American Chamber of Commerce, a purely American organization, in-

---

[61] *Senate Hearings, Philippines,* pp. 147, 148, 151.
[62] *Ibid.,* p. 210.
[63] *Ibid.,* p. 212.

cluding eighty firms and individuals. Mr. Orth stated that "there is no body of men in the United States which has a more intimate or better grounded knowledge of the affairs of, and the facts connected with, the Philippines than we have." His whole case rested, he insisted, on the realities of the situation. "The fact that the Department of Commerce officially gives the Philippine Islands fifteenth rank in a list of sixty-eight countries from which we buy things is, I submit, sufficient indication of the fundamental importance to the United States of existing trade with the Philippine Islands." [64] When the question of interested motives was raised, Mr. Orth did not seek to evade it: "Assuming for the purpose of the argument that our interests are selfish, I ask in what respect do they differ from the interests of the representatives of other organizations which have appeared before your committee? . . . I also ask if the right of self-preservation is denied by any American law or code of morals to any American citizen or body of citizens." [65]

After a long colloquy, in which Mr. Orth frankly stated that his organization had been engaged in legitimate propaganda against the immediate granting of independence to the Philippines, Senator Hawes sought to strike the balance in this manner: "To put it on a selfish basis, if you please, 5,000,000 union men, represented by their national organizations; all the farm organizations in the United States; and all the dairy organizations in the United States; and, in so far as it could be given, the beet sugar raisers of eleven states, the cane sugar industry of one state, and capital representing not millions, but two billions, as I understand it, of American money invested in Cuba, have all expressed their views. Put those things on a selfish basis. I hope this thing will be settled on a higher basis than that, but all these interests take a position exactly contrary to your own, on a selfish basis." [66]

In spite of any inferences that might be made from the simple catalogue of interests formulated by Senator Hawes, no conclusive balance sheet was drawn showing profit or loss on this basis, with respect to national interest in the retention or in-

[64] *Ibid.*, p. 185.
[65] *Ibid.*, p. 184.
[66] *Ibid.*, p. 196.

dependence of the Philippines. The ramification of industrial and agricultural and investment operations represented at the hearings was apparently too complicated for any such statistical determination of the problem. Was it possible to show upon minute examination that an increase of buying power among the stockholders and employees of industrial and trading concerns engaged in Philippine business under the free trade policy would more than offset by additional domestic buying power any loss that might come to American farmers from the competition of Philippine agricultural products? On the other hand, on inquiry, could the case be reversed? Could it be made to appear that the elimination of Philippine agricultural competition would raise the buying power of American farmers to such an extent that they could take the surplus cotton and other manufactures for which an outlet is now found in the Philippines? Neither the data presented at the hearings nor the debates in Congress produced a mathematical solution of the problem in the economic terms employed by the parties to the argument.[67]

[67] Indicative of the trend toward particular "balance sheets" of national interest is the article written for the *Harvard Business Review* by Rufus S. Tucker, formerly on the staff of the United States Department of Commerce. This article was incorporated in the subsequent debates in Congress on Philippine independence. In making the article part of the record, Senator Cutting called it the "profit and loss of our ownership and government of the Philippine Islands." This article, entitled "A Balance Sheet of the Philippines," makes a summary analysis of Philippine-American relations touching the Philippines as a market for American exports; as a source of materials; as a center of distribution for trade with Asia; and as a field for investment. It includes also some observations on the strategic value of the Philippines to the United States; and a summary of the costs of American occupation. Although the writer indicates the many uncertain factors entering into such a "balance sheet," he arrives at some definitive conclusions. "The total gain from United States sovereignty to all classes of United States citizens adds up to less than $10,000,000 a year, which represents all the economic gain susceptible of numerical expression, including some that is made at the expense of other Americans." While on the other hand, the value of the privileges received by the Filipinos from the American relationship totals $71,000,000. "Withdrawal . . . [from the Philippines] . . . would mean an annual saving to the United States Government of at least $4,000,000 in addition to a sum many times as large saved from naval expenditures and a still further saving of approximately $22,000,000 annually to the American consumers of Philippine products other than sugar. It seems obvious that, so far as material advantages are concerned, not only is the present arrangement much more beneficial to the Philippines than to the United States but also the cost to the United States far

At the congressional hearings on the Philippines the spokes-men of industry and the spokesmen of agriculture contented themselves with expressing their own interests frankly and bluntly, making little or no reference to any supreme concep-tion of national interest rising above their particular concerns. But other values not at all susceptible of statistical weight and measurement have been brought into discussions at various hearings. Transcending the results of an economic balance sheet and the merits of the controversy between agriculture and trade is the strategy of national defense—a fixed and en-during national interest. What relation does the question of the Philippines bear to this supreme exigency? According to the testimony of military and naval experts, before and after the issue of independence became acute in 1931, the prime purpose in acquiring the Philippines was to secure a basis of operations in the struggle among the powers for Oriental trade. No one contended that the Islands were necessary for the effective de-fense of the continental United States against invasion. What-ever may have been the moral obligation to hold the Philip-pines, the Navy's argument was economic—the enlargement of American naval power over Oriental commerce. It was necessary, ran the thesis, to cope with occasional disorders in China which threatened American interests and to have a base from which to make demonstrations in order to command au-thority among the armed rivals for dominance in Asia. Other-wise, it was said, American commerce in the Orient would find the door closed and China partitioned into spheres of influ-ence.

In essence this thesis was an economic argument pertaining to Oriental commerce, not to the strategy of defending the con-tinental United States. In realization it involved as a matter of course the perils of war in the Far East; and nothing short of a powerfully fortified naval base in the Philippines supple-mented by adequate naval strength could have removed the hazards thus raised. Yet the Anglo-Japanese alliance formed in 1902, to say nothing of hidden combinations which might be

exceeds the commercial benefit derived or likely ever to be derived." For the full text of the article as incorporated in the Senate proceedings, see *Cong. Rec.*, (day to day proceedings) June 8, 1932, pp. 12640–12645.

turned against the United States, made it clear to the directors of policy in Washington that no such dominant position would be granted to the American Navy without the possibility of a severe struggle—of dubious outcome and still more dubious economic value. It was probably the recognition of this fact which induced the United States Government at the Washington conference to agree to undertake no new fortifications and to make no increases in existing defenses in the Philippines. By this action it surrendered the right to make the Philippines an impregnable base for operations in case of a major war in the Far East. Hence, by a single stroke, the party of the restoration repudiated one of the primary purposes in acquiring the Philippines originally, namely, the establishment of a strong naval base in support of American commerce in the Orient. Its effect upon the strategy of security for the United States was immediately grasped by naval authorities and students of the sea power.

Writing in 1918, even before the Washington conference, Theodore Roosevelt declared that the Philippines constituted a spot of fatal weakness in our national defense lines. "I have never felt," he said, "that the Philippines were of any special use to us. But I have felt that we had a task to perform there and that a great nation is benefited by doing a great task." Referring specifically to the policy to which the Democratic administration had committed the country by passing the Jones bill, Mr. Roosevelt continued: "I hope, therefore, that the Filipinos will be given their independence at an early date and without any guaranty from us that might in any way hamper our future action or commit us to staying on the Asiatic coast. I do not believe that we should keep any foothold whatever in the Philippines. Any kind of position by us in the Philippines merely results in making them our heel of Achilles if we are attacked by a foreign power. They can be of no compensating benefit to us. . . . Inasmuch as we have now promised to leave them, and as we are now abandoning our power to work efficiently for and in them, I do not feel that we are warranted in staying in the islands in an equivocal position, thereby incurring great risk to ourselves without conferring any real compensating advantage, of a kind which we are bound to take into account, on the Filipinos themselves." [68] If such was the case before the surrender of the right of fortification, it was made doubly impressive by that naval retreat. Another plank in the platform of imperial advance was shattered by events.

NATIONAL INTEREST IN THE NEW DEAL

By the autumn of 1932 it was generally apparent that the official thesis of national interest was not working out in practice as expected and promised. The tariff was high, lavish aids were being bestowed upon shipping, the agencies of trade promotion were ready for action, the Navy was fairly adequate, the overseas possessions were intact, backward places needed American goods, impecunious borrowers were prepared to take loans if funds were forthcoming. And yet outlets could not be found for the "surplus" of American goods, machinery, capital, and technical skill. Either the devices employed in giving effect to the thesis were faulty, or sufficient energy and pressure had not been applied, or the economic analysis implicit in the thesis had been wrong. With endless reiteration the American people had been informed that only the engines of economic expansion could drain off the "surplus" which glutted and stifled the American market. The engines had been established and set in motion; but when they were running full speed an explosion occurred which ended in a new glut in the domestic market, a sharp decline of foreign trade, and a staggering drop in the indices of "prosperity." What was the cause? What could be done? Was a renewal of foreign trade promotion the only way out of the impasse or was it necessary to chart another course? Or did governmental action, after all, have any fundamental influence on the fortunes of domestic economy and foreign commerce?

In the midst of this crisis, while such questions were facing the country, the campaign of 1932 was waged. And from a careful review of campaign "literature" it may be said that neither of the political parties came squarely to grips with the issues thus presented. The Republicans had been in office

[68] *Senate Hearings, Philippines*, p. 94.

when the explosion occurred and they could not charge the administration in power with neglecting the application of the official thesis in any of its essential parts. They could not now offer the official thesis as a program for finding ever-expanding outlets for the "surplus" of American goods and capital and giving employment to domestic enterprise. So far as Republican leaders touched upon this delicate subject, they were inclined to diminish their emphasis on foreign commerce and to speak of "recovery" through stimulants applied to domestic economy, especially in the form of credits.

Nor could it be said that the Democrats presented to the public a clear and consistent view of the national interest to be realized in actions affecting foreign policy. With respect to this matter, there was a gradation from wing to wing. On the one side were a few Democrats, notably Cordell Hull, who took the old agrarian view that a reduction of the tariff would move American commodities abroad; with what precise repercussion on domestic economy was nowhere demonstrated. On the other side this doctrine was either rejected or glossed over and the impression given that nothing important was to be expected from freer trade and the internationalism that accompanied it.

Speaking generally on the nature of government, Franklin D. Roosevelt, the Democratic candidate, made it clear, however, that he believed *interest* to be a prime mover in politics and that the *nation* was the center of consideration. He asserted that the Democratic program was essentially a "national program," and laid stress on the "interdependence of all groups, of all sections, of all economic interests." Referring to "the American system at its best," Madison's view [69] of the various interests which compose society and the relation which government should bear to those various interests, Mr. Roosevelt declared: "It is not in ignoring the fact that there are different interests and different parts of the country, and different people with different needs, that we build a nation; it is in recognizing them, looking at them, seeing them, consulting them, helping them, always with a view to the larger interest

[69] *Federalist,* Number X.

—the interest of the nation." [70] What is the "interest of the nation" in such particular matters as the tariff, the question of empire, "international coöperation" and so on?

According to the Democratic party platform, the tariff is to be a "competitive tariff for revenue," with a fact-finding commission free from executive interference. The instruments by which this conception of tariff is to be realized include "reciprocal tariff agreements with other nations" and "an economic conference designed to restore international trade and facilitate exchange." Interpreting his party's stand upon the tariff, Mr. Roosevelt declared that the tariff must be kept high enough "to equalize the difference in the cost of production" at home and abroad, and "to maintain living standards which we set for ourselves." Intimating that there is no fixed rule likely to govern the raising and lowering of tariffs, other than the equalization of the costs of production and the maintenance of living standards "which we set for ourselves," Mr. Roosevelt explained: "Policy needs to be dominated by the realities we discover and by the national purposes we seek." [71]

In the concrete case of the Philippines, the Democratic platform expressed an attitude toward empire which had been rather consistently held by the party ever since Jefferson first asserted the principle upon which expansion of the national territorial domain should rest. [72] While the platform declared for the "independence of the Philippines," it also favored "ultimate statehood for Porto Rico." More explicit is Mr. Roosevelt's attitude respecting the subjects of empire and those of national interest. Speaking of President Hoover, he suggested that the President "turn his eyes from his so-called 'backward and crippled countries' and turn to the great and stricken markets of Kansas, Nebraska, Iowa, Wisconsin, Illinois, and other agricultural states." [73] There is certainly indicated in this remark a primary solicitude for things constituting national interest which does not apply either to the

[70] Speech at the Metropolitan Opera House. New York *Times*, November 4, 1932.
[71] Speech interpreting party platform at Albany. New York *Times*, July 31, 1932.
[72] See Chap. III, *ante.*
[73] Metropolitan Opera House, Speech, *loc. cit.*

implications of empire or to any duty owed by the United States to "benighted peoples."

The same attitude is revealed with regard to other issues. In the matter of a plan for the rehabilitation of agriculture, the Democratic platform favored any project that will provide "effective control of crop surpluses so that our farmers may have the full benefit of the domestic market." And while he declined to adopt any plan which would lead to retaliation from abroad on the ground of dumping, Mr. Roosevelt, in outlining the requirements for a plan for agriculture, maintained that it must raise staple prices in the United States above world market prices.[74] On a number of occasions, Mr. Roosevelt decried the "mobilization of business as the President practices it by promotion and advertising methods." [75] One illustration of these "promotion" tactics bearing upon the national interest, a procedure Mr. Roosevelt condemned, is "the usurpation of power by the State Department in assuming to pass upon foreign securities offered by international bankers, as a result of which billions of dollars in questionable bonds have been sold to the public upon the implied approval of the Federal Government." [76] There was a certain vagueness about his attitude on the "war debts." The platform declared against "cancellation" but left the door open for revision; while in his Albany speech interpreting the party platform, Mr. Roosevelt explained: "The debts will not be a problem—we shall not have to cancel them—if we are realistic about providing ways in which payment is possible" and these ways are "lowered tariffs and the resumption of trade."

Touching other international problems, the platform proposed "no interference in the internal affairs of other nations" and upheld "the sanctity of treaties and the maintenance of good faith and of good will in financial obligations"; but "the Pact of Paris . . . [is] . . . to be made effective by provisions for consultation and conference in case of threatened

[74] Cited in New York *Times,* October 30, 1932, by Charles Merz, item: "The Major Issues: The Campaign Summed Up."

[75] Particularly in his Columbus, Ohio, speech. New York *Times,* August 21, 1932.

[76] Speech interpreting party platform. New York *Times,* July 31, 1932. Reiterated in Mr. Roosevelt's Columbus, Ohio, speech, *loc. cit.*

violation of treaties." Picturing in a broad résumé the conditions alleged to have been brought about by eleven years of government under the theories of the Republican party, Mr. Walsh, in his address as permanent chairman of the Democratic National Convention, asserted: "The occasion called for the most liberal international coöperation. Too late it has come to be realized that our prosperity is intimately bound up in that of the rest of the world." Instead of coöperating with the rest of the nations, "we pursued a policy of selfish isolation." [77]

But there is no indication in the campaign speeches of Mr. Roosevelt that he was as much concerned with so-called "international issues" or "world interdependence" as were other speakers under Democratic auspices during the campaign. It is true that he reiterated the platform pronouncements touching international affairs but in almost every instance the international aspect was stated reluctantly while emphasis upon the American national interest was clearly put. This attitude is repeatedly apparent in his treatment of empire, the tariff, the war debts, and proposals for a solution of the agricultural problem; and it is implied in his condemnation of government activities in relation to the flotation of foreign bonds in American security markets.

The same "mild" endorsement of international activities appears in Mr. Roosevelt's views on the stabilization of international exchanges. In his Albany speech he stated: "The United States could well afford to take the lead in asking for a general conference to establish less changeable fiscal relationships and to determine what can be done to restore the purchasing power of that half of the world's inhabitants who are on a silver basis, and to exchange views regarding governmental finance." There is here, however, no implication of necessity, no feeling of compulsion due to the "interdependence" of nations; while on the other hand such vague expressions as "could well afford" are used. If this were an isolated instance of apparent indifference to international aspects, there would be no justification for emphasizing the point made, but the same tone ran through all of Mr. Roose-

[77] New York *Times,* June 29, 1932.

velt's campaign speeches. Without doubt he expressed an essentially "national" point of view, which, while not denying a place to international aspects, nevertheless clearly indicated that they were secondary and largely incidental to the "intranational" approach to the solution of domestic problems.

NATIONAL INTEREST UNDER THE ROOSEVELT ADMINISTRATION

Owing to the dramatic circumstances under which Mr. Roosevelt assumed the Presidency no genuine indication of policy could emerge during his first months of office. Shaken by the closing of banks throughout the State of Michigan, other states soon followed in declaring bank "holidays" for various periods until it became a matter of nation-wide necessity to close them all. With such a situation demanding immediate action almost wholly domestic in character, there was neither time nor occasion for the assertion or execution of any broad policy other than to relate acts of expediency to some very loose conception of the national interest. Undoubtedly this is all the explanation given at the time for the gold embargo proclaimed during the banking crisis under the unrepealed powers granted to President Wilson in the World War and subsequently confirmed in the Emergency Bank Relief law hastily passed on March 9, 1933.

While intently fixed upon measures touching domestic issues and legislation, President Roosevelt received the representatives of several foreign governments for informal "discussions" concerning economic affairs scheduled to come before the London Conference in June. But no implication of President Roosevelt's attitude on the relation between national interest and foreign affairs could be drawn from the fact of his reception of, and discussions with, these representatives, since there were enough other reasons to warrant their visits to this country. And no definite understandings were reached, no declarations of policy were made, at the conclusion of the several visits, from which the future course of the American Government could be ascertained. At most these visits appeared to be little more than an interlude in the intense preoccupation of the President with the domestic situation. It was a situation undoubtedly like that which would follow, if a valued friend or relative, making a visit either for business or for pleasure, should arrive, unfortunately, at his host's ménage at the precise moment the house had caught on fire. The head of the house would extend a cordial welcome, to be sure, but his attention would be directed elsewhere.

It was during this period that Secretary of State Hull spoke for the new administration. In a public address, he indicated some of the broad principles which he intended to follow in the conduct of his office.[78] He declared that "The restoration of fair, friendly and normal trade relations among nations at present would not only avoid serious economic, military and political differences between countries in the future, but would go far toward composing those now existing." Deploring the "policy of economic isolation" followed by all important countries since the War without satisfactory results, he asserted that "business recovery must be preceded by the restoration of international finance and commerce, an alternative to which is a continuance of the unsound economic policies under the operation of which the entire world since 1929 has been in the throes of an unspeakable depression." In Mr. Hull's opinion, ". . . the destiny of history points to the United States for leadership in the existing grave crisis." It is a satisfaction to realize how "in meeting the problems that are our daily portion, the interests of our government and our people seem so clearly to coincide with the interests of humanity." Concluding his address, he declared that "no nation is sufficient unto itself. . . . The normal life of a nation . . . [as of an individual] . . . is one of association with others . . . [conducted] . . . of necessity . . . in accordance with certain standards which we may term international ethics." [79]

About two weeks later President Roosevelt found time to send an appeal to the fifty-four nations participating in the General Disarmament Conference at Geneva and the World Monetary and Economic Conference scheduled to he held in London. "The world cannot await deliberations long drawn out," he said. "The conference must establish order in place

[78] Text in New York *Times*, April 30, 1933.   [79] *Ibid.*

of the present chaos by a stabilization of currencies, by free-ing the flow of world trade, and by international action to raise price levels." Immediately he added: "It must, in short, sup-plement individual domestic programs for economic recovery, by wise and considered international action." [80] After sug-gesting three steps which, he thought, could be agreed upon in the field of disarmament, the President proposed a fourth step "concurrent with and wholly dependent on the faithful fulfillment of these three proposals and subject to existing treaty rights: "That all the nations of the world should enter into a solemn and definite pact of non-aggression; . . . re-affirm the obligations . . . to limit and reduce their arma-ments; and . . . [under certain conditions] . . . individually agree that they will send no armed force of whatsoever na-ture across their frontiers." [81]

Shortly after President Roosevelt's world-wide appeal, Nor-man H. Davis, in a statement made May 24, 1933, informed the delegates at the Disarmament Conference that the United States proposed to set forth its policy in the matter of con-sultation with other governments "by a unilateral declaration." Illustrating the form such a declaration might assume, Mr. Davis stated that "the United States of America declares that, in the event of a breach or threat of a breach . . . [of the

[80] At this date the following bills had been passed by the United States Congress: Emergency Banking Relief law, Economy law (maintenance of Government's credit), law permitting the manufacture and taxing of beer, Emergency Agricultural Relief law including farm mortgage relief, currency issuance and regulation and inflation, Reforestation Unemployment Relief bill, Wagner-Lewis Emergency Relief law, Muscle Shoals and Tennessee Valley De-velopment Act, and the Supervision of Traffic in Securities law. Among the more important bills not then passed by the Congress were the following: Small Home Owners' Refinancing Act, Railroad Reorganization and Relief law, Wagner National Employment Service law, Gold Repeal Joint Resolution, and the National Industrial Recovery Act.

Commencing in the latter part of March, 1933, business made some progress. Both production and distribution indexes advanced steadily. Retail trade im-proved markedly. Prices of both commodities and securities had begun to rise. The banking situation had eased considerably. With some exceptions, domestic conditions had materially improved since the month of March. The dollar sus-tained a further drop abroad and foreign trade remained unfavorable. For a more detailed statement of general conditions and the statistics upon which the conviction of sustained internal improvement rested, see *Survey of Current Business,* issued by United States Department of Commerce, Washington, D. C. (May to July), Vol. 13, Nos. 5-7.   [81] N. Y. *Times,* May 17, 1933.

Pact of Paris] . . . it will be prepared to confer with the view of the maintenance of the peace. . . . In the event that a decision is taken by the conference powers in consultation in determining the aggressor with which, on the basis of its independent judgment, the Government of the United States agrees, the Government of the United States will undertake to refrain from any action and to withhold its protection from its citizens who engage in activity which would tend to defeat the collective efforts which the states in consultation might have decided upon against the aggressor."

Following this pronouncement no significant statement on foreign policy came from the Roosevelt administration until the World Economic Conference had convened in London. Before examining the nature and upshot of that international convention, however, it is relevant to consider briefly the position on foreign relations established by President Roosevelt and those associated with him from the beginning of the campaign in the previous year until the opening of the Conference, and to analyze more closely the division of opinion within the Democratic party to which reference has been made (p. 411).

That division had appeared early in the history of the party and had become more and more marked in the course of time. With the change in American life from the agricultural base to a base predominantly industrial, there had risen in the Democratic ranks many prominent leaders, sometimes called Eastern Democrats, who were drawn from other than agrarian ranks. They were affiliated with commercial and banking centers—with interests concerned with the export and import of goods and capital; and after the fashion of these interests, they were inclined to favor, besides tariff reductions facilitating the movement of goods in the international market, policies calculated to widen export markets, and to speak of the "desirability" of foreign loans, branch factories, and other activities associated with commercial expansion in the national interest.

It was natural for this group of Democrats to be "internationally minded," and to seek in foreign trade an escape from the economic crisis which paralyzed national economy. An obvious quickening of international life, through travel, the radio, aviation, and the press, as well as through such institutions as the League of Nations, seemed to give substance and warrant to the conviction. Moreover, the eager quest of the late President Wilson for ways and means of avoiding a repetition of the World War and the high moral principles which he had announced in his search for pacification lent sanction to the belief in international coöperation as a good in itself and a source of economic advantage to all participants. Memories of the War and of his teachings had not perished from the earth.

Having this background for their thinking, members of this group favor a reduction of tariffs and a lowering of trade barriers, although in what manner and according to what principles, is not clear. They desire a restoration of foreign markets, without specifying the contents of the new export and import business. They favor a resumption of foreign lending—"sound loans" on more secure principles of lending, not closely defined. They are inclined to believe in a "world interdependence" which makes recovery in each country dependent upon general recovery. They would stabilize prices and exchange on a world basis, as a condition precedent to extended international commerce. Yet they have retained the old traditions of a certain "national" solidarity, a possible "national" equilibrium, a "national" character for American economic life.

Thus the members of this group appear to be between two worlds. They reject the nationalism of the Republicans who would make the United States a manufacturing autarchy and employ all engines of diplomacy and war to thrust the national interests of the United States through and through the structures of world economy. They have cast off this kind of nationalism without going all the way over to the internationalism of free trade and *laissez faire*. They look abroad for the escape from the dilemma presented by periodical economic crises, without offering any machinery for giving certain effect to their hopes or any policies guaranteed to work, which will command the whole-hearted support of their party colleagues of the other wing.

The second group of leaders in the Democratic party appears to be smaller, but of greater influence in official circles. To this group the old possibility of a distinct national life and character—envisaged by Jefferson, grounded in tradition, and tested by such issues as immigration and the question of empire—remains a living and vital force. They emphasize domestic issues. To them, the fact that foreign trade is less than 10 per cent of the total United States trade activity does not represent the margin between mere existence and prosperity, but it illustrates the importance of the domestic market and shows how little we are dependent upon foreign countries.

This group is not averse to a lowering of tariffs—some of its forerunners did not shrink from free trade—on the underlying belief that if a rounded, balanced, "national" life is attained, almost any system is likely to serve for the exchange of a genuine "surplus" of goods. Always wary of international arrangements—whether political or economic—this group remained reluctant under the drive toward "internationalism" instituted under Woodrow Wilson.[82] An attitude of reluctance toward a complete acceptance of a larger political affiliation than the national state has characterized this section of the Democratic party since the World War. It does not reject the obvious realities of the physical interdependence of the several national states, but—and this is an important element in its attitude—it regards international relationships as incidental to the primary interests, the distinctive completeness, of the national state.[83] Prominent in the leadership of this group, dominating it in contemporary politics, acknowledged titular head of the whole Democratic party, is President Franklin D. Roosevelt.

Throughout his campaign he made declarations which brought him rather clearly within the second group of Democrats, who may be said to express a distinctly "national" point

[82] It should be observed that Woodrow Wilson's "internationalism" is neither that of the 1934 Democratic platform, nor that of the "national" group above described; it can only be explained adequately in the light of the exigencies of the World War and of the conditions under which the peace and immediate post-war adjustments were made.

[83] If one scratches the surface of the old "states' rights" doctrine, the same belief in the sufficiency of the *state,* and the same aversion to the larger, centralized, *national state,* may be seen as a positive force in the attitudes of a prominent section of the Democratic party.

of view. He revived traditions of the "national" character and gave them freshness and vividness of expression. He frequently descended from airy generalizations about political principles and talked of politics as a clash of interests, at home and abroad. While referring again and again to foreign trade and affairs, he kept sounding the note that the United States could go a long way toward setting its house in order, toward escaping from the economic crisis, by domestic measures, taken for domestic purposes. All in all, there was no doubt about the center of his emphasis. He did not, to be sure, make a clear distinction between "nationalism" and "internationalism"— two foggy words which confuse mankind—and thus did not alienate the internationalist wing of his party, but he did let it be known that his primary intention was "to sweep his own doorstep"—employ domestic instrumentalities to the utmost in seeking a way out of the economic ruin. In emphasis, then, Mr. Roosevelt's policy marked a certain departure from the verbiage of the platform and the policies espoused by the other wing of his party.

Yet the emphasis was not sharp enough to reveal a hopeless division within the party, although in fact a sharp antithesis of policies was both explicit and implicit. Only the test of concrete action and decision could show the irreparable cleavage. The test came at the London Economic Conference. And instead of defining positions and healing the breach, if possible, the administration chose another course. It allowed each faction to indulge in its sentiments and then decided in favor of the nationalist wing.

Enjoying a free hand, apparently, Secretary Hull, while recognizing nationalism, leaned toward internationalism in his address delivered before the conference.[84] In this keynote speech he declared: The "success or failure of this conference will mean the success or failure of statesmanship everywhere. . . ." He spoke of the "panic-ridden world," the "audience of humanity everywhere," "distressed peoples in every land," "world-wrecking economic policies," and the necessity for a "spirit of coöperation . . . in this conference

[84] Except where otherwise noted the above excerpts are taken from the text printed in the New York *Times,* June 15, 1933.

that will carry hope to the unnumbered millions in distress throughout the world."

Secretary Hull contended that ". . . all nations have strenuously pursued the policy of economic isolation." No nation can "by bootstrap methods, lift itself out of the troubles that surround it"; and then, as if conscious of the necessity of accounting for the sustained rise in American domestic economic life since the latter part of March without any significant contributions from changes in the international sphere, he added: "Each nation by itself can, to a moderate extent, restore conditions by suitable . . . steps. Thus the administration of President Roosevelt has within three months adopted an effective domestic program to promote business improvement in the fullest possible measure." After this brief interlude, Secretary Hull swung back into the international theme. Deriding the "isolationist" for his failure to see the "international character" of the depression, for his belief that relief may be achieved by local action, he arraigned "economic nationalism" for its destruction of business ever since the War.

Quoting statistics in support of his convictions relative to the "indispensable nature of foreign trade," to the degree to which many nations are dependent upon foreign trade, and setting forth the statistical evidence to show the "strangulation of international trade" by the "disastrous policies in operation during the post-war period," Secretary Hull struck the central theme of his argument in the assertion: "Honest intelligence now compels the admission that nations are substantially interrelated and interdependent in an economic sense, with the result that international coöperation today is a fundamental necessity." Indicating his conception of the conflict between "nationalism" and "internationalism"—national economy and world economy—he continued: "The opposing policy of self-containment has demonstrated its inability to either avoid or arrest or cure the most destroying depression in all the annals of business."

If an incongruity was really involved, it did not occur in that light to Secretary Hull when he declared ". . . that trade between nations does not mean the displacement of established home production and trade of one country by that of another." "International trade," he continued, "is chiefly barter or a mutually profitable exchange of surpluses by different countries, either directly or in a triangular manner." It contemplates "that an enterprising nation goes out into the world and locates and develops new markets for the goods it effectively produces"; while the excesses of tariff and other trade barriers are readjusted to a moderate level. Such a program, Mr. Hull believed, avoids the two extremes of economic internationalism and economic nationalism, launching every nation upon "a sane, practical middle course," by reciprocally supplementing "efficient home markets with capacious foreign markets." After asserting that the tariff truce already agreed to by at least a dozen nations must be continued, and urging the nations to remove all excesses in the form of trade barriers, Secretary Hull closed his address with an appeal for cooperation and unified leadership.

Elaborating later these general views, Secretary Hull brought out their implications for American economic life: [85] "We must not expect to protect the limited industries, the products of which are not important in volume or equal in excellence to what our foreign customers have. Nor shall we establish monopolies to the detriment of the consumer." It was in this address that Secretary Hull, unwittingly perhaps, revealed something of the division in the attitudes held by the two groups in his party which have been described above. "Every country can," he stated, "get along in some sort of fashion by depending almost entirely upon its domestic market." "Such a process, however, *means a reconstruction of the country's whole domestic economy. To agriculture it implies the cutting of acreage; to industry, the curtailment of production. . . .*" [Italics mine.] *Now, in fact, this was the precise program set in motion by President Roosevelt and adopted by the Congress in the United States,* through such acts as the National Industrial Recovery bill, the Farm-Relief Inflation bill, the Gold Repeal Joint Resolution, the Supervision of Traffic in Securities law and other supporting legislation. This program expressed the "national" attitude of the apparently smaller, but more influential, group of Democratic leaders headed by

[85] Text in New York *Times*, June 16, 1933.

President Roosevelt. It gained the almost overwhelming support of the Congress. And though there may be some doubt about the understanding of the program which prevailed among the people at large, it was evident that the country as a whole endorsed the trend of affairs. As unwittingly brought out by Mr. Hull, such a process was diametrically opposed to the course which he was trying to follow at London in accordance with the views expressed by him in his initial address before the conference.

This conflict grew more acute as the economic situation improved in the United States, without any apparent help from foreign trade, and while the dollar was left to shift for itself under the assaults of the international exchanges. The two attitudes led to a preliminary clash when, on June 17, 1933, a memorandum on tariffs was submitted by the United States delegation to the economic commission of the World Economic Conference. This memorandum dealt with the reduction of trade barriers by multilateral agreements; it proposed a 10 per cent horizontal reduction in import duties, corresponding liberalization of import restrictions other than tariffs, a regulation of quota and licensing systems, an extension of the customs truce, and encouragement for the making of bilateral tariff agreements between the nations "on the most-favored-nation principle in its unconditional and unrestricted form." [86]

The grounds for aversion to this "proposal" were not disclosed; but the incident occasioned a sharp controversy.[87] Senator Key Pittman, another member of the United States delegation, denied that the suggestion for a general 10 per cent tariff reduction which was submitted to the economic commission of the World Economic Conference came from the United States delegation.[88] In his statement, he explained that the "technical advisers of the . . . [American] . . . delegation may have drafted their ideas to form the basis of discussion for the agenda of the economic commission," but the "suggestions" were not officially given out by the American delegation itself.

[86] For the text of this proposal see New York *Times,* June 18, 1933.
[87] See successive issues of the New York *Times* following June 17, 1933.
[88] New York *Times,* June 19, 1933.

Granting the accuracy of the technical point, as well as the triviality of the incident, the affair was one of the first indications that the division in the Democratic party at home was to appear in London. Commenting upon press dispatches reporting a "most penetrating observation" made by Senator Couzens, as a member of the American delegation, the New York *Times* stated editorially: [89] "The gist of it was that the official attitude at Washington indicates a severe conflict between internationalism and 'our national economic programs.' In the opinion of the Michigan Senator 'we cannot carry through both. Sooner or later we shall have to decide which we are to follow.' "

On this division of opinion respecting fundamentals, the World Economic Conference was finally wrecked. From the moment the conflict was brought into the open by the publication of the memorandum on tariff proposals, it affected every issue that arose until it reached a climax on the question of monetary stabilization. The American delegation continued to function as if no change had occurred, but it was clear that the atmosphere of the conference was charged with this major controversy. It was only a question of when and upon what particular issue the conflict would be definitively resolved as far as the conference was concerned. Senator Pittman's silver proposal was made as if no such conflict existed.[90] The care with which the Trade Resolution introduced before the conference by Secretary Hull was phrased showed the influence of the conflict, for while it revealed many of the attitudes taken by Mr. Hull in his first address to the conference, it was sufficiently general and ambiguous not to create any reaction at home.[91]

But the fires of conflict were smoldering beneath the appearances of things. This became evident in the radio broadcast by Secretary Hull on June 27, 1933. A comparison of his views on the tariff in this broadcast with his views on the same subject in his initial address to the conference (and with the "suggestions" on the tariff put forward by the technical ex-

[89] New York *Times,* June 21, 1933.
[90] Text in New York *Times,* June 20, 1933.
[91] For the text of the resolution, see New York *Times,* June 23, 1933.

perts of the American delegation) clearly shows that he was
no longer in full command of the direction in which events
were to move. "You must understand," he said in his broadcast, "that we are not in London to plunge into the com-
plexities of tariff revision."

His answers to questions put to him by William Hard show
a studied effort to maintain the views advanced by him earlier
in the conference while at the same time adjusting them to
the implications of the conflict that had arisen and to the
rapidly changing domestic situation in the United States. "In
America we have organized an elaborate program for the
benefit of industry and agriculture,[92]. . . if other countries
will undertake a similar program . . . they, too, will have a
similar improvement in commodity prices. . . ." "Our object
is . . . to stimulate international business." But this does not
mean putting the whole world on a free trade basis; "it merely
means that . . . we should reach a declaration of policy that
will start commerce going and keep it moving." By such
generalities, utterly lacking in supporting detail, by temporiza-
tion and qualification, throughout this radio broadcast, Secretary Hull revealed the divided opinion and temper which
beset the American delegation at the conference.

It would be an exaggeration to imply that the conflict of
attitudes in the Democratic party, in the administration, involving the American delegation to the conference, and even
in the wider sphere of American life generally, was solely
responsible for the confusion that beset the conference and
impeded positive and rapid progress.[93] This conflict had its
counterpart in other countries as well. Admitting the strength

[92] It should be recalled here that this program, especially that designed for
agriculture in the farm bill and for industry in the National Industrial Recovery
Act, contemplated moving in the very direction Mr. Hull had deplored when
he said earlier (New York *Times,* June 16, 1933) that while every country might
possibly depend almost entirely upon its domestic market, "such a process,
however, means a reconstruction of the country's whole domestic economy,"
implying for agriculture "the cutting of acreage; to industry, the curtailment
of production." The Democratic platform itself had declared for "effective
control of crop surpluses so that our farmers may have the full benefit of the
domestic market."

[93] As intimated subsequently, for example, by Sir Arthur Salter in his article
"Would Halt Parley Till Our Policy Is Clear," New York *Times,* July 23, 1933.

of its influence at the conference, there were other matters which contributed to the confusion and delay. The aggressive and sustained attempt of a number of countries, notably those referred to as the "Gold Bloc" countries,[94] to give precedence to monetary stabilization over all other issues at the conference, had much to do with the futile outcome. Moreover, the persistence with which that issue was kept before the conference precipitated a temporary closure of the division within the American delegation. In view of the nature of the situation and of the antecedent conditions, this settlement, or clearing of the atmosphere, had to come in the form of a message from President Roosevelt.[95]

"I would regard it as a catastrophe amounting to a world tragedy," he began, "if the great conference of nations . . . should . . . allow itself to be diverted by the proposal of a purely artificial and temporary experiment affecting the monetary exchange of a few nations only. . . . Such action, such diversion, shows a singular lack of proportion and a failure to remember the larger purposes for which the economic conference originally was called together." This was the prelude to the heart of the message, which is contained in the sentence: "The sound internal economic system of a nation is a greater factor in its well-being than the price of its currency in changing terms of the currencies of other nations." Here is the point of view, not of the "nationalism" so popularly discussed, but of the "national attitude" which regards internationalism only as subsidiary, as secondary or incidental, to a strong national solidarity based upon a distinctive conception of American society and its interest. It is a resurrection of the basic relationship between nationalism and internationalism implied by the discussions in the *Federalist*,[96] contemplated in Washington's Farewell Address,[97] and made the cornerstone of Jefferson's philosophy concerning the pattern of American so-

[94] Principal among these were: France, Holland, Italy, Poland, Switzerland, and Belgium.

[95] For the full text of the President's message, see New York *Times,* July 4, 1933.

[96] Especially Nos. XI and XL.

[97] Particularly the passage commencing "Harmony, liberal intercourse with all nations are recommended by policy, humanity, and interest," etc.

ciety. For President Roosevelt it was a definitive reassertion of the opinion which had run like a steady current throughout his campaign addresses and underneath all the measures proposed by him to the Congress for the reconstruction of internal economic life. It rejected the anomalous confusion of the Democratic platform and established—among "first things first"—the supremacy of the "national" or domestic point of view in American policy.[98]

For thus making clear and sharp his point of emphasis, namely, that a "sound internal economic system" is a *greater* factor in the nation's well-being than the price of its currencies in terms of the currencies of other nations, President Roosevelt was sharply criticized, especially by the gold-bloc countries, and charged with "wrecking" the conference. In this way responsibility for the outcome was placed squarely upon the United States, apparently on the assumption that otherwise the conference would have produced fruitful results, would have led the way to "recovery," would have found an escape from the economic crisis.

A few facts must be brought within the picture before the criticism can be appraised. First of all, it must be remembered that President Roosevelt did not call the conference. Nor did his representatives participate in preparing the Agenda. The American delegation at the preparatory conference, led by academic economists, had been selected by President Hoover. In the second place, the Agenda, after revealing a faith in the healing power of *laissez faire* in economy, displayed certain contradictions in economic conceptions. In the third place, there is no ground in the preliminary history for assuming that the other nations were ready to make drastic reductions in trade barriers, to stabilize currencies on a fixed basis, or to rely mainly on some form of international adjustment as the one available or more effective means of escaping from the economic crisis. That many economists believed in the primacy of tariff reductions, currency stabilization, and debt-scaling as opening

[98] An editorial in the *Herald-Tribune* caught a glimpse of the relationship contemplated by President Roosevelt, when it observed a few days before the Roosevelt message, "There is no fatal opposition between a strongly nationalistic policy of self-sufficiency and amicable trade relations with other peoples" (July 1, 1933).

avenues of escape from the economic dilemma cannot be doubted; but that such was the view of the official representatives of the various nations at the London conference is nowhere demonstrated, cannot be demonstrated.[99]

In the circumstances, it seems safe to say that the conference was foredoomed to failure on account of the fact that each of the participating delegates, advisors, and statesmen was at war with himself in his own bosom, had not clarified his own mind on the supreme question: "Is the well-being of my nation dependent primarily on foreign trade or can it make a fairly satisfactory escape from the economic crisis and maintain a high standard of life by domestic activities involving the lowest possible degree of dependence on foreign trade?" And it so happened that President Roosevelt had decided in his own mind where the emphasis and responsibility lay—on vigorous domestic measures attacking the crisis at home. In his campaign, he had given indications of his opinion, despite some confusion of thought; and in the selection of his personal advisors at home he had prepared to make war on the domestic crisis, without waiting for, or placing over-confident reliance on, conclusions reached by diplomatic agents in any kind of international conference. Moreover, between his inauguration and the collapse of the London conference, he had won from Congress an amazing program of legislation looking to the supreme end in view—a vigorous attack on the depression on the home front. This was not the old internationalism or the old nationalism of the outward thrusts, but a new kind of nationalism singularly unaggressive and implying no necessary threats to the security or economic life of other countries.

In one significant respect, then, it may be said that the London Economic Conference was not a failure. It furnished the occasion on which President Roosevelt disclosed his conception of American national interest in the first major, concrete test of his policy, and indicated to the participating nations the possibility of a conception of national economy which does not turn primarily on foreign trade, accompanied

[99] For an analysis of the Agenda of the London Economic Conference see Beard and Smith, *The Open Door at Home* (1934).

inevitably by trade rivalries, as the principal support of the standard of life. President Roosevelt's conception is one that fixes clearly the center of gravity for American policy in the United States itself, envisages the possibilities of a more intense exploitation of American resources, contemplates a more evenly balanced productivity between agriculture and industry and among different industries, seeks in principle a more equitable distribution of real wealth within the country, and accepts with reluctance and care only the minimum of international action which life under modern conditions impels.[100] This conception is amply illustrated in many directions. Besides the national program in the farm and industry legislation, there are the Muscle Shoals and Tennessee Valley Development program, the reforestation plans, the public works projects, the implications of the Corporation of Foreign Security Holders authorized in the Securities Act for the relief of American owners of foreign bonds, the refusal to accord any privileged position under the Recovery Act to exporters,[101] and the declared intention of Secretary of Commerce Roper to close twenty-one of the fifty-three offices maintained abroad by the Commerce Department's foreign service:[102] Such a course may be called the "national attitude," or it may be termed "isolation" or "nationalism," according as those terms are interpreted by various observers; but no matter what name may be applied, the policy itself is clear and appears in connection with every concrete issue to which either of two historic approaches—the national and the international—is made. Under the challenge and amid the exigencies of a new economic situation, the Roosevelt administration moved aggressively to the execution of the broad powers granted to it by an extraordinary session of Congress, and the country, turning from foreign affairs and the wider aspects of international life, became engrossed in working out its typically "national" pro-

[100] This philosophy, at least the domestic part of it, underlies President Roosevelt's Appeal to the Nation, New York *Times*, July 25, 1933. The part bearing upon international affairs is elsewhere expressed in the text above.

[101] For an intimation of the policy on this point, see New York *Times*, July 23, 1933, item, "Threat to Export in Recovery Bill."

[102] For the list of offices closed, see New York *Times*, June 15, 1933, item, "Roper to Close 21 Offices Abroad."

gram, adopting by the very character of its activities and routine the Roosevelt conception of national interest in which international action, though necessary to some degree, is regarded, nevertheless, as an incident to domestic life and progress.[103]

From the above historical survey of national interest in commercial expansion and contemporary policy, the following conclusions are drawn:

1. From the establishment of the Constitution to the close of President Hoover's administration, the Federalist-Whig-Republican conception of national interest contemplated heavy reliance upon foreign trade, a limitation of imports by high duties, and the expansion of foreign markets by the vigorous use of all the engines of government, including the Army and Navy. This conception of national interest proceeded on the assumption that the continuous expansion of foreign markets for American goods is *necessary* to prevent gluts of surpluses at home and is in fact *possible* of attainment; an assumption rudely challenged by the crisis which opened in 1929.

2. During a large part of this span of years, the Jeffersonian party also laid heavy emphasis on foreign trade as a means of marketing agricultural produce and securing cheap manufactures. This was a conception of national interest which conformed in general to the Manchester doctrines of political economy and assumed the possibility of the kind of internationalism contemplated by the Cobden-Bright school.

3. After the collapse of the economic structure in 1929, a new conception of national interest in foreign commerce appeared—a conception that a high standard of national well-being is possible with a minimum reliance on foreign trade and is desirable besides. Under this conception, the principal avenue of escape from economic crisis lies, not in adjustments made at international conferences, not in outward thrusts of commercial power, but in the collaboration of domestic interests with a view to establishing the security which may come from integrated economic activities and a more efficient distribution of wealth or buying power. If this new nationalism runs

[103] See Beard and Smith, *The Future Comes: A Study of the New Deal* (1933).

counter to the Cobden-Bright internationalism of *laissez faire,* it is far from being the old nationalism of imperialism based on *Machtpolitik,* which supports outward thrusts of American economic power and sustains them by diplomacy and arms. Whatever reactions and reversals may come, it may mark, not a swing of the pendulum, but a new stage in the development of national interest and international relations. At all events, it does not assume that outward thrusts of national power too strong to be controlled at home can be subdued at international conferences of diplomats representing governments incapable of conquering at home the very forces whose impacts abroad they seek to master through treaties, agreements, and conversations. It is ostensibly a non-imperialistic nationalism.

Yet it would be a mistake to assume that the emphasis placed on domestic recovery by President Franklin D. Roosevelt meant a reduction in the pressures of outward thrusts in every direction. On the contrary, a number of events indicated an intensification of those thrusts, westward into the Pacific, and southward into Latin America. First of all was a renewal of the building program for the Navy with a view, it was alleged, to reaching the "parity" and limits set by the naval treaties. To be sure, in the official explanation, stress was laid on the aids to industry and employment which the huge outlay would give, but obviously this was merely a pretext, for the same amount of money could have been devoted to the domestic program, with the same or better results in terms of industrial activity and employment. The domestic crisis was the occasion, not the cause, of the new naval construction in 1933.

In embarking on naval construction, the Roosevelt administration was running in the course of *Machtpolitik,* and contrary to the policy of former President Hoover, the supposed heir to the Federalist-Whig-Republican tradition. Repercussions abroad were immediate. Japanese imperialists found justification for even more feverish activities and laid out a new navy program designed, it was alleged, to bring the Japanese navy up to treaty limits, for the purpose of defending the Japanese sphere. British naval writers at once lamented the sad state of the British navy and demanded speedy action on the part of the British government—the adoption of a huge building program. Meanwhile, the historic methods of propaganda for naval rivalry were revived; news and editorials resounded with cries for "preparedness" in the old style. Thus the advocates of *Machtpolitik* were once more placed in the saddle and given an opportunity to ride. All that had been gained by moderation and naval limitation was jeopardized at home and abroad, with what wide consequences no one could foresee, save the certain result that naval rivalry continued and intensified would sooner or later culminate in a conflict irrelevant to national interest conceived in any realistic terms.

With reference to Latin America, events also moved rapidly in the opening months of the Roosevelt administration. Through the intervention of the ambassador of the United States in Cuba, the Machado régime was overthrown or at least its downfall was hastened. If responsibilities here assumed by the Government of the United States fell within the scope of Caribbean obligations carried by previous administrations, Democratic and Republican alike, it was clear that there would be repercussions throughout Latin America, as usual. Other signs of renewed southward thrusts appeared in connection with preparations for the 1933 Pan-American Conference and especially for offsetting the anomalous advantages obtained by the British government in Argentina by a clever stroke of economic diplomacy. In this way an effort was made to widen the American stake abroad at the probable expense of Great Britain, at the very moment when a renewal of naval rivalry appeared on the horizon.

There was, accordingly, no warrant in the nature of things for assuming that the preoccupation of the Roosevelt administration with domestic recovery through economic action at home had suppressed or even curtailed the particular interests that throve by the pursuit of *Machtpolitik,* by outward thrusts of economic and naval power. In other words, all phases of foreign policy were not assimilated to the implications of the National Recovery Program; and untoward events southward in the Caribbean or beyond Hawaii could be precipitated by operations conducted along old lines, resulting in a grand diversion—a diversion that might not be unwelcome, should the domestic recovery program fall far short of its aims. In such circumstances, it was impossible to discover from occurrences themselves how far efforts on the part of the Government of the United States to interpret national interest primarily in terms of domestic economy would go in practice. Faith in the possibility of acquiring ever-expanding markets for growing "surpluses" by outward thrusts of national sovereignty was weakening; but the future of domestic "self-containment" was uncertain, and out of the heritage of ancient rivalries carried on in the name of national interest the flames of a new world conflagration might spring.

EPILOGUE

What general conclusions relevant to the problem in hand emerge from the statements, declarations, practices, and tendencies surveyed in this volume? The following seem to be necessary and fundamental:

Since the foundation of the Republic, statesmen and publicists have written and spoken of national interest as if it were a kind of transcendent unity, even when they use the term "national interests," "American interests," or "our interests." They have treated it as a postulate which automatically provides rules for controlling policies and actions in foreign affairs, in general and in particular. Judging from their assertions and usages, the advancement of national interest is a binding obligation on American statesmen—the supreme obligation, with other considerations employed occasionally as features of policy.

The content and implications of both terms in the formula —"national" and "interest"—have undergone transformation in the process of American development. The word, national, does not appear in the Constitution. Leaders among the framers of that document used it, but owing to the jealousy of the states it later became inexpedient to speak too freely of the Government of the United States or of American society as "national" in character. Whether there was, in fact, an American nation or a mere confederacy of sovereign peoples, whether either the nation in process of making or the Union itself would perdure was a question that was not settled until the close of the Civil War. Only after 1865 did it become both expedient and patriotic to speak of the Federal Government as "national." The term "general" was long recommended by discretion.

In the course of American history, the conception of nationality as such has also been modified. At the outset, it was generally agreed among the founders of the Republic that the American nation possessed a certain ethnic unity—was an aggregation of people bound together, in the main, by common physical characteristics, popularly called racial, language, law, traditions, ideas of liberty, social practice, and government. There was likewise general agreement among the founders that immigration should be restricted with a view to preserving this type of nationality; very early the importation of Negroes as slaves was prohibited. During the nineteenth century, however, under the pressure of industrialists demanding laborers and land speculators calling for settlers, the gates of immigration were thrown open to all peoples; America was proclaimed "the asylum for the oppressed of all lands"; and as a result decided shifts were made in the racial composition of the American nation. Finally, in the immigration legislation of the twentieth century, enacted under vigorous drives of the American Federation of Labor, the racial composition of 1920 was made the basis of American nationality; henceforward it was to be limited primarily to north European stocks, with concessions to certain Latin American regions providing cheap labor for American agriculture and industry and to the insular possessions of the United States.

Very early in the history of the country appeared two fairly clear-cut conceptions of the term "interest," which may be, for the sake of convenience, called Jeffersonian and Hamiltonian.

With respect to the question of territorial expansion, the Jeffersonian conception favors the acquisition of contiguous regions, unoccupied or largely unoccupied, which can be exploited by American farmers and planters; and it opposes the annexation of non-contiguous regions inhabited by races that cannot be easily assimilated and must be defended by expensive naval establishments likely to burden the country and involve it in unprofitable and ruinous wars.

Touching the subject of domestic economy and foreign commerce, the Jeffersonian conception is equally positive. Agriculture is the only secure basis for a republic, the nursery of liberty, and the guarantee of popular institutions. The maintenance of agricultural predominance is thus a prime consideration in national interest. From this follows commercial policy: the foreign policy of the United States should be directed to finding and maintaining outlets for agricultural produce to be exchanged in the best markets for manufactures. As corollaries, tariffs are to be low and mainly for revenue, the carriage of goods on the high seas is to be entrusted to the cheapest carriers, and large military and naval establishments can thus be, and should be, avoided.

In contrast, the Hamiltonian conception of national interest, although not originally explicit on the point, has been employed (a) to oppose the annexation of contiguous territory which may be occupied by American farmers and planters and thus "overbalance the commercial interests" in the Union, and (b) to support the acquisition of distant territories offering naval bases and opportunities for the extension of American commerce, even if inhabited by races that cannot be easily assimilated to American nationality.

The elements of the Hamiltonian thesis touching domestic economy and foreign commerce are likewise definite. Domestic economy is to be diversified by the development of manufacturing as well as agriculture, even if the development leads to the predominance of industry, in terms of capital employed and number of inhabitants engaged. Foreign trade is not to take a "natural course," but is to be deflected by tariffs, subsidies, bounties, and regulations designed to foster American industries and enterprises. The whole weight of the Federal Government, including an efficient naval establishment, is to be thrown into the operation of promoting the export of American goods and the importation of materials that will not "harm" American industries. Since the rise of great technology, the Hamilton conception has been elaborated to mean that the continuous expansion of foreign outlets for American goods and capital is *necessary* to take care of ever-mounting "surpluses," in other words, to keep the American industrial machine running at an ever-higher tension. Thus, foreign trade is not to be "free," but "controlled," and the civil, military, and naval engines of the United States are to be employed in outward thrusts of power for the enlargement of trade outlets.

Like all theses advanced by statesmen, neither of these conceptions of national interest, pushed to its logical conlusion, has ever been precisely and fully applied in practice, but for a long time they served as frames of reference for the formulation of policy and the determination of action by the respective political parties that divided the country after the administration of President Washington. As the years passed, however, the social and economic actualities of the United States, on which they were predicated, underwent revolutionary transformations. Despite the efforts of Jeffersonian leaders, manufacturing did become dominant in domestic economy; the Democratic party acquired a large urban following, including importing and exporting merchants and bankers; and its once clean-cut conception of economy and commercial policy became assimilated more or less to the Hamiltonian conception. In other words, the frames of reference, separate in the beginning, began to overlap and to become confused, and by the third decade of the twentieth century it was impossible to discover, in the pronouncements of statesmen, any sharp distinction between them.

In the meantime the social and economic state of other nations throughout the world, with which American commercial and diplomatic relations were carried on, was also radically changed by a kindred revolution in production. Great Britain found other large sources of agricultural produce and raw materials. Countries once agricultural became industrial and entered into competition with the United States in all the markets in which expanding outlets were sought for American goods and capital. Other naval powers began to dispute the supremacy of Great Britain and the United States in distant sea zones. In fine, the world conditions, in which either the Jeffersonian or the Hamiltonian thesis of national interest, or any hybrid conception, could be, and had to be, realized, if

pushed by the Government of the United States, were profoundly altered by the industrial revolution, the rise of mass
production, and the appearance of intense rivalries carried
on in the name of national interest by European and Oriental
powers. Everywhere, even in Great Britain, the conception
and practice of controlled trade, as distinguished from *laissez
faire*, are now dominant, and present a solid front to all efforts
at realizing the national interest of the United States in foreign
commerce and policy, as historically conceived.

In the great depression following the crash of 1929, the
fundamental *possibility* assumed by both the Jeffersonian and
Hamiltonian conceptions of national interest was challenged
by stubborn facts. Was it really possible, by any policy and
action, to find ever-expanding foreign outlets for the ever
increasing "surpluses" of agricultural produce, manufactures,
and capital, especially in view of the increasing competition of
other great powers for the same markets? If so, why had the
policies and measures vigorously pursued by the Harding-
Coolidge-Hoover administrations, in the Federalist-Whig-
Republican tradition, failed to accomplish that end?

In this situation, fragments of a new conception of national
interest appeared in the policies and measures of President
Franklin D. Roosevelt. Amid them was the central idea: by
domestic planning and control the American economic machine
may be kept running at a high tempo supplying the intranational market, without relying primarily upon foreign outlets for "surpluses" of goods and capital. To give effect to this
idea, legislation which may be deemed almost revolutionary
was adopted in 1933 and administered with great energy.
But no corresponding adjustment was made in foreign policies
inherited from the past, nor was it clear, from the pronouncements and actions of the President, whether any such adjustment was deemed appropriate to the new domestic conception.
On the contrary, enormous funds were allotted to naval construction as if the policy of *Machtpolitik*, favored by Hamilton
and utterly condemned by Jefferson, was still to be followed,
despite the repudiation of the assumptions respecting foreign
trade upon which it rested.

Evidently, then, the two inherited conceptions of national

interest are in process of fusion and dissolution. A new conception, with a positive core and nebulous implications, is rising out of the past and is awaiting formulation at the hands of a statesman as competent and powerful as Hamilton or Jefferson.

APPENDIX

THE AMERICAN STAKE ABROAD

BEARD and Smith pointed out in the original (1934) edition of *The Idea of National Interest* that Americans have, by various processes, acquired many assets in other lands—of which branch factories and the right to be paid for exports are representative. The authors grouped such tangibles together to form what they called "the American stake abroad." [1] While they admitted the term "stake" was "more popular than scientific," they felt it was an appropriate one for characterizing American operations abroad that involved taking chances or risks with valuable property.

Altogether, Beard and Smith devoted two chapters (VII and VIII) and the Appendix to the discussion of "the American stake abroad." However, so much of this material, the bulk of it prepared by Smith, had become seriously outdated by 1962 that he suggested its elimination before the book appeared again. [2] In deference to his request, these three parts have been replaced in this reprint by a single new Appendix, [3] covering roughly the same general ground but in a much abbreviated and updated manner.

THE CAPITAL ACCOUNT

A major component of "the American stake abroad" consists of the long-term private *capital* Americans have poured into enterprises located in other countries. For statistical purposes this capital is

---

[1] Beard and Smith borrowed this term from others, giving these examples of prior use: Max Winkler, "America's Stake Abroad," Foreign Policy Association, *Information. Service,* February 4, 1931, and Harriet Moore, "The American Stake in the Philippines," *Foreign Affairs,* April 1933, pp. 517-20.

[2] Letter dated May 1, 1962, from Smith to William Beard.

[3] Since Charles A. Beard passed away in 1948 and George H. E. Smith in 1962, the work of preparing this Appendix devolved upon Beard's son, William, who had worked with his father on several volumes and was familiar with his style and methods.

commonly divided into two classes on the basis of the rights created by it.[4] The category of "direct" investments covers capital outlays that have provided Americans with a substantial degree of effective control over the management of foreign enterprises. "Portfolio"[5] investments, on the other hand, consist of foreign stocks and bonds acquired by Americans primarily to obtain dividends and interest rather than managerial control.

Private "Direct Investments": Overall Growth. In 1900 American private long-term "direct investments" in other countries totalled $455,000,000. By 1912 this figure had grown to $1,740,000,000, and in 1929 it reached $7,477,735,000.[6] Then followed a period of relative stagnation as a severe economic depression in the 1930's and the wholesale destructiveness of World War II combined to interfere with American investments abroad for nearly two decades. Indeed, the total American private long-term direct investment abroad in 1946 amounted to only $7,200,000,000, or somewhat less than the 1929 figure. For a time after 1946, large amounts of American capital went into the rehabilitation of American-owned enterprises hard hit by the war, into the development of oil fields in the Middle East and Latin America, and into other ventures, raising the total of direct investments to $11,800,000,000 in 1950. Later, the climb was faster, the total of American private long-term direct investments reaching $29,700,000,000 in 1959.[7] By the end of 1963, the figure was up to $40,645,000,000,[8] and it subsequently went still higher.

Private "Direct Investments": Managerial Results. How much influence do Americans wield abroad, through their private long-term direct investments? According to a government survey, almost three quarters of the approximately $24 billion so invested, as of 1957, was in enterprises in which Americans clearly dominated the management by owning 95 per cent or more of the equity (that is, stock, surplus, and branch accounts).[9] Moreover these same Americans controlled the use of most of the additional $18 billions in long-term capital that had been contributed locally by foreigners to these enterprises, since this capital had been largely exchanged for evidences

[4] For the manner in which the dividing line was drawn between the two classes in a major survey, see U.S. Department of Commerce, *U.S. Business Investments in Foreign Countries* (1960), pp. 73, 76-7.

[5] Among other things, the word "portfolio" means a list of the securities held by an individual or corporation.

[6] *The Idea of National Interest,* 1934 ed., p. 209.

[7] U.S. Department of Commerce, *op. cit.,* p. 1.

[8] U.S. Secretary of the Treasury, *Annual Report for the Fiscal Year ended June 30, 1964,* p. 666.

[9] U.S. Department of Commerce, *op. cit.,* pp. 6, 26.

of debt, such as bonds,[10] that did not ordinarily entitle their holders to a voice in management.

Private "Direct Investments": Types of Enterprises. As the table below indicates, the two biggest factors in the growth of American private direct investment abroad between 1929 and 1959 were the expansion of petroleum and of manufacturing operations. Contributing to the "oil boom" were highly successful American exploratory techniques and the keen desire of foreign governments to acquire their own sources of a basic fuel and obtain oil royalties for their hard-pressed national treasuries. In the case of manufacturing, Americans often found that by building plants abroad they could save so much in shipping charges and in labor costs, and avoid so many political obstacles, that they could remain competitive in distant markets which American exporters were finding it difficult, or impossible, to tap at a good profit.

AMERICAN PRIVATE LONG-TERM "DIRECT" INVESTMENTS ABROAD
CLASSIFIED AS TO TYPES OF ENTERPRISE [11]

Industry	1929	1959
Raw Materials		
Petroleum	$1,117,000,000	$10,423,000,000
Mining and Smelting . . .	1,185,000,000	2,858,000,000
Agriculture . . .	880,000,000	662,000,000
Manufacturing	1,813,000,000	9,692,000,000
Public Utilities	1,610,000,000	2,413,000,000
Trade	368,000,000	2,039,000,000
Other	555,000,000	1,648,000,000
Total, all fields	7,528,000,000	29,735,000,000

Private "Direct Investments": Regional Trends. In the table below, the distribution of American long-term "direct" investments abroad among major regions has been given for three widely separated years. It is apparent at a glance that Americans have made their heaviest investments in their own hemisphere, with Canada early taking the lead as the outstanding absorber of American capital and increasing that lead very substantially. Contributing to Canadian predominance were the country's similarities with the United States in culture and economy, its vast natural resources capable of serving American industrial needs, and its growing domestic markets. Next in size in

[10] *Ibid.,* p. 26.
[11] U.S. Department of Commerce, *op. cit.,* p. 93.

1959 were investments in other lands of this hemisphere, with European investments ranking third in size.

Private "Portfolio" Investments Abroad. Besides pouring billions of dollars of private long-term capital into "direct investments" abroad,

AMERICAN PRIVATE LONG-TERM "DIRECT" INVESTMENTS ABROAD
CLASSIFIED BY REGIONS [12]

REGION	1900	1929	1959
Canada	$150,000,000	$1,960,320,000	$10,171,000,000
Other Western Hemisphere . .	290,000,000 [13]	3,518,739,000	9,944,000,000
Europe	10,000,000	1,352,753,000	5,300,000,000
Asia, Australia, New Zealand, and the Pacific Islands . . .	5,000,000	543,694,000	3,029,000,000
Africa	......	102,229,000	843,000,000
Grand totals .	455,000,000	7,477,735,000	29,735,000,000 [14]

Americans have put billions into "portfolio investments." At the close of 1930, for example, private foreign "portfolio investments" made by Americans totalled $7,204,218,000, the majority of it ($4,895,-970,000) in the form of bonds issued by foreign governments.[15] According to preliminary figures for the end of 1963, Americans had by then increased their private "portfolio investments" in foreign countries to $17,611,000,000, of which a smaller portion ($8,131,-000,000, or less than half) consisted of bonds.[16]

Foreign Government Obligations Held by the United States Government. To complete the "Capital Account," there must be added to the billions of dollars of private American capital invested abroad the further billions loaned by the government of the United States to other lands. The oldest of these loans were made during and after World War I, chiefly to enable foreign governments to secure the

[12] Data for 1959, *ibid.,* p. 89; data for 1900 and 1929 from *The Idea of National Interest,* 1934 ed., p. 209.

[13] Includes Puerto Rico.

[14] This total includes some items not separately listed above, such as investments in vessels flying foreign flags and roaming the seas at large, which were classified as "international."

[15] *The Idea of National Interest,* 1934 ed., p. 234. The Appendix to the same, pp. 555-63, classified the purposes of foreign loans floated in the United States, 1920-1929, and listed $1,134,460,976 in dollar bonds issued by foreign countries, held by Americans, and in default, March 1, 1933.

[16] U.S. Department of Commerce, *Survey of Current Business,* August 1964, pp. 8-14, 24.

foodstuffs, munitions, and other supplies they needed for armed combat and for the relief of the war's victims after the fighting ceased.[17] The status of these loans as of June 30, 1964, is given in the table below:

STATUS OF THE INDEBTEDNESS OF FOREIGN GOVERNMENTS TO THE UNITED STATES GOVERNMENT, ARISING OUT OF WORLD WAR I, JUNE 30, 1964 [18]

Country	Original debt	Unmatured principal	Principal and interest due but unpaid
Armenia . .	$ 11,959,917.49	......	$ 38,753,000.86
Austria . .	26,843,148.66	$ 3,530,505.24	22,494,034.35
Belgium . .	419,837,630.37	219,980,000.00	441,603,077.60
Cuba . . .	10,000,000.00	......	......
Czechoslovakia .	185,071,023.07	91,875,000.00	170,359,566.62
Estonia . .	16,466,012.87	10,036,000.00	25,333,770.81
Finland . .	8,999,999.97	5,248,698.99	16,433.19
France . . .	4,089,689,588.18	1,958,692,869.71	4,497,040,314.61
Great Britain .	4,802,181,641.56	2,701,000,000.00	6,600,759,301.93
Greece . . .	32,499,922.67	9,100,000.00	36,054,445.10
Hungary . .	1,982,555.50	1,212,085.00	2,789,866.05
Italy . . .	2,042,364,319.28	1,282,900,000.00	953,638,159.34
Latvia . . .	6,888,664.20	4,230,300.00	10,429,822.04
Liberia . . .	26,000.00	......	......
Lithuania . .	6,432,465.00	3,859,007.00	9,300,913.56
Nicaragua . .	141,950.36	......	......
Poland . . .	207,344,297.37	128,375,000.00	314,269,604.20
Rumania . .	68,359,192.45	35,084,000.00	74,300,491.07
Russia . . .	192,601,297.37	......	631,050,470.42
Yugoslavia . .	63,577,712.55	38,895,000.00	41,448,593.78
Totals . .	12,193,267,338.92	6,494,018,465.94	13,869,641,935.43

After its unfavorable experience with direct loans in World War I, the United States government chose to supply the needs of its associates in World War II via the alternate "lend-lease" route, at a cost of more than $50 billion. After the end of World War II, the United States settled its lend-lease accounts in such a way as to create a new

[17] *The Idea of National Interest,* 1934 ed., pp. 235-36.
[18] U.S. Secretary of the Treasury, *Annual Report on the State of the Finances for the Fiscal Year ended June 30, 1964,* p. 674.

round of debt which foreign governments were obligated to discharge by making periodic payments to the U.S. Then, under "foreign aid" programs to help war-devastated lands rebuild, to combat communism, to assist in the modernization of relatively undeveloped countries, to promote trade, and for a variety of other purposes, the U.S. government loaned further billions abroad. The composition of the debt of $16.6 billions accumulated by these operations, as of the middle of 1964, is presented below:

OUTSTANDING INDEBTEDNESS OF FOREIGN GOVERNMENTS TO THE UNITED STATES GOVERNMENT (EXCLUSIVE OF WORLD WAR I OBLIGATIONS) AS OF JUNE 30, 1964 (IN MILLIONS OF DOLLARS) [19]

Source	Europe	Asia	Latin America	Africa	Oceania	United Nations and unspecified
Under Export-Import Bank Act . . .	$ 652	$ 890	$1,845	$133	$4	......
Under Foreign Assistance and Related Acts . .	1,478	2,514	788	361	......	16
Under Agricultural Trade Development and Assistance Act	707	1,339	163	318	......	......
Lend-Lease, Surplus Property, and Related Settlements [20] . .	1,428	643	10	19	1	......
Other Sources . .	3,168	6	......	......	......	112

Summary: The Capital Account. The components of the capital account, previously separately discussed, have been brought together in the table offered next, to present an overall picture of American long-term capital at work abroad in a sample year. While it is difficult to predict at this stage how much money loaned by the United States government abroad it will ultimately recover, it is also true that the official loans fit very well the Beard and Smith concept

[19] U.S. Secretary of the Treasury, *op. cit.*, pp. 676-77.
[20] Includes $322 million due the United States government from the Soviet Union, of which $120 million had been collected and $52 million was past due. *Idem.*

of the American "stake" abroad as being composed of tangibles being "risked, or hazarded" in other lands.

AMERICAN LONG-TERM CAPITAL AT WORK ABROAD IN 1963

Private investments: [21]		
Direct	$40,645,000,000	
Portfolio	17,611,000,000	
Private investment total . .	58,256,000,000	$58,256,000,000
Loans made by the United States government abroad: [22]		
World War I debts, unpaid principal	11,433,000,000	
Subsequent debts (lend-lease, foreign assistance programs, etc.) . .	15,591,000,000	
Government capital, total . .	27,024,000,000	27,024,000,000
Grand total		85,280,000,000

Partially offsetting the foregoing American placement of capital abroad has been a reverse investment of foreign capital in the United States. In 1963, for instance, foreign direct investments of $7.9 billion and foreign portfolio investments of $13.2 billion, made in American enterprises,[23] amounted to almost a quarter as much as the $85.3 billions of American capital that had been put to work abroad.

THE CURRENT ACCOUNT

Besides risking long-term *capital* abroad, Americans may be found at any given moment engaged in spending and receiving *ordinary funds,* as when they pay for imports out of current business incomes or receive credit abroad in foreign currencies for delivered exports. Uses of "current" funds in this fashion make up what is here called the "current account."

Is the current account really a part of the "American stake abroad"? Arguing in the affirmative, Beard and Smith pointed out in 1934 that such items as "cargoes of American merchandise in foreign ports" are "tangible things" risked abroad, thus satisfying their definition of a stake. Moreover, given the tendency to regulate international

---

[21] Taken from totals given earlier in this Appendix.
[22] U.S. Secretary of the Treasury, *Annual Report on the State of the Finances for the Fiscal Year Ended June 30, 1963,* pp. 712-15.
[23] U.S. Secretary of the Treasury, *Annual Report for the Fiscal Year Ended June 30, 1964,* pp. 666-67.

trade through quota, license, and reciprocal tariff agreements, they remarked that it is "not difficult to conceive" of important ingredients of the current account becoming "the foundation for vested property rights" and hence being "part of a stake" abroad. While the authors also reviewed the case against including the current account in the American stake abroad, they concluded that there are "enough elements" of both tangible value and risk in the current account "to bring it within the purview" of their survey. In deference to this decision, and as a practical aid to present-day students of international "balance-of-payments" problems, the current account has been covered as a part of the American stake abroad in this Appendix.

American Foreign Trade: Magnitude and Ratio Between Exports and Imports. Historically, the chief ingredient of the current account has been American foreign trade—the flow of imports and exports. After occupying a prominent place in the first quarter-century of the nation's independence, foreign trade became of lesser importance to the country's economy for the succeeding three quarters of a century. Then, in the closing years of the nineteenth century, it began to draw increasing attention and to exert a stronger influence on American life. While American foreign trade fell off substantially in the depression years of the 1930's, it revived during and after World War II and has since been a conspicuous feature of the American economy. Fluctuations in the size of this trade, and its distribution between exports and imports, are given in the following table for a considerable

TOTAL EXPORTS, IMPORTS, AND BALANCE OF TRADE OF THE
UNITED STATES [24] (IN MILLIONS OF DOLLARS)

Yearly average or year	Merchandise exports, including re-exports	General imports	Balance of trade, excess of exports over imports
1896–1900	$1,157	$ 742	$ 416
1910–1914	2,166	1,689	477
1915–1920	6,521	3,358	3,163
1926–1930	4,777	4,034	744
1936–1940	3,220	2,482	738
1946–1950	11,829	6,659	5,170
1956–1960	19,204	13,650	5,544
1964	26,438	18,685	7,754

[24] From *The Idea of National Interest,* 1934 ed., p. 247, and U.S. Bureau of the Census, *Statistical Abstract of the United States, 1965,* p. 852.

span of time. As a glance at the extreme right-hand column indicates, America has normally had what is called a "favorable balance of trade," that is, an excess of exports over imports, to this extent bringing more money into the country than goes out of it. Yet, despite the variations evident in the table, the percentage that American exports have constituted of the movable commodities produced in the United States has been surprisingly steady. It was 9.7 per cent in 1914, 9.8 per cent in 1929, and 9.9 per cent in 1957.[25]

Foreign Trade: Composition. In the next table, the total volume of American exports and imports is broken down into five major categories. As one would expect in a country as technologically advanced as the United States, raw materials have long been imported in large volumes and heavy shipments of manufactured goods have been sent to other lands. In 1896-1900 imports of raw material (crude materials and crude foodstuffs) constituted 44.6 per cent of all imports. This percentage subsequently rose to almost 50 per cent of all imports, then fell off after World War II to 29.4 per cent of all imports in 1964, less than the percentage existing at the close of the nineteenth century. The figures for exports of manufactured goods tell a very different story. A spectacular growth in the export of finished manufactures, from 21.3 per cent of all exports to 57.1 per cent of all exports, occurred between the close of the nineteenth century and 1964. Indeed, if exports of manufactured foodstuffs, semifinished goods, and finished manufactures are combined, over three quarters of all American exports in 1964 were manufactured articles. Meanwhile, the proportion of American exports consisting of raw materials has declined drastically, and since 1950 there has been a marked rise in imports of finished manufactures—as varied as Parisian fashions, small cars, fine liquor, and inexpensive transistor radios—some representing special skills and luxuries and others production costs abroad that are less than those in the United States.

Some of the foreign trade just described is essential to the maintenance of current American standards of living. For example, raw coffee, bananas, crude rubber, and cocoa beans consumed in the United States are imported because they can be grown to best advantage only in tropical lands. Even the expansion of American industry—a vast consumer of raw materials that in some cases are growing somewhat scarce at home—is partially dependent on imports. For example, in 1962 some 89 per cent of the aluminum ore

[25] Figures for 1914 and 1929 are from *The Idea of National Interest,* 1934 ed., p. 245; the figure for 1957 is from U.S. Bureau of the Census, *Historical Statistics of the United States, Colonial Times to 1957* (1960), p. 542.

and 34 per cent of the iron ore and concentrates used in the United States came from other countries.[26] Obviously, if these items are to be paid for without excessive drainage on American funds, then at least a corresponding volume of exports is necessary.

FOREIGN TRADE IN MERCHANDISE BY ECONOMIC CLASSES [27]
(IN MILLIONS OF DOLLARS)

EXPORTS

| Yearly average or year | Total value | Percentage of total value | | | | |
		Crude materials	Crude foodstuffs	Manufactured foodstuffs	Semimanufactures	Finished manufactures
1896–1900	$ 1,136	26.1	18.9	24.0	9.6	21.3
1910–1914	2,130	33.5	5.9	13.8	16.0	30.7
1921–1925	4,310	27.5	9.7	13.9	12.5	36.3
1926–1930	4,688	24.4	6.4	9.7	14.1	45.3
1931–1935	1,989	30.2	3.9	8.8	14.5	42.6
1941–1945	9,922	5.8	1.7	11.9	9.4	71.3
1950	10,142	18.6	7.5	6.3	11.1	56.6
1960	20,349	12.7	8.1	5.5	17.3	56.4
1964	26,086	11.1	9.7	6.5	15.6	57.1

IMPORTS

1896–1900	742	29.5	15.1	15.9	13.4	26.2
1910–1914	1,689	35.2	12.0	11.5	18.2	23.1
1921–1925	3,450	37.4	11.1	13.0	17.7	20.9
1926–1930	4,034	36.8	12.6	9.9	18.9	21.9
1931–1935	1,704	28.9	15.6	13.7	18.7	23.0
1941–1945	3,476	33.0	16.4	11.5	21.1	18.0
1950	8,743	28.2	20.0	10.3	24.3	17.2
1960	14,650	20.6	11.7	10.7	21.1	35.9
1964	18,600	18.5	10.9	9.7	21.4	39.4

In certain instances, however, foreign trade that benefits one group of Americans may work a hardship on another. For example, between 1928 and 1931 about $768,000 in tobacco machinery, much of it for

[26] U.S. Bureau of the Census, *Statistical Abstract of the United States, 1965*, p. 876.
[27] Data from 1896 through 1930 from *The Idea of National Interest*, 1934 ed., p. 251. Data since 1930 from U.S. Bureau of the Census, *Statistical Abstract of the United States, 1965*, p. 877.

making cigarettes, was exported by Americans to China, thus bene-
fiting both the Chinese, who were thereby enabled to make their
own cigarettes, and the Americans who exported the equipment, but
sharply reducing the exports of another group of Americans—the
cigarette makers who saw their sales to China slashed in the same
period from an annual volume of 8,654,000,000 cigarettes to only
133,000,000.[28]

Cargo Movements. Most of America's foreign trade is carried in
ships and aircraft. In the early days of the republic, American vessels
hauled 92 per cent of the nation's imports and 88 per cent of its
exports. Beginning in 1830, however, a steady decline set in which
brought the proportion of the nation's foreign trade hauled in American ships down to a mere 9.3 per cent.[29] Later, aided by heavy war-
time shipbuilding programs and government subsidies, the percentage
climbed substantially. Indeed, in the year 1945, after the sinking of
many foreign vessels, 68.4 per cent of the nation's foreign trade tonnage
was carried in American ships. Then once more the figure shrank,
until in 1964 the percentage by weight of American foreign trade
carried in American ships was only 9.9 per cent.[30] Haulage by ship
has been supplemented in recent years by considerable freight movement by air, and here the American position is stronger. In 1964, for
example, 46.0 per cent of American imports and 38.5 per cent of
American exports, by weight, moving by air, were taken by American
carriers.[31]

Obviously, when Americans send goods abroad and foreigners dispatch goods to the United States on American carriers, money goes
into American hands, and conversely, when foreign carriers are used,
dollars end up in foreign hands. Thus the great decline in the use
of American ships, offset to only a limited degree by a better American
position in the air, works to the disadvantage of the United States
in terms of the international movement of funds. A decrease of
American carrying capacity can also be a serious handicap in times
of war.

Travel. American ships and airplanes also compete with foreign
carriers for the passenger trade. If, to the sums Americans have spent
for going abroad on foreign vessels and aircraft, one adds their actual
travel outlays within other countries, one finds that via this route
large sums of money have passed into foreign hands since World

[28] From the 1934 edition, pp. 258-60.
[29] *Ibid.,* pp. 307-08.
[30] U.S. Bureau of the Census, *op. cit.,* p. 598.
[31] U.S. Bureau of the Census, *op. cit.,* p. 595.

War II. In 1947, $628 millions were paid by American travelers to
foreigners in this fashion, a figure which rose to $1,633 million in
1957 and $3,486 million in 1964, when 2.2 million residents of the
United States went abroad. By contrast, foreigners paid to American
carriers and spent in the United States for travel only $1,350 million
in 1964,[32] with the net result that, as far as travel was concerned,
the international flow of cash was heavily outward from the United
States to other lands.

Foreign Aid Programs of the United States Government. While
private interests were influencing the "current account" through
foreign trade and travel in the manner described above, the United
States government was also exerting a powerful effect on it. Altogether, from the start of the foreign aid program in April 1948
through June 30, 1964, approximately $69.8 billion [33] had been dis-
tributed by the U.S. to ninety-eight countries—twenty-four in the
Western Hemisphere, twenty-one in Europe, twenty in Africa, seven-
teen in the Near East and Southern Asia, and sixteen in the Far East
and the Pacific.[34] Part of this total consisted of loans, covered above
in the "capital account" record. The remainder—made up of grants
subject to repayment in only very limited and special cases—is given
for representative years in the table below. Additional money has
flowed into the local economies of many countries from American
military forces and their dependents stationed overseas.

TOTAL OF U.S. GOVERNMENT ECONOMIC AND MILITARY ASSISTANCE GRANTS
TO FOREIGN COUNTRIES (IN MILLIONS OF DOLLARS) [35]

Fiscal years ended June 30	Economic assistance	Military assistance	Total of all grants
1950	$3,451	$ 56	$3,507
1953	1,932	4,159	6,091
1955	1,624	2,396	4,020
1960	1,302	1,697	2,999
1963	953	1,765	2,718

Other Elements in the Current Account. In addition to the activities covered above, there are numerous others which produce significant transfers of money or its equivalents between the United

[32] U.S. Department of Commerce, *Survey of Current Business,* May 1964,
pp. 22ff., and June 1965, pp. 25ff.
[33] U.S. Bureau of the Census, *op. cit.,* p. 863.
[34] U.S. Bureau of the Census, *Statistical Abstract of the United States,*
1964, pp. 860-61.
[35] *Ibid.,* p. 859.

States and foreign countries. Many immigrants, for instance, send some of their earnings back to relatives in the lands of their births, and American plants located overseas share some of their profits with the United States. Payments of dividends and interest on foreign securities owned in the United States flow to America, while similar payments go overseas to foreign holders of American securities. Americans license foreign corporations to use their patents and operational knowledge, and foreigners do likewise to obtain fees from American licensees. Because of the number and complexity of these and other operations, however, and the difficulty of obtaining satisfactory statistics for all of them, no table has been prepared for this the last group of items comprising the current account.

THE BALANCE-OF-PAYMENTS PROBLEM

Writing in 1934, Beard and Smith concluded their survey of the American stake abroad by declaring that "the whole weight of governmental activities" in the United States has been brought into play "to strengthen and increase" the American stake abroad "on the hypothesis, and no doubt the conscientious belief, that the 'national interest' is thereby advanced." [36]

So large did that stake later become, however, and so serious were the balance-of-payments problems created by it, that the government of the United States eventually began to have some very realistic second thoughts about the above hypothesis. Concretely, the American stake abroad reached the point, after World War II, where foreign claims against American dollars were often substantially larger than American claims against foreign currencies. True, this balance-of-payments situation could be, and has been, met in part by heavy shipments of gold by the United States to foreign lands out of the national government's bullion supply. However, as indicated in the accompanying table, the government gold stock had shrunk by August 1965 to $13.9 billion, against which foreigners held $27.7 billions [37] in unsatisfied claims, more than could be met even by a complete delivery of all that was left of the American gold supply.

In trying to find partial solutions to the balance-of-payments problem, the national government had, by the fall of 1965, taken a number of steps which limited the growth of the American stake abroad. For example, early in 1965 President Lyndon B. Johnson and the Secretary of Commerce pleaded with American businessmen to reduce

[36] *The Idea of National Interest,* 1934 ed., Chapter VIII, last sentence.
[37] *Time,* September 10, 1965, p. 86.

the flow of American capital into "direct" investments abroad and to try to secure a greater portion of their funds from local investors overseas.[38] To discourage Americans from exporting dollars to buy foreign stocks and bonds as "portfolio" investments, the "interest

STOCK OF GOLD HELD BY THE UNITED STATES GOVERNMENT
AT THE END OF EACH LISTED PERIOD
(IN MILLIONS OF DOLLARS) [39]

Year	Stock of gold
1948	$24,399
1949	24,563
1952	23,252
1955	21,753
1960	17,804
1963	15,596
August 1965	13,900 (roughly)

equalization tax" had been imposed on certain purchases of this nature, running as high as 15 per cent of their value in some cases.[40]

Turning from the capital account to the current account, President Johnson urged Americans to see their own country rather than spend their dollars abroad in travel. He urged them to ship their cargoes and to ride on American vessels and aircraft rather than contributing dollars to foreign carriers. For its part, the national government had made strong efforts over a span of several years to reduce the expenditure of dollars at American military installations overseas, slashing this dollar drain by some $500 million a year between 1960 and 1963.[41] Techniques, too, were developed to conserve dollars when distributing foreign aid.[42]

Although not designed as tools for solving balance-of-payments problems, certain other actions by the national government also had some effect on the American stake abroad. In this class lay the pro-

[38] "Stanching the Dollar Outflow," *Business Week*, July 3, 1965, pp. 38ff.
[39] U.S. Bureau of the Census, *Historical Statistics of the United States, Colonial Times to 1957*, p. 649; *Statistical Abstract of the United States, 1964*, p. 855; *Time*, September 10, 1965, p. 86.
[40] 26 United States Code § 4911ff.
[41] U.S. Secretary of the Treasury, *Annual Report for the Fiscal Year Ended June 30, 1964*, p. 267.
[42] The exchange of commodities by the United States government for native goods and services the government would otherwise have to pay for in dollars is one such technique. U.S. Department of Agriculture, *Farmer's World: The Yearbook of Agriculture, 1964*, p. 399.

hibitions placed on American trade with Red China, Cuba, North Korea, and North Vietnam, and the licensing restrictions imposed on trade with other communist countries.[43] Even the quotas that had been placed on imports of oil, sugar, cotton, and other commodities contributed their part to a reduction in the flow of American dollars overseas through the current account.[44]

In short, it looked as if, in the fall of 1965, American businessmen were coming to the end of a free and easy era when they could count on governmental backing for expansionist plans almost anywhere, and were joining their colleagues in other lands where the foreign activities of native businessmen had long been subjected to extensive governmental control.

WILLIAM BEARD

[43] 50 United States Code § 2021ff.; U.S. Secretary of the Treasury, *Annual Report for the Fiscal Year Ended June 30, 1964*, pp. 117-18.
[44] "Quotas Shake Up Oil Industry," *Business Week*, July 11, 1959, pp. 137-38; U.S. Department of Agriculture, *op. cit.*, pp. 371, 377.

INDEX

Commerce enlarged, 130; efforts made to arouse interest in foreign trade and to consolidate interest of country for conquest of world's markets, 130; conditions at end of, 143, 144; outburst of naval construction, during, followed by lull, 320; fighting strength of Navy at end of, 323

Yorktown, American war vessel ordered to intercept filibustering movement against Diaz, 179

Zelaya, José Santos, lumber concession secured from, 171-173; struggle between, and revolutionary government set up at Bluefields, 174; efforts of, to put down revolution, 176; resignation of, 176; message of, ascribing responsibility for revolution to "hostile attitude of a powerful nation," 176

Zimmermann, Erich, on "vegetable civilizations" in contrast with "mineral civilizations," 167

QUADRANGLE PAPERBACKS

History

Thomas A. Bailey. *Woodrow Wilson and the Lost Peace.* QP1
Thomas A. Bailey. *Woodrow Wilson and the Great Betrayal.* QP2
Charles A. Beard. *The Idea of National Interest.* QP27
Ray A. Billington. *The Protestant Crusade.* QP12
John Chamberlain. *Farewell to Reform.* QP19
Chester McArthur Destler. *American Radicalism, 1865-1901.* QP30
Elisha P. Douglass. *Rebels and Democrats.* QP26
Herman Finer. *Road to Reaction.* QP5
Felix Frankfurter. *The Commerce Clause.* QP16
Ray Ginger. *Altgeld's America.* QP21
Louis Joughin and Edmund M. Morgan. *The Legacy of Sacco and Vanzetti.* QP7
Edward Chase Kirkland. *Dream and Thought in the Business Community, 1860-1900.* QP11
Adrienne Koch. *The Philosophy of Thomas Jefferson.* QP17
Walter LaFeber. *John Quincy Adams and American Continental Empire.* QP23
David E. Lilienthal. *TVA: Democracy on the March.* QP28
Arthur S. Link. *Wilson the Diplomatist.* QP18
Huey P. Long. *Every Man a King.* QP8
Gene M. Lyons. *America: Purpose and Power.* QP24
Jackson Turner Main. *The Antifederalists.* QP14
Ernest R. May. *The World War and American Isolation, 1914-1917.* QP29
Henry F. May. *The End of American Innocence.* QP9
George E. Mowry. *The California Progressives.* QP6
Frank L. Owsley. *Plain Folk of the Old South.* QP22
David Graham Phillips. *The Treason of the Senate.* QP20
Julius W. Pratt. *Expansionists of 1898.* QP15
Richard W. Van Alstyne. *The Rising American Empire.* QP25
Willard M. Wallace. *Appeal to Arms.* QP10
Norman Ware. *The Industrial Worker, 1840-1860.* QP13
Albert K. Weinberg. *Manifest Destiny.* QP3
Bell I. Wiley. *The Plain People of the Confederacy.* QP4
Esmond Wright. *Causes and Consequences of the American Revolution.* QP31

Philosophy

James M. Edie. *An Invitation to Phenomenology.* QP103
George L. Kline. *European Philosophy Today.* QP102
Pierre Thévenaz. *What Is Phenomenology?* QP101

Social Science

George and Eunice Grier. *Equality and Beyond.* QP204
Martin Oppenheimer and George Lakey. *A Manual for Direct Action.* QP202
Egon Schwelb. *Human Rights and the International Community.* QP203
Clarence Senior. *The Puerto Ricans.* QP201